# FUN WITH THE FAMILY

## Michigan

Praise for the *Fun with the Family* series

"Enables parents to turn family travel into an exploration."
—Alexandra Kennedy, Editor, *Family Fun*

"Bound to lead you and your kids to fun-filled days, those times that help compose the memories of childhood."
—Dorothy Jordon, *Family Travel Times*

## Help Us Keep This Guide Up to Date

We would love to hear from you concerning your experiences with this guide and how you feel it could be improved and kept up to date. Please send your comments and suggestions to:

editorial@GlobePequot.com

Thanks for your input, and happy travels!

# FUN WITH THE FAMILY

## Michigan

### Hundreds OF Ideas FOR Day Trips WITH THE Kids

SEVENTH EDITION

**Bill Semion**

travel

Guilford, Connecticut

To my parents, who first stirred my pilgrim soul.
And thanks to Scott Renas for his assistance.

All of the information in this guidebook is subject
to change. We recommend that you call ahead to
obtain current information before traveling.

To buy books in quantity for corporate use
or incentives, call **(800) 962-0973**
or e-mail **premiums@GlobePequot.com.**

Text design: Nancy Freeborn and Linda R. Loiewski
Maps: Rusty Nelson © Morris Book Publishing, LLC
Spot photography throughout © Photodisc and © RubberBall Productions

ISSN 1540-8744
ISBN 978-0-7627-5069-6

Printed in the United States of America
10 9 8 7 6 5 4 3 2 1

# Contents

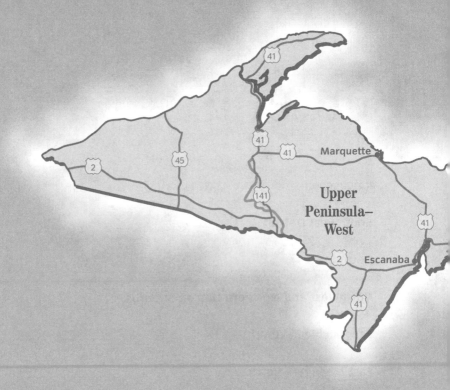

MICHIGAN

# Introduction

The unmistakable sound of children's laughter on a miles-long sand beach on a mid-July day.

The swoosh of skis against some of the purest snow on earth as they cut through woods so perfect you'd swear you were on the set of the latest Hollywood fantasy epic. Or the swoosh of skis on some of the Midwest's most friendly or most challenging downhill runs.

The sound of silent appreciation of a master's work in the halls of a great museum, and the ethereal sound of a trout rising to a gossamer mayfly on yet another perfect June evening on one of the best fishing streams east of the Mississippi.

That and more will be your reward for exploring the following pages, and for exploring this state that I call home.

From the tip of the Keweenaw Peninsula in the north, dipped in autumn brilliance and summer greenery, to the Lake Erie shoreline on its south; from Lake Michigan's white-sand beaches on its west to the public fishing piers and quiet resort towns along Lake Huron on its east; from its huge expanses of state and national forests—which number among the nation's largest tracts of publicly held land—to its fun-loaded cities with excitement for the family that's found nowhere else. This is a place that stands up to the cliché "something for everyone."

One of my earliest memories is of crossing the Straits of Mackinac on one of the big ferryboats that took cars between the peninsulas as the Mackinac Bridge was being built.

We spent a part of each summer along Lake Huron, frolicking on the beach and enjoying the lake's offerings, including perch fishing and driving its magnificent shoreline.

We Michiganians take our Great Lakes for granted. When foreigners or even those from other parts of the nation catch their first eyeful of Huron, Michigan, or, especially, mighty Superior, they're awestruck. And they grow incredulous when they realize that no, you really can't see across them. Did you know, for example, that Lake Michigan is more than 80 miles across at its widest point and more than 900 feet deep at its deepest point? And that scientists now think of Lake Superior, more than 1,000 feet deep, as more of a freshwater ocean than a lake?

I am lucky to have a job that allowed me to continue my family's tradition of travel. Over the last thirty-plus years, I've helped introduce my children and others to the wonders that are found in our state so that they, too, will have an appreciation someday of what Michigan offers.

I hope this book enlightens you, whether you're a Michigan resident or a first-time visitor who doesn't know Saginaw from Manistee—at least not yet. I hope to convince you of the bounty of activities that my state has to offer the family. And in the next pages, I've touched on only a sampling of the thousands of attractions you'll find.

There are plenty more adventures awaiting you and your family if you're willing to explore and open new doors to discovery. Try a Michigan adventure or two, no matter the season.

You'll learn more about our beautiful state and perhaps about yourself in the process. And by introducing your family to travel, you'll be helping them learn to appreciate the wonder all around them, no matter where they go.

See you on the road!

## Lodging, Restaurant, and Attraction Rates

The dollar signs listed for lodgings and restaurants (in the Where to Stay and Where to Eat sections), as well as for attractions, offer a guide to each facility's prices. Lodgings include prices for rooms with a double bed and no meals, unless otherwise indicated, and the restaurant pricing structure is based on both lunch and dinner entrees. If you do not find a restaurant or lodging listing for a particular area, please refer to the surrounding towns for information on the best family-friendly restaurants and lodgings in the area.

Because admission fees change frequently, this book offers a general idea of the prices charged for the daily admission of a single visitor ranging in age from child to adult.

Keep in mind that even though many museums and events offer **free** admission, a donation is often expected to help the facility with the costs of maintenance and keeping the attraction open to the public.

### Rates for Lodging
| | |
|---|---|
| $ | up to $50 |
| $$ | $51 to $100 |
| $$$ | $101 to $150 |
| $$$$ | $151 and up |

### Rates for Restaurants
| | |
|---|---|
| $ | most entrees under $5 |
| $$ | entrees $5 to $10 |
| $$$ | entrees $11 to $20 |
| $$$$ | entrees over $20 |

### Rates for Attractions
| | |
|---|---|
| $ | under $5 |
| $$ | $5 to $10 |
| $$$ | $11 to $20 |
| $$$$ | over $20 |

# Attractions Key

The following is a key to the icons found throughout the text.

| | | | |
|---|---|---|---|
| **SWIMMING** | | **FOOD** | |
| **BOATING/BOAT TOUR** | | **LODGING** | |
| **HISTORIC SITE** | | **CAMPING** | |
| **HIKING/WALKING** | | **MUSEUMS** | |
| **FISHING** | | **PERFORMING ARTS** | |
| **BIKING** | | **SPORTS/ATHLETIC** | |
| **AMUSEMENT PARK** | | **PICNICKING** | |
| **HORSEBACK RIDING** | | **PLAYGROUND** | |
| **SKIING/WINTER SPORTS** | | **SHOPPING** | |
| **PARK** | | **PLANTS/GARDENS/NATURE TRAILS** | |
| **ANIMAL VIEWING** | | **FARMS** | |

# Southwest Detroit

Only a few minutes' drive south and west of downtown Detroit's skyscrapers is one of the country's top universities, nestled in a town that has attractions ranging from the offbeat to the educational. The region takes in Monroe, Washtenaw, and western Wayne Counties.

## Monroe

Monroe is one of the state's oldest cities, founded in 1780 by the French. The last major city in southeast Michigan before the Ohio border, Monroe is home to manufacturing (if you're reading this in a La-Z-Boy recliner, the company is headquartered here) and recreation provided by nearby Lake Erie.

### Tradewinds Fishing Charters (ages 6 and up)
**Off I-75 at exit 11, at Flying Eagle Marina, 1370 Lake Dr.; (800) 983-9463 or (734) 243-2319.**

Lake Erie's walleye fishing is nothing short of fantastic. And, whether you want to show your fishing expertise to your kids or want to introduce them to the sport, here's one of the best ways to do it: Take them on a party-boat trip. No, not that kind of party boat, but a fishing boat like Captain Jim Ulrich's craft. Each day, his three Coast Guard–approved 30- to 32-foot boats head out after walleye in Lake Erie near Monroe. Ulrich and his captains know where the fish are, and lately that's been only a few miles out of the harbor. Once they find a "hot spot" on their fish finder, the engines are off, and you're ready to bait up. The captain will tell you how many seconds to let your bait sink. Two tips so that your kids will be almost guaranteed to catch 'em: (1) "Jig" (raise and lower) your fishing rod a bit while slowly reeling in to attract fish, and (2) try to cast your line on the windward side of the boat; that way it will freely drift  past your quarry, rather than being tugged under the hull first. Once you feel a nibble, pull back a bit to set the hook and reel steadily. Tell your kids not to pull too hard, lest the hook pull out of the walleye's mouth. Ulrich or his

# SOUTHWEST DETROIT

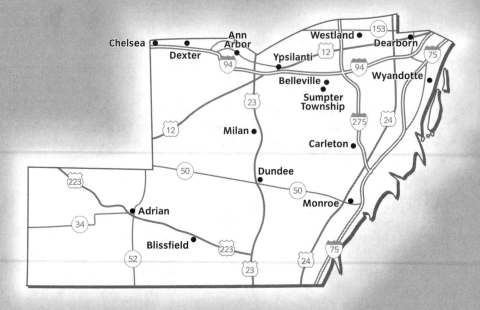

Chelsea • •     Ann Arbor    Westland •   153   • Dearborn
Dexter      94    Ypsilanti   12    94    75
        Belleville •     Wyandotte •
    23    Sumpter Township
12    Milan •      275   24
      Carleton •
   50    Dundee •
223     50   Monroe •
34   • Adrian
   Blissfield •   223
52      23    24   75

captains will be there to net your catch, put it in the cooler, and help you get ready for more action. When the walleye stop biting, usually in mid- to late Aug, Ulrich targets tasty perch.

### River Raisin Battlefield Visitor Center (ages 5 to 16)
**At 1430 Elm Ave.; (734) 243-7136; www.co.monroe.mi.us/monroe/default.aspx?PageId=107 and www.riverraisinbattlefield.org. Visitor center open 10 a.m. to 5 p.m., Tues through Fri, June through Aug; open weekends only in Apr, May, and Sept; grounds open year-round. Free, but donations are accepted.**

The center commemorates the battle that occurred here during the War of 1812, in which Americans suffered one of their worst defeats of the war. Of 934 Americans who fought a force of British and Native Americans led by the famed warrior chief Tecumseh, only thirty-three escaped death or capture. "Remember the River Raisin" became a rallying cry to American troops for the rest of the war. Exhibits include a map showing troop movements and dioramas depicting the midwinter battle.

### River Raisin Canoe Trips (ages 6 and up)
**From Raisin River Canoe Livery, located east of Monroe, 4 miles east of Dundee on Plank Road; (734) 529-9029; www.riverraisincanoelivery.com.**

Choose your craft—from canoe, to kayak, to family-size pontoon boat—for a leisurely one- to eight-hour trip down the quiet River Raisin. The current is slow and gentle, with plenty of opportunities to fish for bass. Trips end at the riverside livery. Life jackets, paddles, and cushions are provided. Pontoons are by reservation only, and primitive camping is also available.

### River Raisin Jazz Festival (ages 3 and up)
**For information, call (800) 252-3011.**

In mid-Aug downtown is alive with the sounds of jazz during this festival, which brings the best of local artists to play at St. Mary's park adjacent to downtown in early Aug. National performers as well as artists from the Michigan jazz scene take the stage for two days from noon to 10 p.m. Pull up a lounge chair or sit on a blanket, bring a picnic basket, and enjoy what's been called the Great Lakes region's fastest-growing jazz event. Be sure to catch the fine art fair, too.

### George Armstrong Custer Statue (all ages)
**At the southwest corner of Monroe Street and Elm Avenue, downtown.**

No matter what you think of him, Custer called Monroe home before riding off to meet his fate and doom at Little Bighorn. At least twenty-three sites are marked as connected to the general in some way, from the home where his wife lived, to the Monroe County Historical Museum (located in a former post office at 125 South Monroe; (734) 240-7780; www.co.monroe.mi.us/museum/), containing Custer family memorabilia along with other aspects of county history.

Pick up a brochure on Custer at the Monroe County Convention and Tourism Bureau (see listing below).

## Lake Erie Metropark  (all ages)

**32481 West Jefferson, Brownstown, north of Monroe; (734) 379-5020; www.metroparks .com. From I-75, take exit 29, Gibraltar Road, east. Turn right onto Jefferson, go about 2 miles, and turn into the park. Admission $ daily or $$$ annually per car. Wave pool $.**

Located where the Detroit River flows into the basin creating Lake Erie, this park, one of thirteen Metroparks ringing southeast Michigan, has just about everything except a beach. A giant wave pool creates 3-footers, satisfying those hungry for swimming, and has a zero-depth entry so youngsters can enjoy wavelets, too. The boat launch allows access to the river and lake. A nature center teaches about the life of the area's wetlands. No boat? Fish from a pier jutting into the lake. At certain times in summer, climb on board a tour boat to learn about wildlife, including bald eagles, in the surrounding area, including Humbug Marsh, another area that was saved from development. You can also enjoy picnicking, ice fishing in winter, hiking, bird-watching, eighteen holes of golf (another course is at neighboring Willow Metropark), and court games. The park is also part of the Detroit River International Wildlife Refuge (www.fws.gov/midwest/detroitriver/).

## Where to Eat

**Bob Evans.** I-75 at exit 15 (Highway 50); (734) 289-4225. Good budget chain food for breakfast, lunch, dinner. Children's menu. $

**Bolles Harbor Cafe.** 13986 La Plaisance Rd., at I-75, exit 11; (734) 457-CAFE. Great breakfasts, lunches, and dinners with wide variety in an out-of-the-way setting near Lake Erie. $–$$$

**Café Classics.** 29 South Monroe St., downtown; (734) 242-8286. Serving a variety of family-friendly grilled sandwiches, salads, wraps, soups, desserts, coffees, and other drinks. $–$$ Next door, Bapa's Coney Island and Inga's Bakery Shoppe, owned by the same family, also are good bets.

**Joe's French–Italian Inn.** 2896 North Dixie Hwy. Take I-75, exit 15, then head east 2 miles on Highway 50; (734) 289-2800. A landmark in the region since 1932, specializing in seafood, steaks, and (guess what?) Italian dishes. Children's menu available. Lunch and dinner served. $$$

**Monroe Street Grill.** 2 West Front St. downtown; (734) 241-1112. Casual dining for breakfast through dinner featuring some unusual treats like its specialty pistachio and artichoke chicken. Children's menu. $$

## Where to Stay

**Best Western Prestige Inn.** Off I-75 at exit 15; (734) 289-2330; www.bestwestern .com/prestigeinn. Motel features 111 rooms and five family suites, an outdoor pool, and extensive continental breakfast; light dinner available Tues through Sat. Restaurants nearby. $$

**Holiday Inn Express Hotel and Suites.** Off I-75 at exit 15; (734) 242-6000; www .hiexpress.com/monroemi. Property has 161 rooms and new suites, heated indoor pool, and other typical Holiday Inn amenities. Breakfast bar included with stay. Restaurants nearby. $$–$$$$

**Sterling State Park.** Exit off I-75 at Highway 50 (exit 15), turn east to the park entrance; (734) 289-2715; www.michigan.gov/dnr, then follow the links under "Recreation, Camping & Boating." One of the state's most modern parks features a 256-site campground (mostly open sites); a large boat launch area, day-use beach, and convenient parking lot; several miles of biking/hiking nature trails; and bridges over the park's colorful marshes. See everything from typical marsh birds and ducks to even bald eagles.

# Carleton

## Calder Dairy Farm  (ages 2 to 12)

**Take Telegraph Road to South Stony Creek Road, head west about 5 miles to Finzel Road, then go south, and watch for the signs; (734) 654-2622; www.calderdairy.com. Open 10 a.m. to 8 p.m. in summer; 10 a.m. to 7 p.m. in winter. Visits to the farm are free.**

The ability to experience life on the American family farm is becoming a rare commodity these days, and here's where you can take your family to experience a real, working dairy farm. A visit to Calder Dairy Farm—located near Carleton in Monroe County, between Detroit and Monroe—will answer all your kids' questions about where milk and ice cream come from. The farm makes out-of-this-world chocolate milk, holiday eggnog so thick it's like liquid ice cream, milk that's still sold in glass bottles, and twenty-two flavors of ice cream and also offers tours to show kids and others how the milk that's in the fridge gets there. Your family can stroll the 180-acre farm to see and pet the Holstein and Brown Swiss cows. Kids can help hand-feed the farm's calves starting at 3 p.m. and see the milking process from 4 to 5 p.m. daily. They can also see and pet more than a hundred other animals, such as waddling ducks and honking geese.

Afterward, take your gang to the farm's small on-site store, where they can sink their teeth into a huge Calder ice-cream cone. You can also head to the main store in Lincoln Park, near Detroit, to buy everything from great cottage cheese to old-fashioned buttermilk.

Group tours available by appointment.

# Dundee

Long a quiet farming community, incorporated in 1855, the town is now a suburb of Toledo, Ohio, as gentleman farmers move in and the main crop has become housing.

## Cabela's  (all ages)

**At the US 23 Dundee exit 17; 110 Cabela Blvd., East Dundee; (734) 529-4700; www.cabelas .com, then choose "retail stores," then "Dundee, MI." Open Mon through Sat 8 a.m. to 9 p.m.; Sun 10 a.m. to 6 p.m.**

At 225,000 square feet, this store can be seen from miles away along the freeway. It's the largest outdoor store in the state. An estimated six million people visit each year.

Huge bronze sculptures adorn the exterior, and the parking lot is packed with cars no matter the season. Relax around a six-acre human-made lake. Traveling with a dog? There's a kennel for Rover while you're inside strolling over a river brimming with trout, past an aquarium with Michigan and Great Lakes fish, a shooting gallery, posed trophies, and even a 250-seat restaurant with wild game and kids' meals. It sells everything out-doorsy imaginable, from the tiniest trout fly to boats and all the gear you'll need for that family expedition into the wild. There's even RV/boat service to install items purchased inside. Find bargains in the "cave." Special activities include seminars and even Santa over the holidays.

### Splash Universe River Run  (all ages)
**At the US 23 Dundee exit 17, attached to the Holiday Inn Express, 100 Whitetail Dr.; (734) 529-5100 or (800) 445-6343; www.splashuniverse.com. $$$.**

While the parents are in Cabela's (see above), the kids can be shepherded to this indoor water park, which brings another level of fun to the same Dundee exit. Slides and rides all feature an outdoorsy theme.

## Where to Eat

**River's Edge Pizza Pub & Grill.** 135 Riley St. (M-50) in downtown Dundee; (734) 529-2445. Great pizza and other kid-friendly fare. $$

**Tamarack Cache Deli.** In Cabela's, 110 Cabela Blvd. East, off US 23 at exit 17; (734) 529-4700. Open Mon through Sat 8 a.m. to 9 p.m., Sun 10 a.m. to 6 p.m. Sandwiches feature fixin's from turkey to ostrich. $$

## Where to Stay

**Country Inn & Suites by Carlson Dundee.** 665 Tecumseh St., off US 23 at exit 17; (734) 529-8822. Hotel has seventy rooms with an indoor pool, continental breakfast, and Internet service, and is near Cabela's. $$–$$$

**Holiday Inn Express.** 100 Whitetail Dr., off US 23 at exit 17; (734) 529-5100 or (800) 445-6343; www.hieusa.com. Designed to complement Cabela's, this outdoor-themed hotel has seventy-seven rooms, including some spa and family suites and indoor pool. Breakfast included with stay. Splash Universe is attached. $$–$$$

## For More Information

**Monroe County Convention and Tour-ism Bureau.** 111 East First St., Monroe 48161; (800) 252-3011; www.monroeinfo .com. Information on the area includes a list of charter operators. Along northbound I-75, near the city at the 10-mile marker, a state-operated welcome center has more informa-tion on Michigan and the area.

# Blissfield

Blissfield is along US 223, reached off US 23, south and west of Monroe.

Take the family on board the railroad and then introduce them to the way small-town life used to be in Blissfield and its next-door neighbor, Adrian. Blissfield was settled about the same time as Adrian and remains Michigan's biggest village.

## Old Road Dinner Train (all ages)

**Leaves from the Blissfield East station in downtown Blissfield along US 223; (517) 486-5979 or (888) GO–RAIL-1; www.murdermysterytrain.com. Family-oriented trips are available. Ride the rails the first Sat of the month, and the Easter Bunny is on board in spring. Daytime trips $$ for adults and $ for children 12 and under. Dinner trips $$$$ per person.**

Step on board the restored 1940s-era, air-conditioned and heated coaches of the Adrian & Blissfield Railroad. It's the longest continually operated quality dinner train in the nation. Your kids will be amazed as the diesel engine enters the station. Then they'll sit back and be treated to a ninety-minute trip through the countryside past manicured, tilled farm fields and over at least two old trestles across the River Raisin. If they watch out the window, they might even see a deer or two. The route follows a segment of the old Erie & Kalamazoo Railroad, which began operations in 1836, making it one of the first railroads west of the Allegheny Mountains.

# Favorite Events in Southwest Detroit

- **Ann Arbor Folk Festival** (Jan), Ann Arbor, (734) 761-1451
- **Black History Month Blues Concert** (Feb), Monroe, (734) 241-5277
- **Flower and Garden Show** (Mar), Ann Arbor, (734) 998-7061
- **Antique Market** (Apr), Saline, (734) 662-9453; www.annarborantiques market.com
- **Orphan Car Show** (June), Ypsilanti, (734) 482-5200 or (734) 483-4444
- **Elvisfest** (July), Ypsilanti, (734) 483-4444; www.mielvisfest.org
- **Ann Arbor Art Fairs** (July), Ann Arbor, (734) 995-7281; www.artfair.org
- **Canton Liberty Festival** (June), Canton Township, (734) 394-5460
- **Heritage Festival** (Aug), Ypsilanti, (734) 483-4444
- **Rod Custom Car Show** (Aug), Belleville, (734) 699-8921
- **River Raisin Jazz and Shadow Art Fair** (Dec and July), Ann Arbor, (734) 480-2739
- **Monroe Holiday Parade** (Nov), Monroe, (734) 242-3366
- **New Year Jubilee** (Dec), Ypsilanti, (734) 483-4444

Themed rides take place throughout the year. Santa himself makes an appearance on every trip in Dec to take toy orders from the kids. A special "Ghost Train" appears during the two weeks before Halloween.

The interactive dinner murder mystery trip is the most popular. The owner rates it PG-13, so children under ten shouldn't attend. Up to a hundred persons are served dinner on china and linen in two dining cars.

## Where to Eat

**Hathaway House (ages 8 and up).** 424 West Adrian (US 223); (517) 486-2141 or (888) 937-4284; www.hathawayhouse.com. Reservations requested. This beautifully restored 1851 mansion serves finely prepared meals, including specialties like potato-crusted whitefish and prime rib or rack of lamb. $$$

**Main Street Stable and Tavern.** Behind Hathaway House; (517) 486-2144. If the kids are in tow and aren't in the mood to sit still, head for burgers in the former carriage house for lunch and dinner. $$

# Chelsea

Settled in 1820 and named after Chelsea, Massachusetts, the town was a farming center until Ann Arborites discovered it, and it was developed into a suburb.

## Chelsea Milling Company (ages 6 and up)

**Take I-94 west from Ann Arbor to the Chelsea exit and head north—you'll soon see the company's silos; (734) 475-1361; www.jiffymix.com. Chelsea Milling Company's free tours take place Mon through Fri between 9 a.m. and 1:30 p.m. Reservations are required.**

Such a deal! The kids will think you're taking them on another one of your educational tours. It's that, yes, but there's a special treat at the end that will make them eager to learn how grain is made into the flour that makes the brownies, cakes, and muffins at the Chelsea Milling Company.

The company began when "Grandma Mabel" Holmes came up with the idea of a flour that's ready to use for making pancakes, biscuits, and other goodies without having to mix all the ingredients first. Today as many as 18,000 visitors a year—split between children and adults—stroll through the plant where Jiffy All-Purpose Baking Flour and sixteen other products are produced.

Tours last up to two hours, depending on the size of the crowd. First you'll be treated to a slide show that starts with a history of the company and how Grandma Mabel's idea in 1930 launched the Jiffy line of mixes.

The slide show over, tour guides then take you to the packaging operations, where you'll see boxes made and filled with what's being produced that day, everything from corn-muffin mix to pizza dough.

The last stop on the tour is a treat for both adults and kids. Grown-ups receive a **free** package of muffin, cake, or frosting mix and a recipe booklet, while the kids can latch onto a box of brownie mix or pizza dough that they can take with them and bake at home. You might even see grandson Howdy Holmes, the former Indianapolis 500 driver, who now oversees the plant.

### Purple Rose Theatre (ages 13 and up)

137 Park St.; (734) 433-7673; www.purplerosetheatre.org. Ask about current productions and schedules. Occasional productions may be too intense for children under 16, so check before making reservations.

Plan to take in a performance of mostly original plays at this newly restored theater. Who knows? You might even see Chelsea resident and Hollywood actor/playwright/singer Jeff Daniels, who has starred in such recent movies as *Good Night and Good Luck, RV,* and a remake of *The Goodbye Girl.* He is part owner and writes some of the plays presented here. The theater is very popular, so call early for seat information.

### Chelsea Teddy Bear Company (all ages)

400 North Main St.; (734) 433-5499; www.chelseateddybearcompany.com Open noon to 6 p.m. Mon through Sat, noon to 5 p.m. Sun. **Free** tours every nonholiday Sat at 11 a.m., 1 p.m., and 3 p.m.

Who can resist **free** tours of a teddy bear factory, regardless of your age? See what's billed as the world's largest teddy bear, standing more than 10 feet tall, and its cousin, a 7-foot-tall grizzly look-alike. On tours, see how teddies are assembled and stored, see antique bears, and, in the museum, learn the history of the bear named after President Teddy Roosevelt.

### Waterloo Recreation Area (all ages)

Take I-94 west of Chelsea and watch for signs to the Eddy Geology center, or take exit 147, 150, 156, or 157; (734) 475-8307; www.michigan.gov/dnr. A state park motor vehicle permit ($) is required for entry.

The Lower Peninsula's largest state park, Waterloo Recreation Area, features more than 20,000 acres of camping from modern to primitive, including rustic cabins for rent, and a riding stable. More than 45 miles of biking trails, plus picnicking and swimming, are available. The recreation area contains a section of the longest hiking trail in southern Michigan. An adjacent Audubon Society preserve often hosts sandhill cranes.

## Where to Eat

**Common Grill.** 112 South Main St.; (734) 475-0470. Lunch and dinner. Closed Mon. The city's best restaurant welcomes children, too. It features a casual atmosphere with an original pressed-tin ceiling, hardwood floors, and a zinc bar. Well-prepared meals feature a variety of seafood and meats and vegetarian items, and a children's menu and Sun brunch are also available. $$$

## Where to Stay

**Chelsea Comfort Inn.** 1645 Commerce Park Dr.; (734) 433-8000; www.choicehotels .com, then follow the prompts. Take I-94 to exit 159N. Turn left at Brown Drive and turn right on Commerce Drive. This hotel has eighty rooms. Pets OK. $$

**South House Chelsea.** 120 South St.; (734) 475-9300. An 1887 Victorian home behind the Common Grill and near the Purple Rose Theatre. Four rooms with private baths and television; full breakfast. Rooms are traditionally decorated. $$

## For More Information

**Chelsea Chamber of Commerce.** (734) 475-1145; www.chelseamichamber.org.

# Adrian

Settled in 1826 by a railroad tycoon and his family, Adrian, nicknamed the City of Maples because of its downtown greenery, was the site of the first railroad in Michigan. Horses pulled the cars initially, and the first steam engine west of the Alleghenies was placed in use in 1837, when Michigan became a state. There's lots to do on a visit to Adrian, which also claims the Irish Hills for its own (see separate entry).

### Antique Alley  (all ages)

**Roughly the area in and around Adrian and the Irish Hills; for more information and maps, call (800) 536-2933 or visit www.visitlenawee.com and look under "things to do."**

Looking for a perfect Queen Anne piece of furniture? How about an antique toy to start your kids' own collection? You can find lots here in Adrian and neighboring Blissfield (see entry), Tecumseh, Clinton, and other towns—an area that is appropriately nicknamed "Antique Alley." More than two dozen antiques stores await in the city and surrounding villages. In early Aug Michigan's Longest Garage Sale takes place along nearby US 12, where you can also shop for bargains, including some possible hidden treasures in someone else's trash.

### Croswell Opera House  (ages five and up)

**129 East Maumee, in downtown; (517) 264-7469; www.croswell.org. Check the playbill for child-appropriate productions.**

Enjoy great locally produced musicals and other plays at the Croswell Opera House, which was established in 1866 and is recognized as the oldest continuously running theater in Michigan and the third oldest in the country. Mostly family-oriented plays are performed just about year-round. It's a great venue to introduce kids to live plays.

## Where to Stay

**Carlton Lodge.** 1629 West Maumee; (517) 263-7000. Ninety-eight rooms with **free** wireless Internet service, indoor/outdoor pool, exercise area, and continental breakfast. $$

**Holiday Inn Express.** 1077 West US 223; (517) 265-5700; reservations, (800) HOLIDAY. Sixty rooms and two suites with indoor pool. $$

# Dexter

Located just northwest of Ann Arbor. From I-94, exit at Baker Road and head north into town. Dexter, until it became a western suburb of Ann Arbor, started out as a small farm community.

### Delhi Metropark (all ages)

**Located on the Huron River's banks on Huron River Drive (Ann Arbor), which skirts the river a good way and is a beautiful drive in itself; (800) 477-3191; www.metroparks.com. To reach the park from Dexter, head east on Huron River Drive. Open 8 a.m. to 10 p.m. $.**

Picnic facilities and canoe rentals are available here (see Huron River Canoeing), as well as fishing in the Huron River. This park is part of the Huron-Clinton Metroparks system, which rings metro Detroit.

### Dexter-Huron Metropark (all ages)

**Along Huron River Drive, downstream from Hudson Mills; (800) 477-3191; www.metroparks .com. Open 8 a.m. to 10 p.m. $.**

A great 125-acre park along the Huron with picnic facilities and baseball diamonds. It's a favorite picnic spot for paddlers on the river as well as for families seeking a quiet, uncrowded park.

### Hudson Mills Metropark (all ages)

**8801 North Territorial Rd.; (800) 477-4191; www.metroparks.com. From Ann Arbor, take US 23 north to North Territorial Road, and then head west. The park is open year-round 7 a.m. to 10 p.m. $.**

The largest of the three related parks, Hudson Mills, also along the Huron River, includes a golf course, bicycle and cross-country ski rentals, bike and ski trails, picnic areas, and disc golf, plus camping for organized groups and canoeists making overnight trips on the Huron.

### Huron River Canoeing (ages 1 and up)

**Headquartered at Delhi Metropark, Ann Arbor; (734) 769-8686. Rent canoes and kayaks mid-May through Oct. All life jackets are provided. There are small, beginner-type rap-ids. Maximum number of people in a canoe is two adults and two nonpaddling children. $$$–$$$$.**

This is a wonderful way to introduce the family to a taste of the outdoors only a few minutes outside the city. Starting from Delhi Metropark, the livery will drive you upriver to nearby Hudson Mills Metropark to begin your journey. Paddlers put in at the park and cruise the river for about three hours. In fall a great stop is the **Dexter Cider Mill** in downtown Dexter, where you can enjoy a break and some cider and doughnuts, or you can stop for a picnic at Dexter–Huron Metropark, downstream.

### Spring Valley Trout Farm (all ages)

12190 Island Lake Rd.; (734) 426-4772; www.springvalleytroutfarm.com. Take I-94 to Baker Road (exit 167). Turn right and go 2 miles. Road ends at Main Street. Turn left. At stoplight continue straight, 4 miles to the farm. Hours vary by season so call ahead. The farm opens for the season in early May and then is open Memorial Day to Labor Day 9 a.m. to 6 p.m. Wed through Sun. Adults $, children under 5 free. Children under age nine must wear life jackets, which are provided. Pets not allowed.

What better way to introduce kids to fishing than to catch a feisty, plump trout or catfish?

Delighting kids since 1970, the farm is on twenty acres of grounds with nine spring-fed ponds and even a children's pond reserved for anglers under age ten.

Trout average 12 to 16 inches in length and about one pound in weight and usually serve up to two persons. Catfish average up to two pounds, and you're encouraged to bring your own rod for those. Admission charge includes cane pole rental and picnic ground use. Purchase fish by the pound, and cleaning is 30 cents extra per trout, 50 cents per catfish.

## Where to Eat

Choose from small local restaurants in towns described previously, or head for more selections in nearby Ann Arbor.

## Where to Stay

See listing of accommodations under Ann Arbor, which is a few miles east on I-94.

# Ann Arbor

Imagine about as eclectic a city as you can, catering to all tastes with theaters and street performers, surprising restaurants, and a vibrant atmosphere unlike any other in the state, and you've just described Ann Arbor, the home of the University of Michigan. This is a great place for families to explore. All University of Michigan museums are free and open to the public. To get to Ann Arbor's campus area, take the State Street exit north off I-94. Main Street shopping is a few blocks to the west.

What's as tall as a house and has rows of huge, sharp teeth? What animal that's a cousin of the elephant once roamed Michigan and other parts of the United States? Ever see a real Egyptian mummy? At the museums you'll find the mummy's tomb (minus the curse) and dinosaurs straight out of *Jurassic Park,* plus a lot more finds worthy of any aspiring Indiana Jones.

### Exhibit Museum of Natural History (all ages)

Corner of Geddes Road and Washtenaw on the campus's east side; (734) 764-0478; www .lsa.umich.edu/exhibitmuseum. Open Mon through Sat from 9 a.m. to 5 p.m., Sun noon to 5 p.m. Free.

Hundreds of families come here, especially on weekends, to entertain and teach their children at the exhibits at two museums. First on the list to visit should be this treasure storehouse of prehistoric Michigan and other discoveries that will appeal especially to kids. The museum houses the most extensive prehistoric-life collection in the state. What excites kids the most is when they come face-to-face with the fossilized bones of a snarling allosaurus standing over its kill, a fossilized stegosaurus like those that roamed the earth millions of years ago and were unearthed near Cleveland, Utah. At another exhibit they can stand next to a skeleton of a huge, elephant-like, 10,000-year-old mastodon that was found in a Michigan farmer's field near Owosso.

Kids marvel at the long, deadly claws of the rapacious deinonychus, relative of the velociraptors of *Jurassic Park* and other movies. There also are more than 700 rock and mineral specimens in the geology section. Other exhibits on the third floor are presented through dioramas that create a picture of what Michigan was like at various times through prehistory and what you might find in the region's forests and ponds today. There is also a planetarium that presents weekend shows.

A new permanent exhibit, said to be the largest of its kind in existence, focuses on the evolution of whales, with six skeletons of prehistoric cousins to the world's largest mammals that were unearthed in China, Egypt, and Pakistan by university scientists. It includes a complete cast of a fifty-six-million-year-old whale ancestor.

At the well-stocked museum store, kids can take home smaller, model versions or books that provide more details about what they saw inside, or they can go home wearing a deinonychus T-shirt. There's also a planetarium with regularly scheduled shows.

## Away for the **Weekend**

Ann Arbor is my pick to headquarter your stay in the region. It's a short drive south to shopping at Dundee via US 23. Chelsea is only a few minutes west by I-94, and the Irish Hills, with everything from auto racing to tourism attractions and lakes (see the East Michigan–South chapter), is just to the south and west via US 12. In Ann Arbor proper, kids will enjoy the city's museums and live theater. Even Detroit's downtown attractions (see the Detroit chapter) are only a forty-five-minute drive away via I-94.

Downtown Ann Arbor is alive with sidewalk restaurants and cuisine ranging from African to American. And just a few minutes from city center are great motels with all the fun a kid could dream of. It's simply the place to be in the region.

# Ann Arbor **Art Fairs** (all ages)

This popular attraction draws hundreds of thousands of families to Ann Arbor each year and virtually closes the city's downtown to traffic. It may be crowded, noisy, and occasionally offbeat, but it's fun for the entire family. It's an annual gathering of more than a thousand artists who take over downtown for four days, usually in the third week of July. Although the event is collectively known as "the art fair," there are actually four simultaneous art festivals. While the fairs may be separate, each flows into the other, which makes walking the entire area easy.

The **State Street Art Fair** runs the length of the State Street shopping district and has grown so large since its beginning in 1967 that it's spilled over into four surrounding streets. The **Summer Art Fair** is spread out along Main Street and adjoining avenues. While it's been known as more commercial in years past, it's come a long way in the past few summers.

Artists' booths are set up along the middle of each street, with passages wide enough for wheelchairs and strollers despite the crowds. Only a few tents ask that children be carried, owing to cramped quarters. As you peruse the artwork, you'll find everything from original pottery and woven clothing to wildlife art and photography. If your teens are into beads, they'll find plenty, along with amulets for make-your-own necklaces.

At the **Ann Arbor Street Art Fair,** the oldest of the fairs, dating from 1959, face-paint experts deftly design flowers, flags, and hundreds of other forms on willing young faces, and youngsters can even try their own hand at the easel with watercolors. There's a **free** family art activity center at the Summer Art Fair, too, with lots of chances for kids to create the next art craze. Running at the same time is the **South University Art Fair.**

Much of the entertainment isn't at the booths, however. At intersections between each fair and along the expanse of grass and diagonal sidewalks along State known as the "diag," magicians, jugglers, and other street buskers love to coax child "assistants" from the crowds, and the kids love it, too. They're trying to earn a living at it, and they often pass the hat at the end of each show. In addition, local merchants use the event as an excuse to offer discounts and sidewalk sales.

For more information, contact the Ann Arbor Street Art Fair at (734) 994-5260 (www.artfair.org), the State Street Art Fair at (734) 663-6511, the Summer Art Fair at (734) 662-2787, and South University Art Fair, (734) 663-5300.

### University of Michigan Museum of Art (all ages)

Located at 525 South State St.; (734) 7l64-0395; www.umma.umich.edu. Gallery hours are 10 a.m. to 5 p.m. Tues, Wed, and Sat, 10 a.m. to 10 p.m. Thurs and Fri, and noon to 5 p.m. Sun. **Free,** but a $ donation is suggested.

The recently reopened museum sports a 53,000-square-foot, $41 million expansion, which more than doubles exhibit space. Collections include Asian, African, European, and American painting and sculpture, both old school and contemporary.

### Kelsey Museum of Archaeology (all ages)

434 South State St.; (734) 764-9304; www.lsa.umich.edu/kelsey. Open 9 a.m. to 4 p.m. Tues through Fri; 1 to 4 p.m. Sat and Sun. Closed Mon. **Free,** but donations are accepted.

The Kelsey opened a new wing in 2009, along with major renovations of its exhibits, which house nearly 10,000 objects from civilizations bordering the Mediterranean. Among the ones that get kids most excited is the sarcophagus of Djheuty Mosc, a priest who lived in southern Egypt between 685 and 525 B.C. Rotating exhibits include displays of Roman antiquities.

The new wing allows the museum to display more of its works, many of which had to be stored because of lack of space.

### Hands-On Museum (toddlers and up)

220 East Ann St.; (734) 995-5437; www.aahom.org. From US 23, take Main Street south to Huron and turn left. Hours are Mon through Sat from 10 a.m. to 5 p.m., Sun from noon to 5 p.m. Closed major holidays. Adults $$, children under 2 **free.**

One of the state's oldest and one of the top museums catering to children of all ages, Hands-On is a place where, as one eleven-year-old noted, kids can learn and have fun at the same time.

Opened in 1982 in the city's renovated, red central fire station, it has been expanded to take in neighboring buildings and contains more than 250 exhibits. One gallery is just for tots age four and under, who can develop their motor skills and at the same time start on the road to discovery about how things work. Other parts of the museum are divided into subject areas.

One section teaches kids about their bodies and how they work. Among other things children can measure their heartbeat and try to beat the clock to measure their reaction time.

Another section shows how technology can turn today's trash into tomorrow's electricity. In a special room a strobe light flashes, and kids are amazed as their own shadows are captured on the opposite wall. They can learn about physics and nature in another area, from building an arch and exploring fossils, to exploring light and optics through holograms. And they'll find out what really happens when they flush a toilet. The bubble chamber is the most asked-for exhibit, where kids can be enveloped in giant bubbles. Or they can create their own TV show. Explanations are offered for everything, but the kids seemingly ignore them, as they flit from one exhibit to another. Don't worry, though. They are learning without even knowing it.

The museum also has unique overnight programs for kids, including camp-ins, birthday programs, and special weekend activities, such as Sciencepalooza every month, featuring some aspect of science, from how a car's brakes work to space travel. On Sat afternoon there's always a science show. Other activities include maze making, exploring potential careers, and long-distance learning opportunities. You'll want to come back, guaranteed, and they will, too.

### Burton Memorial Tower  (all ages)
**In the middle of campus on South Thayer; (734) 764-2539. Free.**

Just look for the multistory pinnacle of this University of Michigan landmark and follow the music during weekly concerts at 10:15 a.m. on Sat during the school year. Lorie Tower on the North Campus also has concerts on Mon at 7 p.m. in June and July. Burton Tower is open to watch the fifty-five-bell Baird Carillon played weekdays from noon to 12:30 p.m. during the school year.

### Domino's Farms  (all ages)
**To get here, exit US 23 at Ann Arbor–Plymouth Road, go east, and follow the signs. For dates of activities, call (734) 998-0182; www.pettingfarm.com. Adults and children 2 and older $, children under 2 free.**

Located next to the Frank Lloyd Wright–inspired headquarters of Domino's Pizza, Domino's Farms depicts an early 1900s Michigan farm. Its fifteen acres host a plethora of programs geared to youngsters.

Come Easter, for instance, there's an annual egg hunt for the wee ones, as up to 1,500 eager youngsters divided into four age groups are set loose to scour the grounds for 20,000 plastic eggs containing candy, stickers, or coupons redeemable for age-appropriate prizes. And of course there's a visit by the Easter Bunny, as well as face painting, hayrides, and other entertainment.

In summer, drive the kids to a pasture fence to peer at a herd of buffalo. Wait to see the look in their eyes when you tell them that these huge woolly beasts weigh as much as a car and can run nearly as fast.

In the petting farm area, kids can stroke the chickens, sheep, goats, peacocks, pot-bellied pigs, and ponies. They can feed the ducks, too. Events appealing to the older set include arts-and-crafts shows and annual classic-car meets.

### Gallup Park  (all ages)
**3000 Fuller Rd., on the city's near-north side; (734) 662-9319; www.a2gov.org/canoe.**

From Apr through Oct, rent a paddleboat, a canoe, or a kayak and enjoy one of the city's best parks along the banks of the Huron River. Sorry, no swimming. Rental prices are as follows: canoes, kayaks, and paddleboats, $$$ for two hours; bikes, $$ per hour.

### Ann Arbor Folk Festival  (all ages)
**Presented in late Jan for two nights to support the Ark, the renowned coffeehouse/small-stage concert venue at 316 South Main. Usually takes place at Hill Auditorium, the great**

# Ann Arbor Pow Wow,
# Dance for Mother Earth (all ages)

The annual event takes place in late Mar or early Apr at Crisler Arena, 333 East Stadium Blvd., just east of the University of Michigan stadium. Adults $–$$, weekend passes $$, and family passes $$$$; children under 3 **free.** www.umich.edu/~powwow. Call (734) 763-9044.

Each year, as Mother Earth once again begins to shake off the pall of winter, more than 1,000 Native American dancers, drummers, and singers gather from Fri through Sun under the arena dome to pay homage.

There are grand entrances each day as dancers in full regalia make their way onto the arena floor, as well as competitive dancing and lots of handmade crafts. The powwow is an exciting and authentic way to introduce children to Native American culture.

concert hall of the University of Michigan. Tickets are $$–$$$, depending on seating desired. Call (734) 761-1800 for information on the event and the Ark; www.theark.org.

Got a hankering to introduce your kids to the sounds of your youth? Hear both old and new artists perform one after the other during this festival, which has taken place in the city for about thirty years now. Everything from acoustic folk to Cajun zydeco is performed, you're guaranteed a great time, and you'll be introducing the kids to the roots of their own music as well as widening their horizons. The Ark itself also presents performances by local and nationally known artists, as well as shows for kids.

## Matthaei Botanical Gardens and Nichols Arboretum (all ages)

1800 Dixboro Rd.; (734) 647-7600; www.mbgna.umich.edu. To get here, exit US 23 at Ann Arbor–Plymouth Road, go east to Dixboro Road, turn right, and go ¼ mile. The gardens are on the left side. The gardens themselves are open daily 8 a.m. to dusk. Touring the grounds is **free** every day. Conservatory admission $, under age 5 **free** and **free** for everyone on Wed from noon to 8 p.m.

Nichols Arboretum is a 123-acre living museum of Michigan flora as well as other plants from around the world, while the Matthaei is a 300-acre site with grand outdoor display gardens; an indoor conservatory featuring more than 1,200 plants from everywhere, from the desert to the tropics; and miles of nature trails to explore outside.

They use beneficial insects to control harmful bugs instead of insecticides. It's a great spot to wind down and let the kids blow off steam.

# Where to Eat

Ann Arbor is eclectic when it comes to restaurants. From the tried-and-true American
to Indian, Korean, German, and African, there
are hundreds of places to eat here.

Here's a sample:

**Argerio's.** 300 Detroit on downtown Ann
Arbor's north side; (734) 665-0444. A small,
family-run restaurant using family recipes for
great Italian fare from sausage to eggplant for
lunch and dinner. $$

**Blue Nile.** 221 East Washington in Ann
Arbor, east of Main Street; (734) 998-4746.
It's a rare treat to try ethnic food like this.
Ethiopian food is prepared using low-fat,
low-cholesterol methods and is served either
all vegetarian (spiced spinach, squash, and
potatoes with carrots are among the items)
or with spicy beef, chicken, and lamb on a
bed of *injera*, a spongy, soft flat bread. Kids
will get a kick out of eating here because
there are no utensils. Everything's served
family style, with an all-you-can-eat option,
and begins and ends with hot towels to clean
your hands. Try the spiced cinnamon tea. $$

**Gratzi.** 326 South Main St.; (734) 663-5555.
Sidewalk, first floor, even balcony seating.
Don't just expect spaghetti and meatballs at
Gratzi. Lunch and dinner. $$$

**Grizzly Peak Brewing Co.** 129 West Wash-
ington, just west of Main Street, downtown;
(734) 741-7325. Eclectic menu with pizzas,
pastas, ribs, and burgers. Watch as eight vari-
eties of beer are made on premises. Freshly
made root beer also available. Children's
menu. $$–$$$$

**Joe's Crab Shack.** 3020 Lohr Rd.; (734) 662-
7091. From I-94, take exit 175 (Ann Arbor–
Saline Road). Turn left, then left again onto
Lohr Road. A fun eatery where the kids have
their own playground and can watch the wait-
staff dance, while adults can choose from all
manner of seafood. $$

**Krazy Jim's Blimpy Burgers.** 551 South
Division at Packard; (734) 663-4590. A Uni-
versity of Michigan math student who either
had too much time on his hands or wanted
a challenge once calculated that you could
order well over a million variations of burgers
here. Any way you do, they've been great
since 1953. It's the oldest burger outlet in the
city, and they're all made to order. Want a
fried egg on top? You got it. Olives? Coming
up. Offering four different buns, from one to
five patties, and up to seven cheeses, Krazy
Jim's has been consistently picked by national
publications from *USA Today* to *GQ* as one
burger you have to try before you die.

**Le Dog.** 410 East Liberty St., and in the mall
at 30 South Main St.; (734) 665-2114 or (734)
327-0091. Open for lunch only. The origi-
nal Le Dog is the brainchild of owner Jules
VanDyck-Dubos, who just wanted to open
a hot dog stand. He did, but the unpreten-
tious red take-out stand with two ordering
windows blossomed into an eatery offering
food for kids as well as adults with a more
educated palate. It serves everything from
dogs to lobster bisque and bouillabaisse, to
summer gazpacho and New Orleans–style
jambalaya and was voted as having the city's
best soups. Treat your kids to one of Le Dog's
famous Yo-Berries, yogurt with four kinds of
berries. $–$$

**Metzger's German Restaurant.** 305 North
Zeeb Rd.; (734) 668-8987; wwwmetzgers.net.
Originally located in downtown Ann Arbor
beginning in 1928, this authentic German restaurant disappeared a few years ago, only to
reopen with an expanded menu that includes
steaks, fish, and the like, but still with a decidedly German accent to its menu. $$–$$$

**Seva Restaurant.** 314 East Liberty; (734)
662-1111. A vegetarian restaurant featuring
imaginative lunch and dinner. $$

**Stucchi's.** 320 South State St.; (734) 662-1700. Great locally made ice cream. $

**Washtenaw Dairy.** 602 South Ashley, just west of Main; (734) 662-3244. There's hardly a kid—or a parent—alive who can resist a single-dip ice-cream cone (for $2.50) that's the same size as a triple at national-brand stores. Giant cones, as well as doughnuts—in other words, all the staples a kid needs—are the fare here.

**Zingerman's Delicatessen.** 422 Detroit, on downtown Ann Arbor's near north side; (734) 663-3354; www.zingermans.com. You have to experience a Zingerman's sandwich at least once, and you'll want to come here to shop as often as your wallet allows. This deli may look like it's been here forever, but it opened in 1982. It has one of the largest selections of imported and local cheeses, meats, and breads you'll find in the state, although prices are somewhat expensive. This is a Sat tradition for many locals, so expect some lines, especially in the morning. Restaurant includes a "kids' room" with a special menu. $$. Also try Zingerman's Roadhouse at 2501 Jackson Ave., on the city's west side; (734) 663-FOOD; www.zingermans roadhouse.com.

## Where to Stay

**Hampton Inn South.** 925 Victors Way, northwest of I-94 exit 177; (734) 665-5000; www.hamptoninn.com. One of two in town, featuring 149 rooms with heated indoor pool, **free** hot breakfast, and movies. Near Briarwood Mall. Kids under eighteen stay **free.** $$–$$$

**Red Roof Inn.** 3505 South State St., off I-94 at exit 177; (734) 665-3500. One hundred nineteen rooms with continental breakfast, wireless Internet, and on-site laundry. Near Briarwood Mall. $$

**Red Roof Inn.** 3621 Plymouth Rd., at US 23 and Plymouth Road; (734) 996-5800. Typical Red Roof budget-minded amenities, wireless Internet in some rooms, and in-room movies. Restaurants nearby. $$

**Weber's Inn.** 505 Jackson Rd., off I-94 at exit 172; (734) 769-2500 or (800) 443-3050; www.webersinn.com. One hundred fifty-eight poolside or other rooms and suites. Indoor pool and recreation area with fitness and game centers and poolside cafe. Weber's restaurant is an Ann Arbor tradition that serves American cuisine. Great place for family getaways. Weekend packages available. $$$

## For More Information

**Ann Arbor Convention and Visitors Bureau.** 120 West Huron, Ann Arbor; (734) 995-7281 or (800) 888-9487; www.annarbor .org.

# Milan

This small farming community south of Ann Arbor along US 23 has two reasons to visit, neither one of them being the local federal prison.

### Milan Dragway (ages 8 and up)

Located 4 miles east of US 23 at exit 25, about 10 miles south of Ann Arbor; (734) 439-7368; www.milandragway.com. Open from Apr through late Oct. Bring earplugs for kids, as some of the dragsters can be very, very loud. Adults $$, kids ages 7 to 12 $; **free** for ages 6 and under. Admission prices may be higher for special events, so call the dragway and listen to the tape-recorded message.

Watch as the best of Michigan—and on special weekends, nationally ranked—drag racers burn up the ¼-mile track here. Special weekends salute devotees of Fords, Chevys, and Chrysler products. In late June the biggest event of the season comes to town with the Michigan Top Fuel Invitational, bringing several "funny" car dragsters capable of hitting close to 300 mile per hour. Local racers who have driver's licenses can see how fast the family van can go every Wed and Fri, when the track is open to all for an entry fee, and at times, even kids compete in special miniature drag cars. Not only is the car watching fun, but the people watching is often just as entertaining.

### Clean Water Beach (all ages)

**Off US 23 at exit 22. Follow the signs from the exit; (734) 439-1818. Adults $–$$, kids under 8 free. Season passes available. Open every nice day from Memorial Day through mid-Aug, then weekends until Labor Day.**

An attraction that started as a result of freeway construction decades ago is now a regional summer fun institution. When US 23, visible from the beach, was being poured, builders needed fill and got it by digging "borrow pits" close to the right-of-way.

In 1962 Milan resident Charles Heath saw workers dig up a six-and-a-half-acre hole in the ground in his horse pasture, watched it fill with water, and got an idea. With encouragement from friends, Heath made improvements to his family swimming hole and opened it to the public, and beachgoers have been returning each summer to enjoy what he created.

## Where to Eat

**Lighthouse Coffee Co.** 9 West Main St.; (734) 439-3623. Features their own baked goods in Ann Arbor and gourmet coffees, homemade pastries, and more. Open for breakfast, lunch, and dinner daily. $

**Roy's BBQ-n-Burgers.** 25 Wabash; (734) 439-1737. Half-pound burgers and barbecue sandwiches are served in a diner setting daily except Sun. $

## Where to Stay

See Ann Arbor and Ypsilanti entries for nearby accommodations.

# Ypsilanti

Home of Eastern Michigan University and its landmark brick water tower, the city was one of the mainstays of what President Franklin Roosevelt called the Arsenal of Democracy during World War II.

The giant Willow Run bomber plant poured out B-24 "Liberator" bombers at the rate of about one an hour. Later the plant, which was the largest factory under one roof, was home to several auto companies. Willow Run is still an active airport and home to one of the city's major attractions.

### Elvisfest  (all ages)

In historic Depot Town in Ypsilanti; (734) 480-3974; www.mielvisfest.org. Take exit 183 off I-94 (Huron Street) and head north. Then just follow the signs.

This annual salute to "the King," which outdoes even Las Vegas for Elvis spotting, takes place in mid-July. During this weekend event hundreds of fans squeeze into white caped jumpsuits, leather jackets, and, of course, wigs to see how close they can come to resembling Presley. Enjoy fan memorabilia and food as you listen to various interpreters of "His" music belt out his famed hits. While you're trying on your own jumpsuit, the kids can do rock climbing, watch magic acts and stilt walkers, do crafts, and perhaps even don a wig and sideburns and learn the famous Elvis hip gyration.

Don't laugh. You'll even see babies in mini-Elvis capes and sideburns. Now laugh.

### Michigan Firehouse Museum  (all ages)

110 West Cross St.; (734) 547-0663; www.michiganfirehousemuseum.org. From I-94 take exit 183 (Huron Street) and go north. Turn left on Cross Street and get in the right lane. Turn right onto Washington Street. Street parking is available. Open 10 a.m. to 4 p.m. Tues through Sat, noon to 4 p.m. Sun. Admission $, children 5 and under **free.**

Kids and anyone who has ever said, "I want to grow up to be a fireman," will love going through this museum, located in the city's former 1898 firehouse. It was founded to honor the men and women who battle fires across the state and to teach fire safety and prevention. Exhibits include a 1918 hand- or horse-drawn pumper, other antique apparatuses, and antique brass fire bells.

### Wiard's Orchards and Country Fair  (all ages)

5565 Merritt Rd.; (734) 482-7744; www.wiards.com. Take Huron Street, exit 183, off I-94 and go south, following the signs. Open daily in fall. The "Ultimate Haunted Barn" is not recommended for children under twelve. $.

Each weekend in Sept and Oct, up to 15,000 people head for Wiard's for its annual harvest celebration, topped off by a salute to Halloween. Kids are catered to farmwide, with goats and pigs to feed, pony rides, minigolf, and a "straw mountain" kids can play in. There are wagon rides and fire engine rides through the orchard past trees heavy with fruit and fields of ripe pumpkins. Kids get a kick out of yanking apples right off the tree and picking out the family jack-o'-lanterns. They also have fun in a maze cut into a cornfield. In Oct there's a haunted evening hayride through the orchard, plus the "Ultimate Haunted Barn" for teens and adults who like their surprises definitely scarier. Mom and Dad can try karaoke, pick nine varieties of apples, taste a glass of fresh-squeezed cider, or head for the bakery.

## Where to Eat

**Haab's.** 18 West Michigan Ave.; (734) 483-8200. Lunch and dinner, including children's menu and seniors' discounts and special Haab's anniversary with prices reduced to 1934 levels for three items. At the location since 1934. $$

## Where to Stay

**Ann Arbor Marriott Ypsilanti at Eagle Crest.** I-94 and Whittaker Road, south of exit 183; (734) 487-2000. Upscale property has 242 rooms, indoor pool, and other amenities, including a weight room and a restaurant. Also home of Eastern Michigan University's Eagle Crest university golf course. $$–$$$

## For More Information

**Ypsilanti Convention and Visitors Bureau.** 106 West Michigan Ave., Ypsilanti; (734) 483-4444; www.ypsilanti.org.

# Belleville

Suburbia has eaten into the neighboring farmlands in this Detroit-area community, but Belleville still retains a small-town feel—and the downtown festival that makes the area famous every Father's Day.

## National Strawberry Festival (all ages)

From I-94, take the Belleville Road exit and turn south into town. There's **free** parking at the Wayne County Fairgrounds, with shuttle rides to the festival; for a festival information recording, call (734) 697-3137; www.nationalstrawberryfest.com. For picking information, call Rowe's Strawberry Farm at (734) 482-8538 (see www.rowesproducefarm.com) and Potter's at (734) 461-6348. The farms are within only a few minutes of downtown.

Come Father's Day weekend, the farm fields around this part of southern lower Michigan blush bright red as one of the state's most luscious crops comes into its prime. It's strawberry-picking time. Two farms offer pick-your-own family fun. Rowe's Farm, with twenty-seven acres of berries, and Potter's, with two acres, offer row upon row of the luscious fruit over the picking season. Berries, best picked in the morning, are sold by the pound, and considering their size, it doesn't take long before you and your kids are lugging four or five pounds of the beautiful, ripe red treats up to the weigh-in center. Rowe's Farm also offers raspberries until the first hard frost.

The picking, though, is just a prelude to the festival, which each year draws up to 175,000 berry lovers to Belleville over the weekend and closes downtown to traffic.

Organizers pride themselves on making the entire festival a family affair, with lots of kids' events and even a family circus. At games designated especially for young children, players can win prizes by reaching for a plastic duck, blowing the biggest bubble gum bubble, or joining in a tug-of-war. There are pony rides and places where young hands can make arts-and-crafts items. Carnival rides at two locations include a special section just for the youngest. A parade is held on Saturday.

Even if the local crop isn't quite ready yet, there are strawberry treats everywhere you turn, from shortcake and pies to sundaes. Whatever they can put strawberries in, they do. Fresh strawberries also are sold by the quart or case, in case you got to the party too late to join the picking.

### Yankee Air Force Museum  (all ages)

On the west side of Willow Run airport; (734) 483-4030; www.yankeeairmuseum.org. To reach the museum from I-94, exit at the Willow Run Airport exit (exit 186) and turn right onto Tyler Road; then follow directions to hangar 2. From the east, leave I-94 at exit 185. Turn onto the west access road. Go to Tyler and turn left, and then follow the directions to hangar 2.   Tours are provided Tues through Sat 10 a.m. to 3 p.m.

A devastating fire in late 2004 destroyed the museum's original home, which it had occupied since 1981. That former hangar had been used during World War II as a school for mechanics, when B-24 "Liberator" bombers were produced in what was then the world's largest plant under one roof. Six historic planes were lost. The group is raising funds for a new home. Two of the museum's flyable craft—a B-17 bomber and a B-25 bomber—are available for rides.

### Taste of Belleville  (all ages)

In downtown Belleville, along High Street; (734) 697-7151. The fourth Thurs of Aug. $.

Taking place in conjunction with the annual Belleville Bridge Walk over the bridge on Belleville Lake, the event features tastes of offerings at area restaurants, along with entertainment. Most of the restaurants will serve along High Street.

## For More Information

**Belleville Area Chamber of Commerce.**
248 Main St., Belleville; (734) 697-7151; www
.bellevillech.org.

# Sumpter Township

Sumpter Township has a distinctive country atmosphere. It was named for the Revolutionary War hero General Thomas Sumter, but a spelling error by a nineteenth-century clerk gave it its different name, and no one bothered to change it.

### Crosswinds Marsh Wetland Interpretive Preserve
(all ages)

Take I-275 south from I-94 to exit 8, Will Carleton Road. Head west 3³⁄₁₀ miles until it becomes Oakville-Waltz Road. Turn north on Haggerty, and the entrance is ½ mile on the left; (734) 654-1220; www.waynecountyparks.org, and follow the links. Call for hours. **Free.**

Sometimes something good comes from "progress." Built to replace wetlands lost by Detroit Metropolitan Airport's expansion, Crosswinds' 1,059 acres make it one of the largest artificially created wetlands in the country. Any threatened plants and animals were moved from the construction zone to this preserve, which ironically was farmland that originally was a wetland. The result is a bird-watchers' paradise in spring and fall, with more than 200 species spotted, including egret, heron, osprey, white pelican, and a pair of resident bald eagles that in the last decade have produced seven eaglets.

There are 4½ miles of bridle paths (bring your own horse). Five hiking loops, from ³⁄₁₀ mile to 5 miles, take visitors over boardwalks, through marshland, and past two fishing docks. A 2-mile canoe trail includes a stop at an island and features interpretive markers for paddlers to follow and learn. Canoe rental is **free,** as is binocular rental.

There are ungroomed cross-country ski trails open in winter, weather permitting, and interpretive programs offered for groups Apr through Oct. It's a great spot for quiet hikes so close to one of the nation's major metropolitan centers.

# Westland

This city may be the only one in the country named after a shopping mall. What used to be called Nankin Township changed its name when the mall, one of the region's first enclosed shopping centers, was built at its center. It's now a typical Detroit suburb but has some interesting stop offs for visitors, besides that mall, which expanded.

### Westland Shopping Center (all ages)

At the corner of Wayne and Warren Roads at 35000 Warren Rd.; (734) 425-5001; www .westlandcenter.com. Hours are10 a.m. to 9 p.m. Mon through Sat, 11 a.m. to 6 p.m. Sun. Strollers may be rented for a small fee.

The mall features eighty-eight stores, plus an arcade to keep the teens busy while you shop. Anchor stores include Macy's, Sears, and JCPenney.

### Wayne County Lightfest (all ages)

Between Westland and Dearborn Heights on 4½ miles of Hines Drive; (734) 261-1990; www .waynecounty.com/parks, and follow the links. Runs between mid-Nov and Jan 1 (closed Christmas night). Minimum donation ($) per car to help keep the fest operating. Traffic is one-way after the roadway is closed from 7 to 10 p.m., following rush hour. Enter at Hines Drive and Merriman, 2½ miles south of the Merriman/I-96 exit.

Nearly one million lights grace sweeping arches and tree-lined straights of Hines Drive in what is billed as the Midwest's largest drive-through holiday light show. Drive past more than thirty-five displays that shine nightly, sponsored by regional businesses.

Refreshments are available.

### William P. Holliday Forest and Nature Preserve (all ages)

Entrances off Cowan Road west of Westland Center, off Newburgh Road north of War- ren Road in Westland, and three other locations; (734) 261-1990; www.waynecounty.com/ parks/pickpark. **Free.**

This 503-acre nature preserve in the midst of the state's most populous area is a gem. It is located along the banks of Tonquish Creek, named for the Native American chief who is buried within its borders. Part of the Rouge River system, the preserve has more than 10 miles of hiking trails, and nature walks are offered regularly.

## Where to Eat

**Famous Dave's Barbecue.** 36601 Warren Rd.; (734) 595-1000; www.famousdaves.com. Great barbecue, served family style or by the plate. Choose from chicken, ribs, brisket, pulled pork, and even fish. Try the bread pudding and key lime pie desserts. $$–$$$

# Dearborn

About a mile south and then east about 12 more miles from Westland is Dearborn, the city that Henry Ford's car built. Here two museums are dedicated to what Ford admired most: middle America. Lots of other activities draw tourists here, too.

### The Henry Ford (all ages)

**20900 Oakwood Blvd.; (313) 271-1620; www.thehenryford.org. From I-94, exit to the Southfield Freeway (Highway 39) northbound and go 3 miles to northbound Oakwood, and then continue about 2 more miles to the entrance. Admission to the museum and/or village can be purchased together or separately. Combined admission is $$$, children under five free. Call for details and dates for special events, like the antique auto muster, sheep shearing at Firestone Farm, and more.**

This complex, begun by Henry Ford, today is much more than what even he had envisioned when it opened in the 1930s. From the Lincoln in which President John F. Kennedy rode in Dallas on Nov 22, 1963, to the Ford that became the first American vehicle to win the famous Le Mans twenty-four-hour race in France, to the chair President Abraham Lincoln sat in at Ford's Theatre on Apr 14, 1865, to the tiny clapboard bicycle shop in Ohio where two brothers taught the world how to fly, this gathering of more than a hundred historic buildings and one of the world's great museums makes the ninety-three-acre complex in Dearborn one of the state's top family tourist destinations.

At the entrance to the grounds stands the Henry Ford Museum, surrounded by the Ford Motor Company. Inside, be sure to take the youngsters, who may have possibly never seen a drive-in, to the miniature version showing old film clips. It's right next to the full-size old-fashioned service station. Peer inside a real New York diner and one of the first rooms of what then was a new motel chain, Holiday Inn. Walk past the museum's collection of more than a hundred antique and classic cars, including the only remaining 1896 Duryea, America's first production vehicle. And wait until the kids stand dwarfed next to the giant, 600-ton steam locomotive.

Greenfield Village is dedicated to the history of small-town America and American inventiveness. See where the Wright brothers designed their first airplane and where they lived. Then step into the laboratory where Thomas Edison invented the lightbulb. Edison's chair remains just as the inventor left it. That's because his friend Henry Ford nailed it to the floor when Edison visited to celebrate his most famous invention's fiftieth anniversary.

There's a log cabin similar to the one in which scientist, inventor, and teacher George Washington Carver grew up; another exhibit depicts how African Americans lived both before and after slavery. Take a carriage or steamboat ride aboard the *Suwanee* in summer, or if you visit in winter, ride in a horse-drawn sleigh when the snow cooperates.

Walking tours are offered in fall.

## IMAX Theater (ages 5 and up)

**Located on the west side of Henry Ford Museum, 20900 Oakwood Blvd.; (313) 271-1620; www.hfmgv.org. From the Southfield Freeway (Highway 39), exit at Michigan Avenue. Turn south at Oakwood to the museum entrance, or if headed south on Highway 39, exit at Michigan and continue on the service drive. Turn west at the village entrance on Village Road. Theater entry fees vary by showing, $$. Admission is separate from the museum and village.**

Welcome to the future of moviegoing. Located on the grounds of the same museum that pays homage to American inventions and, in particular, one of the pioneers of the motion picture, Thomas Edison, the IMAX Theater is something that Tom would be proud of. It's one of the crowd-pleasing additions to the museum.

The theater boasts a panoramic 60-by-80-foot screen. It's capable of showing both two- and three-dimensional films, with seating for 400 persons and a sound system that will put any teenager's boom box to shame.

Outside the entrance there's a great gift shop with museum and theater-related items. The theater is a great addition to an already great museum, the world's largest indoor-outdoor museum. You can't miss it.

## Ford Rouge Plant Tour (all ages)

**Leaves from the Henry Ford; (313) 271-1620 or, for tickets, (313) 982-6001; www.thehenry ford.com, then click on the Rouge Tour tab. Online discount ticket coupons available. Adults $$$, ages 3 to 12 $$, under 2 free.**

Come see a Detroit icon. The Rouge, built in the early 1900s, at its peak employed 100,000 workers. During that period the plant brought in raw materials at one end and manufactured everything from tires to glass to put on the cars that came out the other end. The complex currently builds pickup trucks and features a state-of-the-art "living" roof to lessen the plant's environmental impact. A two-hour tour, which involves all your senses, starts in two theaters and then goes into the plant. You'll learn about the history of the automobile in Detroit and at Ford and the Rouge.

There's also a gift shop. It's an impressive trip.

## Automotive Hall of Fame (ages 8 and up)

**Adjacent to the Henry Ford at 21400 Oakwood Blvd.; (313) 240-4000; www.automotivehall offame.org.   Call for hours and days open. Admission $, under age 5 free. The Hall of Fame and Henry Ford Museum offer a combination ticket allowing visits at a reduced price. $–$$, 4 and under free.**

The Hall of Fame honors the greats in the auto industry, including some who've until now gone unsung. In mock-ups of the inventor's workshops, kids can push buttons and hear portrayals of industry greats. Through hands-on displays kids can learn how pioneers like

Chevrolet, Chrysler, Ford, Honda, Mack, and Benz lent their names to their vehicles. The hall is not dedicated just to those who created auto accessories, but also to the pioneers who led the fight for workers' rights in the 1930s.

The Hall of Fame includes a classic-car display, displays on famous racing cars, and annual outdoor displays of cars considered industry milestones.

There's also a gift shop.

## Fair Lane (ages 8 and up)

**On the campus of the University of Michigan at Dearborn, off Evergreen Road north of Michigan Avenue; (313) 593-5590; www.henryfordestate.org. From the Southfield Freeway (Highway 39), head west on Michigan and north on Evergreen, and then follow the signs. Closed Mon. Adults $$, children under 4 free. Self-guided ground maps are $2. Call to check on tours, as they vary by season.**

The mansion where Henry Ford entertained luminaries of his day, from Lindbergh to President Hoover, and where he died, offers one-and-a-half to two-hour tours. The tours include a look through the restored powerhouse, which once more produces enough electricity using the Rouge River to light the home, plus part of the university campus. Built in 1914, the mansion, which has six levels, features a cornerstone laid by Thomas Edison.

In a restoration of Henry Ford's personal garage, see eight historic vehicles, especially his first vehicle, the quadracycle; his Model T; and the Model A he was riding in the day he died, plus miniature cars created for his children. Also there is the 1920s camper that Ford, Edison, and other friends (such as tire maker Harvey Firestone and naturalist John Burroughs) vacationed in and which many credit with starting the camping and RV industry. You'll also see the cutter sleigh that Henry and wife, Clara, used at the estate; a prototype electric car that he was to build with Edison; an early Fordson tractor, the vehicle that helped modernize the American farm; and the just-added Sweepstakes, a 1901 race car with whose winnings he started the Ford Motor Company.

The estate's gardens have been totally restored and include waterfalls and meadows designed by renowned landscape architect Jens Jensen. There's also a restaurant, the Pool, which was built over Ford's original indoor swimming pool; it is open for lunch Tues through Fri.

## Homecoming (all ages)

**In Ford Field Park, north of Michigan Avenue at the end of Monroe; (313) 943-2285. Takes place the first weekend in Aug. $ for carnival rides and food. Concerts and fireworks are free.**

This annual late-summer festival draws thousands to the park along a branch of the Rouge River and is considered the city's largest annual event. Former big-name recording artists are always a draw when they perform in a natural near-bowl formed by the river valley. There are carnival rides for the kids and food from various Dearborn-area civic groups and restaurants.

### Arab American National Museum (all ages)

13624 Michigan Ave., in the heart of East Dearborn, nearly across from City Hall; (313) 582-AANM; www.theaanm.org. Open 10 a.m. to 6 p.m. Wed, Fri, and Sat, 10 a.m. to 8 p.m. Thurs, and noon to 5 p.m. Sun. Admission $, 5 and under **free.**

Learn about the accomplishments, inventions, celebrities, and other facts about the nation's Arab Americans. Dearborn is home to the largest Arabic-speaking community outside of the Middle East and hosts an annual festival where your can chow down on great Middle Eastern food and learn more about one of the country's newest immigrant groups.

### Ford Community and Performing Arts Center (all ages)

15801 Michigan Ave. at Greenfield Road; (313) 943-2354; www.cityofdearborn.org, then follow the links.

Dearborn's crown jewel of entertainment is also an exercise and aquatic center with two pools, a gymnasium, and a 1,201-seat theater that plays host to conventions, meetings, and entertainment from musicals to concerts. The complex is billed as the largest municipally owned civic center in North America. There's also a small fast-food restaurant inside. Entry is **free,** but ticket prices for events vary.

## Where to Eat

**BD's Mongolian Barbecue.** 22115 Michigan Ave., in the Shoppes at West Village, West Dearborn; (313) 792-9660; www.gomongo.com, and find the location. Kids and adults have fun concocting their own stir-fry blend of meats or seafood with veggies and various spices, and watching one of several cooks stir up their creation in a giant wok using wooden utensils. Either enjoy one helping or pay for all you can eat. There are suggested combinations if you don't want to be adventurous. $–$$

**Big Fish.** 700 Town Center Dr., on the south side of the Fairlane Town Center shopping mall complex, between Michigan Avenue and Hubbard Drive; (313) 336-6350. A great place to treat the family to fresh seafood dinners, including seafood pastas and whole fish. $$$

**Eagle Tavern.** Inside Greenfield Village (village admission required); (313) 271-1620. If you want to show the kids what an 1850s stagecoach stop might have looked like, head here, where you can sample fare of the era and be greeted as if you are city slickers just off the stage, right down to the comments about those "strange city clothes" you're wearing. It's one of six restaurants in the complex. $$$

**Fifty One Oh One.** 5101 Evergreen Rd. (in the student center on the campus of Henry Ford Community College, just north of Fair Lane and U of M Dearborn on Evergreen Road between Ford Road and Michigan Avenue); (313) 845-9642; www.hfcc.edu/about_us/5101.asp. Serving lunch Tues through Thurs at 11 a.m. and 12:15 p.m.; dinner Wed at 6 and 7:15 p.m. Great inexpensive meals because you pay only the cost of the food. Meals are concocted by culinary arts students. $$

**Kowloon.** 22905 Michigan Ave., east of Outer Drive; (313) 565-4521. Inexpensive Cantonese and some Szechuan Chinese dishes. $$

**La Penguina Deli.** 4838 Greenfield Rd.; (313) 945-6633. Open Mon through Fri 8 a.m. to 4:30 p.m. Great cold and hot sandwiches, soups, and pasta salads, plus Calder chocolate milk (see entry for Calder Dairy Farm). Stop at the Italian bakery next door, too. $

**La Pita.** 22681 Newman St., between Outer Drive and Military; (313) 563-7482. Introduce your family to Middle Eastern food at this friendly restaurant in a small shopping center across from Sacred Heart Church. Try the chicken shawarma, either lunch or dinner portion. It's roasted, shaved chicken with sauce and even a pickle slice wrapped in pita bread. Lots of other dishes, too, plus tasty, freshly made fruit smoothies. Children's menu includes burgers and chicken. $–$$$

**Richter's Chalet.** 23920 Michigan Ave., just east of Telegraph Road; (313) 565-0484. Serves great authentic German cuisine. When they're available, try the great bacon, applesauce, or sour cream potato pancakes. Park in rear. $$

## Where to Stay

**Dearborn Inn & Marriott Hotel.** 20301Oakwood Blvd., just south of Greenfield Village complex; (313) 271-2700. Built by Henry Ford to accommodate travelers using his Ford Tri-Motor airplanes landing across the street at the complex, which is now a Ford test track, the inn has 222 rooms and serves breakfast, lunch, and dinner in two restaurants. For a treat, try staying in one of five cottages built as replica homes of famous Americans. $$$

**Hyatt Regency Dearborn.** Fairlane Town Center, at the northwest corner of Michigan Avenue and Southfield Freeway (Highway 39); (313) 593-1234. A thirteen-story modern hotel with 786 rooms, with open interior balconies for each floor. Dining rooms, coffee shop, and deli for breakfast, lunch, and dinner. Also a pool, hot tub, sauna, and fitness club. $$$

**Red Roof Inn.** 24130 Michigan Ave., near the corner of Telegraph Road; (313) 278-9732. Inexpensive lodging in 111 rooms with Red Roof quality. Continental breakfast. $$$

**Ritz Carlton–Dearborn.** 300 Town Center Dr., at the southwest corner of Hubbard Drive and Southfield Freeway (Highway 39); (313) 441-2000. Going north, exit Southfield at Michigan Avenue and continue north on the access drive to Hubbard, and then go west about 1 block. Going south, exit Highway 39 at Ford Road and continue on the access road to Hubbard, and then head west about 1 block. Elegant rooms located within walking distance of the Fairlane Town Center shopping mall. The property has 308 rooms and dining rooms that serve expensive breakfast, lunch, and dinner. Head for other mall-area restaurants off Town Center Drive and in the mall if your budget doesn't allow eating at the Ritz. $$$$

## For More Information

**Dearborn Chamber of Commerce.** 15544 Michigan Ave., Dearborn ; (313) 584-6100; www.dearbornchamber.org.

# Wyandotte

This city, which once was known only for its odoriferous chemical plant and steel mills, has undergone a renaissance that has transformed it into a bustling recreational community and close-knit Detroit suburb south of Dearborn. Take the Southfield Freeway

# Wyandotte **Art Fair** (all ages)

Nearly as big as the one in Ann Arbor, Wyandotte's annual fair is another street celebration, with the lower Detroit River providing a beautiful watercolor background. Hundreds of artists set up stalls as streets close and the city parties. The fair takes place in downtown every mid-July.

Call (734) 324-4500 for information.

(eventually it becomes Southfield Road) to its end at the Detroit River at Jefferson Avenue. Turn right and parallel the river a few miles, and you're there.

## Ford–MacNichol Home and Wyandotte Museum (ages 5 and up)

2610 Biddle Ave.; (734) 324-7297; www.wyandotte.net/historical-museum. Hours: Thurs through Sun, noon to 4 p.m. $.

The historic home is decorated in the style of the Victorian era. The basement museum chronicles the history of the city from the early 1800s, when it was a Native American village, to the 1900s, when it was a smoky chemical- and steelmaking center.

## Detroit River Kayak Tours (ages 12 and over in their own boat with adults; under 12 must be in a tandem kayak)

Located at Riverside Kayak Connection. 4016 Biddle Ave.; (734) 285-2925; www.riverside kayak.com. Cost includes kayak, paddle, life jacket, and whistle. Paddlers must wear life jackets. $$$$.

Take a kayak tour of the lower Detroit River and see some of the diverse wildlife that is part of the Detroit River International Wildlife Refuge. Several tours are offered, based on experience levels and weather conditions. You've got a good chance to see a bald eagle or two. You read that correctly. That's how much the water quality has improved here along the river.

## Where to Eat

**Porto Fino.** 3445 Biddle Ave., on the Detroit River; (734) 281-6700. Specializing in Italian cuisine and seafood. Dine indoors or on the dock next to boats tying up at riverside. Great atmosphere. The dock tends to be a bit congested and noisy, especially on weekends, but the river views are worth the wait. $$$

**Speedboat Bar.** 749 Biddle Ave.; (734) 282-5750. Look for the bow of a boat that seemingly has propelled itself onto the roof of this landmark neighborhood downriver eatery. Specialty is chili. $$

## For More Information

**Wyandotte City Community Relations Office.** 3131 Biddle Ave., Wyandotte; (734) 324-4505; www.wyandotte.net.

# Detroit

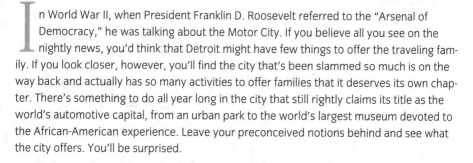

I n World War II, when President Franklin D. Roosevelt referred to the "Arsenal of Democracy," he was talking about the Motor City. If you believe all you see on the nightly news, you'd think that Detroit might have few things to offer the traveling family. If you look closer, however, you'll find the city that's been slammed so much is on the way back and actually has so many activities to offer families that it deserves its own chapter. There's something to do all year long in the city that still rightly claims its title as the world's automotive capital, from an urban park to the world's largest museum devoted to the African-American experience. Leave your preconceived notions behind and see what the city offers. You'll be surprised.

## Top
## FamilyAdventures in Detroit

1. **Charles H. Wright Museum of African American History, in the Cultural Center.** An eye-opening showcase of the struggle and triumph of African Americans, with great rotating and permanent exhibits. www.maah-detroit.org.

2. **Belle Isle Park, in the Detroit River.** A unique island park with everything from a nature zoo to beaches.

3. **Detroit's Coney Islands, on Lafayette Avenue.** Bite into a Coney dog, and you've tasted the essence of the city.

4. **Auto Shows, Cobo Center.** What else says more about Detroit than cars? www.naias.com and www.autorama.com.

5. **Detroit's Cultural Center, near the Wayne State University Campus.** One of the nation's leading universities, surrounded by the symphony, art, science, and historical museums.

# DETROIT

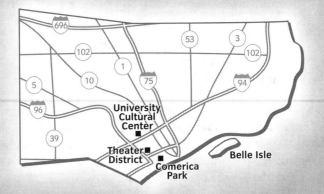

University
Cultural
Center ■

Theater ■
District
Comerica
Park ■

Belle Isle

# Belle Isle

Welcome to America's largest city-owned island park, reached by a gracefully arching ½-mile-long bridge. Located in the middle of the Detroit River, the island is reached by exiting I-75 at Jefferson Avenue and heading east. Turn right and cross onto the island by the Douglas MacArthur, or Belle Isle, Bridge from Jefferson Avenue.

Belle Isle is Detroit's downtown playground, home to its own herd of deer, within sight of the state's tallest buildings. On the 985-acre island in the middle of the Detroit River are so many family attractions that you couldn't do justice to them in an entire summer. There are about 8 miles of roads on the island, with top speed limits of 20 miles per hour in most areas, including a 5½-mile drive circling the perimeter. You'll find plenty of picnic and other relaxing opportunities, including a beach on the calm, quiet side of the Detroit River. Many of the activities are within walking distance of one another. Just park your car along one of the tree-lined boulevards and enjoy.

### Belle Isle Nature Zoo  (all ages)

Located on Central Avenue; (313) 852-4056; www.detroitzoo.org/visitors/nature_center. $.

The motto of the new "zoo," really more of a nature center, is "bringing the wilds of Michigan to the heart of Detroit," and the zoo does just that. Its newest exhibit is "Deer Encounter." Kids enjoy getting close to fallow deer, part of a herd that roamed the island freely until only a few years ago. Interpreters from the Huron-Clinton Metroparks present a variety of nature programs.

### Whitcomb Conservatory  (all ages)

Located in midisland; (313) 331-7760; www.bibsociety.org. Open daily from 10 a.m. to 5 p.m. Call for details on upcoming flower shows and hours. Free.

Surrounded by grounds from which you can see giant oceangoing and lake freighters pass by in the Detroit River, the domed conservatory houses a unique display. It's a great place to explore the world of plants through more than 2,000 species, from desert settings for cacti to tropical humidity for ferns, palms, and banana trees. The conservatory's annual winter orchid and mum shows, two of six special events mounted here annually, are spectacular.

## The **First Tee**  (ages 6 and up)

Call (313) 852-4086 for clubhouse, (313) 852-4106 for driving range. The Belle Isle golf course has been redesigned and improved to bring the game to everyone. A public-private partnership between Ford Motor Company, the city, and the World Golf Foundation (part of the PGA) renovated the existing course into a new nine-hole course, with a training center for kids and adults, a driving range, and a putting green.

## Dossin Great Lakes Museum (all ages)

Located on Strand Drive, on the southwest shore; (313) 852-4051; www.detroithistorical .org. Open Sat and Sun 11 a.m. to 4 p.m. and weekdays for groups by appointment. Adults $, under 4 **free.**

This is a city treasure. While the marine radio crackles with the sounds of river traffic, kids can stand in the working wheelhouse of a former Great Lakes ore carrier in the Ford fleet. Marvel at the Gothic Room, with more than 7½ tons of hand-carved oak work taken from a 1912 Great Lakes steamer, and see the first boat to break the 100-mile-per-hour barrier on a closed course. There's a great model display, too, along with terrific views of passing vessels during the summer shipping season.

## Kids Kingdom Playscape and Scott Fountain (all ages)

Located on Belle Isle; (313) 852-4075. **Free.**

Two of the island's favorites are the Kids Kingdom and Scott Fountain. Kids Kingdom is made for romping, with lots of safe play surfaces.

The white-marble Scott Fountain, a gift to the city by the eccentric James Scott, offers colored light shows from dusk to 11 p.m. from Memorial Day to late Sept.

## Detroit International River Days (all ages)

Located along Detroit's new RiverWalk, between Rivard Plaza and Hart Plaza; (313) 963-8418; www.detroitriverdays.com. Detroit's neighbor across the river—Windsor, Ontario, another auto town—hosts an annual summer fest as well, with a downtown carnival; rides are extra.

Taking place in late June and billed as the replacement for the aging Freedom Festival, this new annual event makes best use of the city's reviving waterfront, which is sprouting new parks, bikeways, and fun things to do for the entire family. Like the Freedom Fest it culminates in a huge fireworks show on the Detroit River and coincides with Windsor, Ontario's Summer Fest, running the same time across the river (remember, proper identification is required to cross into Canada), reachable via the Ambassador Bridge or the Detroit-Windsor Tunnel. River Days spotlights the parkland that has been made by the Rivard Plaza and also takes in the General Motors Plaza and Promenade, festooned with rows of fountains. Eventually, parks and walkways, a bike rental kiosk, and even a carousel that kids can ride will stretch to Belle Isle. The festival gives families the opportunity to enjoy the RiverWalk project and Hart Plaza. The fun includes a carnival, live Detroit Symphony performances and other music, and a special family-fun zone, plus food from Detroit restaurants. It's organized by the Detroit Riverfront Conservancy, one of the forces behind the riverfront's growing renaissance from an industry base into a ribbon of parkland that organizers hope will stretch from Lake St. Clair to Lake Erie.

## Campus Martius Park (all ages)

Located along Woodward Avenue in downtown Detroit; (313) 962-0101; www.campus martiuspark.org. Call or check the Web site for specifics and events. **Free.** Ice skate rental is $; if you bring your own skates, shoe storage is $.

# Chrysler-Jeep Superstores **APBA Gold Cup** (ages six and up)

The boat races usually take place in mid-July. Race-day tickets range from $$ to $$$$ (for the best seats). Pit passes also are available to watch the giant boats lifted in and out of the water and to see the crews and drivers up close. If you can afford it, it's a great way to show the kids these complex machines, now powered by turbine engines. If you're near the course, earplugs might be a good idea, especially for younger kids All ages are welcome, but older children may be more interested. Call (586) 774-0980 for updates on future dates, or visit www.gold-cup.com.

Bring along a cooler, spread out a blanket or grab a grandstand seat, and enjoy the day as the shore between the mainland and Belle Isle is taken over by race mania. There, the river's tricky waves are tested by up to a dozen Unlimited-class hydroplanes. An estimated 400,000 fans come to watch the boats, turning the event into a giant picnic beside the water. These boats are built to skip across the river surface with a high-pitched whine, shooting giant columns of water called "rooster tails" into the sky.

During the race, drivers navigate a difficult course, encapsulated in cockpits like fighter jet pilots. They compete in several heats around a 2½-mile modified oval, running up to 225 miles per hour in the straights. Boats compete on both Sat and Sun, with qualifying heats starting before noon. Top finishers rack up race points, and those with the highest totals earn a spot in the afternoon championship heat. Smaller boats powered by automobile engines, as well as classic racing boats, also compete on their own white-knuckle rides around the river, which, because of the peculiar waves formed by break walls, can be treacherous at times.

This rejuvenated park has become the heart of a renewed downtown along Woodward Avenue. In summer, enjoy monthly concerts, while in winter the boards go up and the ice goes down on the park's skating rink, one of the highlights of the season. Families join downtown workers for an evening or weekend skate, especially when the city Christmas tree twinkles atop the park's fountain. The rink usually opens in Nov and is open until 9 p.m. weekdays, until 11 p.m. Fri and Sat, and until 8 p.m. Sun.

## Mexicantown International Welcome Center and Mercado (all ages)

In Detroit's Mexicantown area, at 2835 Bagley Ave.; (313) 967-9898; www.mexicantown .org. Admission is **free.** To reach Mexicantown, exit I-75 southbound at Clark Street, take the service drive to Bagley, and head west a few blocks and look for the banners along Bagley. From northbound I-75, exit at Springwells, head north to Vernor, and turn right. From I-96, exit at Michigan Avenue and take the southbound service drive to either Vernor or Bagley.

You can let the kids pour on the hot sauce over authentic Mexican fare and test their palates, find a toy among the craftspeople, or join in the folk-dancing demonstrations at this facility hosting several events throughout the year in the heart of the city's Latin community. And don't forget the great restaurants for inexpensive Latin fare that's as mild or wild as you wish (see Where to Eat).

### African-American World Festival  (all ages)

At Hart Plaza the third weekend in Aug. Hours are noon to 11 p.m. Fri through Sun during the festival. Admission is **free.** For specifics and events for each year's festival, call the Charles H. Wright Museum of African American History at (313) 494-5800; www .maah-detroit.org.

More than 200 vendors from around the world gather to sell their wares. There's African, Caribbean, and Haitian cooking. Storytellers, performers, and activities are in the Children's Village.

# Theatrical Adventures

Just up the street from the Coney emporiums (see Cultural Center Attractions), mostly along Woodward Avenue, a miniature renaissance is taking place in what once was Detroit's glittering theater district.

Detroit is home to a surprising number of venues that offer plays from classical to the avant-garde. If your youngest kids can sit still for performances such as these, it's a grand way to widen their horizons in music and the arts as early as possible. However, be considerate of fellow theatergoers and judge accordingly whether your child should attend. If you bring your family here just once for a movie or concert, their visit to these restored complexes will stay with them the rest of their lives.

### Fox and Fillmore Detroit Theaters  (all ages)

Fox, (313) 961-5451 for the Fillmore; www.olympiaentertainment.com/venues/FoxTheatre .jsp for the Fox, and www.livenation.com/venue/the-fillmore-detroit-formerly-state-theatre-tickets/ for the Fillmore.

The Fox Theatre is the world's largest surviving 1920s movie palace. From the gold-leafed lobby set off by magnificent simulated columns that evoke a scene from the movie *The Ten Commandments* to the huge, 5,000-seat auditorium with gargoyles and other characters staring down from everywhere under a tentlike dome, the Fox is a tribute to its architect, C. Howard Crane, and those who rescued this beauty from sure ruin. Your kids will instantly recognize that this is no mall multiplex.

Holiday family shows, as well as big-screen movie epics shown each summer, draw crowds into the area.

The Fox's success has led another theater, geared to youths, to open next door. The Fillmore Detroit presents local and nationally famous alternative rock groups.

### Detroit Puppet Theater (up to age 13)

**25 East Grand River Ave.; (313) 961-7777; www.puppetart.org. General performances take place at 2 p.m. each Sat, with special events as scheduled on its Web site. $.**

Master puppeteers trained in the former Soviet Union emigrated to the city in 1998 and have been wowing kids and adults alike with their skills and their creations for the miniature stage ever since. The troupe performs puppet plays and fairy tales from around the world. It's one of the activities that make Detroit unique.

### Music Hall Center (all ages)

**350 Madison Ave., at Brush; (313) 887-8500; www.musichall.org. Take I-75 and exit at Madison Avenue. The theater is 3 blocks to the left. $$.**

Music Hall Center is the scene for acts and entertainment traveling to Detroit, from nationally known dance troupes to live music and other stagecraft. Each summer the hall presents "Camp Broadway," a one-week opportunity for students to work with national dance companies and attend low-cost performances.

In about half of the productions, performers answer questions from the audience after the shows.

### Gem and Century Theatres (ages twelve and up)

**333 Madison Ave., across from the Music Hall Center; (313) 963-9800; www.gemtheatre.com.**

Some of the best live theater in the Midwest takes place on the twin stages of the Gem and its little sister, the Century Theatre, in the same building. The Gem is a 450-seat theater with both cabaret table seating on the first floor and traditional seats in the upper level, while the Century is a more intimate setting, with 200 cabaret-style seats. Age limits for children depend on the play's subject matter. Check with the box office to see if performances are appropriate.

### Fisher Theater (all ages)

**West Grand Boulevard and Second Avenue, in the heart of the city's "New Center," across from the original General Motors building; (313) 872-1000; www.nederlanderdetroit.com.**

Located inside the art deco Fisher Building, this is one of the city's premier theater showcases, where, along with numerous other shows, touring Broadway companies often present their best.

### Masonic Temple Theatre (all ages)

**Just west of Woodward; turn west at Temple and go 2 blocks to Cass; (313) 832-2232; www.olympiaentertainment.com/venues/masonictemple.jsp. Parking is adjacent, either on the street or in a lot. $.**

Another of the city's old theater landmarks is this huge hall owned by the Masons, which is home to Broadway musicals, concerts, and other entertainment.

### Hilberry Theatre (all ages)

**4743 Cass, at Hancock, a block south of Warren, on the Wayne State University campus; (313) 577-2972; www.hilberry.com. Exit I-75 at Warren and head west to the campus, then south on Cass.**

Plays feature Wayne State drama students and are a great way to introduce kids to live theater. Plays here have included Agatha Christie's *The Mouse Trap* and other classics, including those by Shakespeare.

### Bonstelle Theatre (all ages)

**3424 Woodward, ½ block south of Mack; (313) 577-2960; www.theatre.wayne.edu. From I-75, exit at Warren and head west to Woodward. Turn south.**

Also featuring budding drama students from Wayne State University, this larger, traditional theater presents several plays per year. Plays recently performed here include *Dracula* and other contemporary classics.

### Chene Park (all ages)

**On the river off Atwater, south of Jefferson, at Chene; (313) 393-7827; www.chenepark detroit.com. From Jefferson, turn south on Chene.**

Under a giant tent up to 5,000 people can enjoy outdoor concerts in summer. The music is usually jazz in all its forms.

# Auto Shows

### North American International Auto Show (all ages)

**Held in mid-Jan at Cobo Center, downtown; www.naias.org. To reach Cobo, take the southbound Lodge Freeway (Highway 10) downtown and follow the exit signs to the Jefferson exit; rooftop or underground parking at the convention center. Parking is also available in**

# Favorite Events in Detroit

- **North American International Auto Show** (mid-Jan), Cobo Center, (248) 643-0250; www.naias.org

- **Detroit Boat Show** (early Feb), Cobo Center, (734) 261-0123 or (800) 932-2628; www.mbia.org

- **Target Riverfront Fireworks** (late June), downtown along the riverfront, (313) 923-7400; www.theparade.org

- **Chrysler-Jeep Superstores APBA Gold Cup** (mid-July), Detroit River off Belle Isle, (586) 774-0980; www.gold-cup.com

- **Michigan State Fair** (mid-Aug through Labor Day), at the fairgrounds, Woodward and Eight Mile Road, (313) 369-8250; www.michiganstatefair .com

- **Detroit International Jazz Festival** (Labor Day weekend), at Hart Plaza, (313) 963-7622

- **America's Thanksgiving Day Parade** (Nov), downtown along Woodward Avenue, (313) 923-7400; www.theparade.org

- **Noel Night** (Dec), Detroit Institute of Arts, (313) 577-5088; www.detroitmid town.com

street-level lots. Crowds can be heavy on weekends, so it might be wise to plan a week-night visit. And because of the crowds and the excitement, be sure to keep track of your kids, or arrange to meet the older ones periodically at predetermined sites. $$.

Visiting this show is like entering the world's largest new-car showroom, as each maker hires dancers, singers, and models and carts out glitzy rides that kids and grown-ups alike stand in line to try. Everywhere, kids walk by with bags full of advertising brochures and line up for a chance to sit behind the wheel of a new Mustang, Camaro, or other sporty models.

Other showstoppers include the concept cars that are always introduced at this event, exhibits that show youngsters how auto engineers work to design next year's models, and drawings of concept cars done by local college and high school students.

On Cobo's lower level the kids will also be able to bounce on the sofa beds and try out the TVs in the latest van conversions or grab a snack at the concession area.

### Autorama (all ages)

Held in early Mar at Cobo Center; (248) 373-1700; www.worldofwheels.com. See directions under North American International Auto Show. Adults $$$, children 6 to 12 $$, 5 and under free. Discount tickets are available at local venues around town.

Everyone from preteens to grown-ups will marvel at seeing favorite custom cars that have appeared in national auto magazines. Lacquered hot rods with gleaming chrome engines, side pipes, and wheels—pinstriped beauties that run the gamut from 1934 Fords and 1969 Corvettes to modified Mercedes—are polished and awaiting the car aficionado's review. Up to 500 custom models cover the display floor at Cobo.

Most of the entries are the pride and joy of average shade-tree mechanics who've worked on the cars in their own garages for a chance at showing them off. The show also features special exhibits, such as a display of nearly a hundred Harley-Davidson motorcycles and specialty cars from recent movies. Got a hankering to own a piece of Detroit muscle? There's a car corral with vehicles for sale by private owners as well.

Along with the stars of steel, stars of sports and television are present to sign autographs. Past appearances have included nationally known soap opera stars and sports celebrities. Best of all, with your admission comes the chance to pick out a favorite car and vote for it as best of the show. Other judges award trophies to winners in each class.

# Cultural Center Attractions

Located adjacent and within a few blocks of Wayne State University, one of the nation's largest urban higher education schools, Detroit's Cultural Center attractions are some of the best of their kind in any city. The area is reached by exiting I-94 at Woodward/John R Avenue and heading south on either John R or Woodward about ½ mile to Kirby. From I-75, exit at Warren Avenue and head west to Woodward, and then go 2 blocks north.

### Detroit Historical Museum (all ages)

**5401 Woodward Ave., at Kirby; (313) 833-1805; www.detroithistorical.org. Hours are 9:30 a.m. to 3 p.m. Wed through Fri, 10 a.m. to 5 p.m. Sat, and noon to 5 p.m. Sun. Adults $, 4 and under free. Parking is available on the street and in nearby lots and costs about $5.**

This museum's focus on the city's past and future is made especially appealing for youngsters, who have fun while exploring the city's history at the same time. If you haven't been here lately, there are six new exhibits, including the "Fabulous Five," an homage to five things that make Detroit world famous.

The museum's trademark is on the lower level. In a darkened streetscape lit by "street lamps," visitors walk the cobbled streets of a mock-up of what the city looked like in the 1800s, before the automobile transformed it forever. You can peer into the homes and businesses, almost expecting the mannequins to come alive as they sit, counting out the day's receipts, or make purchases.

A 12-by-34-foot miniature train layout delights kids. Four 600-foot loops of track continuously operate. The layout changes regularly and may depict a small-town scene, circus trains, or even a rodeo coming to town. A popular feature is its "train-cam," a miniature camera mounted in the engine that displays its view on a nearby television monitor. In conjunction with the layout, there's also an annual train show in late Dec.

On the first floor is "The Motor City," an interactive display that includes a 70-foot section of the assembly line of the old General Motors Detroit Cadillac assembly plant, with an operating "body drop," where the body of a car is slid onto the chassis. Also included is an exhibit where kids can actually crank and start a replica Model T Ford.

Check into the series of tours to historic Detroit sights hosted by the museum. Historic churches and strolls through communities and sites along both Detroit's and Windsor, Ontario's segment of the Underground Railroad (across the Detroit River) are among those available.

The museum publishes a list of events, programs, and tours twice a year. Some take all day, so small children probably wouldn't last.

## Detroit Institute of Arts  (all ages)

**Kitty-corner from the historical museum at the corner of Woodward and Farnsworth; (313) 833-7900; www.dia.org. Parking is behind the building and underground on the south side. The Detroit Film Theater, in the institute's auditorium, shows avant-garde, European, and other movies Fri through Mon. Call for what's showing, along with other special programs and concerts there. Hours are 10 a.m. to 4 p.m. Wed and Thurs, 10 a.m. to 10 p.m. Fri, and 10 a.m. to 5 p.m. Sat and Sun. Tours take place at 1 p.m. Wed through Sat and 1 p.m. and 2:30 p.m. Sun. Admission $$. There are Brunch with Bach concerts every third Sun $$$–$$$$ (museum admission included), but the series isn't recommended for children not used to sitting quietly. Food is served on paper plates—not to be economical, but to reduce table noise during the music.**

Now, before the kids wrinkle their noses up at the uncool thought of going to an art museum, tell them to be patient. This one is different. While many museum employees gulp when they see kids coming, the DIA has plenty of exhibits that invite youngsters to touch and explore on their own and that start them on the road to appreciating art in all its forms. There are drop-in art workshops, gallery drawing, and storytelling and family music performances, too, especially on Sun, which are dedicated to families, with puppet shows, live music, and storytellers.

There are several sure-bet draws for kids inside: armor, mummies, a spiral staircase, the American house, the "donkey," and a special treasure-hunt game, "The Mystery of the Five Fragments." The game motivates young visitors to discover the museum and its art with enthusiasm, overcoming any reluctance by sending them throughout the galleries in search of clues to solve the mystery. Another way to get the kids involved while you enjoy works from Warhol to Rembrandt is through the DIA's interactive computer programs. Two art games and a history timeline allow young people and older folks alike to correlate art from Egypt, to art from Asia and North America from the same time period.

The most popular exhibit for kids, however, is the display of ancient Egyptian art and artifacts. Included is a beautifully preserved, gilded, masked mummy. It is now in a display case with four jars once used to store the mummy's internal organs.

## Detroit Science Center (all ages)

5020 John R Ave. at Warren Avenue; (313) 577-8400; www.sciencedetroit.org. From I-75, exit at Warren and go west to Brush. Turn right, and then go left. Center hours change with the season, so call ahead. IMAX shows are presented hourly. $–$$.

After you finish exploring the Detroit Institute of Arts, walk 1 block on the DIA's south side and visit the colorful Detroit Science Center, which offers fun for everyone, from toddlers on up. One of the highlights is taking a seat before the three-and-a-half-story-high IMAX Dome screen, reached after traveling through a rainbow of neon colors on the 80-foot-long escalator tunnel to the lower level. Then, on the huge domed screen, lights dim as sixteen loudspeakers erupt, and you are taken on a seat-of-the-pants flight aboard the space shuttle, on a flight skimming over a canyon frothing with white water, on a 200-mile-per-hour ride in an Indy racing car, or on some other spectacular film excursion. You'll leave awed but ready for the next adventure, just upstairs on the upper floor.

The planetarium features the renowned Dassault Systemes. In the 120-seat planetarium, sit before the 50-foot-wide, three-story-high screen and watch the universe unfold all around you. Young astronauts can explore planets, nebulae, supernovae, and galaxies far, far away with the help of a guide.

On the four floors of the center, there are six science labs that explore matter and life sciences, including a new space laboratory where kids can learn about the size and scope of the universe we are part of. Be sure to see the science shows at the DTE Electricity Theater. The newest exhibit is the Toyota Engineering Theatre. An addition will soon house a charter middle school, new lobby, gift shop, and welcome center.

## Museum of Contemporary Art Detroit (all ages)

4454 Woodward Ave., just south of the Wayne State University Campus; (313) 832-6622; www.mocadetroit.org. Hours are 11 a.m. to 5 p.m. Wed, Sat, and Sun and 11 a.m. to 8 p.m. Thurs and Fri. Parking is adjacent. Free.

The MOCAD is Detroit's newest museum, dedicated to all forms of contemporary art, from sculpture to movies as well as educational programs for kids. Local as well as international art is on display. There's also a museum store.

## Charles H. Wright Museum of African American History (all ages)

315 East Warren Ave., directly east of the Detroit Science Center; (313) 494-5800; www .maah-detroit.org. Parking is adjacent. Hours are 9 a.m. to 5 p.m. Tues through Sat and 1 to 5 p.m. Sun. During the holidays there's a special presentation on Kwanzaa. $–$$.

This museum features some of the most extensive interactive exhibits of any museum in the nation. Twenty-six stations make up a hands-on learning "dictionary" for preschoolers through fourth graders to introduce the histories and cultures of Africa. Kids can learn by doing, for example finding out what it feels like to lift a thirteen-gallon bucket of water from a simulated 98-foot-deep well.

Detroit's African-American roots run deep, and visitors learn about everything from the African continent's history as the cradle of human life, to the tragedy of slavery here in America, to the city's role in the Underground Railroad, and up the present.

# Detroit's **Rising Stars**

Rivertown, Foxtown, Midtown, Greektown, and Mexicantown—they all are unique areas in the city. Many are former industrial or entertainment districts that are staging comebacks. Pubs, microbreweries, and restaurants are sprinkled throughout the Rivertown District along Orleans, Riopelle, Rivard, and Joseph Campau, the location of the Stroh River Place. Foxtown is buoyed by the return of the revived Detroit Tigers at Comerica Park, while right next door, the Lions' Ford Field attracts even more people and businesses downtown to the area and neighboring Greektown.

One of the newest hot spots is a restaurant owned by the Red Wings' perennial defenseman Chris Chelios. Mexicantown, with its great restaurants and entertainment, has brought much to the area near the Ambassador Bridge, where there is talk of adding a second span and more attractions. New townhomes have risen just north of downtown, and old mansions are being restored. These clusters of new businesses, including those along the revived Woodward Avenue, give more hope to bringing downtown back to its former grandeur. Detroit's downtown is laying the groundwork for a comeback, make no mistake.

## Gateway to Freedom International Memorial to the Underground Railroad (all ages)
**On Hart Plaza along the Detroit River.**

The statue of a slave family pointing to Canada and freedom commemorates the hundreds and perhaps thousands of escaped slaves who crossed the Detroit River to Canada (and to freedom) in the years before the Civil War. Detroit was a major depot on the Underground Railroad, and residents helped slaves escape bounty hunters by rowing them across the river. Another monument at the spot where many made it to final freedom is on the Civic Esplanade across the river in Windsor, Ontario.

## Lafayette and American Coney Islands (all ages)
**Lafayette Coney Island, 118 West Lafayette (313-964-8198); American Coney Island, 115 Michigan Ave. (313-961-7758). From the southbound Lodge Freeway (Highway 10), exit at Howard Street, continue 1 block, and turn left onto Lafayette. The restaurants are 3 blocks apart, 1 block east of the U.S. courthouse. They're open twenty-four hours a day, every day. $.**

Home of the "Coney Island dog," which has been imitated by others, but if you're in the Motor City, the Lafayette and American Coney Islands are the places to try 'em.

Since 1918 both eateries have served millions of tube steaks in a bun, slathered in a meaty chili that's just spicy enough, then layered with onions and topped with mustard that's deftly applied by the grill man with a wooden spoon. It's been that way for generations of Detroiters who've pounded down Coneys accompanied by orange soda or other pop.

Grab a seat and order a chili dog or two accompanied by a bowl of chili, or try something completely different: a Coney burger, loose ground beef in a bun and, again, smothered in chili and onions. Then listen as the waiter sings out the song of the Coney: "Six on four, one no onions, four Cokes." Translation: two plates with two Coneys on each and two with one each. And these are real skin-on franks that pop when you bite into them. Those brave enough to risk a be-chilied shirt pick them up, while the more practical and the suit-and-tie crowd cut them with a fork.

# Holiday Traditions and Other Pastimes

### America's Thanksgiving Day Parade (all ages)

**Annually each Thanksgiving Day starting around 9 a.m., running along Woodward Avenue from the Cultural Center to Jefferson downtown; (313) 923-7400; www.theparade.org, or for shuttle transportation information, call (888) D–DOTBUS. General grandstand seats are located in the Comerica Park area; Jubilee Grandstand Seats, located in the TV zone, include a commemorative seat cushion. $$$$ Or find a spot along Woodward early—by 6:30 a.m.—to watch free at streetside.**

It may be officially called America's Thanksgiving Parade, but veteran Detroiters still remember it as the Hudson's Parade, named for the downtown department store that once sponsored the entire event. The store is long gone, but for many Detroiters and surburbanites, this is *the* parade.

Televised nationwide, the more-than-eighty-year-old event signals the traditional kickoff to the holidays. The excitement of floats, marching bands, and balloons amid the city skyscrapers on a crisp Nov morning—and finally, the sight every child waits for, Santa's sleigh—is all here. The fun starts at in front of the Detroit Public Library at Woodward and Putnam. It then heads downtown on Woodward, ending at Congress.

### Motown Historical Museum (all ages)

**2648 West Grand Blvd., on the south side of the road; (313) 875-2264; www.motownmuseum .com. From the Lodge Freeway (Highway 10), exit at the Milwaukee/West Grand Boulevard exit and head west on Grand Boulevard. Hours vary by season, so call ahead. $–$$.**

Want a museum with a different beat? Check out one of Michael Jackson's famed sequined gloves and the cramped studio where the likes of Diana Ross, the Temptations, Marvin Gaye, the Four Tops, and Stevie Wonder put Detroit on the world's music map. In two side-by-side homes, composer and producer Berry Gordy lived and produced hits for those and scores of other performers from Detroit's neighborhoods who went on to recording glory in the studios he named "Hitsville, USA." With Motown hits playing in the background, guided, wheelchair-accessible tours lead past the gift shop and other rooms where the raw talent Gordy discovered was refined to the point that they eventually performed in front of heads of state worldwide.

## Model T Heritage Automotive Complex (all ages)

**461 Piquette Ave., in the New Center Area; (313) 872-8759; www.tplex.org. From downtown, take Woodward Avenue north. Turn east onto Piquette and travel three blocks. Open the first and third Sat, May through Oct 10 a.m. to 4 p.m. $$. Group tours available.**

See where the auto industry in American got rolling at pioneer Henry Ford's first large production facility. The venerable Model T was designed and built here before production moved to larger facilities. Examples of vehicles built at the plant, as well as the spot where Ford Models B, C, F, and finally, the famous T, where conceived.

## Comerica Park (all ages)

**2100 Woodward Ave.; (313) 962-4000; www.detroittigers.com. Take Lodge Freeway downtown to Woodward, and turn north. Go about 1½ miles to the park. There is parking around the ballpark.**

From opening day in early Apr to the last game in the fall, the 40,000-seat stadium is a magical place where the smells of steamed hot dogs and peanuts mix with the crack of the bat and the roar—or boos—of the crowd.

Comerica Park is a cozy, state-of-the-art park with a scoreboard that lights up the sky when the home runs fly. Home base looks out toward Detroit's skyline, and passersby can even catch a glimpse of the game outside.

Seats range from the venerable bleachers to expensive corporate skyboxes and even to special seats for die-hard Tiger fans who will pay extra to be in those spots. In the plaza outside there's a Ferris wheel and carousel and several restaurant choices. The Tigers beefed up the team but haven't forgotten the kids inside, either. Watch for the special promotional days when youngsters get **free** Tigers gear ranging from hats and beach towels to gloves and backpacks.

Paws, the Tiger mascot, is usually found roaming the plaza before the game and heads into the stands during play to cheer on or cheer up the crowd, depending on who's winning. And, of course, everybody joins in singing "Take Me Out to the Ball Game" during the seventh-inning stretch. The Tigers were at the city's old ballpark since the early twentieth century. Look for them to be here for a long, long time, too.

## Redford Theater (all ages)

**17360 Lahser Rd., between Grand River Avenue and Seven Mile Road; (313) 537-2560; http://theatreorgans.com/mi/redford/index.htm. To reach it, exit the Southfield Freeway**

(Highway 39) at Grand River, turn west to Lahser, and then head north. $–$$$. Theater tours also are available. Call for a recorded schedule, or watch the *Detroit News* or the *Free Press* movie guides.

It's the amazement at hearing the throaty blasts of a nearly seventy-year-old theater organ introducing a movie classic. It's watching Humphrey Bogart in *Casablanca* or *The African Queen* on the big screen, or the spectacle of *Lawrence of Arabia*. It's blithely "nyucking" along with the crowd at the antics of the Three Stooges. Enjoying classic movies in an old-time, neighborhood theater setting is a practice that's still alive and well here. The Redford caters to families with its series of ageless flicks.

Before each feature the kids will get a kick out of encountering something they—and possibly you—have never experienced: a thirty-minute concert performed on the giant 800-pipe, ten-rank Barton Golden Voice theater organ, which can imitate everything from a tuba to a classical orchestra.

## Joe Louis Arena (all ages)

**600 Civic Center Dr., on the Detroit River; (313) 983-6606; www.olympiaentertainment.com/ venues/joelouisarena.jsp. Follow the Lodge Freeway south to Detroit and to the Joe Louis Arena exit.**

The arena plays host to the NHL Detroit Red Wings hockey team from fall through late spring.

## Renaissance Center (all ages)

**On Jefferson Avenue, just east of Woodward and adjacent to Hart Plaza; (313) 568-5600.**

The dream of Henry Ford II, who helped push construction of these five glass towers, the Ren Cen's office towers have ironically been taken over by General Motors.

There's a new Wintergarden atrium on the river side of the Ren Cen with more restaurants and shops, along with walking and bike paths along the river. In the middle is the seventy-story Marriott Renaissance Center Hotel, which overlooks the river and the city.

## Ford Field (all ages)

**2001 Saint Antoine Dr.; (313) 962-4285; www.fordfield.com.**

This 65,000-seat domed stadium marks yet another milestone in the resurgence of downtown as the place to be for pro field sports. Located due east of the Tigers' Comerica Park, the field is the home of Detroit's NFL

Lions, Super Bowl XL, and the 2009 NCAA Final Four. The stadium features lots of restrooms, legroom, and cup holders for each seat. Fans hope the state-of-the-art stadium will give the team new incentive to become competitive with the rest of the league; after all, they last won the championship fifty years ago. Right now, all fans can do is hope and keep the faith. The park also hosts big-name rock concerts when the Lions aren't playing. Inquire about stadium tours.

### Michigan State Fair (all ages)

**Located at the State Fairgrounds at Woodward and Eight Mile Road on the city's northern border (313-369-8250; www.michigan.gov/mistatefair). Hours are 10 a.m. to 10 p.m. daily. Adults $$, children under 12 $, under 2 free. Ride the rides all day for $$–$$$. Most concerts are included with fair admission.**

The fair, one of the nation's oldest, has undergone a facelift to upgrade facilities and make it family friendly. Visit the Miracle of Life, where kids can see baby farm animals from chicks to larger critters get their first glimpse of the world. Walk into the dairy barn and, for 25 cents, treat your kids to a bottomless glass of chocolate milk from a recipe mixed exclusively for the fair. There are contests for the best livestock and even home-brewed and microbrewed beers. Midway rides and food from corn dogs to those flat, sugar-coated fried dough pieces called elephant ears are the fare of the day here. A highlight of the fair is the free concerts by nationally known groups from rock to gospel at the outdoor band shell.

### Greektown (all ages)

**On downtown's near east side, between Beaubien and St. Antoine, about 2 blocks north of Jefferson Avenue. Watch for signs to the area along Jefferson just east of Woodward and across from the Renaissance Center.**

Learn the meaning of "Ooopa!" here when you order a flaming cheese appetizer at any of several Greek restaurants in this lively downtown entertainment district.

There's shopping for Greek treats like baklava and other Greek goodies.

### Diamond Jack's River Tours (all ages)

**Tours depart Rivard Plaza and downriver at Bishop Park in Wyandotte; (313) 843-9376; www.diamondjack.com. Tours run mid-June through early Sept, Thurs through Sun at 1 p.m. and 3:30 p.m. Two tours are available, one of the upper and one of the lower Detroit River. The lower tour leaves from Wyandotte's Bishop Park off Jefferson Avenue (call Diamond Jack's for directions). Adults $$, children under 6 ride free.**

Two-hour tours aboard the Diamond Jack take in the history, both that of long ago and that currently being made, of the city and its Canadian neighbor, Windsor. Among the sites, the boat will pass under the Belle Isle Bridge and along the Windsor waterfront before turning at the Ambassador Bridge, just upstream of the mills that made Detroit the Arsenal of Democracy, Historic Fort Wayne, and the Detroit skyline, before returning.

### *Detroit Princess* (all ages)

**Departs from Hart Plaza from May through New Year's Eve; (877) 338-2628; www.detroit princess.com. Tickets include the cruise, a meal, and entertainment. $$. Children under 12 regularly go for half price. On Sun afternoons, children under 12 ride free with a paying adult, and those ages 13 to 17 are half price.**

Cruising since 2005, the *Princess* offers buffet lunches and dinners and moonlight cruises for as many as 1,800 at a time. It's a great addition to the riverfront, brought to the city by the same folks who run the *Michigan Princess* in Lansing (see listing).

# People **Mover** (all ages)

The People Mover is an automated elevated monorail that links downtown. In fact, a ride's a good way to get acquainted with various parts of the area, from the entertainment and restaurants of Greektown to a trip through the vast exhibit space of Cobo Center. $; kids under 5 **free**. For more information, call (800) 541-RAIL or go to www.thepeoplemover.com.

## Where to Eat

There are so many places to choose from in and around Detroit that it's hard to recommend only a few. But here are some:

**Elwood Bar & Grill.** At the corner of Adams and Brush downtown; (313) 961-7485. "Bar" may be in its name, but the Elwood is suitable for all family members. Booths and tables are available. City landmarks don't have to be big. The Elwood's claims to fame include not only its great burgers but also its flashy art deco architecture. And lucky for it, it's right near both Comerica Park and Ford Field. Call for current hours. $$

**Evie's Tamales.** 3454 Bagley in Mexicantown; (313) 843-5056. Open Mon through Sat 8 a.m. to 6 p.m. and Sun 8 a.m. to 3 p.m. Serves inexpensive authentic Mexican lunch and dinner items daily. $

**Fishbone's Rhythm Kitchen Cafe.** 400 Monroe, at the corner of Brush; (313) 965-4600. Open Sun through Thurs 6:30 a.m. to midnight and Fri and Sat 6:30 a.m. to 2 a.m. No one under twenty-one allowed after 10 p.m. Fri and Sat. A bit of New Orleans in the Motor City, right down to the alligator tail and crawfish appetizers, hot sauces, and that bread pudding. Fun and noisy for breakfast, lunch, or dinner. Children's menu available, too. $$$

**Hard Rock Cafe.** 45 Monroe, inside the Compuware headquarters; (313) 964-7625. Open Sun through Thurs 11 a.m. to 11 p.m., Fri and Sat 11 a.m. to 1 a.m. Detroit's version of this ever-popular restaurant chain featuring rock star memorabilia. This one includes instruments and clothing worn and played by some of Motown's greats. $$

**Hockeytown Cafe.** 2301 Woodward Ave.; (313) 965-9500. Open Sun and Mon 11 a.m. to 9 p.m., Tues through Thurs 11 a.m. to 11 p.m., Fri and Sat 11 a.m. to midnight. Run by the Ilitch family, who owns the Detroit Red Wings. The theme here is sports, and Red Wings through and through. Besides good food Wings fans can bask in hockey memorabilia throughout. Don't miss the mini hockey rink of ice that helps keep beverages cool at the bar. $$

**Sinbad's.** Upper Detroit River at East Jefferson and Marquette; (313) 822-8000. Open Mon through Fri 11 a.m. to midnight, Sat and Sun 11 a.m. to 1 a.m. Watch for the sign for the Roostertail and turn south from Jefferson onto Marquette, and then follow it to 100 St. Clair. Watch the boaters come and go in summer, or enjoy the river's quiet times for lunch or dinner and Sun brunch. Children's menu. Specializes in steak and seafood. $$$

**Traffic Jam and Snug.** 511 West Canfield, at Second; (313) 831-9470; www.traffic-jam .com. Open Mon through Thurs 11 a.m. to 10:30 p.m., Fri and Sat 11 a.m. to midnight, Sat and Sun 11 a.m. to 8 p.m. From the Lodge Freeway, exit at Warren and head east to Second, then south to Canfield. Parking is across the street. Dine beneath the barnlike timbers while rubbing elbows with professors from nearby Wayne State University. Take home bread baked on the premises and enjoy dishes from traditional to vegetarian. Children's menu, too. $$

**Union Street.** 4145 Woodward, just south of the Wayne State University campus; (313) 831-3965. Open Mon through Fri 11:30 a.m. to midnight, Sat 5 p.m. to 4 a.m., Sun 11 a.m. to 8 p.m. In a classic building with a pressed-tin ceiling, enjoy a large choice of casual dining options for lunch or dinner, from sandwiches to seafood and pasta. Large imported beer list, too. $$

**Xochimilco.** 3409 Bagley, in Mexicantown; (313) 843-0179. Open 11 a.m. to 2 a.m. daily. You can't go wrong with any of the restaurants in this part of town if you enjoy food from south of the border. This restaurant, in the heart of Mexicantown, has great authentic Mexican food. $$

## Where to Stay

Downtown Detroit's array of hotels and motels just got glitzier with the addition of three new casino hotels, and classier, too, with the reopening of two classic beauties from the last century. Here's a glimpse of what's available now.

**Atheneum Suite Hotel and Conference Center.** 1000 Brush and Lafayette, in the Greektown entertainment district; (313) 962-2323. This property has 174 suite-style rooms, exercise facilities, and dining. Also adjacent to Fishbone's and other Greektown restaurants. $$$$

**Courtyard by Marriott.** 333 East Jefferson; (313) 222-7700. Located across from and connected via walkway to the Renaissance Center in the Millender Center, this hotel has 255 rooms with indoor pool, exercise area, and racquetball and tennis courts. It's also a few

blocks south of Greektown. A modern, very nice hotel for the money. $$$

**Detroit Marriott Renaissance Center.** At the Renaissance Center; (313) 568-8000. The city's largest hotel, with 1,342 rooms overlooking downtown and the riverfront. Package plans available. Restaurants within the hotel and the Ren Cen. $$$$

**Detroit Riverside Hotel.** 2 Washington Blvd., at Jefferson Avenue, near Cobo Center; (313) 965-0200. This property has 437 rooms, outdoor pool open in summer, exercise room, and restaurant. $$$

**Hilton Garden Inn Detroit Downtown.** 351 Gratiot; (313) 967-0900; www.hiltongardeninn.com, then search for downtown Detroit. Located only a block from both ballparks and many downtown attractions like Greektown, the hotel features a pool, fitness center, two restaurants, and 198 rooms. $$–$$$

**Holiday Inn Fairlane/Dearborn.** Ford Road and the Southfield Freeway (Highway 39); (313) 336-3340. Located much closer to Dearborn attractions than those downtown but still in the Detroit city limits, this property has 347 rooms, a large atrium lobby, indoor and outdoor pools, and an exercise room. Kids age eleven and under eat **free,** and under nineteen stay **free,** with dining room and sports bar and other restaurants adjacent. **Free** shuttles to Greenfield Village and the Henry Ford. $$$

**Omni Detroit Riverplace.** 1000 River Place; (313) 259-9500. From downtown, head east on Jefferson about 1½ miles and turn south on McDougall. The property has 108 rooms on the Detroit River with a good restaurant and others nearby. $$

**Westin Book Cadillac Hotel.** 1114 Washington Blvd.; (313) 442-1600. In the heart of downtown, this is what can happen to change the face of a city when $200 million is used to renovate a once glorious hotel to make it so once more again. The world's tallest hotel in 1924, now restored to its original splendor and more, the Book Cadillac features 453 unique guest rooms that come standard with LCD televisions and Internet access, and five restaurants including its signature dining spot, Roast. A great place to stay downtown. Along with the equally renewed Doubletree Guest Suites Fort Shelby, the Book Cadillac is sure to make an impact on the city's future. $$$

## For More Information

**Metro Detroit Convention and Visitors Bureau.** 100 Renaissance Center, Suite 1950, Detroit 48243; (800) 338-7648; www.visit detroit.com.

# Northwest and Northern
# Detroit
## Suburbs

This region of southeastern Michigan skirts metropolitan Detroit's northern suburbs, taking in parts of western Livingston, eastern Wayne, and Oakland, Macomb, and St. Clair Counties, at the base of Michigan's Thumb. In summer this is the region's "concert central," home of outdoor venues that bring in some of music's greatest stars. In contrast, though, it also offers visits to the baronial mansions of auto pioneers as well as beautiful beaches and parks that entertain families year-round.

## Top
# FamilyAdventures
### in Northwest and Northern Detroit Suburbs

1. Motorsports Museum and Hall of Fame of America, and tours of the Corvette engine plant, Novi. Speed demons can get their fill of track history, then see high-performance engines being hand-built at a GM plant nearby.

2. Detroit Zoological Park, Royal Oak. A great family institution open year-round.

3. Huron-Clinton Metroparks. They're headquartered between Milford and Brighton but are scattered all around the region, offering golf, beaches, aquatic centers, marinas, and more.

4. Skiing! At Mount Brighton, near Brighton; Alpine Valley, Milford; Pine Knob, Clarkston; and Mount Holly, Holly. On any winter night the family can have dinner and be skiing in an hour's time from nearly anywhere in metro Detroit.

5. DTE Energy Music Theater, Meadow Brook Summer Music series, and Freedom Hill. Bring the best of recording entertainment to the city.

# NORTHWEST AND NORTHERN
# DETROIT SUBURBS

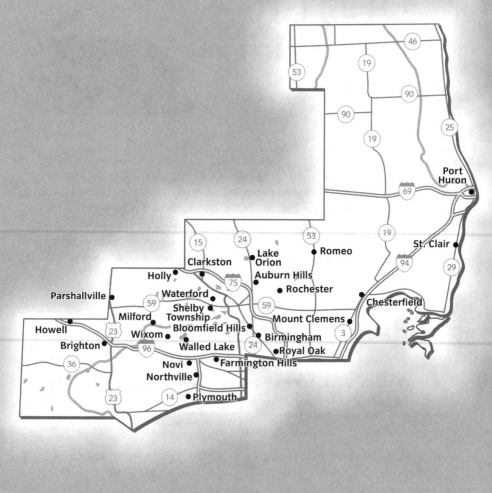

# Farmington Hills

This northwest Detroit suburb of chic office buildings and clusters of shops also has an attraction unique to Michigan and perhaps the region.

**Marvin's Marvelous Mechanical Museum** (all ages)
31005 Orchard Lake Rd.; (248) 626-5020; www.marvin3m.com. To reach it, take Orchard Lake Road north from I-696. Turn left into the Hunter's Square shopping center at Fourteen Mile Rd. Hours are 10 a.m. to 9 p.m. Mon through Thurs, 10 a.m. to 11 p.m. Fri and Sat, and noon to 9 p.m. Sun. Free admission. Games cost extra.

It's a great name for one of the most interesting and peculiar collections of things that whir, click, toot, and tick that you'll ever see. Started by Marvin Yagoda, a pharmacist with a definite fascination for things mechanical, the museum is filled with seemingly every coin-operated nickelodeon or other carnival coin-swallowing machine that's ever been made. See what your future holds according to Madame Zelda, a 1917 fortune-telling machine, or bat against the baseball players of yesteryear in a 1937 World Series game. Also on display are a forty-seven-piece nickelodeon band and a "mechanical brain." Modern videogames also are part of the fun.

## Where to Eat

**Kerby's Koney Island.** 21200 North Haggerty Rd., at I-275 and Eight Mile, Northville; (248) 449-7088. One of a number of coney dispensers modeled after those in downtown Detroit but with larger menus. Great dogs and loose burgers and Greek salads for lunch or dinner. $

**Max and Erma's.** 30125 Orchard Lake Rd.; (248) 855-0990. Good selection of family fare like burgers, pasta, salads, and steaks. Children's menu. $–$$$

## Where to Stay

**Comfort Inn Farmington Hills.** 30715 Twelve Mile Rd., Farmington Hills, at the I-696/Orchard Lake Road exit; (248) 471-9220. This hotel has 135 rooms, continental breakfast, and in-room movies. Restaurants nearby. $$

**Courtyard Marriott.** 31525 West Twelve Mile Rd., just north of I-696 and Orchard Lake Road; (248) 553-0000. Modern hotel with easy access to freeway; has indoor pool and whirlpool, and restaurant. Several other restaurants adjacent. $$$

**Holiday Inn Hotel and Suites.** 37529 Grand River Ave., at I-96 and I-275; (248) 477-7800. Take the Grand River exit off I-96. This hotel has 137 rooms with microwaves, plus indoor pool, exercise area, and dining room. $$$

**Red Roof Inn–Farmington Hills.** 24300 Sinacola Court; (248) 478-8640. From I-96, take the Grand River exit. This property has 108 rooms. Coffee and papers available in the lobby. Restaurant nearby. Typical Red Roof, comfortable. Children under eighteen stay free. $$

# Plymouth

Plymouth was once known as the BB-gun capital of the world because it was the head-quarters for Daisy Air Rifle before the plant moved south. Since the surrounding farm-lands became expensive subdivisions, the city has undergone lots of changes, but it works hard to live up to the vision of its founders, who named it for the Massachusetts town of their ancestors. Quaint shops cluster around a great downtown park. A second, smaller downtown, called the Old Village, is just north of the main shopping district.

### Plymouth International Ice Sculpture Spectacular  (all ages)

**Held annually in mid-Jan downtown; (734) 459-9157; www.plymouthice.com. To reach Plymouth, follow I-275 to Ann Arbor Road, and then turn west and go about 1½ miles. Turn north on Main Street, find a parking spot, and follow the crowds downtown. Everything's free and open twenty-four hours a day until the festival closes.**

Imitated but never duplicated, the festival draws more than 500,000 persons to the streets of this normally placid colonial downtown to ogle hundreds of sculptures carved from 400-pound blocks of ice. The event is one of the best of its kind. Carvers chip, chop, smooth, grind, and buff their way through town as they form works of fleeting, crystalline art. Adjacent to the main display, a special exhibit for kids usually includes up to twenty fantasy ice sculptures.

### Green Street Fair  (all ages)

**Downtown Plymouth, May 1–3.; www.greenstreetfair.com. Free.**

This unique fair takes place in early May in downtown to educate and inform about the benefits of living green. Stroll past more than 150 vendors showing ecofriendly products.

### Plymouth Orchards and Cider Mill  (all ages)

**10685 Warren Rd.; (734) 455-2290. West of the city in the rolling farmland. From the Plymouth-Canton area, take Ford Road west to Ridge Road and follow the signs. Open during harvest season, usually Sept through early Nov. Free.**

## Away for the **Weekend**

Enjoy a leisurely early-American weekend getaway in the cities of Plymouth and Northville. Great shopping; festivals such as the midsummer Art in the Park and the end-of-summer Fall Festival in Plymouth and Victorian weekend in Northville; unique downtowns, with a large city park in Plymouth and cute shops in Northville; cozy restaurants and theaters; Fri concerts, June through Sept, in downtown Plymouth; bed-and-breakfasts and hotels—all this and more make them great places to relax and explore.

Treat the family to a hayride, let the kids pet farm animals from horses to turkeys, pick apples from dwarf trees, and end the outing by sipping some freshly squeezed cider with a sugar-cinnamon doughnut or two. For the perfect sugar overload, top it off with a caramel apple. It's a fall tradition. The petting zoo is **free,** as are trips into the orchards, but picking price varies by the season, as does the price for cider, sold in quarts, half gallons, gallons, and by the cup. Picnic-table seating is inside.

### Penn Theatre  (all ages)

**760 Penniman Ave.; (734) 453-0870; www.penntheatre.com.**

Opened three days before Dec 7, 1941, the Penn is a downtown Plymouth fixture, presenting classic movies as well as first-run pictures in an old-fashioned movie house setting.

## Where to Eat

**Compari's.** On Main, downtown across from Kellogg Park; (734) 416-0100. Great Italian dishes with outside seating in season. $$–$$$$

**Grand Traverse Pie Company.** 41640 Plymouth Rd.; (734) 459-9200. Open 8 a.m. to 9 p.m. Mon through Sun. Great lineup of sandwiches, potpies, and quiche, with those great fresh-baked cream and fruit pies for dessert or to take home. $

**Little Bangkok.** 545 Forest Ave.; (734) 414-8696. Introduce the kids to spicy Thai food at various levels of heat. $$

**Plymouth Crossing.** 340 North Main, just north of the railroad tracks; (734) 455-3700. Upscale dining in this former BB-gun factory. Prime rib, seafood, and other dishes please the palate here. Children's menu available upon request. $$$

**Station 885.** 885 Starkweather, in the Old Village area of shops; (734) 459-0885. Take Main Street north from downtown and turn north on Starkweather. Trains rumble by this replica of the old city passenger station as you enjoy your lunch or dinner. Besides steaks and seafood the house specialty is the Veal Station 885, sautéed veal with garlic, olives, and

shrimp. Also available are a children's menu and Sun brunch. $$$–$$$$

## Where to Stay

**Comfort Inn Plymouth Clocktower.** 40455 Ann Arbor Rd., just off I-275; (734) 455-8100. This property has 123 rooms and an outdoor pool. Several restaurants are nearby. $$

**Plymouth Hilton Garden Inn.** 14600 Sheldon Rd.; (734) 354-0001. One hundred fifty-seven rooms with **free** movies, restaurant, indoor pool, and exercise room. Kids under eighteen stay **free** in parents' room. $$$

## For More Information

**Plymouth Chamber of Commerce.** 386 South Main St., Plymouth 48170; (734) 453-1540; www.plymouthchamber.org.

# Northville

Plymouth's twin sister to the north, built on a hill and settled in the 1830s, is now known for its compact old downtown's quaint shops and fine homes, some of which are now restaurants, and some unique attractions. To find Northville, exit I-275 at Eight Mile Road and head west; turn south at Center Street.

## Favorite Events in Northwest and Northern Detroit Suburbs

- **Plymouth International Ice Sculpture Spectacular** (Jan), downtown Plymouth, (734) 459-9157

- **Erie Ice Daze** (Jan), Lake Erie Metropark, north of Monroe, (734) 379-5020

- **Annual Detroit Camper and RV Show** (Feb), Rock Financial Showplace, Novi, (248) 348-5600

- **Spring Festival** (Apr), Kensington Metropark, Milford, (248) 685-1561

- **Art in the Park** (July), Kellogg Park in downtown Plymouth, (734) 454-1540

- **Blue Water Festival** (July), Port Huron, (810) 987-8687 or (800) 852-2828

- **Target Harmony in the Metroparks** (July), Detroit Symphony performs in Kensington and other Metroparks designated each summer, (810) 227-2757

- **World's Second Largest Garage Sale and Antique Show** (July), Royal Oak, (248) 547-4000

- **Armada Fair** (Aug), Armada, (810) 784-5488

- **Howell Melon Festival** (Aug), downtown Howell, (517) 546-7477

- **Michigan Renaissance Festival** (Aug and Sept), Holly, (800) 601-4848

- **Victorian Festival and Art Market** (Sept), downtown Northville, (248) 349-7640

- **Plymouth Fall Festival** (Sept), downtown Plymouth, (734) 453-1540

- **Michigan Peach Festival** (Sept), downtown Romeo, (586) 752-6633

- **Chili Cook-Off** (Oct), Kellogg Park in downtown Plymouth, (734) 453-1540

- **Fantasy of Lights Parade** (Nov), downtown Howell, (517) 546-3920

- **Rochester Community Christmas Parade** (Dec), (586) 752-6633

- **Christmas Parade** (Dec), downtown Marysville, (810) 364-6180

## Marquis Theater (ages 3 and up)

**135 East Main St.; (248) 349-8110. $$.**

Got a budding child actor in the house? This might be his or her chance to break into the big time. Since 1983, in a facility nearly a century old in quaint downtown Northville, the unique theater has been producing drama that makes stars out of children.

Owner-producer Inge Zayti began the Marquis featuring adult actors but later found her niche introducing children to the stage. In addition to spending the summer working with would-be actors, she presents children-oriented plays from Mar through Dec. Recent performances have included *The Princess and the Pea, Peter Pan,* and *Heidi,* all performed by children between eight and eighteen. In summer Zayti cultivates new talent by offering a two-week day camp that features acting and singing activities for kids who want to give the bright lights a whirl. She's assisted by five instructors.

## Mill Race Historical Village (all ages)

**On Griswold south of Eight Mile Road; (248) 348-1845. Exit I-275 at Eight Mile Road, go west to Griswold, and then head south. Grounds are open year-round except when private functions are taking place. The buildings are open Sun 1 to 4 p.m. from June through Oct. Informational signs outside give some of the history when the buildings are closed. Free.**

Nine white clapboard homes and buildings make up this replica community, created in 1972 on the site of a former gristmill. All structures except the gazebo looking over the branch of the Rouge River were moved here from various nearby locations. The New School Church, for example, was built in 1845. Wash Oak School is one of the state's last surviving one-room schoolhouses, built in 1873. Another building was the waiting room at Newburgh and Eight Mile Roads for the Interurban, a rapid, electric mass transit rail line. Call for information on the special events that often take place here.

## Maybury State Park (all ages)

**On Eight Mile Road, west of Beck Road, west of Northville; (248) 349-8390; www.michigan .gov/dnr. A daily or annual motor vehicle entry permit is required. Open 8 a.m. to dusk daily, year-round. $.**

Michigan's first urban state park is 70 percent covered in forest, making it a wonderful spot to bring the family any time of year. Cross-country ski or hike in winter, road or mountain bike or horseback ride ($$$) in summer, and enjoy the colors of fall or the rebirth of spring. There are 6 miles of dirt hiking trails and 4 miles of paved bike trails, plus naturalist-led hikes and activities, along with a petting farm. Pamphlets help you teach youngsters to identify trees and plants along the way. There is no camping, however.

## Hines Park (all ages)

**To reach the park from downtown Northville, take Center south to Seven Mile Road and turn east, and then veer to the right, and you're at the entrance. For park information, call the Wayne County Parks, (734) 261-1990; www.waynecountyparks.org. Open year-round. Free.**

This 16-mile-long park offers picnic areas, swings, slides, softball diamonds, a remote control off-road model-car track, and three artificially created lakes (unfortunately, they are not open for swimming). Farther east, Newburgh Lake is now stocked with game fish. Many restroom facilities in the park have been renovated.

From summer through fall, a portion of the park is closed to vehicles, and only bicycles and other nonmotorized vehicles are allowed during "Saturdays in the Park." If you miss the weekend, try the bicycle trail, which covers the entire length of the park. Near Nankin Mills in Westland, summer activities include outdoor movies. The mill is now a nature center with naturalist-led hikes and other activities planned, including bicycle rental.

In winter sledding is available at Cass Benton and many other hills along the park when the snow allows, as is cross-country skiing. Also see the listing under Westland for Wayne County Lightfest.

## Where to Eat

**Doc's Sports Retreat.** 19265 Victor Parkway; (734) 542-8162; www.docssportsretreat .com. Hours 11 a.m. to 2 a.m. Mon through Sat, noon to 2 a.m. Sun. Enjoy what may be the state's best pizza, plus innovative sandwiches, great soups and other items while keeping your eye on your favorite sports team on any of 101 televisions. Outdoor and indoor seating both available. $$

**Genitti's Hole in the Wall.** 108 East Main St.; (248) 349-0522; www.genittis.com. You can let the kids get a bit rowdy in this eatery, which began as a grocery. A hole was knocked out of one of the building's walls when the restaurant opened, hence the name. Expansions brought more and more for the seven-course Italian, please-pass-the-pasta family-style dinners . Genitti's Little Theater features interactive performances where audience members get in on the act with a professional cast. Comedy acts and other kids' shows also are featured. All ages. Family dinners with entertainment. $$$$

**Guernsey Farms Dairy.** 21300 Novi Rd.; (248) 349-1466. From downtown Northville, go north on Center, then east on Eight Mile Road about ¼ mile to Novi Road and turn north. The dairy is about ½ mile on the right. The ice cream here may be the best ice cream on the planet. The restaurant serves meals from breakfast on. $

**Zoup! Northville.** 20065 Haggerty Rd.; (248) 374-1000; www.zoup.com. The name says it all. Wonderful, hearty meat, low-fat, and veggie soups, chili, and the like. $$

## Where to Stay

See Novi listings.

# Novi

This community is located at the intersection of Novi Road, Grand River Avenue as it makes its way from Detroit west, and I-96. Interesting name, eh? It's actually derived from Roman numerals. "No. VI" used to be stagecoach stop number six between Detroit and Lansing. The name was even further abbreviated to Novi, and the town is now  one of Detroit's bedroom communities.

## Rock Financial Showplace (all ages)

46100 Grand River Ave., 1 mile west of the Novi freeway interchange (exit 162); (248) 348-5600; www.rockfinancialshowplace.com. To get to the center, leave I-96 at Novi Road, and go south to Grand River. Turn right, go 1½ miles, and watch for signs.

This megacomplex expo center replaces the former Novi Expo Center just to the east. Larger and with better access, the center hosts events throughout the year, including home improvement and cat shows, camper shows, train shows, the annual Outdoorama, Native American powwows, and car auctions.

## Motorsports Museum and Hall of Fame of America (all ages)

Currently located on the north side of the old Novi Expo Center, which the Showplace (see preceding entry) replaced; (800) 250-RACE; www.mshf.com. The museum is open Tues through Sun 10 a.m. to 5 p.m. $.

Got a need for speed? This museum pays tribute to all motor sports and is a must stop during any Detroit-area visit.

Introduce your kids to the sport/hobby you may have enjoyed as a kid with a run on the hall's eight-lane slot car track ($), where scale model electric-motor cars held onto the track by a pin inside a slot (hence the name) race; or climb into the coin-operated video simulation race car that pits you against another driver.

Inside the main exhibit area, changing displays include thirty-five racing vehicles, from current Indy-style cars, stock cars, and drag strip models to turn-of-the-twentieth-century vehicles, including motorcycles, powerboats, and a racing airplane.

Kids can have their picture taken in the driver's seat of a real Winston Cup stock car—a treat they'll remember for a long time. Four video screens play race footage throughout the display area, while a gift shop supplies everything from die-cast model cars to T-shirts and other wearables, collector cards, videos, and more.

## GM Powertrain Performance Build Center Tours (ages 12 and up)

Tours are 9 a.m. to 11 a.m. and 1 to 3 p.m. Mon through Fri. Reservations are required. Call (734) 564-9565 or (248) 668-2401. Free.

After you've toured the Motorsports Museum, sign up for a tour to watch high-performance engines for ZO6 and ZR1 Corvettes being hand-built at this sparkling General Motors facility. Learn about the evolution of the Corvette's engines from the 1950s. No photography is allowed, and tour takers must wear pants with no open-toed shoes. For tour package information, call the Staybridge Suites (see listing below), (248) 349-4600.

# Where to Eat

**Don's of Traverse City.** 48730 Grand River, just east of Wixom Road, between Novi and Wixom; (248) 380-0333. Music from the 1950s and 1960s, malts, and burgers rule here in this dinerlike incarnation of the original drive-in in Traverse City. $

## Where to Stay

**Crowne Plaza Novi.** 27000 Sheraton Dr., at I-96 and Novi Road, across from Twelve Oaks Mall; (248) 348-5000. This property has 217 rooms, indoor and outdoor pools, exercise area, and restaurant. $$$

**Doubletree Hotel Detroit/Novi.** 42100 Crescent Blvd., at the I-96 and Novi Road exit; (248) 344-8800. This property has 148 rooms, indoor pool, and dining room. $$

**Sheraton Detroit Novi.** 21111 Haggerty Rd., at the northwest corner of I-275 and Eight Mile Road; (248) 349-4000. You can't miss this white edifice rising seven stories. There are 239 rooms with indoor pool, exercise room, and dining. $$$

**Staybridge Suites–Novi.** 27000 Providence Parkway; (248) 349-4600; www.staybridge.com/novimi. From I-96, take the Beck Road exit. Turn south to Grand River Avenue. Go west. The hotel is just past the hospital. This new facility has 108 rooms, indoor pool, outdoor jogging track, and **free** breakfast buffet and Internet. For the GM plant tour package, the hotel will arrange your tour (see listing above). $$

## For More Information

**Novi Chamber of Commerce.** 47601 Grand River Ave., Novi; (248) 349-3743; www.novichamber.com.

# Wixom

Wixom is another small farming community that is fast becoming a community of subdivisions.

## Proud Lake State Recreation Area  (all ages)

From I-96, take Wixom Road north about 6 miles; (248) 685-2433; www.michigan.gov/dnr. A state park vehicle permit is required for entry. Camping is extra. $.

Including a portion of the upper Huron River, the park contains more than 3,600 acres. There are more than 21 miles of trails offering warm-weather hiking. Part of the trails are open for cross-country skiing in winter. Also featured are a beach and swimming on a portion of the river and canoeing, as well as camping and a boat launch area on Proud Lake. The area is the site each spring of a release of large hatchery rainbow and brown trout available for catch and release fishing until opening day of trout season (always the last Sat of Apr).

## Alpine Valley Ski Area  (all ages)

Located on the north side of Highway 59 at 6775 East Highland Rd., White Lake; (248) 887-4183; www.skialpinevalley.com. From I-96, take Milford Road exit north to Highway 59 and head west. The ski school can accommodate children ages six and older. There isn't, however, child care available for younger children. Alpine Valley has cafeteria-style food.

Here is a southeast Michigan ski area with a true "up north" feel due to the tree-covered slopes along many of its twenty-five runs. Like nearly all ski areas in the state, Alpine

Valley is constantly updating its rental equipment, including "shaped" skis that help all levels of skiers improve their skills. The facility offers snowboard rentals so skiers can try their hands—and whatever else hits the snow when they're learning—at it.

### Environmental Discovery Center at Indian Springs Metropark
(all ages)

**5200 Indian Trail, White Lake; (248) 625-7280; www.metroparks.com, then pick the park. The park is open 7 a.m. to 10 p.m. Apr to Nov, then to 8 p.m. through Mar. Exit I-96 at Milford Road and go north. Turn west onto Highland Road (Highway 59), then right onto Ormand Road, right onto White Lake Road, and left onto Indian Trail into the park. A daily or annual vehicle entry permit is required. $–$$**

One of the Metroparks' newest facilities, the Environmental Discovery Center is surrounded by sixty acres of restored and native ecosystems. The highlight is a trip underwater via a pond viewing room, giving visitors an underwater view of pond life including native Michigan fish.

## Where to Eat and Stay
See Novi listings.

# Royal Oak

Let's jump east a few townships to this unique community. From I-696, take the Royal Oak exit and head north on Woodward to North Main into downtown. Lost in the doldrums of urban sprawl for decades, Royal Oak is suddenly one of southeast Michigan's hot spots to live and play. Restaurants line streets like Main and Washington, and in between are chi-chi shops next door to vintage clothing stores.

### Detroit Zoological Park  (all ages)

**West Ten Mile Road and Woodward Avenue; (248) 541-5717; www.detroitzoo.org. From I-75, take I-696 west and watch for the zoo directional signs near the Woodward Avenue exit. The park is open year-round except some holidays, and hours vary by season. Adults and children ages 2 to 18 $$, children under 2 free. Parking $. There's a picnic grove west of the Penguinarium, where grills are allowed, along with a playscape playground for kids.**

Wise planners placed this 125-acre park here in 1928, the first in the nation to use barless exhibits, place animals in settings as close to their natural environment as possible, and confine them using dry or water moats for an unobstructed view.

One of the zoo's most popular features isn't an animal at all. It's the Tauber Family Railroad. On weekends the train transports nearly a half million passengers per year. It's 1¼ miles from the Main Station near the front gate, through a tunnel, to Africa Station, at the farthest corner of the park.

Other popular attractions include the bear dens; the Holden Museum of Living Reptiles; the National Amphibian Conservation Center; and the Wildlife Interpretive Gallery, a large building housing a butterfly and hummingbird garden, Pacific fish aquarium, and free-flight aviary with a waterfall and hundreds of live plants that create a junglelike environment for more than thirty species of birds. Other favorites include the snow monkeys' hot tub antics in winter; the Great Apes of Harambee, where you can view chimps in forest, meadow, and rock-outcropping settings, all resembling their natural habitat; and the Penguinarium, with its underwater views of the flightless birds.

The newest attraction is the "Australian Outback Adventure," where you and the kids can actually get face-to-face with the zoo's seventeen red kangaroos and wallabies along a winding path bordered by knee-high cables, while the 'roos are free to bounce wherever they wish. Kids can also handle Australian artifacts and musical instruments.

Then, head to the great "Arctic Ring of Life," North America's largest polar bear exhibit. It includes a spectacular 70-foot-long clear tunnel that kids love to walk through. Look up at the seals—although it doesn't look it, they're protected from their natural predators, the bears—and 1,000-pound polar bears as they cavort in the water and watch

## Cruisin' the Woodward Dream Cruise

If your household is full of car nuts, Woodward Avenue through Royal Oak is classic-car central during the third weekend of Aug. The annual Dream Cruise, billed as the world's largest one-day car show, features up to 45,000 cars, from the '30s on up, tooling up and down this boulevard highway from Detroit to Pontiac, but Royal Oak is considered the epicenter.

"Trailer queens"—cars that hardly ever leave their transport trailers—as well as daily drivers (some from as far away as California, New York, and Florida) come to celebrate Detroit rolling sculpture in this homage to the car that must be experienced to be appreciated. Spectators set up lawn chairs along the road and cheer on the hot rods, as police on every block monitor speeds and keep everything family friendly. Entertainment and vendors set up shop all along the route, along with those selling official fund-raising T-shirts to help keep the event going each year. There also are car shows on several main roads crossing Woodward. Although the cruise isn't officially until the third Sat in Aug, the cars get rolling the weekend before. For more information, go to www .woodwarddreamcruise.com.

you. Displays in the four-acre space also include a replica of an early 1900s Inuit Village. There's a great place for a family picnic in the zoo's large wooded grove. Adult roller chairs and "kid kabs" are available for rent year-round at the entrance near the Zoofari Market ($).

### Bluewater Chapter of the National Railway Historical Society
(ages 6 and up)

**Since the society has no museum or other headquarters to visit, getting there, in this case, is all the fun. For information on all trips, call (248) 541-1000 or visit www.bluewaternrhs .com. $$$$.**

Take your family back to the time when railroad passenger service was the only way to travel, with a series of historic train trips offered by the National Railway Historical Society. You don't have to be a member of the society to join the thousands who have traveled with the group since 1983.

Trips range from a few hours to overnight journeys with stays and meals at charming hotels in some of the prettiest towns Michigan and surrounding areas have to offer.

## Where to Eat

If you like food, you've come to the right place. Royal Oak has restaurants of all types. Check out restaurant row on the parallel streets of Main and Washington.

**Gayle's Chocolates.** 417 South Washington; (248) 398-0001. Did someone say chocolates? Hand-dipped masterpieces mixed with less-cholesterol-laden menu items mirror the mix of the city. Good selection of coffees, fresh juices, and teas. $

**Lily's Seafood Grill Brewery.** 410 South Washington; (248) 591-LILY; www.lilysseafood .com. Great seafood as the name implies, with made-on-premises root beer available for the kids, who eat **free** on Tues. Children's menu available. $–$$$

**Memphis Smoke.** 100 South Main; (248) 543-4300. With a name like that, ribs have got to be the featured meal, and they are. That, and turkey and other items roasted over wood. Children's menu available for lunch and dinner. There's late-night blues entertainment, too. $$$

**Mongolian Barbeque.** 310 South Main; (248) 398-7755. Open for lunch and dinner. Make your meal your way. Step along the offerings, scoop 'em on your plate, and take it to the huge wok, where cooks prepare your food. You can have it vegetarian, too. If you don't want to improvise, there are suggested combinations of goodies posted. $$$

## Where to Stay

**Travelodge.** 30776 Woodward Ave.; (248) 549-1600. Seventy-seven rooms, from which you can view the Woodward Cruise. Restaurants nearby, continental breakfast. $

See also the listings for Birmingham.

## For More Information

**Royal Oak Chamber of Commerce.** 200 South Washington, Royal Oak 48067; (248) 547-4000 or (248) 544-EVENTS; www .royaloakchamber.com or www.downtown royaloak.org.

# Bloomfield Hills

Consistently ranked among the top five or ten wealthiest communities in the nation, Bloomfield Hills has long been the retreat for auto barons beginning in the 1920s. Gracious, and not always large, homes line streets where many southeast Michigan residents enjoy driving past and ogling the fancy digs.

### Cranbrook Institute of Science  (ages 6 and up)

**39221 North Woodward Ave., in the Cranbrook complex; (248) 645-3200 or (877) 462-7262; http://science.cranbrook.edu. Hours are 10 a.m. to 5 p.m. daily, except on Fri, when hours are 10 a.m. to 10 p.m. Closed major holidays. The observatory, weather permitting, is open Sun from 1 to 4 p.m. and Fri from 8:30 to 10 p.m. Admission is $$ adults, $ children. Children under 2 enter for free; however, there is an extra charge for exhibits such as the Bat Zone. There are a small cafe and a science-oriented gift shop.**

With other kid-friendly displays from meteorites that flew in from space to the Bat Zone (open Sat and Sun), where kids can get up close and personal with the leathery-winged critters along with displays on physics and biology that encourage investigation, this venerable Detroit-area institution is bound to knock every kid's socks off.

### The Planetarium  (ages 6 and up)

**Inside the Cranbook Institute of Science; (877) 462-7262. Planetarium shows are on the hour from noon to 4 p.m., plus 7 to 9 p.m. on Fri. Children under 3 are admitted free; however, there are age restrictions for some shows, so call ahead. The cost of all shows is over and above regular museum admission. Because of multiple opening hours, be sure to call for current shows, or explore http://science.cranbrook.edu. $.**

Young children may remember for the rest of their lives their first steps into the Planetarium at the Cranbrook Institute of Science. As the lights slowly melt into darkness in the seventy-five-seat theater, the star guide takes you on a journey around the Milky Way galaxy. Shows change several times a year, so chances are your next visit will hold something completely different. The Planetarium also presents annual special holiday programs, special events that introduce the heavens to children, and weekend music and spectacular laser shows set to music, which are especially popular.

## Where to Eat and Stay

See Birmingham listings.

# Birmingham

One of the Detroit area's ritziest suburbs, Birmingham and neighboring Bloomfield Hills and West Bloomfield are consistently ranked among the richest communities per capita in the nation. It has a great downtown shopping area; stores range from T-shirt shops to high fashion. Parking is available on the street or in covered lots ($ per hour). If you choose the street, be aware that the meter maids are always watchful here.

## Where to Eat

**Cupcake Station.** 136 North Old Woodward; (248) 593-1903; www.cupcakestation .com. What kid or parent can resist this? Scores of varieties are available, and you also can order with your choice of frostings and toppings. $

**Max & Erma's.** 250 Merrill; (248) 258-1188. A large variety of dependable entrees available from steak to pasta, seafood to burgers. Children's menu includes corn dogs, pasta, chicken fingers, and grilled cheese. $–$$$

**Olga's Kitchen.** 138 Old Woodward; (248) 627-2760. Great family restaurant serving pita-style wraps with flair. Try the Lamb Olga. $–$$

## Where to Stay

**Holiday Inn Express.** 35370 North Woodward; (248) 642-6200. This hotel has sixty-four rooms with fitness center, **free** breakfast, and other restaurants nearby.

**Radisson Hotel Bloomfield Hills.** 39475 Woodward; (248) 644-1400. Great luxury hotel with 151 rooms, indoor pool, and great restaurant. $$–$$$

# Auburn Hills

Named for the hills making up this area of Oakland County, this Detroit suburb is now home to a shopping megamall and an automotive history museum.

## Walter P. Chrysler Museum  (all ages)

Located at Chrysler headquarters, 1 Chrysler Dr.; (888) 456-1924; www.chryslerheritage .com. Take I-75 to exit 78, and then follow the signs. Open 10 a.m. to 5 p.m. Tues through Sat, noon to 5 p.m. Sun. Closed holidays. $–$$, children 5 and under, as well as Chrysler employees and retirees, **free.**

Yeah, it's got a hemi. Or two or three. This metro Detroit museum honoring Chrysler motoring pioneers is on Chrysler's  modern campus.

Spread over three levels and a garage housing famous Chrysler racing products and an assortment of Jeeps and other vehicles, the museum portrays the company history, including its role in producing for the military, and the people who made it what it is today, and includes perhaps its most famous modern-day addition to the roadway, the family minivan. There are lots of hands-on displays, a theater, and a gift shop.

## Great Lakes Crossing  (all ages)

4000 Baldwin Rd.; (877) SHOP–GLC; www.shopgreatlakescrossing.com. Take I-75 to exit 84, Baldwin Road. The mall is adjacent.

More than 200 stores, both discount oriented and regular price, line the hallways of this huge complex. They include the five-football-field-big Bass Pro Shops store, where you can buy a lure or a boat and ogle the huge aquarium, as well as the large Neiman-Marcus Last Call discount outlet. There are several restaurants (see below) and a great food court, a multiscreen movie theater, and a unique glow-in-the-dark minigolf course for the whole family when you need a spending break. Package stays at seven nearby accommodations are available.

## Where to Eat

**Joe's Crab Shack.** 4975 South Baldwin Rd.; (248) 393-7319; www.joescrabshack.com. Near Great Lakes Crossing. From I-75, go north on Baldwin Road. Fish and crab are staples here, plus steaks. A children's menu also offers pizza, chicken, and macaroni. $$–$$$

**Rainforest Cafe.** Located inside Great Lakes Crossing mall; (248) 333-0280; www.rainforestcafe.com. Great atmosphere with plenty of greenery and a variety of menu offerings, including soups, salads, ribs, and chicken. Children's menu. $$

## Where to Stay

**Fairfield Inn.** 1294 Opdyke Rd.; (248) 373-2228 or (800) 228-2800. The inn has 119 rooms and an outdoor pool. Hot complimentary breakfast; restaurants nearby. $$

**Hyatt Place.** 1545 Opdyke Rd.; (248) 475-9393. Take I-75 to exit 79 (University Drive) west, to Opdyke and turn right. It has 126 rooms with indoor pool and food bar. $$$. Packages for Great Lakes Crossing available.

## For More Information

**Auburn Hills Chamber of Commerce.** 1 South Squirrel Rd., Auburn Hills 48321; (248) 853-7862; www.auburnhillschamber.com.

# Rochester

This region of rolling, forested hills wasn't just recently discovered by those looking for a home in the 'burbs. It has been a favorite country playfield of the rich and famous of Detroit industry since the early twentieth century. One home in particular still draws attention year-round. The city is also the home of several of the region's most popular cider mills.

### Meadow Brook Music Festival (all ages)

**On the campus of Oakland University at 3554 Walton Blvd.; (248) 377-0100; www.palacenet .com. From I-75, exit at University Drive (exit 79) and head east to Squirrel Road. Take Squirrel Road north to Walton Boulevard and turn right onto Walton. Take Walton east, ¾ mile to the main entrance. Parking ($) is in addition to admission. The season runs roughly from Memorial Day through late Sept. $$$–$$$$**

Meadow Brook's lawn-seating atmosphere is genteel, restful, and family-oriented. Families heading for the 5,300 lawn seats—actually just a grassy place to spread your blanket—can carry in some food items, but beverages must be purchased on the grounds. If you want to picnic with your own drinks, plan to tailgate in the parking lot before the concert starts. Then stretch out and enjoy music by former Motown greats  and other popular artists, plus occasional concerts by the Detroit Symphony. The uncovered pavil-ion seating holds 2,200. Specific concerts at Meadow Brook cater to families, with **free** lawn admittance for children age twelve and younger when accompanied by an adult for select concerts. Picnicking on the lawn is one of the best, laid-back aspects of concerts here. Don't pass it up.

### Addison Oaks County Park  (all ages)

**1480 West Romeo Rd., Leonard, 9 miles north of Rochester; (248) 693-2432; www.oakgov .com/parksrec, then pick the park. From Highway M-59 in downtown Rochester, head north on Rochester Road, then west on Romeo Road. Open year-round.**

This scenic and nearby 1,141-acre park features two lakes with swimming, boating, camp-ing, and log cabins available to rent; a twenty-four-hole disc golf course plus 12 miles of cross-country ski and mountain bike trails, including one lighted for night touring and special events.

## Where to Eat

**Paul's on Main Street Family Restau-rant.** 630 North Main St.; (248) 656-0066. Good family fare. $$

**Rochester Mills Beer Company.** 400 Water St.; (248) 650-5080. This local brewpub caters to families and even carries house-made root beer on its children's menu. Louisi-ana jambalaya, fish and chips, and shepherd's pie are specialties. $$–$$$$

## Where to Stay

**Royal Park Hotel.** 600 East University Dr.; (248) 652-2600; www.royalparkhotel.net.

There are 143 guest rooms and several larger suites in this luxury hotel, which also has a restaurant. Definitely not for the economy minded. $$$

**Spartan Motel.** 1100 Main St.; (248) 651-8100; www.spartanmotel.com. This cozy motel features microwaves in rooms and Internet access. Restaurants nearby. $$

## For More Information

**Rochester Downtown Development Authority.** 308½ Main Street, Rochester 48307; (248) 656-0060; www.downtown rochestermi.com.

# Rochester Hills

### Yates Cider Mill  (all ages)

**1990 East Avon Rd. (Twenty-three Mile Road and Dequindre); (248) 651-8300; www.yates cidermill.com. Open Aug through Nov daily from 9 a.m. to 7 p.m. except Thanksgiving Day. Free.**

Up to 600 dozen doughnuts an hour come through the 8 feet of cooking vats at this mill. Oh, and there's great cider, too.

### Goodison Cider Mill  (all ages)

42965 Orion Rd.; (248) 652-8450. From I-75, exit north on Highway 24, and then head east on Silver Bell Road to Goodison. Open during the fall crushing season, usually from early Sept–Labor Day through mid-Nov. **Free.**

This mill is along the beautiful Paint Creek Trail (see detailed entry on the trail in Lake Orion section).

## Where to Eat

See Rochester listings.

## Where to Stay

**Best Western Concorde Inn.** 1919 Star-Batt Dr., at the junction of Highway 59 and Crooks Road, only a few miles southwest of downtown Rochester in Rochester Hills; (248) 299-1210. The inn has 120 rooms with **free**

and pay-per-view movies and **free** continental breakfast and evening snacks, plus indoor pool. Packages available. $$

**Red Roof Inn Detroit–Rochester Hills.** 2580 Crooks Rd., at the junction with Highway 59 in Rochester Hills; (248) 853-6400. The inn has 111 rooms with **free** and pay-per-view movies. Pets OK. $$

# Lake Orion

To reach Lake Orion, leave I-75 at exit 81 and go north on Highway 24. Once considered too far outside metro Detroit to count as a suburb, it has rapidly become that as metro Detroit expands outward.

### Olde World Canterbury Village  (all ages)

2369 Joslyn Court; (248) 391-5700 or (800) 442-9627; www.canterburyvillage.com. From I-75, take exit 83 (Joslyn Road) north about 3 miles. The village is open from 10 a.m. to 8 p.m. Mon through Sat, from 10 a.m. to 6 p.m. Sun, and from 10 a.m. to 5 p.m. on Christmas Eve and New Year's Eve.

On a registered state historic site, this mall—with a combination of gift, Christmas, and specialty shops—used to be the 3,000-acre Wildwood Farm estate of publishing magnate William E. Scripps in the early 1900s. Canterbury Toy World is every boy's and girl's dream, filled with educational toys and books with hands-on testing and demos, while Canterbury Gifts has plenty of items for the home. The Royal Confectionary tempts the palate with chocolates.

### Bald Mountain State Recreation Area  (all ages)

Headquarters are at 1350 Greenshield Rd.; (248) 693-6767. To reach the park area, exit I-75 at Highway 24 and head north to the first unit. Another section of the park is east of downtown Lake Orion. This is a day-use area only, no camping available. Entry is with state park vehicle permit. $.

It's hard to believe that a touch of northern Michigan can be found so close to metropolitan Detroit, but here it is. Encompassing more than 4,600 acres, the recreation area straddles Highway 24. In the southeastern section is Lower Trout Lake, called by many the best swimming beach for children in the region because of its long, sandy, gradual slope. There are canoe, paddleboat, and horse rentals, too.

Hikers can find nearly 14 miles of trails, and anglers will find bass and panfish. Fly fishermen may be amazed that there are brown trout in Trout and Paint Creeks.

### Paint Creek Trail  (all ages)

**A limestone trail that runs 8.9 miles between Lake Orion and Rochester, paralleling Paint Creek and through small portions of the Bald Mountain State Recreation Area. There are entrances in Lake Orion with parking off Clarkston Road, east of Highway 24; in the Goodison area southeast of Lake Orion; and in Rochester off University Drive, west of Main. For the status of the trail, call (248) 656-4673 or (248) 651-9260; www.paintcreektrail.org; e-mail the group for a free brochure and map.**

Actually a former railroad grade, the trail meanders through fields, woods, and some of the highest elevations in southeast Michigan. Use on foot, on a bike, on horseback (in certain areas only), or on cross-country skis (in winter). There are access points along the trail to try fishing for Paint Creek's trout.

## Where to Eat

**Buffalo Wild Wings.** 770 North Lapeer Rd.; (248) 814-8600. Good wings, ribs, and other fare. $$

## For More Information

**Orion Area Chamber of Commerce.** P.O. Box 236, Lake Orion 48361; (248) 693-6300.

## Where to Stay

See Rochester and Rochester Hills listings.

# Romeo

Located along Highway 53 and Thirty-two Mile Road in northwest Macomb County, Romeo was founded in 1838. This little village retains its small-town atmosphere, thanks in part to attaining National Historic District stature. Lots of fine antiques shops grace the old downtown, which features brick-paved sidewalks.

### Wolcott Mill Metropark  (all ages)

**63841 Wolcott Rd., Ray, between Twenty-nine and Thirty Mile Roads; (810) 749-5997 or (800) 477-3175; www.metroparks.com. From Highway 53, head east on Twenty-eight Mile Road. Continue east to Jewell Road, and then head north to Twenty-nine Mile Road and then east 6 miles to Kuntsman Road, to the Historic Center. The Farm Center is on Wolcott Road, north 1½ miles off Twenty-nine Mile Road. It's open daily from 9 a.m. to 5 p.m. spring through fall. Hours and days open vary in winter. Call ahead. Entrance $; annual permit $$$.**

# Armada Fair (all ages)

Armada is off Highway 53, northeast of Romeo in Macomb County.

Every Aug this small town, at the base of Michigan's Thumb, welcomes upward of 50,000 visitors to what's generally regarded as Michigan's best county fair. The Armada Fair has been crowding 'em in for more than 125 years now, and depending on who's bragging, it's either the third- or fourth-oldest county fair in the state. The fun includes everything county fairs should include, from judging the best 4-H sheep, steers, and other four-footed farm inhabitants to the big midway with enough flashing lights to make any child's eyes open wide. But there's more that this fair also brings to the table. Up-and-coming country-and-western stars and other top-name acts entertain in the grandstands each evening, and there are always tractor pulls and other contests. $–$$, two and under free. For information on the next edition of the fair, call (586) 784-5488; www.armadafair.org.

Wolcott Mill is an 1847-era gristmill that was operational until 1967 on the banks of the North Branch of the Clinton River. It was developed into the Huron-Clinton Metroparks system's only historical facility. The sounds of grinding millstones still fill the old mill as you learn the history of milling in Michigan. There's an eighteen-hole golf course, and special events include a boo-barn around Halloween, hayrides and harvest activities, a corn maze, and other events such as a Civil War muster.

The park's Farm Center is a real, modern operating farm that shows visitors the importance of farming today. See a dairy herd during their daily 10 a.m. milking, spring through fall (5 p.m. the rest of the year), plus draft horses, sheep, and demonstration vegetation plots. Special events also take place here. Call the park for information.

## Where to Eat

**Juliet Chocolates.** 66870 Van Dyke St.; (586) 752-4335. Now, who could resist stopping by, with a name like that? More than eighty varieties of handmade chocolates. $

**Office Pub & Cookery.** 128 South Main St.; (586) 752-6680. Serving pitas, burgers, and the like for lunch and dinner. $

**Romeo Coney Island.** 130 South Main St.; (586) 752-5730. When the suburbs expanded, Detroiters took their likes with them, including downtown-style coneys. Breakfast and lunch. $

## Where to Stay

**Hudson Inn.** 198 West St. Clair; (248) 703-1450; www.hudsoninn.com. Well-behaved kids are welcome in this 1901 Queen Anne–style abode with five rooms and game hookups. $$$

**Prospect Hill Bed and Breakfast.** 439 Prospect; (586) 336-1527. From Highway M-53, turn west onto West St. Clair Street, go 3 blocks to Prospect, and turn north. This 1870s-era mansion features feather beds and full breakfast for families with kids age fifteen or older. $$

## For More Information

**Romeo Washington Chamber of Commerce.** 228 North Main St., Romeo; (586) 752-4436; www.rwchamber.com.

# Milford

Named for the mills that once churned along the Huron River, Milford is another bedroom community for metro Detroit. Along I-96, west of Novi, Milford is the site of several canoe liveries that offer day and overnight trips on the Huron.

**Kensington Metropark.** (all ages)

**The main entrance is off I-96, at Kent Lake Road, one exit past Milford. There is another entrance off the I-96 Kensington Road exit. The headquarters is at 2240 West Bund Rd.; (248) 685-1561; www.metroparks.com. The park is open from 6 a.m. to 10 p.m. daily. Call for a locator map of all Metroparks and their facilities, including eight eighteen-hole golf courses. A daily ($) or annual ($$$) motor vehicle permit is required for entry.**

Kensington Metropark, in the far western Detroit suburbs, is a 4,400-acre gem.

Located on a 1,200-acre lake created by a dam on the Huron River, it's a year-round family attraction that by itself draws millions of visitors annually. Where else can you sled and toboggan or cross-country ski in winter, swim and sunbathe in summer at two beaches, and launch your own boat? In the fall you can enjoy Michigan's sweeping autumn color show by driving or biking roads overlooking the lake, exploring secluded nature trails on your own, or joining weekend naturalist-guided hikes. You can also board the thirty-seven-passenger pontoon boat *Island Queen II,* which operates through mid-

## Geocaching, Anyone?

Ever heard of geocaching? It's one of the hottest new sports around, but no one in your family needs to be a star athlete to participate. All you need is a handheld GPS, and to be close to a cache location, such as one of the metro Detroit Metroparks. Here's how it works: Get a brochure, printed new every year, or go to www.geocaching.com and find a park.

Each park contains a "cache," or a small box of trinkets and messages left by others. It's custom that if you take something from the cache, you leave something in return. Your family's job? Using your handheld GPS, track down the location of the cache by following the longitude/latitude and other clues in the brochure. The cache could be in a hollow tree stump, as ours was, or hanging in a tree, or even on a branch over a river.

Oct, to catch the area's fall color season. There is great fishing here, too, for warm-water species like bass and panfish, and the entire lake is under a no-wake rule. In spring, take the children to witness the annual rite of the season as thousands of waterfowl return to the park's outdoor center. Kids can meet the animals at the farm, as well. The farm admission is **free** with entry.

The park's newest addition is Splash 'N' Blast, two waterslides, plus a spray pad for the little ones. You can also geocache here (see "Geocaching, Anyone?") as well as rent a canoe or kayak at nearby Heavener Canoes (248-685-2379).

Golfers will enjoy a 6,300-yard, eighteen-hole course laid out along the western shore of the lake. In winter sleigh rides are offered, too, as long as there's a 4- to 6-inch base of snow.

## Where to Eat and Stay

See Brighton listings.

# Brighton

Brighton is located along I-96 at US 23. There are exits to the city on both freeways. Brighton was settled in the 1830s. Until a few years ago, it was just another farm and resort lake community on the route between Lansing and Detroit—until it was discovered by suburbanites.

### Brighton Recreation Area  (all ages)

**Located at 6360 Chilson Rd., Howell; (810) 229-6566. From I-96, take exit 147. Travel west about 6 miles to Chilson Road, then go south about 1½ miles to Bishop Lake Road and follow the signs to the park. A daily or annual state park motor vehicle entry permit is required, $. Camping is extra.**

This is one of the most popular recreation areas in the region. Bishop Lake is a longtime favorite for metro-area swimmers, with two beaches, one there and another on Chilson Pond. There are four campgrounds that include primitive cabins. You can fish in several lakes for panfish, and in Appleton Lake for trout. Hiking, snowmobiling, and cross-country skiing also are available.

### Imagination Station  (all ages)

**In downtown Brighton at the Mill Pond; (810) 227-5086. Free.**

While you explore the shops of downtown, the kids can feed the waterfowl and explore this 10,000-squarefoot wooden castle and fortlike structure adjacent to the pond that once powered the town's mill. Next to the Imagination Station, Tridge, the three-pronged bridge, crosses part of the millpond. Sundays in summer, there are **free** concerts in the nearby gazebo.

# Mount Brighton Ski Area (ages 7 and up)

Mount Brighton is reached by exiting I-96 at the Old Grand River Road exit in Brighton. Turn south, and at the first stoplight past the freeway, turn right. You'll see the ski area on the left. Contact Mount Brighton for conditions by calling (810) 229-9581, or go to www.mtbrighton.com. Rental equipment is available. Lift tickets are $$$. Skiing children ages 5 and under schuss free with a full-fare adult.

Metropolitan Detroit is blessed with plenty of things to do when winter arrives, including skiing at four downhill slopes, this being one. Ski areas like Mount Brighton are popular because they make it a point to cater to families, whether they're just starting on the bunny hill or are tackling the toughest black-diamond runs.

If you've never skied before, sign up for "Discover Michigan Skiing" days. This annual program takes youngsters onto the slopes at Brighton and nearly two dozen other areas around the state for beginner lessons. Since the program is geared to first-time and neophyte skiers, the package also represents a great value. In Jan they can quickly advance their skills, progressing through beginner-level lessons taught by a professional instructor during a ninety-minute session. You can even try out snowboarding. Cost includes all rental equipment and beginner lift tickets. The package price is far less than the cost of a lift ticket alone, and renting your equipment the first few visits allows you to try out the sport with hardly any investment. Discover Michigan Skiing offers lesson and rental packages for adults, $$$$, ages 7 to 14, $$$, and $$$$ for snowboarding lessons regardless of age. It's not recommended for kids younger than age seven. However, fourth graders are eligible for another learn-to-ski program called "Cold Is Cool," with free downhill and cross-country ski passes.

A large and well-trained ski school staff will have your family up and shuffling around on slats within minutes. There are plenty of novice and gentle intermediate runs where you can hone new skills. Intermediate and advanced skiers will find plenty of challenging terrain over twenty-six runs. Experienced snowboarders may want to try the expert bumps and pipes in Brighton's terrain park, and there are children's learn-to-ski programs, too.

Nearly two dozen other Michigan resorts—including Alpine Valley, near Milford; Mount Holly, near Holly; and Pine Knob, in the southeastern part of the state—also participate in the program. To learn more, call Michigan Snowsport Industries Association at (248) 620-4448, or go to www.goski michigan.com.

## Huron Meadows Metropark (all ages)

**8765 Hamel Rd.; (248) 231-4084; www.metroparks.com. The park is open 7 a.m. to 10 p.m. Memorial Day to Labor Day and 7 a.m. to 8 p.m. the rest of the year. A daily ($) or annual ($$$) motor vehicle permit is required for entry.**

Rent a boat to fish on Maltby Lake, or fish from a platform, or play the park's great eighteen-hole golf course, or have a picnic. There also are 5 miles of hiking trails. In winter cross-country ski rentals are available, weather permitting, and ice fishing is available in this 1,540-acre park.

## Where to Eat

**E. G. Nick's.** 11600 East Grand River Ave.; (810) 227-2131. Open weekdays for lunch and dinner, weekends for dinner, including ribs, steaks, and fish. $$

**Grecian Island.** 9994 East Grand River Ave.; (810) 229-3101. Open for breakfast through dinner daily. Inexpensive Greek food. $

**Red Robin.** 8522 West Grand River Ave.; (810) 534-1000. Open for breakfast through dinner, this family-friendly chain offers good food, from burgers to wraps and pastas. $$ See also subsequent entries for Howell, a city near Brighton.

## Where to Stay

**Courtyard by Marriott.** 7799 Conference Center Dr.; (810) 225-9200 or (800) 321-2211. From I-96, take exit 145, Old Grand River Avenue. This property has ninety rooms and an indoor pool. Breakfast available. Restaurants adjacent. $$

**Holiday Inn Express.** 8079 Challis Rd.; (810) 225-4300 or (800) 465-4329. From I-96, take exit 145. This property has 106 rooms and an indoor pool. Breakfast with some hot items. Restaurant nearby. Children ages eleven and younger stay **free.** $$$

**Homewood Suites by Hilton.** 8060 Challis Rd.; (810) 25-0200. Ninety-four rooms with indoor pool and complimentary breakfast buffet and weekday manager's reception meal. $$$

See also subsequent Where to Stay listings for the nearby city of Howell.

## For More Information

**Greater Brighton Chamber of Commerce.** 131 Hyne St., Brighton 48116; (810) 227-5086; www.brightoncoc.org.

# Going to **Hell**

No, it's not what you think. This unique townlet actually exists, near Brighton, so-named as a joke in 1841, as the legend goes, the town founder, having some fun when asked what the town name was, told the state to "call it Hell, for all I care . . ." The state obliged. Lots of ice cream is sold here, along with the proverbial T-shirts and the like. Stop by the Dam Site Inn, or canoe and kayak on Hell Creek. Camp at Hell Creek Ranch (734-878-3632; www.hell creekranch.org).

# Parshallville

### Parshallville Cider Mill  (all ages)

8507 Parshallville Rd.; (810) 629-9079; www.parshallvillecidergristmill.com. The cider mill is in what's called downtown Parshallville, even though the mill and a few other buildings are about all that's there. From Brighton, head north on US 23 to the Clyde Road exit. Head west, then north on Old US 23 to Parshallville Road, then go west about 1 mile to the mill. **Free.**

In the center of this tiny hamlet founded in 1835 by Isaac Parshall, North Ore Creek still is dammed up to power the gristmill, which was purchased by the Walker family in 1880. The family milled grain there until 1960. Cider making began several years later. Parshallville remains one of two historic mills in the state that can still operate using waterpower. Besides the pressing operations, there's a small store that sells baked and canned items. Enjoy your cider along the millrace below the building.

### Spicer Orchards  (all ages)

10411 Clyde Rd., Fenton; (810) 632-7692; www.spicerorchards.com. From Brighton, head north on US 23 to the Clyde Road exit. Turn east about ¼ mile. The mill and store are on the left. Admission is **free.**

In a modern setting compared with its neighbor in Parshallville, the farm features apple picking in late summer and fall. The orchard also hosts a **free** mid-Sept harvest festival with pony rides and other activities for the kids.

# Howell

Howell was founded in 1834, and recently it has become a meeting point for commuting families heading west to Lansing and east to the Detroit area. Most of the downtown, however, still retains its rural, country feel. Located along I-96, just west of Brighton, at exit 133 or 137.

### Tanger Outlet Center  (all ages)

On Burkhart Road, just off I-96, exit 133; (888) 545-0565; www.tangeroutlet.com, and pick the center from the list. Open daily 10 a.m. to 9 p.m. Mon through Sat and 11 a.m. to 6 p.m. Sun. From Jan 1 through Feb 28 it is open 10 a.m. to 7 p.m. Mon through Thurs, 10 a.m. to 9 p.m. Fri and Sat, and 11 a.m. to 5 p.m. Sun.

More than eighty name-brand shops offer wares ranging from spatulas to suits and suitcases at discount prices. A food court is set in the middle of the stores.

### Michigan Challenge Balloonfest  (all ages)

In Howell the third weekend of June at Howell High School, 1200 West Grand River Ave.; (517) 546-3920; www.michiganchallenge.com. The festival is **free,** but carnival rides and other ancillary events are $–$$.

Almost a quarter of a century old, one of the largest gatherings of hot-air balloons in the state takes flight over the farm fields of Livingston County during this annual event, as nearly fifty pilots take off during evening mass balloon launches. There are other activities, too, including skydiving demonstrations, stunt kites, and skateboard demonstrations. Kids, bring your own board for open skate times. The carnival also comes to town.

## Where to Eat

**Tomato Brothers.** 3030 West Grand River Ave.; (517) 546-9221. Good Italian lunches and dinners. $$

See also previous Where to Eat listings for Brighton, which is nearby.

## Where to Stay

**Best Western of Howell.** 1500 Pinckney Rd.; (517) 548-2900. From I-96, take exit 137, and then head south on CR D-19. This property has sixty rooms, outdoor pool, and restaurants nearby. Kids ages eleven and younger stay **free.** $$

**Kensington Inn of Howell.** 124 Holiday Lane; (517) 548-3510. This inn has 107 rooms, outdoor pool, and **free** continental breakfast. Restaurants nearby. Pets OK. $–$$

See also previous Where to Stay listings for the nearby city of Brighton.

## For More Information

**Howell Chamber of Commerce.** 123 Washington St., Howell 48843; (517) 546-3920; www.howell.org.

**Livingston County Visitors Bureau.** 123 East Washington St., Howell 48843; (517) 548-1795 or (800) 686-8474; www.lccvb.org.

# Clarkston

### DTE Energy Music Theater  (all ages)

**This outdoor theater is reached from several exits off I-75 north of Pontiac, the most popular of which is northbound Sashabaw Road; (248) 377-0100; www.placenet.com. Open mid-May through late Sept. If sitting in the covered pavilion, bring along ear protection, especially for children. Wheelchair accessible. $$$$.**

To some, it will always be Pine Knob, but DTE now sponsors the facility and owns the name. Whatever name you call it, it's become one of the most successful outdoor music venues in the country. The covered pavilion seats more than 6,400, and the "cheap seats" on the lawn hold more than 8,000. For most concerts, especially the loudest ones, families prefer the lawn seating. Get there early to stake out a spot with your blanket or small beach chairs. Food and drinks must be purchased in the park if you're on the hill. Otherwise, throw a tailgate picnic in the parking area before the show. The seasonal lineup is usually announced in late Apr or early May.

### Pine Knob Ski Area  (ages six and up)

**On the grounds of DTE Energy Music Theater; (248) 625-0800; www.skipineknob.com. Ski rentals and instruction available. There's also a cafeteria. $$–$$$$.**

Once the lights at the theater go out after summer, the lights on the ski hill come on a few months later, usually starting in early Dec. There are about fifteen runs to ski or snow-board. Pine Knob also participates in learn-to-ski promotions, similar to Mount Brighton's (see listing). It's a great place to learn and then go for an after-dinner ski.

## Where to Eat

**The Clarkston Union.** 54 Main St.; (248) 620-6100. Open Mon through Wed 11 a.m. to midnight, Thurs through Sat 11 a.m. to 2 a.m., and Sun 9 a.m. to 2 p.m. and 3 to 9 p.m. From I-75, take the Highway 15 exit and go south about a mile into downtown. Set in a refurbished nineteenth-century church, this restaurant features pub-style food. It's especially known for macaroni and cheese made with sharp cheddar and penne pasta, baked with bread-crumb topping. Adults can sample any of the thirty-five American, European, and Japanese beers on tap as well as teas and coffees. Children's menu. $$–$$$

See also Waterford listings for more restaurants.

## Where to Stay

See Waterford listings.

# Holly

### Mount Holly Ski Area  (ages 7 and up)

**13536 South Dixie Hwy.; (248) 634-8260 or (800) 582-7256; www.skimtholly.com. From I-75, take the Dixie Highway exit and head north on Dixie, or take the Fenton exit and follow the signs. The season generally runs from Dec through late Mar or snowmelt. Plan on spending $$$$ for rental equipment and ski passes; children ages 6 and under get half off. Watch for special learn-to-ski prices in Jan. You can buy cafeteria food or bring your own.**

One of southeast Michigan's premier ski areas, Mount Holly features eighteen runs of fun, with the region's first high-speed, four-seat chairlift, along with two "carpet" lifts just for beginners.

### Michigan Renaissance Festival  (all ages)

**To reach the grounds, turn off I-75 north at exit 106 near Grand Blanc, Holly. Go 2 blocks and turn south onto Dixie Highway for 2 miles. Festival grounds are 1 mile north of Mount Holly. Phone (248) 634-5552 or (800) 601-4848 for more information; www.michrenfest.com. Discounted advance tickets are on sale at area supermarkets. $–$$$, children 5 and under free. Ticket prices include all entertainment, but you pay extra for food and souvenirs. The fair is open rain or shine. Parking's free.**

For seven weekends each year beginning in mid-Aug, these sixteen wooded acres come alive with strolling minstrels, knights in shining armor, lords and ladies dressed to the hilt, and plenty of roasted turkey legs, soup in hollowed bread loaves, and other finger food to gnaw on Henry VIII–style (remember, this is the sixteenth century: no utensils). You don't have to come in costume, but it helps everyone get into the mood, especially if you come dressed as a noble family and make the "serfs" bow and scrape as you go by.

More than 195 craftspeople sell their wares, including beautiful walking sticks with sorcerer-like faces and other fantasy toppings that are made on the spot. Promenade to the competition ring and watch as knights in more than ninety pounds of armor climb onto horses and hold full-contact jousting tournaments, or engage each other in a one-on-one contest on foot, as the queen looks on from her royal booth.

A portion of the park is set aside just for children, including human-powered rides to provide not only a laugh but also a slight historical insight into what city fairs of yesteryear Europe must have been like. There are daily show performances, games, crafts, puppet shows, and more, including daily sightings of a friendly dragon. Entertainment on the festival's eight theme stages includes jugglers, storytellers, a sword swallower, and 200 other costumed performers.

# Waterford

Once a sleepy village in the heart of north Oakland County's lake country, Waterford now is a suburb of metro Detroit, Pontiac, and Flint to the north. It was settled in 1819 and was named for the area's abundant lakes.

### The Fridge at Waterford Oaks Park  (ages 5 and up)

**On Scott Lake Road, between Dixie Highway and Pontiac Lake Road, near Waterford; (248) 858-0906; www.oaklandfridge.com. To get to the park, leave I-75 at Dixie Highway and head south to Scott Lake Road. Turn south and follow it to the park. Hours are 4 to 10 p.m. Mon through Fri, 10 a.m. to 10 p.m. Sat, and 10 a.m. to 8 p.m. Sun, weather permitting. The runs are open New Year's Eve and Day but are closed Christmas Eve and Day. When you call, you can also receive a guide to the ten other Oakland County parks. $$.**

It's like hopping on a giant ice cube at Michigan's first refrigerated toboggan run, at Waterford Oaks, north of Pontiac. A unique refrigeration system ices two flumes of water that drop riders 55 feet before they travel another 1,000 feet, flying over hills, straights, and dips. You don't need anything except warm clothes and a readiness to have a blast. Each of the park's 200 toboggans holds four riders (riders must be at least 30 inches tall; those under 43 inches tall must be accompanied by an adult) and are transported by park staff from the finish back to the start. There's a warming building with a fireplace, a viewing area, concessions, and restrooms.

In summer the park entertains with a wave pool, a water park, and a BMX bicycling course.

### Stony Creek Metropark (all ages)

4300 Main Park Rd.; (586) 781-4242 or (800) 477-7756; www.metroparks.com. To get to the park, from I-696, take Highway 53 north to Twenty-six Mile Road and go west for about 2 miles. Watch for the signs to make a left into the park. Park entry is by daily ($) or annual ($$$) permit.

One of the string of Metroparks surrounding Detroit, this 4,461-acre beauty has everything from swimming and mountain bike trails to a great nature center. There's also a 6-mile-long paved hike/bike trail. Bikes are available for rent, along with canoes, kayaks, rowboats, and paddleboats. Teens and young adults love the disc-golf course, and there's an eighteen-hole regular course, too.

## Where to Eat

For fast food, check exits along I-75 between Pontiac and Clarkston. For other eateries, see Clarkston listings.

## Where to Stay

**Comfort Inn.** 7076 Highland Rd., at the junction of Highway 59 and Airport Road; (248) 666-8555. From I-75, head south about 6 miles on US 24 to Highway 59, and then go west 6 miles. The hotel has 111 rooms with movie and game rental and an indoor pool with game room. $$

**McGuire's Motor Inn.** 120 South Telegraph Rd. (US 24), 2 blocks south of Highway M-59; (248) 682-5100; www.mcguiresmotorinn .com. The hotel, which is 3 miles north of the Fridge, features forty rooms with in-room microwaves and minifridges. Restaurants nearby. Small pets OK. $

# Shelby Township

The township is one of the fastest growing in southeast Michigan, with farm fields disappearing into subdivisions' basements. It is also close to recreation on Lake St. Clair.

### Joe Dumars' Fieldhouse (all ages)

45300 Mount Rd., just north of Highway 59; (586) 731-3080; www.joedumarsfieldhouse .com. To reach it, exit I-75 at Highway 59 and turn east to Mound Road. Hours are 8 a.m. to 2 a.m. daily. Four to eight people can rent an indoor volleyball hard court, $$$–$$$$ per hour, or an outdoor beach volleyball court, $$–$$$ per hour, Apr through Sept.

You just might catch a glimpse of Detroit Pistons great–turned–team exec and Basketball Hall of Famer Joe Dumars at his namesake, a combination play-and-exercise center for both adults and children in this northern Detroit suburb. If you're in shape, you could participate in ten sports in a row at this 70,000-square-foot complex. In addition to six full-size and three half-court hardwood-floor indoor basketball courts, there are minigolf, laser tag, batting cages, and a rock-climbing wall. The field house also houses five hardwood volleyball courts. You can also play touch football or learn golf or rollerblading. Outdoors, beach volleyball courts are open in summer.

The field house is so popular that Dumars opened another in the Michigan State Fairgrounds agriculture building (see State Fair listing for address). It operates fall through spring.

The field house has a full-size roller-hockey rink, complete with leagues for kids age ten and younger, dads and moms thirty-five and older, and everything in between. After the game, head for a workout in the training center run by Beaumont Hospital for an additional charge.

Once you've had enough, offer the kids a meal at Sticks Sports Bar and Grill (810-726-0055), a restaurant inside that serves reasonably priced family fare such as submarine sandwiches, burgers, and pizza, or pick up a souvenir at the pro shop on the way.

### Riverbends Park (all ages)

**From Highway 59, head north on Mound Road for 1 mile; it becomes Auburn Road. Follow Auburn Road to Ryan Road, and turn north to the first unit. For the other unit, continue on Ryan Road to Twenty-two Mile Road and go east 1 mile to the picnic unit. Both units are parts of the same park, but they are divided by the river and are connected by a footbridge. Phone (810) 731-0300. Park hours are 8 a.m. to 8 p.m. or dusk (whichever comes first) from May through Oct, 8 a.m. to 5:30 p.m. from Nov through Feb, and 8 a.m. to 6:30 p.m. Mar and Apr. Free.**

Originally part of a state recreation area, this park is a tribute to Michigan's history and that of the canal-building era of the mid-1800s. Officials, eager to put their young state on the map in 1838, began an ambitious project to link Lake St. Clair and Lake Michigan with a shipping canal between the Clinton River and west Michigan's Kalamazoo.

However, an economic depression soon put an end to this dream. Today, remnants of the 12 miles of canal that were dug are evident, especially in the unit off Ryan Road. Explore the canal and its towpath; walk, bike, or skate 3½ miles of paved trails; go hiking and cross-country skiing or mountain biking on miles more; or try the skateboard/BMX bike park.

## Where to Eat and Stay

See listings under Mount Clemens.

# Sterling Heights

Named in honor of a pioneer settler, the city is now home to auto manufacturing and is a northern suburb of Detroit.

### Kart2Kart. (ages 16 or over)

**42705 Van Dyke Ave., just south of Nineteen Mile Road; (586) 997-8800; www.kart2kart .com. Open 2 to 10 p.m. Mon through Thurs, noon to midnight Fri and Sat, and noon to 8 p.m. Sun.**

If your kids are age 16 or over, bring them here to drive a modern go-kart on an indoor track or take a driving course. Karts can travel up to 40 mile per hour. Heats go for eight minutes, or about fifteen laps. $$ per heat. There are discounts on Fri and Mon, and a special driving academy for budding racers ages 13 to 16 is available. A snack bar also is on the premises

## Where to Eat

**Grand Traverse Pie Company.** 44951 Schoenherr; (586) 323-2743. Open 9 a.m. to 9 p.m. Mon through Sat, 9 a.m. to 6 p.m. Sun. Great selection of sandwiches, potpies, and quiches, plus breakfast and a children's menu, not to mention fresh-baked fruit and cream pies. $

**Loon River Café.** Attached to the Best Western Sterling Inn (see entry below for location); (586) 979-1420. A north-woods-like feel with everything from wild game to fish and pot roast on the menu. $$–$$$

**Nestle Toll House Café.** 13923 Lakeside Circle, outside Lakeside Mall; (586) 566-1313. Cookies chock full of those great chocolate chips are all they do, washed down with coffee and other beverages. $

## Where to Stay

**Best Western Sterling Inn.** 34911 Van Dyke Ave.; (800) 953-1400; www.sterlinginn .com. This family-friendly inn features 246 rooms, metro Detroit's only indoor water park, and dining. $$$

# Mount Clemens

Once famous for its mineral baths, the seat of Macomb County is located off I-94. And although it's located a few miles from Lake St. Clair, its soul feels connected with the water.

**Metro Beach Metropark** (all ages)
**Reached at the eastern end of Metropolitan Parkway, off I-94; (586) 685-1561 or (800) 477-3172; www.metroparks.com. The unguarded beach is open daily from May 1 to Sept 30. Entrance $ daily or $$$ annual pass.**

Another example of the forward-thinking park planners is this Huron-Clinton Metropark system's 770-acre lakeside beauty. On a typical steamy summer weekend day, you'll see thousands of people enjoying the pool, Squirt Zone, and beach, all on Lake St. Clair. A trackless train shuttles families from the parking lot to the point, where anglers fish for bass. Other attractions include the tot lot, where kids as young as age three can have fun; an Olympic-size heated pool with two waterslides; the Squirt Zone, a **free** spray park that kids love; minigolf; and a par-three golf course where you can rent clubs to start kids off in the game. Typically in July there is a **free** Detroit Symphony Orchestra concert (park entry fee required). Naturalist programs start at the park's nature center, where there are seasonal exhibits, displays of waterfowl inhabiting the area, and activities for kids.

### Morley Candy Makers  (ages 6 and up)

**23770 Hall Rd. (Highway 59); (800) 651-7263 or (586) 682-2760, ext. 2218 to reserve a tour time; www.morleycandy.com. Exit I-94 at the Selfridge Air National Guard Field exit, or Hall Road. Turn west to Gratiot, the first light. Cross Gratiot and look for the signs at the Tudor-style building. Free tours are between 10 a.m. and 1 p.m. Mon through Fri and include a video. Or take a self-guided tour without the video. Best of all, there are free samples. Reservations are required.**

What child isn't ready anytime to tour a candy factory? Morley's is Michigan's largest candy maker because of its popularity among charity fund-raising groups. Morley's cooks its chocolate goodies gallons at a time in huge, old-fashioned copper kettles, just like founder Ervin Morley did in 1919, when he created confections out of his original store in Detroit.

On hour-long tours of the facility, visitors walk along a 75-foot observation hallway and bask in the aromas of sugar and cocoa as employees and machines dip and mold each of the chocolates, which will eventually be boxed and ready for sale.

### Selfridge Military Air Museum).   (all ages)

**Near Mount Clemens on Selfridge Air National Guard base, off Highway 59 (Hall Road), near the main gate to Selfridge Air National Guard base; (586) 307-5035; www.selfridgeair museum.org. Open noon to 4:30 p.m. Sat and Sun, Apr through mid-Oct, Memorial Day, and Independence Day. There are train rides connecting to the Michigan Transit Museum (see listing below) Sun, Apr through Sept, and Sat and Sun in Oct. See schedule for details, as late trains don't stop here. Admission is by donation.**

At this static air museum, see twenty of the armed forces' combat and transport planes on display, from World War II aircraft to an F-16 Falcon, paying tribute to America's fighting men and women. You can also enjoy an indoor display, a small gift shop, and a huge air show (usually every other summer

### Michigan Transit Museum  (all ages)

**200 Grand Ave., between Gratiot and Groesbeck Avenues at the tracks; (586) 463-1863; www.michigantransitmuseum.org. Open Sat and Sun from 1 to 4 p.m. Train rides take place in summer, are forty-five minutes long, and leave hourly, not from the museum, but from nearby Joy Park, ¼ mile east of northbound Gratiot Avenue. Admission for adults $$, ages 4 to 12 $, under age 4 free. The trains stop at the Selfridge Military Air Museum (see above) on rides from 1 to 3 p.m.**

See some of the history of early mass transit in Michigan, as well as a glimpse of what travel in the state may be like in the coming decades. Exhibits include a locomotive and an interurban streetcar, one of the first mass transit vehicles that ran between towns.

## Where to Eat

**Bath City Bistro.** 75 Macomb Place; (586) 469-0917. Named for the city's mineral-bath history, the restaurant is in a late nineteenth-century building and features two levels, plus feather bowling, a game imported from Belgium. Steaks, calzones, and mussels are on the menu. $–$$$

## Michi-**fact:**

Michigan's reputation for spectacular fall foliage is well deserved. The number of hardwoods in the state has leaped in the last few decades, and maples make up the majority of the trees you'll see. Since they're the most colorful, it makes for great fall seasons that rival anything New England can offer.

## Where to Stay

**A Victory Inn.** 1 North River Rd., about a mile west of I-94 at the River Road exit; (586) 465-2185. The inn features ninety-nine rooms. $$

## For More Information

**Macomb County Chamber of Commerce.** 49 Macomb Place, Mount Clemens 48043; (586) 463-1528; www.centralmacomb.com.

# St. Clair

Located along scenic Highway 29 on the St. Clair River, this picturesque river town has great shops downtown and is famed for its downtown inn and restaurant overlooking the swift St. Clair. It's also part of a great driving trip on Highway 29, which parallels nearly the entire length of the St. Clair River. Exit onto Highway 29 from I-94 north of Mount Clemens for the longer scenic route. To get to the city, exit I-94 at Rattle Run Road. The river is visible starting near Algonac.

**Algonac State Park** (all ages)

Between St. Clair and Algonac along Highway 29, just south of Marine City; (810) 765-5605. For camping reservations, call (800) MI-4PARKS. $.

Take a lawn seat for this 1,023-acre park's main event, watching the St. Clair River traffic, from oceangoing "salties" to hulking 1,000-foot-long lake freighters riding low with cargoes of grain, iron ore, or coal. There are nearly 300 campsites, which get heavily used in summer, but most are small. The park makes a great weekend getaway, especially for anglers after the river's walleye. There are several trails that lead through a primitive prairie area, and cross-country skiing is available in winter.

## Where to Eat

**River Crab.** 1337 North River Rd. (Highway 29), a few miles north of St. Clair; (810) 329-2261 or (800) 468-3727. Great seafood, fresh fish lunch and dinners, Sun brunch, children's menu available. $$$

## Where to Stay

**Blue Water Inn.** Adjacent to the River Crab; (810) 329-2236. This cozy inn has twenty-one comfortable rooms. $$

**St. Clair Inn.** 500 North Riverside Dr. (Highway 29), in downtown St. Clair; (810) 329-2222; www.stclairinn.com. This Tudor-style inn has seventy-eight rooms, many overlooking the river traffic. Other amenities include indoor pool and whirlpool. The inn's restaurant offers outdoor dining, and a waterslide is open in warm weather. $$$

## For More Information

**St. Clair Chamber of Commerce.** P.O. Box 121, St. Clair 48079; (810) 329-2962; www.stclairchamber.com.

# Port Huron

Located at the eastern end of I-94 on the St. Clair River, the city of Port Huron is one of Michigan's three portals to Canada in Detroit, its near southern neighbor—that's right, by a quirk of geography, part of Ontario actually is south of metropolitan Detroit. Port Huron is one of the state's oldest cities, founded in 1686. Originally a fort to protect the entrance to the lower Great Lakes and the French fur trade, it sits where all Great Lakes water funnels into the narrows at the start of the St. Clair River under the Blue Water Bridge. Near it stands a statue dedicated to Thomas Edison, the town's most famous resident.

## Port Huron Museum and Thomas Edison Depot Museum
(all ages)

There are five museums in town, all under the umbrella of the museum headquarters at 1115 Sixth St., on the south edge of town; (810) 982-0891; www.phmuseum.org. From I-94, exit at Business 69. Go left and travel 6 blocks to Wall Street. Turn left and watch for signs. Adults $, children 6 and younger get in **free.** Museum hours are 11 a.m. to 5 p.m. daily. The Edison Depot is near the Blue Water Bridge and the Thomas Edison Inn (see listing). Call ahead or see the Web site for hours for each location as they vary by season. For detailed hours, call ahead. Museum admission: adults $, children 7 and under **free.**

Port Huron counts Thomas Edison—inventor of the electric light, the movie projector, and the phonograph, among thousands of other things—among its native sons. Edison once sold newspapers on the train between the city and Detroit. To clue your kids in on local history, take in the museum's Edison Depot adjunct facility, under the Blue Water Bridge along Edison Parkway, reached just off I-94 before the Blue Water Bridge.

Museum exhibits depict Edison's boyhood after moving here from Ohio and his work on the trains that left from this very depot. His science successes are highlighted in a sit-down theater, live science presentations, and hands-on activities, plus lots of memorabilia from his later life at his lab in Menlo Park, New Jersey. Other exhibits outside the museum tell the story of the area's first inhabitants.

## Lightship *Huron* Museum and
## Coast Guard Cutter *Bramble*  (all ages)

Located at Pine Grove Park, along the St. Clair River; (810) 982-0891; www.phmuseum.org. Follow I-94 to its end. At the light, follow Hancock Street, and then go south on Pine Grove to the park. Thurs through Mon early Apr to Memorial Day and Sept through Nov, and

# Fishing for Fun

When you come to Port Huron, bring your fishing equipment, regardless of the season. All summer, the St. Clair River produces great walleye action. In spring, anglers drop special pyramid-shaped nets into the river along the walkway south of the Blue Water Bridge to fish for tasty smelt, and charter boats are available to take you into lower Lake Huron for lake trout and salmon. For more information, check with the Blue Water Convention and Visitors Bureau (see listing) or sport shops, including Anderson's Pro Bait (810-984-FISH).

daily 11 a.m. to 5 p.m. Memorial Day through Labor Day. Adults $, children 6 and younger are admitted **free.**

The museum shares the address of the retirement home of the *Huron,* moored along the St. Clair River north of downtown in Pine Grove Park. Until 1970 the *Huron,* actually a floating lighthouse, stood guard to direct ships past shoals north of the St. Clair's treacherous below-bridge currents. Kids can explore the ship to see how its crew of eleven lived on board the vessel for twenty-one days at a time and learn where else the *Huron* served in its half century on the lakes. While you're there, the family can also scramble aboard the Coast Guard cutter *Bramble* for tours. Ask about the historic Fort Gratiot Lighthouse, also part of the Port Huron museums collection.

### Ruby Tree Farm and Cider Mill (all ages)

6567 Imlay City Rd., Ruby, just west of Port Huron; (810) 324-2662. From I-94, follow I-69 west to exit 96. Turn north and follow the signs. The cider mill is open weekends 11 a.m. to 5 p.m. from Aug through Halloween, and tree cutting is on weekends 11 a.m. to 5 p.m. from Nov through Dec.

You can make your children's Christmas even more magical when you take them on a trip to a cut-your-own tree farm like this one. Michigan is one of the nation's leading growers of Christmas trees. At this farm and others like it around the state, borrow a handsaw—no axes or power saws allowed—and haul back your own tree, $$$$.

Ruby's is also a cider mill, and during pressing time there are carnival rides including a carousel open through Halloween, a wax museum featuring a presidential display, a Christmas gift shop, and a petting zoo.

### *Huron Lady II* Boat Tours (all ages)

Sails from 800 Military St., on the south side of the Black River at the Military Street Bridge; (810) 984-1500; www.huronlady.com. From I-94, take exit 271. Follow Business I-69 (Oak Street) to Military, and then go left across the river to Quay Street. Cruises leave daily at 1 p.m. from mid-June to Labor Day, plus Sat at 3:30 p.m. and Sun at 4:30 p.m. in July and Aug. Adults and seniors $$$, children 5 to 12 $$. Under age 5 **free** with paying adult. Add $ for Sun's longer, three-hour cruise.

Step aboard for a two-hour narrated cruise—three on Sun—of the historic St. Clair River and Port Huron, which, during French and English days as Fort Gratiot, guarded the gateway to the Upper Great Lakes and was key to the control of the region. The three-hour tour cruises the swift St. Clair River from the mouth of the Black River to St. Clair and returns. You'll see beautiful waterfront mansions along both the American and Canadian shorelines, and take a trip around picturesque Stag Island. The two-hour tour takes in the Fort Gratiot Lighthouse and the twin Blue Water International Bridges and ventures out a bit into Lake Huron. On either cruise there's a great chance that your family will catch sight of a giant Great Lakes freighter or an ocean ship from a different country. There also are summer dinner cruises featuring a stop at the River Crab. The boat is Coast Guard approved and inspected.

## Where to Eat

**Quay Street Brewery.** 330 Quay St.; (810) 982-4100; www.quaybrewing.com. A diverse menu featuring everything from steaks to eggplant lasagna to fish, served along the Black River. House-brewed beers are on tap, along with homemade root beer. Children's menu. An upper and lower deck offers outside dining in summer. $$–$$$

**Thomas Edison Inn.** 500 Thomas Edison Parkway; (810) 984-8000. Just south of the Blue Water Bridge, adjacent to Thomas Edison's statue, and located inside this riverside hotel of the same name is this upscale restaurant. Look out on the St. Clair River traffic and enjoy prime rib, paella, and other menu items for dinner. Breakfast and lunch also are served. Children's menu. $$$$

## Where to Stay

**Comfort Inn.** 1700 Yeager St.; (810) 982-5500. Leave I-94 at the Water Street exit. This property features eighty rooms and an indoor pool. Continental breakfast served. There is other dining nearby. $$

**Days Inn.** 2908 Pine Grove Ave.; (810) 984-1522. At the end of I-94. The property has 106 nice rooms, an outdoor pool, and continental breakfast. Restaurant nearby. $

**Fairfield Inn by Marriott.** 1635 Yeager St.; (810) 982-8500. Leave I-94 at the Water Street exit. Marriott quality for a family budget. The inn has sixty-three rooms, an indoor pool and whirlpool, and continental breakfast. Dining nearby. $

**Thomas Edison Inn.** 500 Thomas Edison Parkway; (810) 984-8000. See directions in Where to Eat section. The inn has 149 rooms, many overlooking the St. Clair River. Amenities include indoor pool and exercise area with sauna and whirlpool. $$

## For More Information

**Blue Water Convention and Visitors Bureau.** 520 Thomas Edison Parkway, Port Huron 48060, in the old railroad train station next to the Thomas Edison Inn; (810) 987-8687 or (800) 852-4242; www.bluewater.org.

# East Michigan– South

E ast Michigan, which stretches from the Ohio border to the Straits of Mackinac, is the state's breadbasket. Within its borders farmers tend crops on some of the richest land on earth—giant expanses where flat fields that once were home to the world's largest deciduous forest now grow more white, navy, and other beans than anywhere else. To the north are some of the state's richest natural resources, from trout-laden streams and reborn forests to the world's largest limestone quarry. To make it easier, we've split the region into north and south, using Highway 46, which runs east and west, as the dividing line. This chapter covers the south part; the next chapter, the north.

## Irish Hills

The Irish Hills are located along US 12, one of Michigan's designated Heritage Trail highways, between Highway 52 on the east and Coldwater on the west. The region was named, legend has it, by an Irish immigrant minister for its resemblance to his homeland.

The Irish Hills, located in Michigan's south-central Lower Peninsula, have, since the 1930s, been a one-stop vacation attraction for families. Everything from outdoor fun to quirky tourist places can be found within a few miles of one another.

### Mystery Hill  (all ages)
**7611 US 12, Onsted, opposite the entrance to Hayes State Park; (517) 467-2517; www .mystery-hill.com.**

Mystery Hill "tour guides" will take you to a spot where you'll see water running uphill and other illusory feats. Admission price varies by activity. Other fun kid things to do at the Hill include minigolf.

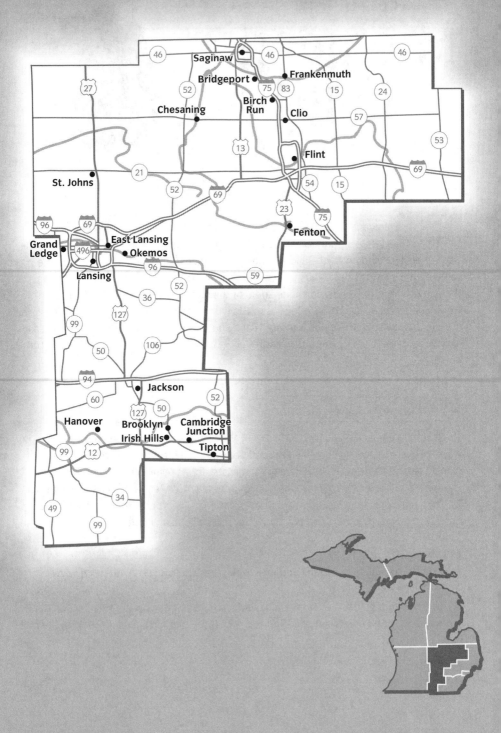

## Where to Eat

See Brooklyn listings, below.

## Where to Stay

The Irish Hills area does not provide many places to stay. For large, modern accommodations, see listings under Jackson, which is just to the north. Also see listings for Tipton.

**Cowboy Creek Lodge.** Located at the former Stagecoach Stop USA, 7203 US 12, Onsted; (517) 467-2300. Stay in a room or treat the kids to a stay in a teepee at this family-fun resort. Rooms and cabins also available. Race dates for nearby Michigan International Speedway are very popular, so book ahead. $$–$$$

**Lakeside Motel.** 110 US 12, Brooklyn, 4 miles west of Hayes State Park; (517) 467-2536. On Wolf Lake the motel has seven rooms with kitchenettes. Dockage for your own boat is available, or rent one with your room. There is a good beach at nearby Hayes State Park. $

# Brooklyn

Located just north of US 12, Brooklyn is one of several small communities nestled in the hills named by immigrants because they reminded them of Ireland.

## Top
# FamilyAdventures
### in East Michigan–South

1. Cascades at Sparks Foundation County Park, Jackson. Great fun with splashing colored water and other events like the big Civil War muster.

2. State Capitol and Michigan Historical Center, Lansing. The century-old State Capitol and legislative chambers, and all there is to know about Michigan, rolled into a few blocks.

3. Irish Hills, US 12. A fun ride through part of the nation's history.

4. The town of Frankenmuth. Chicken dinners, a great list of festivals starting with the Bavarian Festival, great window-shopping, and a grand hotel.

5. Johnny Panther Quests, in the Flint-Saginaw area. Join guide Wil Hufton as he shows you wildlife you never thought would exist so close to two of the state's larger cities.

6. The Michigan State University museums and gardens, East Lansing. Take the kids on a tour that will drive them buggy and teach them about art and flowers, all on campus.

# US 12: **The Heritage Trail**

Cutting a southwest-to-northeast path through the southern Lower Peninsula, US 12 is finally getting recognition as one of the great pioneer routes to what in the early 1800s was the western frontier. The Great Sauk Trail, as it was known, began in Detroit and carried through to Chicago. Eventually, the road continued west all the way to the Pacific, and still does. Historical markers along its route among the huge, stately oaks lining the road in many areas tell the story of how stages and wagons used it for commerce and to head for a new life in the West. The road became the key route between two then-fledgling frontier towns: Detroit and Chicago. It's a great story, and because of it the highway became the state's first designated heritage route in 2004.

### Michigan International Speedway  (all ages)

**12626 US 12; (517) 592-6666 or, for tickets, (800) 354-1010. For area camping and motel information, call (800) 543-2937 or (517) 764-4440. www.mispeedway.com. $$$$.**

For several weekends each summer, the roar of finely tuned stock and Indy car engines that produce more than 900 horsepower each echoes through the heart of Michigan's Irish Hills region, on a 2-mile, D-shaped track that rivals anything the South has to offer. One of the biggest draws is the Michigan 500, the Motor State's version of the Daytona 500, which is billed as the fastest 500-mile race in history. Other races are in June and Aug.

Tickets range from look-over-someone's-shoulders or perch-on-your-camper-top viewing in the infield, to seats in the main grandstands, which are your best choice.

There also are hospitality packages and prerace pit passes with garage access for Indy racers. Grandstand occupants can bring one cooler with them; bring your binoculars, too. Camping packages are available, but come prepared for rustic conditions.

There's also a special wheelchair platform as well as a chance for fans who are eighteen and older to walk the pits on race days (shirt and shoes must be worn, and shoulders and legs must be covered). Seats to witness qualifying heats and practice cost a lot less than on race day.

Area accommodations include a field across from the speedway; camping is **free** but strictly primitive here, with only central cold water and portable restrooms, so you must be pretty self-sufficient. You can also purchase a pass ($$$$ per vehicle) to the limited, primitive camping area in the infield.

### Victory Lane Speedway  (all ages)

**11541 Highway 50; (517) 592-3716. $.**

After the kids have seen the big cars run at Michigan International Speedway, let them practice their own skills here. There are also bumper boats.

### Hayes State Park (all ages)

Entrance is located near the intersection of Highway 124 and US 12, Onsted; call (517) 467-7401 or go to www.mi.gov/dnr for information; visit www.midnrreservations.com to reserve a site. Entrance is $ daily or $$ for annual permit; overnight camping $$$.

One of the most popular state parks in lower Michigan, Hayes's 650 acres encompass parts of two lakes: smaller Round, open to fishing and with camping nearby, and Wampler's, with a large swimming beach. There are boat launches on both lakes, and in fact, you can go from one to the other via a small canal. It's a great spot to bring the kids because the beach deepens very gradually. There's a 210-site campground as well.

### Walker Tavern State Historic Complex (all ages)

13220 Highway 50, Brooklyn; (517) 467-4414; www.michigan.gov/walkertavern. Open Memorial Day through Labor Day from 11:30 a.m. to 6 p.m. Wed through Sun. **Free.**

You can get an inkling of what nineteenth-century stagecoach travel must have been like on the five-day run along the old Chicago Road (now known as US 12) between Detroit and Chicago at this restored former overnight inn that's also known as Cambridge State Historic Park, situated at the junction of two important roads and run then by Sylvester and Lucy Walker.

For years the original inn was known for its famed "Murder Room," the purported scene of what one owner described as a particularly gruesome crime involving a stolen money belt. According to the same owner, the inn hosted such famous guests as frontier author James Fenimore Cooper and statesman Daniel Webster. State officials later surmised that these tales were hoaxes perpetrated by the inn's proprietor, who thought they'd be good for business. (He was right, of course.)

Annual events include the Walk through Time historical reenactment, old-fashioned baseball, a vintage-car show, and Frontier Fest, which shows how settlers lived and produced their own goods on what then was the western frontier. A movie at the visitor center on travel in the 1840s depicts a young boy's journey from New York to Chicago, including an overland ride on a much more rugged US 12 than today's paved version.

## Where to Eat

**Big Boy.** 329 South Main St., Brooklyn, about 3 miles north of US 12; (517) 592-3212. Open 6 a.m. to 10 p.m. Sun through Thurs and 6 a.m. to 11 p.m. Fri and Sat. Chain restaurant serving family meals from spaghetti to its trademark triple-decker burger. $

**Jerry's Pub.** 650 Eagan Hwy., Brooklyn; (517) 467-4700. Open 11:30 a.m. to 9:30 p.m. daily. A cozy place frequented by locals and vacationers alike. It overlooks Wampler's Lake

and offers outdoor dining in warm weather. Specialties include pizza, ribs, seafood, and pasta. Children's menu. $$

**Randy's Roadhouse.** 7305 US 12, Brooklyn, 500 feet from Hayes State Park entrance; (517) 467-2190. Open 4 to 11 p.m. Wed through Fri, and 4 to 10 p.m. Sat. An Irish Hills landmark since 1975, here one finds barbecue, from ribs to pulled pork, plus chicken and salads. Children's menu. $$

## Where to Stay

**Greenbriar Golf and Campground.**
14820 Wellwood Rd., near Wampler's Lake, 1¾ miles north of US 12 on Highway 124; (517) 592-6952. One hundred campsites, some with water and electricity. Heated pool and playground. $

See also listings under Tipton and Jackson.

# Hanover

### The Buffalo Ranch (all ages)

12770 Roundtree Rd.; (517) 563-8249; www.horsesandbuffalo.com. Take US 12 to Moscow Road, go north to Mosherville Road, and turn west to Roundtree; then follow the signs. The ranch is open from 9 a.m. to 4 p.m. Tues through Sun from Apr through Nov 1, then by appointment only. Visit with the herd, $. Horseback rides are $$$$ per hour.

Here's a chance to show your kids a bit of living American history. In the late 1800s the American bison, or buffalo, was on the edge of extinction, reduced in an ongoing slaughter from the thirty to fifty million that once roamed the continent in nearly every region to fewer than 1,000. The future of the buffalo is now secure, however, thanks mostly to private herd ranchers like Terrell and Dana Daniels, owner of the Buffalo Ranch in the heart of Michigan's Irish Hills, which is home to up to sixty-five "buffs."

Visitors can climb on board a hay wagon hitched to a tractor and ride into the pastures to help feed the huge animals ears of corn. Kids 8 and older and adults can also saddle up and play cowboy for a day, riding the ranch and feeding the buffs, with breakfast and lunch included ($$$$).

The Danielses also sell buffalo meat, which they call nature's original health food. In addition to the animal's meat, the Danielses uses just about everything else but the grunt, much as Native Americans once did on the plains. Bones are sold for jewelry; hides for coats, moccasins, and rugs. Native Americans often visit to purchase ceremonial items.

The couple hosts a real buffalo rendezvous each Aug, and it's **free.** Kids can experience a pre-1840s living-history encampment with craftsmen, traders, Native Americans, and, of course, the buffalo. They also offer hayrides and horseback riding.

## Where to Eat and Stay

See listings for Brooklyn, Tipton, and Jackson.

# Tipton

Founded in 1831, this tiny town was first named Tripp Town after its founder, and the name was shortened to Tipton a few years later. It's in the heart of the Irish Hills on Highway 50, a few miles south and east of the intersection with US 12.

### Hidden Lake Gardens (all ages)

**Located 2 miles west of Tipton on Highway 50; (517) 431-2060; www.hiddenlakegardens .msu.edu. Hours are 8 a.m. to 4 p.m. Nov through Mar and 8 a.m. to dusk the remainder of the year. $.**

It's said that Michigan State University's East Lansing campus is one of the nation's most beautiful because of its greenery, and the university continues that tradition in Hidden Lake Gardens, just east of the other Irish Hills attractions. Inside this 755-acre complex, a 6-mile one-way drive takes you through a lush arboretum featuring thousands of trees, nearly all of them labeled; one-hundred-plus acres of plants and shrubs; and displays of special dwarf evergreens.

Under a tropical greenhouse dome, walk past plants from around the world or explore the gardens' 5 miles of nature trails, one of which accommodates wheelchairs.

There's also a picnic area.

### Port-to-Port Adventure Golf

**5768 West US 12; (517) 431-2262; www.porttoportgolf.com. $–$$.**

A great family-oriented spot with minigolf, batting cages, basketball hoops, and a game room.

## Where to Eat

See listings for Brooklyn and Irish Hills.

## Where to Stay

**Hideaway Cove Log Cabins.** 11560 Breyman Hwy.; (517) 431-2594; www.hideaway cove5.com. Five furnished two-bedroom cabins on Evans Lake. $$$

**Ja Do Campground.** 5603 US 12; (517) 431-2111; www.jadocampground.com. Five miles west of Highway 52 and 6 miles east of Highway 50, this facility has 130 campsites, some with electricity and water. Playground and catch-and-release fishing pond, plus weekend activities.

## For More Information

**Brooklyn–Irish Hills Chamber of Commerce.** 221 North Main, Brooklyn 49230; (517) 592-8907; www.brooklynmi.com.

# Jackson

Founded in 1830 and named after Andrew Jackson, the city is the Jackson County seat and remains a manufacturing center. Nicknamed the Rose City for its annual rose festival downtown in mid-June, it was at the crossroads of an old Native American trail and the upper Grand River. It also became one stop on the Underground Railroad, which helped fugitive slaves reach freedom. In the early twentieth century, twenty autos were made here. While many cities lay claim to the title, Jackson citizens say the Republican Party was formed here in 1854 underneath some spreading oak trees downtown, and they have a historical marker there to prove it. The city also lays claim to the dubious distinction as the home of Jackson State Prison, the world's largest walled home for the notorious.

### Cascades at Sparks Foundation County Park  (all ages)

Exit I-94 at exit 138, go south on West Avenue, and follow the signs; (517) 788-4320; www .co.jackson.mi.us/parks. The fountain runs from 8:30 to 11 p.m. nightly from Memorial Day through Labor Day. Adults $, children ages 4 and younger **free.**

Fountains and other watery displays have always been a part of Michigan's towns, and this one is among the state's most spectacular. One of the oldest of its type in the Western Hemisphere, the 500-foot-long, 64-foot-high display, which has delighted families since 1932, celebrated its seventy-fifth anniversary in 2007. Take the kids and watch as water cascades over sixteen falls and three main pools, while lights color the tableau in a constantly changing palette, all set to music.

The park also contains two golf courses, minigolf, picnic areas, batting cages, paddleboats, and the Cascades Museum, where photos trace the history of the building of the fountain.

A Civil War muster takes place at the Cascades in late Aug. It includes battle reenactments between Union and Confederate soldiers, with artillery and infantry demonstrations, living-history docents, and more in a show billed as the Midwest's largest.

Another fun event at the Cascades is the Classic Car Show in early June. For more information, call (517) 787-2065.

### Ella Sharp Museum of Art and History  (all ages)

3225 Fourth St.; (517) 787-2320; www.ellasharp.org. Take exit 138 or 139 off I-94. Follow the green trailblazer signs south to the museum. Museum hours are Tues through Fri from 10 a.m. to 4 p.m. and Sat and Sun from 11 a.m. to 4 p.m.; closed Mon and holidays. Adults $, children under 5 **free.** A restaurant inside the original farm granary is open for lunch Tues through Sat.

It's only a 2-mile drive from the Cascades to the museum of nineteenth-century farm life, a 530-acre site filled with historic local structures and living-history demonstrations around the home of Ella Sharp, who willed the property to the city. There's a one-room school, woodworking shop, and other buildings that have been moved to the site, including a log house and doctor's office. Special seasonal events are held in Mar, Oct, and Dec, when the Sharp residence is decorated for a Victorian Christmas. The visitor center connects to a modern-art gallery; entry to the gallery is included with admission.

### Nite Lites  (all ages)

Jackson County Fairgrounds, 200 West Ganson St.; (517) 788-4405 or (800) 245-5282. From I-94, take exit 139, Cooper Street. Turn left and head downtown. Turn west on Michigan to Ganson. Open nightly from 6 to 10 p.m. from mid-Nov through Dec 30. The per-vehicle donation ($$) helps purchase more lights and compensate the workers.

More than a half million lights (the count rises each year) twinkle on a 1½ -mile drive through the fairgrounds over the holidays. The auto route is lined with lights and guides you through "Candyland" holiday scenes. Vehicles then enter the religious part of the display. Kids can visit Santa on Fri and Sat from 6 to 9 p.m. through the last Sat before

# Favorite Events in East Michigan–South

- **Shrine Circus** (Jan), Saginaw, (989) 759-1330
- **Zehnder's Snow Fest** (Feb), downtown Frankenmuth, (989) 652-6106
- **Sugaring and Shearing Festival** (Mar), Ella Sharp Museum of Art and History, Jackson, (517) 787-2320
- **Storytelling Festival** (May), Jackson, (517) 784-8827
- **Bavarian Festival** (June), Frankenmuth, (989) 652-6106
- **Rose Festival** (June), downtown Jackson, (517) 764-4440 or (800) 245-5282
- **Hot Air Jubilee** (July), Jackson County Airport, (517) 782-1515
- **Car Capital Celebration** (Aug), downtown Lansing, (517) 372-0529
- **Civil War Muster** (Aug), Jackson, (517) 788-4320
- **Great Lakes Folk Festival** (Aug), East Lansing, (800) 648-6630
- **Fall Festival** (Sept), Spicer Orchards, Fenton, (810) 629-2119
- **North Pole Express and Santa's Village** (Nov and Dec), Chesaning, (989) 845-3055 or (800) 255-3055
- **Christmas at Crossroads** (Dec), Flint, (800) 648-7275

Christmas. Those waiting to see Santa can board the **free** trackless train for a short ride to keep them occupied.

## Phyllis Haehnle Memorial Sanctuary (all ages)

**According to sanctuary caretakers there is no street address, as there are no buildings at this location. Just follow the directions, and you'll get there: From I-94, take exit 147 and head north on Race Road for 2 miles. Turn west on Seymour Road and go about 1½ miles, and the parking lot is on the north side of the road; (517) 769-6891. Free.**

The woods, ponds, and wetlands are the site of the state's largest fall gathering of sandhill cranes. On any given day in Oct, more than 2,000 cranes can be seen returning to the marshlands for the night. The 930-acre property is owned by the Michigan Audubon Society.

## The Michigan Theatre (ages 5 and up)

**124 North Mechanic St.; (517) 783-0962; www.michigantheatre.org.**

This restored downtown movie palace opened in 1930 and now shows both classic and first-run movies.

### Dahlem Environmental Education Center (all ages)

**7117 South Jackson Rd.; (517) 782-3453; www.dahlemcenter.org. From I-94, head south at exit 138 on West Avenue. Go east on High, then south on Fourth. Follow Horton Road west to South Jackson, and then turn south to the center. Open from 9 a.m. to 5 p.m. Tues through Fri and noon to 5 p.m. Sat and Sun. Trails open daily 8 a.m. to sunset. Free.**

A bit of nature just outside the city. Five miles of hiking trails to explore fields, forests, marshes, and ponds, including a ½-mile-long "special needs" trail. All-terrain wheelchairs are available on request. The Nutshell gift shop features books, clothing, bird-feeding supplies, and other items. Cross-country skiing is available, weather permitting.

### The Parlor at the All-Star Dairy (all ages)

**1401 Daniel Rd.; (517) 783-1581. To reach the dairy, leave I-94 at exit 138 and go south seven stoplights. At the seventh, turn west onto Wildwood, go two more lights, and veer to the right onto Daniel. The parlor opens at 11 a.m. daily. It closes at 11 p.m. Fri and Sat, as well as every night in summer; the rest of the time it shuts down at 10 p.m. $$.**

Jackson proclaims proudly that the Republican Party was founded there. Now, what can be more American than that? Ice cream, of course. According to voters of all political persuasions, one of the state's best places to sink your teeth into a chocolate-banana sundae is the Parlor, on the city's northwest side.

The huge menu lists nearly two dozen different sundaes and fountain specials, parfaits, and splits—you name it, they'll make it. The pièce de résistance, if you dare, is twenty-one different flavors topped with everything in the place, for $29.99. A "single" cone, actually two scoops, is $2.99, plus tax.

## Where to Eat

**Cascades Manor House Restaurant.** 1970 Kibby Rd., at the corner of Denton Road; (517) 784-1500. Open from 11 a.m. to 2 p.m. Sun for brunch. It caters to private functions other days. Overlooking Cascades Park, the Manor House features reasonably priced items for lunch or Sun brunch. Dishes include two carved meats and four other entrees including fish, pasta, omelets, and shrimp cocktail. Children's rates available. $$

**Finley's American Restaurant.** 1602 West Michigan Ave., at the corner of Michigan and Brown; (517) 787-7440. From I-94, take Business 94 to Brown. Open for inexpensive lunch and dinner, which feature chicken and ribs. Children's menu. $$

**Red Lobster.** 2400 Shirley Dr.; (517) 787-7820. Good, inexpensive seafood. The menu also has steaks and chicken. Children's menu. $$

## Where to Stay

**Baymont Inn.** 2035 North Service Dr.; (517) 789-6000. From I-94, exit northbound on US 127. It's on the west side of the highway. This chain property has sixty-five good rooms with continental breakfast. $$

**Fairfield Inn.** 2395 Shirley Dr.; (517) 784-7877. From I-94, take exit 138 north ½ mile to Springport Road, then head south to Shirley. This inn has fifty-seven rooms with an indoor pool. Restaurant nearby. $$

**Greenwood Acres Family Campground.** 2401 Hilton Rd.; (517) 522-8600. From I-94, exit at Race Road, exit 147. Go south to Ann

Arbor Road, then west to Portage. Turn south to Greenwood, then east, then turn north on Hilton. One of Michigan's largest campgrounds, if not the largest, with 1,160 campsites, many with electricity and water. Pool, beach, tennis, nine-hole golf course and minigolf, restaurant, recreation center, and weekend activities. $

**Holiday Inn.** 2696 Bob McClain Dr.; (517) 788-6400. Take exit 137 off I-94 and turn north. Scheduled to open in summer 20010, the hotel is behind Meijer. Ninety-nine rooms with restaurant, indoor pool, and Internet access.

**Jackson Hotel and Convention Center.** 2000 Holiday Inn Dr.; (517) 783-2681. From I-94, exit at US 127, Springport Road, and head north. This 184-room property has an indoor pool as part of an indoor recreation area with miniature golf and arcade, exercise room, and restaurant. Small pets allowed in rooms for $15 extra. $$

**Motel 6.** 830 Royal Dr.; (517) 789-7186. From I-94, head south on US 127. This basic chain motel has ninety-five rooms. Restaurant nearby. $

## For More Information

**Jackson Convention and Visitors Bureau.** 6007 Ann Arbor Rd., Jackson 49201; (517) 764-4440 or (800) 245-5282; www.visit jacksonmi.com.

# East Lansing

The hometown of Michigan State University runs the gamut of family fun, from festivals to strolling one of the nation's most beautiful campuses. Michigan State University, founded in 1855, was the nation's first land-grant university. The campus is located just to the south of Grand River Avenue—yes, the same Grand River that begins in downtown Detroit.

## Michigan State University  (all ages)

To reach East Lansing and the MSU campus, take I-96 to I-496/US 127 north and follow the signs to the main campus exit, Trowbridge Road. The general university phone number is (517) 355-1855; www.msu.edu. There are no special parking provisions, other than some lots open to faculty only, and meter maids are not stingy with tickets.

And you thought college campuses were only for 18- to 21-year-olds. Think again. If you've got a pre-college-age child who's ready to pick a school, or you just want to go back and relive a bit of your youth, a visit to East Lansing's 5,200-acre campus, with one

## Shopping East Lansing

In downtown East Lansing, stores along Grand River Avenue that cater to students sell everything from MSU-logo clothing to books. Several good restaurants are in the area as well. For free information on the entire Lansing–East Lansing region, call (800) 968-8474.

of the largest student bodies in the nation, makes a perfect weekend getaway. It's considered one of the nation's most picturesque and beautiful college venues. Some liken it to going to school in an arboretum, so majestic are the huge oaks, maples, and pines that cover the old part of the campus. Classrooms and older dorm buildings are draped in ivy for that perfect campus look. The Red Cedar River flows between the buildings. You can join the students taking a study break along the riverbank or rent a canoe for a leisurely float. For a map of the campus area, contact the Greater Lansing Convention and Visitors Bureau (see For More Information under Lansing).

### MSU Horticultural Demonstration Gardens and Teaching Greenhouse (all ages)

**Bogue and Service Road; (517) 355-0348. The gardens are open dawn to dusk May 1 through Nov. Free; for the gardens, children's garden, and butterfly house (see separate listings that follow), admission is $$; parking $ on weekdays, free on weekends and holidays. Tours ($$$), scheduled from June 1 through Sept 10 by appointment, are best for groups.**

The MSU gardens include 18,000 square feet of perennials and the All America Trial Garden, a test site used by companies for annuals that includes more than 1,000 varieties.

### MSU Dairy Store (all ages)

**The original store is on Farm Lane, in the middle of campus; (517) 355-8466; www.dairy store.msu.edu. Open 9 a.m. to 8 p.m. Mon through Fri, noon to 8 p.m. Sat and Sun. There's also a store in the MSU Student Union along Abbott Road on campus.**

Join the kids choosing from thirty-three flavors of ice cream, try some fresh yogurt, or take some cheese from the spot where it's all made. Dairy products come from animals raised in the university's dairy barns, and you can tour the facility from above. Is two giant scoops of creamy delight for $2.65 cheap enough?

## MSU Tours

If you're a prospective university student or the parent of one, sign up to take a tour of one of the nation's most picturesque campuses. Or, if you're not, you can download a self-guided walking or driving tour of the campus. Prospective student tours are at 10:30 a.m. Mon through Sat and leave from the first floor of the MSU Student Union. Tours are conducted by trained student guides who can show you the ropes, and an appointment is needed. Go to www.admissions.msu.edu/events/default.asp for more information. Group tours also are available by calling the Tour Consortium at (517) 432-9508.

### MSU Farms  (all ages)

On the south campus. Open from 8 a.m. to 5 p.m. Mon through Fri. Closed during lunch hour. Call the Department of Animal Science at (517) 355-8383 or (517) 355-7473 for specific visiting times.

MSU originally was strictly an agricultural college, and the presence of the school's animal research and teaching, from veterinary science to farming research, remains a big part of the campus. Many of the buildings are open for touring. There are farms for sheep, cows, horses, and swine. Milking takes place each afternoon at the cow barn. Call first to learn specific times.

### Michigan 4-H Children's Garden  (all ages)

Located on the campus's south side near the Plant and Sciences Building at the corner of Wilson Road and Bogue Street; (517) 353-6692; http://4hgarden.msu.edu. Open daily from sunrise to sunset Apr 1 through Oct 31. Admission is **free,** but there is a parking fee from 7:30 a.m. to 6 p.m. Mon through Fri.

This half-acre garden is one of the favorite places for families visiting the campus to bring children and is part of the university's large Horticultural Demonstration Gardens (see listing). More than sixty differently themed areas show plants kids use in everyday life but may not have seen except in a different form on the dinner table. It is definitely hands on, but no picking or tasting is allowed. Come in Mar and Apr, when students and teachers tending the garden set up a building where live butterflies flit about.

### MSU Bug House  (all ages)

Rooms 146 and 147 of the Natural Science Building, on the northeast corner of Farm Lane and East Circle Drive; (517) 355-4662; www.ent.msu.edu. Programs presented here take about an hour. **Free.**

Ever hear a cockroach hiss? We hope not, but at the Bug House you will witness that variety from Madagascar, as well as hundreds of other species, including giant Florida lubber grasshoppers twice the size of a typical one, walking sticks, millipedes, and more.

### MSU Museum  (all ages)

West Circle Drive. Once on campus, follow the signs to the museum; (517) 355-7474; www .museum.msu.edu. Hours are 9 a.m. to 5 p.m. Mon through Fri, 10 a.m. to 5 p.m. Sat, and 1 to 5 p.m. Sun. Admission is **free.**

Great exhibits on three floors focus on the state's natural history, including fossils and Michigan history. There are exhibits on everything from wildlife art to the now-extinct passenger pigeon, which once darkened the skies over parts of the state. There's a good gift shop, too, with jewelry and educational gifts for kids.

### MSU Beaumont Tower  (all ages)

West Circle Drive, near the MSU Museum on the MSU campus. **Free.**

The forty-nine-bell carillon here is at the site of the Old College Hall, the first building in the nation built for agricultural instruction. There are weekly concerts in summer.

### MSU Kresge Art Museum  (all ages)

Auditorium and Physics Roads; (517) 355-7631; www.artmuseum.msu.edu. Hours are 10 a.m. to 5 p.m. except Thurs, when hours are 10 a.m. to 8 p.m.; in summer hours are 11 a.m. to 5 p.m. Tues through Fri and noon to 5 p.m. Sat and Sun. Closed in Aug. Admission is **free.**

A visit here is like getting an education in 5,000 years of art at MSU's collection, including avant-garde works. There are works by artists such as Salvador Dalí, architect Louis Sullivan, and Andy Warhol, as well as unknown artists who fashioned Grecian urns and bowls, Russian icons, and other works from long ago.

### MSU Wharton Center for the Performing Arts  (all ages)

On the campus's east side, at the corner of Wharton and Center; (517) 432-2000 or (800) 942-7866; www.whartoncenter.com.

Named for one of the university's former presidents, the center has two auditoriums that almost always offer an evening concert or play. There are **free** backstage tours by appointment.

### MSU Abrams Planetarium  (all ages)

Corner of Shaw Lane and Science Road, on the MSU campus; (517) 355-4672 or (517) 355-4676 or, for current sky information, (517) 332-7827; www.pa.msu.edu/abrams/. Open at 8 p.m. Fri and Sat, 2:30 p.m. and 4 p.m. Sun. Tickets are sold a half hour before each show. $.

The planetarium's sky theater presents star shows using a state-of-the-art computerized star projector. Various themes are presented, and there are special shows for the holidays.

Although the shows are for all ages, preschoolers should be taken to a special family show at 2:30 p.m. Sun.

## Where to Eat

**Beggar's Banquet.** 218 Abbott Rd.; (517) 351-4573. From I-69/US 127, take the Michigan Avenue exit. Go 3 miles east, and then turn north on Abbott. Restaurant interior is a rustic natural wood setting. Excellent breakfast. Lunch and dinner feature chili and vegetarian items in very large servings. Children's menu, too. $–$$

**Harper's Brewpub.** 131 Albert St., in downtown East Lansing; (517) 333-4040; www.harpersbrewpub.com. Good selection of food, from burgers and pizza to salmon. Children's menu. $$–$$$

**Hershey's Steak & Seafood.** 2682 East Grand River; (517) 337-7324. Open for lunch and dinner Mon through Sat, plus Sun brunch. Great prime rib and seafood. $$$

## Where to Stay

**East Lansing Marriott at University Place.** 300 M.A.C. Ave.; (517) 337-4440. Across from the MSU north campus area. From I-496, exit at Trowbridge Road, go east, and turn north on Harrison, then east on Highway 43 to Grand River. The property features 180 rooms, indoor pool, exercise area, and restaurant. $$$

**Kellogg Hotel and Conference Center.**
East Michigan and Harrison on the MSU
campus; (517) 432-4000 or (800) 875-5090.
A unique hotel that provides students at the
university's hospitality school a firsthand look
at hotel management, from folding sheets to
working the front desk, and cleaning up juice
spilled by the kids at breakfast. There are
165 rooms and suites, with access to a pool,
tennis, exercise area, golf, and dining on the
premises. $$

## For More Information

See the Lansing listings.

# Lansing

Lansing's place in state history was assured when legislators, trying to decide on a proper
state capital because the then-capital of Detroit was too near Canada, laughingly sug-
gested this tiny town, which consisted of a sawmill and not much else.

When it was approved, they all stopped laughing, knowing they'd have to travel
through almost impenetrable woods to conduct business. Nevertheless, the legislature
and the state survived. Later, Lansing became one of Michigan's industrial powerhouses
and is still the home of two state-of-the-art manufacturing complexes building General
Motors vehicles.

## Impression 5 Science Center  (all ages)

**200 Museum Dr.; (517) 485-8116; www.impression5.org. Open 10 a.m. to 5 p.m. daily, to 8
p.m. on Thurs. $, children under 3 free.**

The Impression 5 Science Center is the state's largest hands-on children's museum and
was judged one of the country's top ten. There's something here for everyone, from tots
to teens, with demonstrations on computers, natural sciences, medicine, and physics,
including a special exhibit on the fish of the Grand River, which flows just outside. Kids can
freeze their shadows on a wall, try to grab a hologram, or explore their senses among the
more than 150 exhibits.

Kids can make their own funny putty or television slime, explore the world of electric-
ity, or have their hair stand on end, literally. There are daily floor demonstrations plus
talks on subjects of displays. Educational programs including camp-ins and displays of
children's art help students explore the worlds of science and art.

## Planet Walk  (all ages)

**Starts outside the Impression 5 Science Center and ends near Potter Park Zoo; (517) 702-
6730. Free.**

Take a tour of a scale model of the solar system as you stroll on a sidewalk. The walk
begins with the sun, which is 20 inches in diameter, and then 179 feet away you'll find
Earth, the size of a pencil eraser. In a little less than an hour, your family will have strolled
over 5 billion scale miles. Total walking distance is about 2 miles. Every footstep will cover
a million scale miles.

## Capitol Complex, Historical Center, and Supreme Court Learning Center (all ages)

**The Capitol is at Capitol and Michigan downtown, (517) 373-2353. The Michigan Library and Historical Center is behind the Capitol at 702 West Kalamazoo St.; (517) 373-3559; www .michiganhistory.org. The Supreme Court Learning Center is at 925 West Ottawa St.; (517) 373-7171; www.courts.michigan.gov/plc/index.htm. All are free.**

You can spend most of a day touring these three facilities, each within walking distance.

Built in 1879, the Capitol is one of the country's first capitols built to model the U.S. Capitol, and it was restored during the state's 150th birthday in 1987. Guided tours take place from 9 a.m. to 4 p.m. Mon through Fri. The Michigan Library and Historical Center contains the state's archives, as well as great exhibits depicting the state's early history. Kids can walk through a mock copper mine and can also learn about the state's contributions in World War II and its outdoor heritage.

The Supreme Court Learning Center gallery includes videos and hands-on computer displays that teach kids about the role of judges and courts and the jury system.

## Lansing Lugnuts (all ages)

**The team plays at Oldsmobile Park, at the corner of Michigan Avenue and Cedar, 2 blocks from the Capitol; (517) 485-4500; www.lansinglugnuts.com. The regular season runs from early Apr through early Sept. The team hosts about seventy home games. Lawn, reserved, and box seats are a true baseball bargain, $. Park in city lots nearby.**

What better way to finish a tour of the capital than with a ball game? The state capital now rings with the crack of the bat and howl of the crowd as the city welcomes its own baseball team, curiously named after the bolts put on the tires at the nearby General Motors assembly plant. The stadium is big, seating 11,000, and that's a good thing, because the 'Nuts have become one of the hottest places to be in summer, not only to enjoy inexpensive, quality baseball but also because of the crazy name. Lugnuts caps and such are valued by collectors.

One of the most fun aspects of a game is seeing the hot dog cannon in action. The hydraulic-powered cannon shoots tube steaks into the crowd from the field, just for the fun of it.

## Potter Park Zoo (all ages)

**1301 South Pennsylvania Ave.; (517) 483-4222. From Michigan Avenue downtown, head east to Pennsylvania and go about 1 block south of the I-496 underpass. Open 9 a.m. to 5 p.m. daily, with extended summer hours. Admission $; parking $.**

Pony rides, even camel rides, and canoe rentals are offered at the compact but well-stocked zoo. Some of the 400 other animals living there include rhinos, penguins, lions, and farm animals. Picnicking and food are available, too.

## Lansing City Market (all ages)

**333 North Cedar St. at Shiawassee, on the banks of the Grand River next to Riverfront Park; (517) 483-7460; www.lansingcitymarket.com. Open year-round 8 a.m. to 6 p.m.**

Tues, Thurs, Fri, and Sat. From Michigan Avenue downtown, head north on Cedar about 2 blocks. Admission is **free.**

Your chance to stock up on fresh veggies, in season, from local farms, along with baked goods, ethnic foods, and crafts in a market built as a Depression-era project in 1938.

### Michigan Walk of Fame (all ages)

On Washington Street in downtown Lansing in front of the State Capitol; (517) 487-3322; www.michiganwalkoffame.com. **Free.**

The walk commemorates famous Michiganians with brass plaques embedded in the sidewalk. Inductees include singer Stevie Wonder, Tiger Hall of Fame broadcaster Ernie Harwell, actor Jeff Daniels, reporter Helen Thomas, and others, with more to come.

### Ranney Skatepark (all ages)

In Ranney Park, a Lansing city park, at 3201 East Michigan Ave.; (517) 483-4277; www .parks.cityoflansingmi.com. Open daily 8 a.m. to 10 p.m. Admission is **free.**

Skateboarders and Rollerbladers will enjoy the city's premier skating facility, designed and built by nationally known skate-park experts Team Pain. The 20,000-square-foot facility takes on all boarders.

### Fenner Nature Center (all ages)

2020 East Mount Hope Rd.; (517) 483-4224; http://parks.cityoflansingmi.com/fenner/fnc .html. Open year-round from 9 a.m. to 4 p.m. weekdays and 11 a.m. to 4 p.m. weekends. **Free.**

The city's nature center features self-guided trails through woods and around ponds, a visitor center and gift shop, and programs throughout the year that help introduce youngsters to such activities as making apple butter in fall and maple syrup in spring.

### Lansing River Trail (all ages)

Winding along the rivers from 300 North Grand River; (517) 483-4277; www.lansingmi .gov/parks. Pick up the trail anywhere from access sites in downtown Lansing. Paved and accessible for strollers and wheelchairs. **Free.**

Traveling over the water in places and in others alongside it, the river trail winds for more than 11 miles along the waterways. Rent a bike for the day at Riverfront Cycle (517-482-8585) and at Michigan State University's bicycle service center (517) 432-3400), about a block off the trail near the Lansing City Market (see entry).

### Brenke River Sculpture and Fish Ladder (all ages)

Along the River Walk near the intersection of Turner and Grand River. Open daily. **Free.**

In fall, see spawning salmon, which have made it all the way from Lake Michigan miles away, fight their way upstream. The event repeats each spring when steelhead, a lake-run rainbow trout, make the journey.

## Malcolm X Homesite Historical Marker (all ages)

**At the corner of Vincent Court and Martin Luther King Jr. Boulevard, downtown; (517) 487-6800. MLK Boulevard is 6 blocks west of the State Capitol. Vincent is to the south. Free.**

Now a registered historical landmark, this site has a historical marker and is where the home of one of the civil rights movement's most influential spokesmen used to be.

## Peanut Shop (all ages)

**117 South Washington; (517) 374-0008. Near the State Capitol. Open from 9:30 a.m. to 5:30 p.m. Mon through Fri, 9:30 a.m. to 4 p.m. Sat. Closed Sun.**

A cute little shop that features more than thirty-six varieties of nuts, roasted on the spot, along with popcorn and other goodies to treat the kids to after your capitol tour. The shop has been here since 1937.

## J&K Steamboat Line (all ages)

**The *Michigan Princess* runs Feb 19 through Dec 31 from Grand River Park. For schedule information, call (517) 627-2154; www.michiganprincess.com. Rates vary by what type of cruise you take, ranging from lunch, dinner, and fall color, to dinner theater (which includes a five-course meal). Ages 3 to 12 are half price. $$$–$$$$. Call ahead for specifics, including cruises of special interest to kids.**

The three-level *Michigan Princess* sails the Grand River during festivals and lunch and dinner dates, including themed meals and special events. Enjoy a leisurely cruise down a portion of the state's longest river, which eventually runs through Grand Rapids and empties into Lake Michigan at Grand Haven.

## Eastwood Towne Center (all ages)

**On Lake Lansing Road, just off US 27; (517) 316-9209; www.lansing.org.**

This mall includes an eighteen-screen theater, stores such as Williams-Sonoma and Banana Republic, and a full complement of restaurants.

# Where to Eat

**Clara's Lansing Station.** 637 East Michigan Ave.; (517) 372-7120. Just east of the Grand River and State Capitol. Open for lunch and dinner daily. The food's good and so is the atmosphere, inside a restored former train station where the freights still rumble by outside. The menu takes in many food styles. The chicken Caesar salad is great, as are the malts. $$

**Fleetwood Diner.** 2211 South Cedar St.; (517) 482-0300. Breakfast, burgers, and baskets are the fare at this fun restored diner.

Chocolate-chip pancakes are the best, say both kids and grown-ups, and if you're a malt fan, plan a stop here. $–$$

## Where to Stay

Always ask about special group discounts, package plans, and weekend and children's rates, as many offer **free** lodging for kids.

**Hampton Inn of Lansing.** 525 North Canal Rd.; (517) 627-8381. From I-96, take exit 93 and go east on Saginaw Street. There are 107 rooms, an exercise room, and continental breakfast. Small pets allowed with deposit. $$

**Lansing Cottonwood Campground.** 5339 South Aurelius Rd.; (517) 393-3200. From US 127, take the Jolly Road exit. Go 1 mile southwest on Dunkel Road, ½ mile west on Jolly, and then head south on Aurelius. Open May 1 through Oct 29. This campground has 110 sites, with fishing, canoeing, paddleboat rental, and a pool. $

**Radisson Hotel–Lansing.** 111 North Grand Ave., downtown; (517) 482-0188. An easy walk 2 blocks east of the State Capitol and near Lansing's Museum Row. The hotel has 257 rooms in eleven stories with an indoor pool, sauna, exercise room, and dining. Downtown Lansing's best and most convenient accommodations. $$$

**Sheraton Lansing Hotel.** 925 South Creyts Rd.; (517) 323-7100; www.sheratonlansing

.com. From I-496, take Creyts Road north, exit 1B. Turn right onto South Creyts Road. This hotel has 212 rooms with indoor pool and fitness center. $$–$$$$

**Sleep Inn.** 1101 Commerce Park Dr., DeWitt; (517) 669-8823. Just north of the intersection of US 27 and I-69, 6 miles north of the State Capitol. The inn has sixty-one rooms, outdoor pool, and complimentary continental breakfast. Dining nearby. Only ½ mile from the Lansing Factory Outlet Mall. $

**Sleepy Hollow State Park.** 7835 Price Rd., Laingsburg; (517) 651-6217. On Lake Ovid, about 15 miles north of Lansing. From US 27, head east on Price Road about 6 miles. Lake Ovid is an artificial lake, part of the Little Maple River, with a great ½-mile-long sand beach with concession stand and picnicking. There are 181 modern campsites in the 2,600-acre park. There also are about 16 miles of trails through the park's woods, and mountain biking is allowed. The lake is perfect for small-boat anglers, as there is no wake allowed. Boat rental is available, too. $

## For More Information

**Greater Lansing Convention and Visitors Bureau.** 1223 Turner St., Suite 200, Lansing 48912; (517) 487-6800 or (888) 2-LANSING; www.lansing.org.

# Grand Ledge

Named for the 300-million-year-old sandstone ledges along the Grand River, Grand Ledge is a popular Lansing bedroom community with a historic downtown.

### Fitzgerald Park (all ages)

**133 Fitzgerald Park Dr. From I-96, take exit 93A and head west on Highway 43 about 6 miles to Jefferson Street. At the sign for Fitzgerald Park, take a right, and the park is down the road on the left about ½ mile. Call (517) 627-7351 for Fitzgerald Park**

information; www.grandledgemi.com/parks. The park is open to all ages. Fitzgerald Park is open 8 a.m. to dark daily. There is a motor vehicle entry fee ($) from Apr through Oct. Wed is free.

Take the family on a self-guided twenty-minute walk along the base of the famous rock ledges that gave the city its name. There's also a connecting trail to Island Park in downtown Grand Ledge. Oak Park, also overlooking the Grand River, features the largest rock outcropping in central Michigan.

## Where to Eat and Stay

See East Lansing, Lansing, and Okemos listings.

# Okemos

A bedroom community for the Lansing and East Lansing area, Okemos is the location of one of its largest shopping centers, the Meridian Mall, along Grand River Avenue.

### Meridian Mall (all ages)

1982 West Grand River Ave.; (517) 349-2030; www.meridianmall.com. Open 10 a.m. to 9 p.m. Mon through Sat, noon to 6 p.m. Sun.

One of the state's largest malls, with 130 stores, including Sears, JCPenney, Macy's, and Dick's Sporting Goods, as well as a food court and stores catering to families.
Stroller rentals are available.

## Where to Eat

**B. D.'s Mongolian Barbecue.** 2080 East Grand River Ave.; (517) 347-3045. Reached by taking the I-96 Okemos exit to Grand River Avenue and heading east. The restaurant is on the north side of Grand River. Open for lunch and dinner. Make up your own meal or use the suggested combinations on the big menu board, and watch as cooks prepare it on a large cooking table. Pay one price for all you can eat, if you wish. $$$

**Grand Traverse Pie Company.** 3536 Meridian Crossing Dr.; (517) 381-7437. Open 6:30 a.m. to 8:30 p.m. Mon through Fri, 8 a.m. to 8:30 p.m. Sat, and 10 a.m. to 6 p.m. Sun. Great sandwiches, potpies, and quiche, with fresh-baked cream and fruit pies for dessert or to take home. $

**Traveler's Club International Restaurant and Tuba Museum.** 2138 Hamilton Rd., downtown; (517) 349-1701. From I-96, take the Okemos Road exit and head downtown. It's at Okemos and Hamilton. Open for breakfast through dinner. An eclectic restaurant that serves ethnic foods, with evening entertainment from folk to jazz. $$

## Where to Stay

**Fairfield Inn by Marriott.** 2335 Woodlake Dr., off I-96 at exit 110. Go north on Okemos Road about ¼ mile; (517) 347-1000. This hotel offers seventy-nine rooms and an indoor pool. $$

**Holiday Inn Express Suites.** 2187 University Park Dr.; (517) 347-6690. Off I-96 at exit 110, head north about ¼ mile on Okemos Road, then east on University Park Drive. This hotel has ninety rooms. $$

See also entries for East Lansing and Lansing.

# St. Johns

St. Johns is the seat of Clinton County, north of Lansing along US 27, which became Old US 27 when the new stretch of freeway bypassing the town opened. The town was infamous in past years for the huge summer holiday traffic jams, one of the reasons for the expressway extension. The county and another town in it, Dewitt, were named after former New York governor Dewitt Clinton, under whose stewardship the Erie Canal was opened, which enabled many of the area's pioneers to settle here.

This is a big agricultural area, with mint being among the largest crops. Hence its nickname: Mint City, U.S.A. In downtown St. Johns, on the second weekend of Aug, more than 60,000 visitors come to enjoy the St. Johns Mint Festival, which includes arts-and-crafts sales, food vendors, a parade with 170 entrants, kids' rides and games, a professional rodeo, and more.

### Uncle John's Cider Mill  (all ages)

**8614 North US 27; (989) 224-3686; www.ujcidermill.com. The mill is 7½ miles north of St. Johns on the east side of the highway. Watch for the signs. Open from 9 a.m. to 7 p.m. May through Aug, 9 a.m. to 8 p.m. in Sept and Oct, and 9 a.m. to 6 p.m. in Nov and Dec. Free admission; extra charges for tours and special attractions.**

In the Beck family for more than a century, the cider mill and farm have been an attraction for area families since 1972. There's something taking place at the farm and mill nearly every weekend. In May there's a garden shop with plants for sale. Summer finds fresh fruit, and starting approximately Sept 1, it's apple season, culminating with pumpkins in Oct. There also is a gift shop, plus a mile-long nature trail that winds past three ponds and a picnic area. Events include an annual Labor Day weekend car show, with more than 500 classic, antique, and collectible cars on display; a kids' fest in late Sept; free tractor rides through the orchard on Sept and Oct weekends; an orchard tour ($); a Halloween costume party; a corn maze ($); and more.

### St. Johns Mint Festival  (all ages)

**The festival takes place throughout downtown and at the Clinton County Fairgrounds in mid-Aug. For more information, call (989) 224-7248.**

The rich fields around this city have been famous for growing peppermint and spearmint. While the landscape has changed a bit since it was the main crop, spearmint farming continues and is feted in this annual festival, which includes a Saturday Mint Parade, and bowls of mint chocolate-chip ice cream and other mint-laced foods, and **free** daily entertainment.

### Maple River State Game Area (all ages)

**Located 8 miles north of St. Johns along Old US 27. For more information, including maps, call the State Department of Natural Resources Rose Lake Wildlife Research Center at (517) 373-9358.**

Take the kids on a "soft" eco-adventure to this 10,000-acre game area, the largest single wetland complex in mid-Michigan and home to thousands of ducks, geese, swans, and other animals throughout the year. Portions of the wetland are created by diking parts of the Maple River, and visitors are welcome to walk the dikes to view the wildlife. There's a barrier-free hunting-photo blind and trail, reached just north of the US 27 bridge in Unit B of the area. There's also an observation tower visitors can climb to look out over the complex. A few words of caution, however. Canals throughout the area are deep, so watch younger children. Trails can get muddy in spring, and the area is open to hunting in fall.

## Where to Eat

**St. Johns Big Boy.** 1408 South Old US 27, in town; (989) 224-6828. Open 6:30 a.m. to 11 p.m. Mon through Sat, 6:30 a.m. to midnight Sun. Chain restaurant serving a variety of foods, from a salad bar to its trademark Big Boy triple-decker burger. $

## Where to Stay

**St. Johns Motel.** 1212 North Old US 27; (989) 224-2321. Located just north of the city on the west side of the road, near the intersection of Highway 21. A quiet, renovated country motel with ten rooms, including two whirlpool suites. Restaurants nearby. $$–$$$

## For More Information

**Clinton County Chamber of Commerce.** 1013 South US 27, St. Johns 48879; (989) 224-7248.

# Fenton

Now travel to the east, to this suburban town smack in the middle between Flint and northern metro Detroit. Originally settled in the 1830s as the end of the line for railroad freight traffic from Detroit, Fenton later counted on using the cement and aggregate business to make its way. Fenton, in Genesee County, also is the site of one of the area's larger lakes, Lake Fenton.

### Balloon Quest Inc. Captain Phogg Balloon Rides (all ages)

**2470 Grange Hall Rd.; (248) 634-3094; www.balloonride.com. To get to Captain Phogg, take I-75 to exit 101, Grange Hall Road. Turn west, go about 4 miles to Holly, and continue through the traffic light. Watch for a traffic light at Fish Lake Road; the entrance is 200 yards past the light to the south. Captain Phogg flies seven days a week, except Christmas Day, weather permitting. $$$$.**

Take your family walking the winds and get a bird's-eye view of the state's scenic landscape, lakes, and wildlife the way the pros do aboard an aerial nature trek with Captain Phogg. The most popular package is "the traditional." From a private launch field on Grange Hall Road, up to eight persons can join the pilot on an hour-long flight wherever the winds take you, setting down in another field and ending with a ballooning tradition, a champagne celebration back at the headquarters.

Got a hankering to get into the sport yourself? Lessons are available, and balloons are for sale. There's even an annual Seven Lakes State Park Balloon Race, which you can participate in if you like, in late July. See Captain Phogg's Web site for details.

## Where to Eat

**Elias Brothers Big Boy.** 3401 Owen Rd.; (810) 629-0541. Take the Owen Road exit off US 23. The restaurant is just to the east. Open Sun through Thurs 6 a.m. to 11 p.m., Fri and Sat 6 a.m. to 1 a.m. Chain restaurant that serves a variety of foods, from a salad bar to the Big Boy burger. $$

**John's Pizzeria.** 1492 North Leroy St.; (810) 629-5060. From US 23, head east on Silver Lake Road into town to Leroy Street. Turn north and go about a mile. Open noon to 10 p.m. Sun, 11 a.m. to 11 p.m. Mon through Wed, 11 a.m. to midnight Thurs through Sat. Winter hours go back one hour. Sit-down restaurant with pizza and pastas. Children's menu. $$

## Where to Stay

**Holiday Inn Express.** 17800 Silver Parkway; (810) 714-7171. This chain property has sixty-nine rooms with indoor pool and continental breakfast. Some rooms have whirlpools. Restaurant nearby. $$–$$$

## For More Information

**Fenton Area Chamber of Commerce.** 114 North Leroy St., Fenton 48430; (810) 629-5447; www.fentonchamber.org.

# Flint

This community rests at the intersection of I-75, US 23, and I-69. The whole of this city's modern history is tied in some way to the wheel. Once it outgrew its simple existence as a river ford, the city was on the road to becoming a major manufacturing center. First there were the carriage shops of downtown, which gave birth to the largest automotive company in the world. General Motors remains a presence in this town, nicknamed the Vehicle City, despite being hit hard by closings. Visitors might wonder about some addresses in Flint that begin with the letter G. This denotes locations outside the city of Flint, but in Genesee County. It's a little confusing, especially when a few addresses might carry identical numbers, except for the G, denoting one as outside the city. As long as you understand that, you won't have trouble getting around.

# Flint **Cultural Center**

This complex is located along East Kearsley Street and Longway Boulevard. Take I-475 to Longway Boulevard, head east to Walnut, then head south. The road dead-ends at the parking lot for the Cultural Center area.

The center features several attractions, including the Flint Institute of Arts, Robert T. Longway Planetarium, and Sloan Museum.

### Flint Institute of Arts   (toddlers and up)

1120 East Kearsley, in the Flint Cultural Center; (810) 234-1695; www.flintarts.org. Hours are 10 a.m. to 5 p.m. Tues through Sat and 1 to 5 p.m. Sun. Closed major holidays. This is a great spot to introduce youngsters to art, but be mindful when bringing young children who may not appreciate a visit here. Strollers are welcome. Admission is **free,** and donations are appreciated.

Nearly 5,000 works of art on display make this one of the largest privately owned museums in the state. Art includes works from the eighteenth century onward, including a unique collection of antique French paperweights. The museum hosts seasonal art fairs, and there's also a gift shop.

### Robert T. Longway Planetarium  (ages 3 and up)

1310 East Kearsley, in the Flint Cultural Center; (810) 237-3400; www.longwayplanetarium .com. The building is open from 8:30 a.m. to 4 p.m. Mon through Fri and noon to 4:15 p.m. Sat and Sun. The display area is **free,** planetarium and light shows $–$$.

Since they may not understand or like sitting in the dark for the shows, very young children should probably not accompany you to these excellent shows about the night sky. Special holiday shows are also offered. The planetarium is the largest in Michigan.

### Flint Children's Museum  (ages 2 to 10)

1602 West University Ave. (Third Ave.), on the city's northwest side; (810) 767-5437; www .flintchildrensmuseum.org.  Open from 9 a.m. to 5 p.m. Mon to Fri, and 10 a.m. to 5 p.m. Sat. Admission is **free** for children younger than age 2. There's also a family pass. $.

More than one hundred hands-on exhibits, from carnival-style crazy mirrors to create-your-own buildings at a Lego table and a real storybook coach. Activities are designed so children can learn while having fun. During the holidays kids can make crafts.  There's also a gift shop.

### Historic Crossroads Village and Huckleberry Railroad  (all ages)

G-6140 Bray Rd.; (800) 648-7275; www.geneseecountyparks.org/crossroadsvillage.htm. Exit I-475 off either I-75 or I-69 to Saginaw Street, exit 13. Take it north to Stanley Road, and then follow the signs to go east on Stanley to Bray and south to the village. There also are signs along the way to direct you. The village is part of the Genesee County Recreation Area and is open pretty much year-round. Crossroads hours aren't the easiest to keep track of. It's best to call ahead. It's open weekends in Sept for special events, from a harvest jubilee to a juried quilt competition. Christmas at Crossroads runs approximately Nov 23–25, Nov 30–Dec 2, and Dec 4–9, 11–16, 18–23, and 26–30. Check schedule for specific dates, as they vary from year to year. Regular admission for the train ride and village is $$. For the train, village, and *Genesee Belle* boat ride, admission is $$$ for adults, $$ for children ages 3 to 12. Christmas at Crossroads admission with the village and train is $$. Village-only admission is less, but the train ride is worth it for the kids' reactions alone. **Free** for children 2 and under.

History of the 1800s in Michigan and elsewhere comes to life at this village alongside Mott Lake, a dammed portion of the Flint River. Everything from a steam-train ride through the countryside—complete with a visit by mock robbers every hour—to a look at what everyday life in the Flint area was like back in the 1860s is in store here.

The complex is part of the Genesee County parks system. Inside, craftspeople demonstrate blacksmithing, spinning, woodworking, and how mothers managed cooking with the right temperatures on woodstoves. Twenty-nine historic buildings make up the village. Kids will especially enjoy the 1910-era Ferris wheel and 1912 carousel.

There are events scheduled every summer weekend, from car shows and history encampments to museum displays. During the holidays the village becomes an especially magical place when more than 600,000 lights decorate the buildings and streets in what's billed as the state's most spectacular moving light display, which you can enjoy Wed through Sun from the day before Thanksgiving to Dec 30. On Mon only drive-through viewing is available.

## Stepping Stone Falls (all ages)

5161 Branch Rd., at the dam forming Mott Lake; (800) 648-7275; www.geneseecountyparks .org/stepping_stone.htm. From Crossroads Village, head south on Bray Road, then east at the end of the lake on Carpenter Road to Branch Road. Head north on Branch to the falls. Open 8 a.m. to 11 p.m. daily. **Free.**

The falls impound 600-acre Mott Lake and feature colored-lighting evenings between May 25 and Oct 31. It's also the site of the docks for the *Genesee Belle*. This sightseeing boat departs from Stepping Stone Falls and Crossroads Village, offering forty-five-minute cruises on the lake. Call (810) 736-7100 or (800) 648-7275 for specific times and prices.

## Steam Railroading Institute and Polar Express Locomotive

(all ages)

Located about 30 miles north of Lansing and 30 miles west of Flint in Owosso at 405 South Washington St.; (989) 725-9464; www.mstrp.com. North Pole Express trips are $$$$. Tours the rest of the year are $, kids 4 and under **free.**

Besides pieces of old rolling stock like cabooses and other gear in various stages of restoration, the institute is home to the Pere Marquette No. 1225, the huge locomotive that was used in the production of the movie *The Polar Express,* which is shown in many large-format theaters around the country, especially during the Christmas holidays.

And now, families can ride the North Pole Express on a three-hour round-trip to the "North Pole." Trips leave weekends at 10 a.m. and 4 p.m. from late Nov through mid-Dec.

You will believe, and the kids will, too. At other times during the year, there are guided hands-on tours of the shop and coaches.

Each July, what's billed as America's largest celebration of railroading takes place at the institute. The three-day festival features up-close looks at both hulking steam and diesel locomotives, including up to seven steam-powered models, along with huge model railroad layouts, vendors, and more. If someone in the family is a railroad buff, this is the place to be.

## Where to Eat

Flint contains a multitude of dining opportunities, including a couple of must-dos and some family favorites.

**Angelo's Coney Island & Grill.** 1816 Davison Rd.; (810) 238-3761. Open daily almost around the clock. Some argue this is the home of the epitome of Coney Island hot dogs. One thing's for sure—it is popular with Flint-area residents and those traveling through. $

**Bill Thomas's Halo Burger.** Eleven locations, including ten in the Flint area: 800 South Saginaw, downtown; 3410 Corunna Rd.; 4474 Richfield Rd.; 3388 South Linden Rd.; 3805 East Court; G-4415 West Pierson Rd.; 11355 Saginaw; 2248 East Hill Rd., Grand Blanc; 1464 North Leroy, Fenton; and the Flint University Center, downtown; plus Birch Run (see listing). A Flint-area tradition since the 1920s, and one of the best burgers you'll ever have, cooked to order. Choose from unusual toppings, including one of my favorites, sliced green olives. $

**Walli's East.** G-1341 South Center Rd., Burton, just south of the I-69 and Center Road exit; (810) 743-9600. Family restaurant for breakfast, lunch, and dinner. $$

## Where to Stay

**Holiday Inn Gateway Centre.** 5353 Gateway Centre; (810) 232-5300. Exit US 23 at Hill Road and turn east. Or, from I-75, head north 1 mile from the I-475 interchange, then 2 miles west on Hill Road. This property has 173 nice rooms, huge lobby, restaurant, indoor pool, and exercise area. Convenient to the entire area's attractions. $$$

**Hometown Inn.** G-3277 Miller Rd.; (810) 733-5910. From I-75, exit at Miller Road and head west. Property has 135 rooms and outdoor pool. Restaurants nearby. $

**Red Roof Inn.** G-3219 Miller Rd.; (810) 733-1660. From I-75, exit at Miller Road and turn west. Inn features 107 simple, comfortable rooms. Restaurants nearby. $

**Timber Wolf and Wolverine Campgrounds.** Both are part of Holloway Reservoir Regional Park on the dammed-up Flint River. Timber Wolf is at 7004 North Irish Rd., in the Genesee County Recreation Area near Crossroads Village and Huckleberry Railroad; (810) 640-1600. Take I-75 to Mount Morris Road and head east about 10 miles to Irish Road. Go south 1 mile to the campground. Timber Wolf features 196 campsites open from early May to mid-Sept, with showers, laundry, and electricity. There's also a small boat launch to explore the Flint River and playground and hiking trails. $

Wolverine Campground is in Holloway Reservoir Regional Park at 7698 North Baxter Rd.; (810) 793-6613. Take I-75 to Mount Morris Road and head east about 14½ miles to Baxter Road. Head south to the campground. Wolverine, open from mid-May through early Sept, has 195 campsites on the 2,000-acre Holloway Reservoir with showers, electricity, and rustic tent camping. There's a boat launch and beach, too. $

## For More Information

**Flint Area Convention and Visitors Bureau.** 519 South Saginaw St., Flint 48502; (810) 232-8900 or (800) 253-5468; www.visit flint.travel.

# Chesaning

Somewhat off the track of most tourists zooming up I-75, this community is worth a westward detour to check out. Downtown Chesaning and stores just west of the city center offer lots of fun for families, along with the famous Showboat.

### Chesaning Showboat (all ages)

**In Showboat Park, just southeast of downtown; (800) 844-3056;www.chesaningshowboat .org. The festival takes place the second full week of July. $$$$.**

Running for more than fifty-six years, this family-style variety show along the water features a big-name entertainer or two each year on the Showboat stage, when the words "Showboat's a-coming" ring out over the park. Past guests have included Sugarland and '60s rocker Tommy James. The stage on land seats 7,000, and it's nearly always filled, so order tickets as early as possible.

## Where to Eat

**Showboat Restaurant.** 244 West Broad St.; (989) 845-2830. Family-style cooking specializing in prime rib and fish. Breakfast through dinner served. $$$

## Where to Stay

**Colonial Motel.** 9475 East Highway 57, ½ mile from downtown; (989) 845-3292. Fourteen rooms with breakfast included. $$–$$$

See also lodging listings for Flint and Saginaw.

## For More Information

**Chesaning Chamber of Commerce.** 218 North Front St., Chesaning 48616; (989) 845-3055; www.chesaningchamber.org.

# Birch Run

Only a few years ago, this tiny community was a local farming center. The biggest event to hit town was when the downtown grain elevator burned to the ground. I remember it, too, for years as the northern end to the I-75 freeway. From this point travelers going north exited onto the four-lane Dixie Highway to head through towns like Saginaw and Bay City on their way to resorts farther north.

That all changed, however, when suburbanites discovered the area, and the first portion of the megamall of discount stores opened here to make it one of the hottest tourist destinations in the state.

## Prime Outlets at Birch Run  (all ages)

12240 South Beyer; (989) 624-6226; www.primeretail.com. Exit I-75 at Birch Run and follow the flying charge cards. This outdoor mall is open from 10 a.m. to 9 p.m. Mon through Sat and 11 a.m. to 7 p.m. Sun. There are often special sales and events, such as deer hunter's Widow's Weekend the first weekend on or after Nov 15.

There are five other factory discount-outlet malls in Michigan, but for anyone's money, this one is by far the largest, offering markdowns on everything from books to toys to tools to brand-name clothes that you would otherwise find only at standard retail malls. True, some items are damaged and some are closeouts, but many are only last season's line or production overruns from this season.

Families, especially around the big summer holiday sidewalk sales, spend the entire day roaming more than 160 stores. You can pick up school shoes for the kids at Nike, luggage for your next trip at American Tourister, and book bags at Eddie Bauer, and then shop at scores of other stores that specialize in everything from knives to books. Some of the stores that specialize in exercise or stereo equipment don't discount at all, so it's a good idea to check prices at other stores before you head here for anything. While sale items at regular retailers may be better priced, most often you won't find brand-name items for less than you can here.

If you get hungry, there are shops that sell everything from real food to fudge—even one for Pepperidge Farm cookie aficionados. Open since 1986, the mall is not enclosed.

## Wilderness Trails Zoo  (all ages)

11721 Gera Rd. (Highway 83); (989) 624-6177; www.wildernesstrailszoo.org. The park is about 2½ miles east and north of the I-75 Birch Run exit. After exiting, turn east, follow the road to the Highway 83 intersection, and turn north; the park is ¼ mile north, on the east side of the road. Open 10 a.m. to 6 p.m. Mon through Sat and 11 a.m. to 6 p.m. Sun, May 1 to Oct 31. Adults, kids ages 3 to 15, and seniors $$, kids 2 and younger free. Family packages available.

Three miles to the east of the outlet stores, one of the best privately owned exhibits in the state introduces young children to the animal kingdom. More than fifty different species from around the world can be seen from gravel trails that weave throughout thirty-eight acres of woods at the park. Show your youngsters everything from black bears, which roam wild barely an hour's drive north, to coyotes, raccoons, otters, and porcupines.

More exotic types you'll see include lions, llamas, bison, and even a Siberian brown bear and Siberian tiger. Spend a quarter for a palmful of feed at a treat station for everything from bears to catfish. There are two walking paths. A ½-mile trail takes you past the front part of the exhibits, while a back trail allows you to see many of the hoofed animals, such as elk and deer (you can see those in the wild in northern Michigan, too), that may be too shy to be seen from the other trail. You pay 50 cents per person to hop on board the horse-drawn covered wagon that takes twenty visitors per trip on half-hour tours of the entire facility. In addition to a petting area where children can see, feed, and touch baby animals, kids can also enjoy a small picnic area and playground.

### Birch Run Expo Center  (all ages)
**11600 Beyer Rd.; (989) 624-4665; www.birchrunexpos.com. From I-75, exit at Birch Run Road and head west to Beyer, and then drive north to the facility. Hours and admission vary by show.**

This 109,000-square-foot facility hosts everything from RV and camping shows to bridal displays.

## Where to Eat

Besides the national chain fast-food restaurants at the Birch Run exit, here are some local favorites:

**Bill Thomas's Halo Burgers.** 9130 East Birch Run Rd.; (989) 624-5441. From I-75, take the Birch Run exit and head east to the driveway. Open from 7 a.m. to 10 p.m. Sat through Thurs, 7 a.m. to 11 p.m. Fri, and 10:30 a.m. to 9 p.m. Sun. The same great fixed-to-order, old-fashioned burgers that are available at several locations in Flint. $$

**Tony's.** 8781 Main St., just west of I-75, on the north side of the road; (989) 624-5860. Humongous servings and low prices. Order a BLT, and you'll get a pound of bacon with lettuce and tomato packed between Italian bread a quarter of a loaf thick. Other items, like famous Italian sausage sandwiches, are equally huge. Serves breakfast, lunch, and dinner. $$

## Where to Stay

**Best Western Birch Run/Frankenmuth.** At the Birch Run exit on I-75; (989) 624-9395. This newly renovated property has 146 rooms and some whirlpool suites with **free** Wi-Fi. Complimentary hot breakfast, an indoor pool, and restaurant attached. Pets OK at extra charge. $$–$$$

**Super 8 Motel.** 9235 East Birch Run Rd.; (989) 624-4440. From I-75, exit at Birch Run and head east. A basic place with 107 rooms. Restaurants nearby. $$

## For More Information

**Birch Run Chamber of Commerce and Convention & Visitors Bureau.** P.O. Box 153, Birch Run 48415; (888) 624-9193; www .birchrunchamber.com.

# Bridgeport

Founded in 1836 and named for the bridges that crossed the Cass River here, Bridgeport has become a suburb of Saginaw.

### Junction Valley Railroad  (all ages)
**7065 Dixie Hwy., at Junction Road; (989) 777-3480; www.jvrailroad.com. To reach the rails, take exit 144 off I-75 and head south on Dixie Highway 2 miles to the first flashing traffic**

light. Open from 10 a.m. to 6 p.m. Mon through Sat and 1 to 6 p.m. Sun from Memorial Day weekend through Labor Day weekend. The train operates from 1 to 5 p.m. on weekends only from Memorial Day weekend to Labor Day. The special Halloween train operates weekends in Oct. Admission varies by date but is generally $–$$. On Father's Day rides for dads are **free** when accompanied by a paying child.

Rain or shine, after or before hitting Birch Run, treat the kids to a ride on the world's largest one-quarter-size railroad, Junction Valley, just east of the Saginaw suburb of Bridgeport. Climb on board the miniature cars as one of eight scale-model diesel locomotives pulls you on the 2-mile ride through woods, over 865 feet of trestles, including the only "diamond crossing trestle" in the world, and even through a 100-foot-long tunnel. A picnic area and a playground are also available. The season starts the weekend before Memorial Day, and special events take place regularly. Halloween "spook train" rides pass thirty-five different scenes, to the light of more than 250 trackside jack-o'-lanterns.

## Where to Eat

See listings for Birch Run, Frankenmuth, and Saginaw, plus fast food locations at the I-75 Bridgeport exit.

## Where to Stay

**Baymont Inn.** 6460 Dixie Hwy.; (989) 777-3000. From I-75, head north on Dixie Highway. Basic property with 104 rooms. Restaurant nearby. $

**Heidelberg Inn Motel.** 6815 Dixie Hwy.; (989) 777-2195. From I-75, exit southbound onto Dixie Highway and drive about 1 mile. There are fourteen rooms in this well-kept motel that dates from the days when Dixie Highway was the main route north and south. Dining is nearby at the I-75 interchange area. $

# Frankenmuth

Barely five minutes east of the Junction Valley Railroad, Frankenmuth is the realm of *gemütlichkeit,* that untranslatable German word that can mean everything from hospitality to down-home friendly. Whatever your interpretation, Frankenmuth will supply.

Founded in 1845 by fifteen German Lutherans who came to this then-wilderness to preach to Native American tribes, the town has held onto its German past while transforming itself into Michigan's top tourist destination. Many towns have tourist attractions. Here, just about the entire town is one. There are two ways to get to Frankenmuth. From the Birch Run exit, head east to Highway 83 and take it north straight into town. From the Bridgeport exit, head south on Dixie Highway to Junction Road, and then go east about 5 miles.

## Bavarian Festival  (all ages)

Throughout the city, usually the second weekend in June; (989) 652-6106; www.franken muthfestivals.com. **Free** admission but there are charges for the beer tents and cooking classes.

Whatever the season or the reason, it seems there's almost always a celebration going on in town. This is the one that started it all and put the city on the map for tourists, a mid-June celebration that draws more than 100,000 visitors for food, parades, and lots of polka music. All events center on Heritage Park, a short walk across the authentic wooden covered bridge from downtown's restaurants and other fun. Dance the polka in one tent or enjoy other music in another. Knock back a bratwurst sausage with a glass of your favorite beverage and join in the fun. This is only one of several events that take place from Jan through Nov.

### Bronner's Christmas Wonderland  (all ages)

**25 Christmas Lane; (989) 652-9931 or (800) 255-9327; www.bronners.com. Just off Highway 83 at the south end of town; you can't miss it. Open nearly every day of the year. Hours are 9 a.m. to 9 p.m. Mon through Sat and noon to 7 p.m. Sun from June through Dec; 9 a.m. to 5:30 p.m. Mon through Thurs and Sat, 9 a.m. to 9 p.m. Fri, and noon to 5:30 p.m. Sun from Jan through May. Admission is** free.

Be ready to share your visit to what's billed as the world's largest Christmas store with lots of folks. They come here by the busload to view the Christmas ornaments, trees, nativity scenes, and more that are up year-round inside, along with a great light display outside. Late owner Wally Bronner started the business downtown as a sideline to his sign business. When it outgrew the two buildings being used, Bronner moved into this huge structure, which has been expanded again. Things are a mite pricier here than at the local discount store, but what the heck, it's Christmas here even when it's ninety degrees outside.

At the south end of the Bronner's parking lot, be sure to see the Silent Night Memorial Chapel, a replica of the chapel in Oberndorf, Austria, where the famous Christmas song was penned.

### *Bavarian Belle* Riverboat Tours  (all ages)

**925 South Main St. at the Cass River; (866) 808-BOAT. Departs daily 11 a.m. to dusk, early May to mid-Oct. Adults $$, children ages three to twelve $, three and under** free.

Take a scenic narrated hour-long cruise on the Cass River as the *Belle*'s captain relates the history of the area.

### Zehnder's Restaurant  (all ages)

730 South Main St.; (800) 863-7999; www.zehnders.com. Open 11:30 a.m. to 9:30 p.m. daily all year. $$.

There are a lot of other items you can order off its menu, but at Zehnder's, most opt for its renowned family-style, all-you-can-eat chicken dinner, which comes complete, from bread and soup to veggies and dessert and platefuls of fried chicken. Be sure to get a side order of the zesty chicken livers.

### Frankenmuth River Place  (all ages)

925 South Main St.; (800) 600-0105; www.frankenmuth-riverplace.com. Open longer hours in summer, but core hours are 10 a.m. to 6 p.m. Sun through Thurs, 10 a.m. to 8 p.m. Fri and Sat. Laser shows take place most nights; check for specific times. Some attractions charge admission. Check individually for prices.

The city's newest shopping experience, this cluster of thirty-five shops and attractions includes an outdoor amphitheater where laser shows take place, plus the *Bavarian Belle* paddle wheel riverboat dock. Young kids have fun exploring River Place Toys, while teens can try the Cosmic Cars bumper car ride or find their way out of the Ultimate Mirror Maze, a modern-day take on the old amusement park funhouse, with a maze of glass and mirrors.

### Bavarian Inn  (all ages)

713 South Main St.; (800) 228-2742; www.bavarianinn.com. Open year-round from 11 a.m. to 9:30 p.m. Sat and 11 a.m. to 9 p.m. weekdays and Sun. $$–$$$.

Across the street from Zehnder's, the Bavarian Inn also serves chicken, but it's most famous for serving German-style meals. Outside, entertain the kids first with a performance of the inn's glockenspiel clock tower, which tells the Pied Piper story in music.

# Zehnder's Snow Fest  (all ages)

This event in the last week of Jan brings thousands of people out into the cold to view massive snow sculptures thrown up around the town's two famous downtown restaurants. There are paths around the works in front of and behind both the Bavarian Inn and Zehnder's restaurants, which are across the street from each other, and tents are available so you can duck in and out of the cold and, if you wish, grab something to eat or something hot to drink. Even if there's no snow on the ground, festival organizers will have plenty available for the champion carvers who sculpt figures out of blocks of snow. Snow sculptures also line Main Street, where there are nearly fifty shops, which sell everything from fresh-ground flour and hand-carved chess sets to made-while-you-shop dolls for the kids.

Each restaurant, incidentally, is owned by Zehnder family members. Be sure to check out the lower-level gift shops in both restaurants. In the Bavarian Inn, have a doll made for your children in about an hour.

## Where to Eat

**Tiffany's.** 656 South Main St., just north of Zehnder's; (989) 652-6881. Open from 11 a.m. to 11 p.m. daily. Where the locals go to ogle the tourists waddling out of Zehnder's. Fresh pastas, pizzas, and grilled items. Children's menu. $$$

## Where to Stay

**Drury Inn.** 260 South Main St., downtown; (989) 652-2800. The inn has seventy-eight comfortable rooms, an indoor pool, and complimentary breakfast. Within walking distance of downtown attractions. Restaurants nearby. $$

**Frankenmuth Bavarian Inn Lodge.** 1 Covered Bridge Lane, 1 block east of downtown across the bridge; (989) 652-7200; www.bavarianinn.com. The lodge has 354 rooms along the Cass River in a European-themed setting. A family-fun center includes five indoor pools and three whirlpools, family suites, an eighteen-hole indoor minigolf center, jogging trails and exercise area, tennis courts, and more. Two restaurants inside. $$$

**Frankenmuth Jellystone Camp-Resort/ MiniGolf.** 1339 Weiss St.; (989) 652-6668; www.frankenmuthjellystone.com. This facility has 250 sites open all year, with a playground, an outdoor pool, game room, theme weekend fun, and a minigolf course. $

**Frankenmuth Motel.** 1218 Weiss St.; (989) 652-6171 or (800) 821-5263; www.frankenmuthmotel.com. This motel has fifty-four rooms, offers **free** continental breakfast, and is close to downtown. $$–$$$

**Zehnder's Splash Village Hotel and Waterpark.** 1365 South Main St., ½ mile south of downtown; (800) 863-7999. This hotel has a four-level waterpark and 152 rooms, plus restaurant, adjacent to Bronner's. $$–$$$$

## For More Information

**Frankenmuth Convention and Visitors Bureau.** (989) 652-6106 or (800) 386-8696; www.frankenmuth.org. A town visitor center is at 635 South Main St., Frankenmuth, near Zehnder's and the Bavarian Inn. It has **free** on-site hotel reservation assistance and attraction information.

# Saginaw

This former rip-roaring lumber town is a bit quieter than it was in the 1800s, when lumberjacks would drive log rafts down the Cass and Tittabawassee Rivers to the city's sawmills. While it still owes much to auto manufacturing, tourism is becoming a major part of its economy. The Saginaw and Tittabawassee Rivers are now famous among walleye anglers nationwide. Each fall and winter, and again in spring, anglers gather to try for walleye, which enter the river system from Lake Huron's Saginaw Bay to the north.

**Johnny Panther Quests Ecotours** (all ages)
**A trip to introduce you to the upper Flint River in fall is $100 per couple, $30 each additional person, with kids under 12 half price. The Saginaw-area trip is $140 per couple, plus**

$50 for each additional adult; kids under 12 half price. For information on the Au Sable River expedition, as well as other trips, call (810) 653-3859; www.jpqat.com. River trips accommodate two to twelve persons.

If you've never taken your kids on a real adventure, here's a good place to start, waiting just down the road, literally, from one of the state's major cities. For within a few minutes of leaving downtown Saginaw, you can enjoy an unspoiled natural habitat that covers thousands of acres of wetlands and that owner/guide Wil Hufton calls Michigan's Everglades. You're almost certain to see a bald eagle flying silently over the water or perched in a tree enjoying a fish dinner, spot a roosting cormorant, hear calling geese and ducks, watch deer bounding through thickets, or hear the slap of a beaver's tail on the water.

Hufton, a Coast Guard–licensed captain, motors one of his two specially built boats into the wilds and then floats through the silence. Much of this wilderness skirts the Shiawassee National Wildlife Refuge, which he explored as a kid. Trips can accommodate any age, from more adventurous types who don't mind a portage to see the beauty to those who just want to float. He'll even let you off to quietly picnic for a few hours before he returns to pick you up in time for your very own sail into the sunset.

## Saginaw Children's Zoo at Celebration Square (all ages)

1720 South Washington; (989) 759-1408; www.saginawzoo.com. To get to the zoo, leave I-675 at the Fifth Street/Sixth Street exit and head south on Washington Avenue approximately 2 miles. The park is on the east side of the street. The zoo is usually open daily from Mother's Day weekend through Labor Day. Zoo hours are Mon through Sat 10 a.m. to 5 p.m., Sun and holidays 11 a.m. to 6 p.m. Adults $, children 2 and under free. Carousel and train rides cost extra ($), with kids 2 and under free with paying adult.

This children's zoo has always been a great summer attraction, and it keeps getting better. Located in a grove of trees on the city's east side near the Saginaw River, the zoo features what's billed as the largest American alligator exhibit in the state, a great garden, and a river otter exhibit that offers underwater viewing of the playful critters. There's also a new exhibit on warm-water South American penguins. This is in addition to twenty-eight other species of animals on the park's more than eight-and-a-half acres, such as monkeys, wolves, and eagles, and a walk-through butterfly exhibit. The Ibershoff Special, a miniature train ride, loops the zoo in a ½-mile trip. You'll also find a souvenir shop and playground. The handcrafted carousel was made locally by volunteers and "seats" twenty-nine riders on horses, bunnies, zebras, and chariots. Painted scenes depict Saginaw County history.

## Mid-Michigan Children's Museum (ages 5 to 12)

315 West Genesee Ave.; (989) 399-6626; www.midmicm.org. Take I-75 exit 149B onto Holland Avenue (Highway 46). Turn right onto East Genesee Avenue into downtown. Cross the Saginaw River and the museum is on the left. Open 10 a.m. to 5 p.m. Mon and Wed through Sat, and noon to 5 p.m. Sun. Free for kids under 2, $$ for ages 2 and above.

Catering to kids under 12, the museum offers a great hands-on introduction to the world of science, art and other areas and without their even knowing they're learning through

# Shiver on the River

Ice or no ice, when the temperature turns wintry here, it's the signal for hundreds of locals and tourists to come into the cold during the annual fishing festival, which not only celebrates the renewed annual runs of hungry walleye but also includes a contest to catch the biggest in the Saginaw River and its main tributaries and Saginaw Bay. Each year, the fish swim into the river from Saginaw Bay to winter and then spawn in spring. The contest usually runs between late Jan and early Feb. And even if there isn't any ice, anglers haul out their boats to brave the sometimes bitter cold for a chance at the prizes.

The top prizes total up to $5,000, and some years there's a special award for any angler who catches a fish setting a state record. Walleye up to thirteen pounds are often landed here. If you come for the fun of it or to teach your offspring about winter fishing, all the equipment you'll need is a license, a stubby ice-fishing rod, an auger or spud to chip through the ice (if there is any), and lots of patience to sit on the ice hoping for a bite.

If you're in it for the money, get the rules, fill out an entry blank for $10 per person at local tackle shops, and head out. Pay attention to weather forecasts, as ice conditions on the river can change quickly.

Best fishing times are usually early morning and late evening, and most anglers use small jigs tipped with minnows. Weigh-ins are all conducted at a local tackle shop. For more information, call (989) 776-9704; www.mlive.com/shiver.

eleven galleries. Even included is a chance to explore Michigan's agricultural roots at Aunt Sugar's Farm, and to explore the city's automotive past at the Car Works.

### Kokomo's Family Fun Center (all ages)

**5200 Kokomo Dr.; (989) 797-5656; www.kokomos.com. From I-675, exit at Tittabawassee Road and head west past Bay Road to Kokomo Drive, and then head north. From early June to late Aug, open 10 a.m. to midnight Mon through Sat, 10 a.m. to 10 p.m. Sun. Late Aug to early June, open 10 a.m. to 9 p.m. Mon through Thurs, 10 a.m. to 11 p.m. Fri and Sat, 10 a.m. to 7 p.m. Sun. Prices for all activities are $–$$, and a wristband good for three attractions may be purchased ($$$).**

A nineteen-hole minigolf course, go-karts, bumper boats, laser tag, and even an ice rink and snacks make a stop here fun. Golfers will find an enclosed driving range with thirty-four stations, indoor putting green, and golf pros to give you pointers. There also is "water wars," a water-balloon game.

## Where to Eat

**Damon's Place for Ribs.** 4960 Towne Centre; (989) 249-7427. Attached to Four Points Hotel by Sheraton (see Where to Stay). Famous for its ribs and prime rib. Seafood and some veggie items are also on the menu. Children's menu. $$–$$$

**First Wok Buffet.** 4624 State St.; (989) 799-3888. Open daily, for lunch 11:30 a.m. to 3:30 p.m., dinner 4 to 9 p.m. Excellent selection of Chinese food served buffet-style. Lunch $, dinner $$, ages three to ten half price.

**Sullivan's West.** 5235 Gratiot (Highway 46); (989) 799-1940. From I-75, exit at Highway 46 and head west. Good family dining. Children's menu for lunch and dinner. $$

## Where to Stay

**Four Points Hotel by Sheraton.** 4960 Towne Centre Rd.; (989) 790-5050. At the junction of I-675 and Tittabawassee Road, north of downtown, this hotel has 156 rooms with complimentary hot continental breakfast, indoor/outdoor pool, fitness area, and whirlpool/sauna. Damon's restaurant (see listing) is attached. Near Fashion Square Mall. $$

**Hampton Inn.** 2222 Tittabawassee Rd., at the junction with I-675; (989) 792-7666. A basic motel with 120 rooms with outdoor pool and dining nearby. Also close to Fashion Square Mall. $$

**Montague Inn.** 1581 South Washington; (989) 752-3939; www.montagueinn.com. From I-675, exit downtown and head west to Washington, and then head south about 1½ miles. The inn has eighteen rooms. What might be one of the best bed-and-breakfast experiences you'll have in the state is waiting inside this former lumber baron mansion overlooking Lake Linton, a lagoon of the Saginaw River. Great Victorian atmosphere as well as a restaurant serving both breakfast and elegant dinners. Choose from two buildings to stay in, and make arrangements to take a Johnny Panther wilderness tour with a stay here. $$

**Motel 6 Saginaw–Frankenmuth.** 966 South Outer Dr.; (989) 754-8414. From I-75, exit at Highway 46, head west to Outer Drive, and then turn north. A basic motel with seventy-nine comfortable rooms. $

## For More Information

**Saginaw County Convention and Visitors Bureau.** 1 Tuscola St., Suite 101, Saginaw 48607; (989) 752-7164 or (800) 444-9979; www.saginawcvb.org.

# East Michigan– North

The northern part of east Michigan drifts from the nation's "beanbasket," which produces more soy, navy, and other bean varieties than any other state, to some of the largest publicly owned tracts of forestland in the nation.

The dichotomy amazes even well-traveled Michiganians, who keep coming back, drawn by the diversity.

## Top FamilyAdventures
### in East Michigan–North

1. Hartwick Pines State Park, Grayling. Kids will be mesmerized by the size of the trees in the park and the history of Michigan logging.

2. Dinosaur Gardens Prehistorical Zoo, Ossineke. Children come face-to-face with one of the great fascinations of kid-dom.

3. Fishing for salmon or lake trout on Lake Huron in Oscoda, Alpena, Rogers City, or Grindstone City, and fishing for perch or walleye in Caseville. With several ports and species to choose from, what could be better than spending a day fishing with your kids?

4. Higgins Lake South State Park, Roscommon. A great place that kids enjoy because of its gentle, sloping beach, where they can get their toes tickled by minnows.

5. Renting a cabin for a week on Lake Huron, between Au Gres and Rogers City. A great way for a family to vacation together.

# EAST MICHIGAN–NORTH

# Bad Axe

Bad Axe is at the intersection of Highway 53, which runs north and south from the Detroit area through the Thumb, and Highway 142. A great way to tour the Thumb is along Highway 25, which runs through many of the area's major communities, as well as along the Lake Huron shoreline in many areas. It is part of a designated scenic drive called the Lake Huron Circle Tour, which includes routes in Ontario, too. Native American rock drawings in Michigan? Yup—in the heart of the state's Thumb, the tip of which makes up Huron County. The county seat got its name innocently from an old ax found on the site by early surveyors. The landscape also is dotted with an increasing number of giant electricity-generating turbines.

## Sanilac Petroglyphs State Historic Park  (all ages)

**To find the park, turn east off Highway 53 onto Bay City/Forestville Road, travel about 4 miles to Germania Road, and turn south. The park is ½ mile farther, on the west side. For more information, contact the Michigan Historical Museum at (517) 373-3559; www .michiganhistory.org, and search the Michigan Historical Museum system section. Open Wed through Sun from Memorial Day through Labor Day. Hours are 11:30 a.m. to 4:30 p.m. Admission is free.**

Estimated to be more than 1,000 years old, the rock carvings, or petroglyphs, were chiseled into the soft sandstone along the north branch of the Cass River. Kids will marvel at these characters, including the figure of a hunter with a bow and arrow, and others that resemble animals. Visitors can also walk a mile-long nature trail through the forested park, where you'll see more marked sites (plan on at least one hour, and take along bug repellent). Forty-five-minute guided presentations on the petroglyphs are given in summer. Check the Web site for occasional special events at the site.

## Pioneer Log Village  (all ages)

**In Bad Axe City Park, downtown; (989) 269-7674 or (989) 269-3084. Open from 2 to 5 p.m. Sun from Memorial Day to Sept 26. Free.**

It's hard to believe when looking over the region that lumbering, not farming, was the major activity here more than a century ago. Huge fires in 1871 (at the same time as the Chicago fire) and 1881 sent lumbermen elsewhere, and this began farming. You'll learn more about the area through the museum. Its log cabins are open by appointment.

Six nineteenth-century log structures have been moved from around the county to the park: a pioneer home, school, blacksmith shop, chapel, store, and barn. Pioneer Log Village is billed as the state's largest collection of restored log cabins.

## Where to Eat

**Big Boy.** 900 North Van Dyke (Highway 53); (989) 269-9515. Family restaurant with food ranging from a salad bar to trademark triple-decker burgers. $$

**The Pasta House.** 339 Main, Kinde, east of Michigan 53 in Kinde, about 10 miles north of Bad Axe; (989) 874-4070. Family-oriented Italian restaurant in the middle of this tiny farm community, across the street from the elevator. Open for lunch and dinner. Children's menu. Walk down the street to the Country Parlor, also owned by the Pasta House, for ice cream and minigolf. $$–$$$

## Where to Stay

**The Franklin Inn.** 1070 East Huron Ave., 7 blocks east of Highway 53; (989) 269-9951. This inn has fifty-nine rooms and a restaurant on the premises. $

## For More Information

**Bad Axe Chamber of Commerce.** P.O. Box 87, Bad Axe 48413; (989) 269-6936.

# Huron City

### Huron City Museum  (all ages)

7930 Huron City Rd. (Highway 25), Port Austin; (989) 428-4123; www.huroncitymuseums .com. To reach the museum, take Highway 25 east from Port Austin about 8 miles. From July 1 to Labor Day, the museum is open Thurs through Mon from 10 a.m. to 5 p.m. The price of admission depends on which of two tours (the town, the Point Aux Barques lifesaving station, or both) you'd like to take. The last tour of the day is at 4:30 p.m.; the last double tour leaves at 3:30 p.m. Adults $$, seniors and anyone 10 to 14 years old $–$$, children 9 and younger **free.**

Catch a glimpse of what local life was like in the early twentieth century at the Huron City Museum, a restored town on the Lake Huron shore at the tip of Michigan's Thumb. From 1893 until 1938, Huron City was the summer home of William Lyon Phelps, a Yale professor, whose relatives created this unique museum.

Each summer families can join guides on one-hour tours of Phelps's restored home, Seven Gables, the restored general store, the church where Phelps preached, an 1837 log cabin, the town's Community House Inn, and the U.S. Lifesaving Station along the beach. The Lifesaving Service was the forerunner of the Coast Guard, and its crew's job was to save passengers and crew from foundering ships along the Thumb's reef-scarred shoreline.

## Where to Eat and Stay

See Port Austin listings.

## Huron County Regional Information

For more information on the county, call the Huron County Economic Development Corporation at (989) 269-6431; www.huroncounty.com. Besides cottages and resorts some private beachfront homes also are rented seasonally. Call (800) 358-4862 for more information.

# Grindstone City

To get to Grindstone City, take Pointe Aux Barques Road east from Port Austin about 4 miles until it ends, turn north, and watch for the signs directing you to the harbor.

To get a little lesson in Michigan history and a big lesson in fishing for the "fightingest" fish in the Great Lakes, visit this tiny town, which once was the nation's grindstone capital. Located at the very tip of the Thumb, Grindstone City was famous nationwide for a century for producing some of the world's finest grinding stones, which were cut from its limestone quarries and sent to markets around the globe.

When other sharpening materials became popular during World War I, the town's two factories closed. Old grindstones ready for export can still be seen lining the roads and driveways in spots.

### Charter Fishing (all ages)

**For Grindstone City charter-boat information, call (989) 738-5271; www.thumbtravels.com, and then go to "fishing." $$$$.**

The grindstone industry may be long gone, but now Grindstone is known for something else: what may be the best early-season salmon and trout fishing on the lakes.

From a cozy, crescent-shaped harbor, up to a dozen charter boats take anglers on morning and afternoon trips in pursuit of chinook salmon, steelhead (a lake-living rainbow trout), and lake trout.

All gear—and instructions when you hook into a big one—is provided. All you need is a state fishing license (children ages sixteen and younger are exempt). The best salmon fishing runs from May to mid-June, and fish that are more than twenty pounds are not uncommon. In summer lake trout fishing is tops, and by July 20 the salmon return. Fishing stays productive through early Sept. Charters are for a half day (usually, morning fishing is best, starting at or before sunup) and take up to six persons, so the cost can be split among friends or family members.

## Where to Eat and Stay

See Port Austin listings.

# Port Austin

Port Austin is located 8 miles west of Grindstone City on Highway 53 at the intersection with Highway 25. This resort town at the tip of the Thumb is pretty quiet, except in summer, when cottage renters and campers populate the environs, especially on weekends.

### Sandy Dunes Adventure Golf (all ages)

**2755 Highway 25, between Port Austin and Caseville; (989) 738-6066. Open daily 10 a.m. to 10 p.m. Memorial Day through Labor Day and weekends through early Oct, depending on the weather.**

Besides a landscaped eighteen-hole minigolf course with waterfalls, you and the kids can also enjoy a game room and a dairy bar.

### Family Go-Karts  (ages 6 and up)

**One mile south of Port Austin on Highway 53; (989) 738-5130. Open daily from Memorial Day weekend through Labor Day weekend. Hours are 10 a.m. to 10 p.m.**

Go-karts for juniors, rookies, and adults are the featured attraction. You'll also find basketball hoop throws, a trampoline, and a gyro fitness test, among other fun activities.

## Where to Eat

Besides these upscale places to eat, there are others in the area that aren't as hard on your pocketbook. But since most people come here on vacation anyway, and many of us like to take the family out for a treat at least once during our stay, here are some in the area that will impress them all:

**The Bank-1884.** On Highway 25, Main Street, 2 blocks south of the harbor; (989) 738-5353. Open Apr through Oct. Built of brick to withstand any repeat of the 1881 fire that swept the Thumb, the bank is now a restaurant that serves great dinners on two floors. Enjoy a variety of entrees from prime rib to fresh walleye. Children's menu. $$$

**The Farm.** 699 Port Crescent Rd.; (989) 874-5700. Two miles west of Highway 53 and about 3 miles south of Port Austin. Since the restaurant is open only seasonally, here is its schedule: open daily except Mon for dinner from Memorial Day to Labor Day, open weekends from Mother's Day to Memorial Day and from Labor Day through mid-Oct. Surprising dinners served in a one-hundred-plus-year-old farmhouse and spiced with herbs and produce grown in the owners' own five-acre garden. Whitefish, pasta, and made-on-premises desserts, breads, and soups. Children's menu. $$$

**Sportsman's Inn.** 8708 Lake St.; (989) 738-7520. In downtown Port Austin on the east side of Highway 25, just south of the traffic light. It may look like a bar at first glance, but there's a separate side entrance to a family dining room that serves pizza, fresh seafood, and ribs at inexpensive prices. $$

## Where to Stay

If you're looking for a posh hotel or motel, this isn't the area to find one. The area prides itself on being one of the last bastions of family-run resorts in the state. If staying in a cottage, don't expect a mansion. There also is a good selection of campgrounds in the mix.

**Kreb's Cottages.** 3478 Port Austin Rd., 9 miles west of the city along Highway 25; (989) 856-2876. Eight cottages from one to four bedrooms, usually renting weekly. Featuring a sandy beach on the lake, with grills. $$$$ weekly.

**Lake Vista Motel and Cottages.** 168 West Spring (Highway 25), ½ mile west of the town light; (989) 738-8612. This facility has fifteen rooms in a motel setting along the beach next to Port Austin's harbor. $$

**Oak Beach County Park.** 3356 Port Austin Rd., west of downtown along Highway 25; (989) 856-2344. Here you'll find fifty-five campsites, a swimming beach, and tent and modern camping. $

**Port Crescent State Park.** About 4 miles southwest of Port Austin along Highway 25; (989) 738-8663. For reservations, call (800) 543-2937. Motor vehicle permits ($ daily or $$$ annually) required to enter are sold at the gate. Port Crescent is not only a place to stay but a place to enjoy on a vacation as well. It is one of the newest and most picturesque state parks in Michigan. At 565 acres it also has one of the last undeveloped stretches of beach along the Thumb. Families can choose from among 138 campsites (try for number 89, a beachside gem nicknamed the "honeymoon site"), roam some of the finest examples of Lake Huron sand dunes in east Michigan, and go for an inland hike on the 6½ miles of nature trails that run along the beach and through the Thumb's surprisingly extensive hardwood forests. The park also includes a fitness trail, fishing access along the Pinnebog River for persons with physical disabilities, and a 3-mile-long beach for daytime use that often is virtually deserted. Port Crescent also features minicabin rentals by reservation. $

## For More Information

**Port Austin Chamber of Commerce.** (989) 738-7600; www.portaustinarea.com.

# Caseville

Caseville is a great little resort town nestled along the beach on Lake Huron, next to a large harbor. The city beach is a wide, popular spot in summer and has a boardwalk.

In mid-May the annual Dulcimer Festival and Art in the Park take place in Sleeper State Park. The annual Auto Festival takes place in mid-July at Caseville Public School, featuring antique and classic cars and hot rods, and there's also a walleye tournament in July.

### *Miss Caseville*  (all ages)

**The new home of the former *Miss Port Austin*, now renamed the *Miss Caseville*, is the Caseville state dock. To reserve a spot on the next voyage, call (989) 856-2650. Fishing trips are $$$ per person, with a discount for families and seniors on weekdays. Rental fishing rods are extra ($). Call ahead for departure times to be sure. If fishing is on the docket, you'll need a Michigan state fishing license (one-day permits are available at area tackle shops; children ages 16 and younger don't need one) and a cooler for drinks. Chances are the boat's mate will help you clean for tips. If only sightseeing is available, call for sailing times and prices.**

After a quarter century of fun taking families fishing off Port Austin's rock reefs, the *Miss* is now moored in Caseville and is doing the same thing here. It's one of the best all-around family fun experiences on Lake Huron. Up to twice a day in summer, the *Miss* sails with up to twenty on board and steers a course toward fun. If the perch, walleye, or bass are in, the boat heads for the fishing grounds. If they're not, you can choose from sightseeing and sunset cruises past structures along the Lake Huron shore, as well as other cruises.

The *Miss* uses an electronic fish-finder to find perch schools. Even if you or the kids have never fished before and have no equipment, you can rent rods for the day and bait up with the minnows on board—the rest is up to you. If nothing's doing at first, the *Miss* will try several spots until the fish start biting. It's a great way to introduce children to the joys of summer on the water, the bird life that typifies the area, and something they can take pleasure from for the rest of their lives.

### Walleye Fishing (all ages)

**Call charter captain Vern Metz at (248) 634-7988 or (248) 459-1001, and he'll show you why Saginaw Bay is known nationwide for its walleye fishing.**

It's estimated that more than a million legal-size fish are finning through the waters off the town. If you don't have a boat or the expertise, Metz will take you. He fits up to six anglers per trip to introduce them to the fish, considered one of the top-tasting freshwater fish around, up close and personal. Best action, he says, runs from May through early Sept. A trip includes tackle and everything except beverages and onboard food.

## Where to Eat

**Bay Cafe.** 6750 Main St.; (989) 856-3705. Open for breakfast, lunch, and dinner. Outdoor dining in summer, with children's menu and family atmosphere. $$

**Giuseppe's Pizzeria Italian American Restaurant.** 6562 Main St. (Highway 25); (989) 856-2035. Enjoy pizza for lunch or dinner with overlooks of Caseville's harbor area. $$$

**Monette's Riverside Roadhouse.** 6540 Main St. (Highway 25); (989) 856-8606. Good food served along the river. $$

## Where to Stay

**Albert E. Sleeper State Park.** Five miles northeast of Caseville on Highway 25; (989) 856-4411. The park is open all year; however, showers and flush toilets are open only from May 1 to mid-Oct. A valid motor vehicle permit is required for use and is sold at the gate. Cost is $4 daily or $20 for an annual pass. One of the oldest and most beautiful state parks in Michigan preserves 700 acres of woods and beachfront and features a walkway over Highway 25 between the campground and the day-use-only beach area. Sleeper has 208 campsites and about 4 miles of nature trails that run through the woods, which actually are made up of old dune areas from when the lake was higher long ago. Trails also are open to cross-country skiing in winter. Unsure about camping? Sleeper and Port Crescent also feature minicabin rentals

by reservation. The cabins are wheelchair accessible and include electricity, bunk beds, and a table and chairs, as well as a grill and fire pit outside. $

**Bella Vista Inn.** 6024 Port Austin Rd. (Highway 25); (989) 856-2650; www.bella-caseville .com. This complex features 700 feet of Lake Huron beach, two outdoor pools, motel rooms, cottages, and suites. The owners also now run the *Miss Caseville* fishing boat (see listing). $$–$$$$

## For More Information

**Caseville Chamber of Commerce.** 6632 Main St., Caseville 48725; (989) 856-3818 or (800) 606-1347; www.casevillechamber.com.

# Bay City

To get to downtown Bay City, from I-75, take Business I-75 east, which becomes Highway 25. Cross the bridge and turn north on Washington, and you're in the heart of downtown. To reach the west side business district, turn north on Highway 13 from Business I-75, then east on Midland Road, and follow it there.

Lumbering and sawmills were so thick along the river in the nineteenth century that even today, when workers lay foundations for new buildings nearby, they still run into piles of sawdust several feet deep. This former rip-roaring lumber town has settled down a bit from when bars along the Saginaw River held trapdoors waiting for unsuspecting lumberjacks who'd just gotten paid and had too much to drink. Today the excitement has shifted to more legitimate action. Bay City, with its scores of Victorian-era buildings and quaint downtown, is the setting for some of the region's best special events, recreational activities, and shopping. The city's business districts are divided into east and west by the Saginaw River, and there's plenty to do on both sides.

The Bay City River Roar, a series of boat races held the third weekend of June on the Saginaw River downtown, draws more than 50,000 spectators to the shores to see hydroplanes powered by automotive engines roar around an elliptical course. A final heat determines the winner. The Fourth of July Fireworks Festival takes place on the riverfront downtown from July 2 through 4. Billed as the largest show in the region, the festival includes a Fourth of July parade. The day is capped by the **free** fireworks show over the water at dusk on July 4 before more than 175,000 pyrotechnics fans.

## Delta College Planetarium and Learning Center  (all ages)

**100 Center Ave.; (989) 667-2260; www.delta.edu/planet. On the river's east side in downtown. Head across the river on Business US 10, and then turn north on Saginaw. It's at the corner of Center and Saginaw. Showtimes vary by season and length. Check the Web site's calendar, or call for specific times. Afternoon shows are perfect for children ages 10 and younger, as the later ones are reserved for older kids. $.**

Funded by NASA, this place is a great one to introduce youngsters to stargazing of the noncelebrity kind. There's a rooftop observatory, along with a state-of-the-art planetarium, where occupants of the 130 seats can actually vote on what to see in the solar system.

## St. Laurent's Nut House  (all ages)

**1101 North Water St., on the city's east side; (989) 893-7522 or (800) 289-7688. From Business I-75, head across the bridge to Saginaw, and head north to Second, then west about a block. Open 9 a.m. to 9 p.m. Mon through Sat and 11 a.m. to 5 p.m. Sun.**

The sign outside says nuts since 1904, and it's right. Stock up on the PB part of PB&J sandwiches here, where all-natural, regular or low-sodium, smooth or crunchy peanut butter is sold in tubs of up to five pounds. Go nuts at the nuts counter, too, while the kids are inside picking out some penny candies.

# Sportfishing in the Bay

At least seven charter boats operate out of the Bay City area, in search of fish from salmon to those famous Saginaw Bay walleye. Check out the list provided by the Bay Area Convention and Visitors Bureau (see For More Information at the end of this section). If you have your own boat, there are several public boat-launch sites around Saginaw Bay, so you can follow the fish through the season. Or visit www.saginawbay.com for up-to-date fishing reports and charter info.

This section along Water Street, incidentally, was the city's most notorious area, known in the nineteenth century as "Hell's Half-Mile" by even the roughest lumberjacks.

### Bay City State Recreation Area (all ages)

Six miles north on the west side, at the end of Euclid Avenue; (989) 684-3020. To reach it from I-75, exit at Beaver Road (exit 168) and drive east 5 miles, or exit from the south at Highway 25/15 to Euclid, then turn north, and follow it to the park. Admission is by vehicle permit ($ daily or $$$ annually). Camping is $$$ nightly.

Formerly Bay City State Park, the park's name was changed because of the great variety of activities it encompasses, including camping in 264 sites and a beach on the bay. Swimmers should be watchful of zebra mussels. Brought in from Europe to the Great Lakes by passing ships, the mussels are now a nuisance in one sense but good in another, as they have cleaned the bay's water. The shells are sharp, however, so swimming is confined to a nice beach at the park's northern end, featuring the gradual slope so attractive to families with young children. The day-use area features new playground structures as well.

The park also includes the Saginaw Bay Visitors Center (989-667-0717) across the road from the day-use area, Hands-on exhibits for kids show  the importance of wetlands to the bay's health. A paved nature trail, including one with Braille signs, leads to two towers with overlooks of the 1,700-acre Tobico Marsh. Bring bug repellent if you go walking in the evening. There are 5 miles of trails in all. The wetland is considered one of the best birding spots in the state.

## Where to Eat

**Great Wall.** 805 North Euclid Ave.; (989) 667-8849. Chinese food served buffet style. $$

**The King Fish.** 1019 Water St.; (989) 894-0772. On the east bank of the Saginaw River, downtown. Great views overlooking the river. Fish is a specialty, but other items, from chicken to ribs, are also served. Children's menu and a popular Sun brunch. $$–$$$

**Mornin' Maggies Omelette Shoppe.** 819 Saginaw St.; (989) 892-3142. As the name implies, the restaurant serves innovative omelets. $–$$

**Turkey Roost.** 2270 South Huron Rd. (Highway 13), Kawkawlin; (989) 684-5200. If one serving of Thanksgiving dinner isn't enough, stop here. Serving tasty, unbelievably inexpensive turkey dinners since the 1950s, along with breakfast and lunch. Try the pies, too. $$

## Where to Stay

**Bay Valley Resort Hotel.** 2470 Old Bridge Rd.; (989) 686-3500. From I-75, exit at Highway 84 and head west about ¼ mile, and then follow the signs north. A full-service resort with a Jack Nicklaus–designed golf course, indoor-outdoor pool, and 150 rooms in a country-club-like setting. Restaurant on premises and other dining nearby. $$

**Doubletree Hotel Bay City–Riverfront.** 1 Wenonah Park Place, downtown; (989) 891-6000. This hotel has 150 guest rooms and suites, an indoor pool, and a restaurant overlooking the river. $$–$$$

**Econolodge.** 6385 West Side Saginaw Rd. (Highway 84); (989) 686-0840. At the junction of I-75 and Highway 84, on the west side of the freeway. The inn has seventy-one rooms with an outdoor pool, next to a Saginaw River tributary. $$

## For More Information

**Bay Area Convention and Visitors Bureau.** 901 Saginaw St., Bay City 48708; (989) 893-1222 or (888) 229-8696; www.tourbaycitymi.org. Also look at www.baycityarea.com.

# Freeland

Freeland, a small community along the Tittabawassee River, is the site of a ski area.

**Apple Mountain** (ages 3 and up)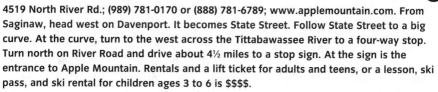

4519 North River Rd.; (989) 781-0170 or (888) 781-6789; www.applemountain.com. From Saginaw, head west on Davenport. It becomes State Street. Follow State Street to a big curve. At the curve, turn to the west across the Tittabawassee River to a four-way stop. Turn north on River Road and drive about 4½ miles to a stop sign. At the sign is the entrance to Apple Mountain. Rentals and a lift ticket for adults and teens, or a lesson, ski pass, and ski rental for children ages 3 to 6 is $$$$.

Originally built next to an apple orchard, this man-made ski hill has twelve runs with ski and snowboard equipment rental, instruction, night skiing, and other amenities.

There's golf in summer, too, plus a restaurant.

## Where to Eat and Stay

See Saginaw and Midland listings.

# Midland

The town that aspirin built has lots to offer the family, from plant tours to the arts to nature study. It has a great compact downtown along the Tittabawassee River, including a unique three-cornered bridge called the Tridge, just beyond the corner of Ashman and Main Streets.

## Midland Center for the Arts (all ages)

1801 West St. Andrews; (989) 631-5930; www.mcfta.org. From US 10, take the Eastman Road exit 2 miles into town. It's at the corner of Eastman and West St. Andrews. Open from 10 a.m. to 6 p.m. Tues through Sat, noon to 6 p.m. Sun. Closed major holidays. Admission $; call ahead for rates for events.

One of the state's first children's museums is included in the galleries. The Hall of Ideas has do-it-yourself displays, computer games, and puzzles, most of which are hands-on activities. Also included are exhibits of the Midland Historical Society, which feature local history and prehistory. The gallery features art collected from around the world.

## Dow Gardens (all ages)

Adjacent to the Midland Center for the Arts, at 1809 Eastman Ave.; (989) 631-2677; www .dowgardens.org. Open 9 a.m. to one hour before sunset. Admission is $, **free** for children 5 and younger.

More than one hundred acres of gardens include displays of rhododendrons, trees, and wildflowers. In season, 20,000 tulip bulbs and 10,000 bedding plants erupt in color along waterfalls and bridges.

## Chippewa Nature Center (all ages)

400 South Badour Rd.; (989) 631-0830; www.chippewanaturecenter.com. To reach the center, take the Business US 10 exit off US 10 and turn south onto Cronkright. Go over the bridge and then north on St. Charles, the first street past the Tittabawassee River. Watch for the sign at the Y in the road, turn left, and drive about 3 miles farther, and you'll see the entrance. The center is open Mon through Fri from 8 a.m. to 5 p.m., Sat from 9 a.m. to 5 p.m., and Sun and most holidays from 1 to 5 p.m. Admission is by donation.

At the center activities focus on humankind's interaction with the planet. One of its most popular events is the Maple Sugaring Weekend, which begins on the third Sat in Mar. Families can tour the 1,000-acre center with a naturalist and follow the process that turns watery sugar-maple sap into thick, luscious syrup in the center's Sugar Shack. Other perfect family activities include nature walks through the center's 14 miles of trails, exploring a restored 1870s farm and log school, and naturalist-led programs such as insect, reptile, and flower identification in summer.

There's a wheelchair-accessible trail as well. The Oxbow Archaeological District contains the site of a monumental territorial battle between two Native American tribes, the Ojibwa and the Sauk. The burial ground was unearthed in the 1930s.

## Pere Marquette Rail Trail (all ages)

From Midland, the trail begins at the Forks, location of the Tridge downtown, where the Chippewa River, coming from Mount Pleasant, and the Tittabawassee River, coming from the north, merge. The trail can be picked up at several parks and other sites along Old US 10. For information, contact the Midland County Department of Parks and Recreation, (989) 832-6870; www.midlandcounty.org, then click on the drop-down "department links" list to find parks and rec. Or contact the Midland City Parks and Recreation, (989) 835-9071; www.midland-mi .org, and look under "services." The city also has a network of mountain biking trails. **Free.**

Grab your bike or in-line skates or just walk a part or all of this 22-mile-long trail, which follows the old Pere Marquette Railroad right-of-way between Midland and Coleman and, eventually, all the way to Clare and even beyond. The paved portion runs between Midland and Coleman along Old US 10, through parks, and over rivers like the Tittabawassee and the Salt, the stream favored by Native Americans for its salt deposits, which supposedly gave Herbert Dow the idea for his operations. It crosses three old railroad trestles. Maps are available from the Midland County Convention and Visitors Bureau (see For More Information at the end of this section). Traversing woods and farmland is a great way to explore the diversity of mid-Michigan.

## Great Lakes Loons  (all ages)

**The Loons play each summer at Dow Diamond downtown, named the best new ballpark when it opened in 2007. Just follow the signs along Business US 10 to 825 East Main St., (989) 837-2255, or (888) 678-2255; www.loons.com.**

Midland and the rest of eastern mid-Michigan have gone looney over the state's newest minor league baseball team. Playing in its new stadium downtown, the Great Lakes Loons host teams from the Midwest League. The Los Angeles Dodgers affiliate team plays seventy games at home.

## Where to Eat

**Bamboo Garden.** 2600 North Saginaw Rd.; (989) 832-7967. From US 10, exit at Eastman Road and head 1 mile south and ½ mile west on Saginaw Road. Very good Chinese food, specializing in spicy Szechuan and Shanghai cuisine for lunch and dinner. Children's menu. $$

**Damon's Place for Ribs.** 6801 Eastman Rd.; (989) 837-7427. From US 10, exit at Eastman. Sports atmosphere, with ribs a specialty for lunch and dinner. $$

**Grand Traverse Pie Company.** 2600 North Saginaw Rd.; (989) 839-4872. Open 7 a.m. to 9 p.m. Mon through Thurs, 7 a.m. to 10 p.m. Fri, 8 a.m. to 10 p.m. Sat, and 9 a.m. to 9 p.m. Sun. Great potpies and well-made sandwiches, along with fresh-baked cream and fruit pies. $

**Pizza Sam's.** Corner of Ashman and Main, downtown; (989) 631-1934. Pizza, sandwiches, and more in a family atmosphere for lunch and dinner. $$

## Where to Stay

**Best Western Valley Plaza Resort.** 5221 Bay City Rd.; (989) 496-2700 or (800) 825-2700. From westbound US 10, take the Midland/Bay City Road exit. From eastbound US 10, exit at Waldo Road. Head 2½ miles south on Waldo to Bay City Road, then turn east, and go about a mile. The resort has 236 rooms with three indoor pools, even a beach and lake for summer swimming, plus bowling alley and billiards, four restaurants, exercise area, and movie theater. $$

**Fairview Inn.** 2200 West Wackerly Rd.; (989) 631-0070 or (800) 422-2744. From US 10, take the Eastman Road exit south to Wackerly, and then head west. The inn has ninety-four rooms, indoor pool, and hot tub. Restaurants nearby. $$

**H Hotel.** 111 West Main St., near downtown's "Tridge" bridge; (800) 282-7778. One hundred thirty-one guest rooms with indoor pool, wireless Internet, and two restaurants. $$$

**Holiday Inn of Midland.** 1500 West Wackerly; (989) 631-4220. From US 10, take the Eastman Road exit south to Wackerly, and then head west. The property has 235 rooms, with indoor pool and recreation area, racquetball courts, and restaurant. $$

## For More Information

**Midland County Convention and Visitors Bureau.** 300 Rodd St., Midland 48640; (888) 464-3526, ext. 2; www.midlandcvb.org.

# Alma

Alma, north of Lansing along US 27, is a small town that up to the early 1900s lived in relative obscurity. As a by-product of drilling brine wells for Midland's Dow Chemical, oil was discovered in the area, and the town became a refinery site.

It's also the site of Alma College, founded by the Presbyterian Church in 1887.

## Alma Highland Festival and Games (all ages)

To get to the festival area, take the Alma exit downtown to the Alma College campus. For more information on the event and other Alma activities, call the area chamber of commerce at (989) 463-8979; www.almahighlandfestival.com. Festival hours are 8 a.m. to 9 p.m. on Sat and Sun. Admission varies by day of events ($$–$$$), with special events costing more. Children ages 5 and younger are admitted **free.**

At this annual late-May festival, you can show your kids that yes, Scotsmen really do wear kilts, even when they compete in contests such as the caber and stone toss—old training techniques dating from the times when the English would not let the Scots have weapons. In these contests of strength and skill, competitors see how far they can flip a piece of wood the size of a telephone pole, and how far they can push a heavy chunk of rock (sizes vary according to class). Scottish-style food, dancing demonstrations and contests, and lots of bagpipe music prevail the entire weekend, as does other fun, including sheepherding demonstrations and arts-and-crafts sales.

Since this is a small town, accommodations around the area fill fast, with some visitors even heading for dorm rooms here and at Mount Pleasant's Central Michigan University, so plan ahead if you intend to attend.

## Where to Eat

**Elias Brothers Big Boy.** 7990 North Alger Rd.; (989) 463-5039. Open Sun through Thurs 6 a.m. to midnight, Fri and Sat 6 a.m. to 1 a.m. Family fare from salad bar to triple-decker burgers. $$

## Where to Stay

**Alma Comfortable Inn.** 3130 Monroe Rd.; (989) 463-4400. The inn has eighty-five rooms with indoor pool. Restaurant nearby. $$

## For More Information

**Gratiot Area Chamber of Commerce.** 110 West Superior, Alma 48801; (989) 463-5525; www.gratiot.org.

## Michi-fact:

Just to the north of Alma, St. Louis is the geographical center of the state, marked by a historical plaque.

# Mount Pleasant

Just to the north of Alma on US 127, Mount Pleasant may not be on much of a mountain, but it is home to Central Michigan University and one of the largest gaming casinos east of the Mississippi, a few miles from where Amish farmers and craftspeople ply their wares to tourists, from baked goods out of a farm kitchen to hand-worked oak furniture and quilts.

Such is the dichotomy here today, and the choice facing tourists, who once would only gas up on their way farther north. Golfers also will find some of the state's best public courses here, scattered along the Chippewa River.

### Museum of Cultural and Natural History  (all ages)

**On the Central Michigan University campus in Rowe Hall, at the corner of East Bellows and Mission Street (Business US 127); (989) 774-3829; www.museum.cmich.edu. Open from 8 a.m. to 5 p.m. Mon through Fri. Admission is free.**

It may not be the largest museum you've ever gone through, but it is one of the most interesting. Located inside a classroom building on campus, the museum explores Michigan's natural history through artifacts and fossils. One room focuses entirely on Native Americans of the Great Lakes, ending in the Native American Gallery, where wonderful contemporary works of art are displayed.

### Chippewa River Canoeing  (all ages)

**Offered by Chippewa River Outfitters in Mount Pleasant; (989) 772-5474 or (888) 775-6077; www.chipoutfitters.com. From US 127 northbound, turn onto Mission Road/Business US 127. Turn west on Bloomfield Road to Lincoln, and then turn north about ¼ mile to the store. From US 127 South, exit at Pickard Road and go west to Lincoln, then south about 1¾ miles. Open May through Oct with reservations. Trip durations range from one to six hours. $$$–$$$$.**

Roll—or in this case, paddle—on the river for one hour or more, or take an overnight trip on this section of the "Chip." There are no rapids, so bring along an inner tube (also available for rent). It's a great, relaxing float.

## Where to Eat

You won't run out of choices here, from family food to fine dining. Here are a few of the city's more than forty restaurants:

**Blue Gator.** 106 Court St.; (989) 772-5456. Cajun food served in a fun, sports pub atmosphere. Children's menu. $$

**Jon's Drive-In.** 1030 South Mission St., off the CMU campus; (989) 773-9172. Treat the kids to a real drive-in like you used to enjoy, right down to the burgers and malts. $

**Mountain Town Station.** 506 West Broadway St.; (989) 775-2337; www.mountaintown .com. Located in a historic train station. Famous for its ribs and handcrafted beers and root beer. Children's menu. Dinner train, too. $$–$$$

## Where to Stay

**Fairfield Inn by Marriott.** 2525 South University Park, next to CMU off Mission Street; (989) 775-5000. Marriott quality for the family budget. The inn has seventy-four rooms, indoor pool, and whirlpool. Restaurant and recreation nearby. $$

**Shardi's Hide-Away Campground.** 340 North Loomis Rd.; (989) 773-4268. From Mount Pleasant, head east on Highway 20, then north on North Loomis Road. Campground has 102 sites, pool, playground, and on-site cabin rentals year-round. $

**Soaring Eagle Convention Center.** 5665 East Pickard St.; US 127 and Highway 20; (989) 772-2905. Connected by name to the nearby casino, this inn has 184 rooms with indoor and outdoor pools, restaurant, tennis, and two eighteen-hole golf courses. Courseside accommodations available. $$

# "Pleasant" Fests

The city puts on lots of different faces throughout the year, many of them family oriented. Admission is charged for most and varies by year. Call the convention and visitors bureau (see For More Information above) for information. Here is a sampling of these activities:

- **Mount Pleasant Summer Festival.** Takes place in mid-June, with fun such as a custom-car show, carnival, music all day, and evening fireworks.

- **Co-Expo World Championship Rodeo.** Takes place the third weekend in June at the Isabella County Fairgrounds, reached by taking tthe Highway 20 exit west off US 127 and then going west on Pickard to Mission; turn north onto Mission, then west onto Old Mission, which leads to the grounds. Cowpokes from across North America come to compete and rack up points in hopes of being recognized as the world's best in events from bull riding to barrel racing.

- **Little Elk's Retreat Indian Powwow.** Takes place the first weekend in Aug on the Chippewa Indian Reservation. Authentic foods, crafts, arts, colorful dancing, and storytelling.

**Soaring Eagle Hotel.** On the Chippewa Indian Reservation, adjacent to the Soaring Eagle casino; (989) 775-7777; www.soaringeaglecasino.com. From US 127, head east 1½ miles on Highway 20 and south on Leaton Road. The hotel has 512 rooms, pool, exercise area, restaurant, cafeteria and deli, and children's programs. $$

## For More Information

**Mount Pleasant Area Convention and Visitors Bureau.** 114 East Broadway St., Mount Pleasant 48858; (888) 772-2022; www .mountpleasantwow.com.

# Clare

This town is just north of Mount Pleasant, about 15 miles off US 127. For decades Clare, named for County Clare in Ireland, was known to travelers as "The Place Where the North Begins," so much that the town adopted the slogan. And it does, as pines and hardwoods envelop the roadsides a few miles north of town.

A few years ago, Amish from Pennsylvania liked the area's low land prices and began moving in. Now, locals hardly take notice of the black buggies parked outside the local supermarket, which has built a spot just for the horses. The Amish residents have prospered not only through their farming but with their craftsmanship as well. A map that features locations of Amish businesses is available from the Clare Chamber of Commerce downtown on Business US 127, just north of the main stoplight. On typical summer weekends, just south of the US 127 freeway overpass, local Amish gather to sell beautifully handcrafted quilts in all colors of the rainbow.

### Yoder's Amish Quilt Auction at Yoder's Farm  (all ages)

**Takes place mid-May and around Labor Day. For more information, call (800) 233-1359; www.clarecounty.com, or also www.claremi.com. To avoid the limited parking at the farm, pick up the free shuttle from downtown at the Doherty Hotel, Carousel Mall, and Big Boy restaurant.**

This annual event gives the family an opportunity to take in a real Amish farm and bid on 300 to 500 handmade quilts made in the area by the Amish. Amish baked goods, food, furniture, and crafts are also for sale. The event takes place Fri and Sat only. Get a map from the convention and visitors bureau (see For More Information) at other times of the year to visit farms where items such as handmade oak furniture are sold.

### Benchley's Amish Furniture and Gifts  (all ages)

**9425 Tobacco Dr.; (989) 386-7951; www.benchleysfurniture.com. From Clare, go east on US 10 to North Loomis Road and follow the signs.**

If you don't have time to track down the area's individual Amish stores, come here for great cherry and oak Amish-made furniture for everything from kids' rooms to entertainment centers and the office.

# Favorite Events in East Michigan—North

- **Tip-Up Town USA** (Jan), downtown Houghton Lake and Prudenville, (989) 366-5644 or (800) 676-5330

- **St. Patrick's Day Parade** (Mar), Bay City, (989) 684-7980

- **Irish Festival** (Mar), downtown Clare, (989) 386-2442

- **Maple Syrup Festival** (Apr), Shepherd, south of Mount Pleasant, (989) 828-5726

- **Michlimackinac Pageant** (Memorial Day weekend), Michlimackinac State Park, Mackinaw City, (231) 436-4100

- **Free** fishing weekend on all Michigan Great Lakes and inland waters (June and Feb, usually first full weekends), (989) 373-2842. No license needed this weekend only

- **Corn Festival** (July), Auburn, (800) 424-5114

- **Bluegill Festival** (July), St. Helen, (989) 389-3725

- **Tawas Bay Waterfront Fine Art Festival and Children's Art Fair** (Aug), Tawas City, (800) 559-8292

- **Bay Port Fish Sandwich Festival in Bay Port,** (989) 551-9929 and Teaseburger in Caseville, (800) 606-1347 (Aug)

- **Fall Art Fair** (Sept), Midland, (989) 662-4357

- **Great Lakes Lighthouse Festival** (Oct), Alpena, (800) 425-7362

- **Festival of Lights** (Nov), Bay City, (888) 229-8696

- **Holiday Walk** (Dec), Flint Cultural Center, (810) 760-1169

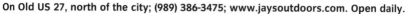

## Jay's Sporting Goods  (all ages)

On Old US 27, north of the city; **(989) 386-3475; www.jaysoutdoors.com. Open daily.**

A sportsman's paradise, Jay's is one of the largest stores of its kind in the Midwest. Here you can be outfitted for the woods or waters from the cap down.

## Where to Eat

**Clare City Bakery.** 521 McEwan; (989) 386-2241. Lunch items and baked goods served. $

**Doherty Hotel.** 604 McEwan; (989) 386-3441. Located downtown. Great food, including special holiday buffets, breakfast, lunch, and dinner. Children's menu. $$

**The White House.** 613 McEwan (Business US 127); (989) 386-9551. This tiny diner is a city institution for breakfast. It's open twenty-four hours a day, and breakfast is served anytime. $

## Where to Stay

**Doherty Motor Hotel.** Corner of Old US 10 and US 127; (989) 386-3441. Here you'll find ninety-two hotel- and motel-style rooms, indoor pool, whirlpool, golf and ski packages. Pets OK. There is a restaurant on the premises. $$

**Econolodge Clare.** 10318 South Clare Ave., just off US 127; (877) 282-5273. This hotel has ninety-six rooms with kitchens, indoor pool, and complimentary breakfast. $$–$$$

## For More Information

**Clare County Convention and Visitors Bureau.** P.O. Box 226, Clare 48617; (800) 233-1359; www.clarecounty.com or www.claremi.com. The CVB shares quarters with the Clare Chamber of Commerce, at 429 North McEwan, Clare 48617; (989) 386-2422; www.claremichigan.com.

# Lake

Along US 10 west of Clare, this small resort community is in the midst of a fast-growing area for retiring baby boomers because of its lakes. The tiny downtown was formerly a stop on a passenger rail line that ran across central Michigan. Snowmobilers now use the trail, which eventually may be linked with a paved trail in Midland.

### Big Al's Restaurant (all ages)

In downtown Lake on Mystic Lake Road, 1 block south of US 10; (989) 544-3502. Open 11 a.m. to 10 p.m. daily. $$

"Big Al" Kuebler, a former Elvis impersonator, may even belt out a tune, or at least a few notes, as you enjoy his good, inexpensive fare for lunch and dinner, from fish to burgers. Elvis memorabilia and black velvet paintings decorate the walls.

## Where to Stay

See Clare listings.

# Linwood

This small town is located on the shore of Lake Huron. From I-75, take Highway 13 north at Bay City.

### National Pickle Festival (all ages)

Takes place annually the third weekend of Aug in downtown Linwood, east of Highway 13 at the stoplight. Call (989) 697-5825 for information.

I know, now you've heard everything. But there really is a reason. The extensive farm fields around Linwood, a few miles north of Bay City, still produce truckloads of pickling cucumbers each summer, so why not a festival? Pickle companies bring in trucks full of fresh pickles. A button ($) gets you into the entertainment tent and a chance to win, yes, a jar of pickles. The Sat pickle parade on Center Street through this tiny town features a 6-foot-tall float topped with Petunia Pickle and eighty to one hundred other parade units. On Sun it's the kids' turn, with a bike parade and small floats, and there's plenty of food, carnival games, and other small-town craziness, just for the fun of it.

### Williams Cheese Company (all ages)

**998 North Huron Rd. (Highway 13), south of Deer Acres; (800) 968-4492; www.williams cheese.com. Hours are 8 a.m. to 6 p.m. Mon through Thurs and Sat, 8 a.m. to 7 p.m. Fri, and 10 a.m. to 6 p.m. Sun. Admission is free.**

The company produces eighty varieties of cheese and sells more than 180 types, many at a discount, at the store in front of its cheese-making plant.

## Where to Eat and Stay

See Bay City listings.

# Pinconning

This east Michigan town may be nicknamed "Michigan's Cheese Capital" because its factories produce the cheddarlike Pinconning cheese, but there's nothing cheesy about its attractions.

### Deer Acres (all ages)

**2346 Highway 13; (989) 879-2849; www.deeracres.com. From I-75 take exit 164 at Kawkaw-lin and go north on Highway 13 for about 10 miles. Open daily early May through Labor Day, from 10 a.m. to 6 p.m. weekdays, 10 a.m. to 7 p.m. weekends, and after Labor Day until Oct 15 on weekends only from 10 a.m. to 6 p.m. Admission $$, rides $.**

Since 1959 this attraction, painted a bright chartreuse and located on the east side of Highway 13, has attracted an average of 40,000 families each summer. Kids love to hand-feed the herds of deer—and the deer love the attention, too. The deer have learned to come running when they hear the sound of the food dispensers clicking all over the park. In Story Book Village kids can meet all their favorite Mother Goose and other storybook characters, like Peter Pumpkin and Jack, the beanstalk-climbing giant killer. Pack a lunch and use the grills and picnic tables, or head for the snack shop. Five amusement rides include a narrated trip past storybook characters and animals from llamas to monkeys, with signs explaining how and where they live in the wild, and a narrated ½-mile-long miniature train excursion. New owners have added go-karts, bumper boats, a cafe, and other attractions in addition to the four-footed residents.

## Where to Eat and Stay

See Bay City listings.

# Au Gres

Long considered the gateway to the Sunrise Side's beaches and resort towns, this city was named after the nearby point jutting into Lake Huron, which in turn was named by French explorers for its stony makeup. Today it's a pleasure-boat port city, with a new twist: island hopping.

### Charity Island Boat Cruises (ages 8 and up)

3660 East Huron Rd. (US 23); (989) 876-8929; www.charityisland.net. Birding tours run late Apr through mid-May and dinner cruises run June to mid-Oct. Dinner tickets are $$$$. Birding tours are $$$$.

Climb aboard one of two forty-eight-passenger Coast Guard–approved vessels and come on a five-hour journey to Charity Island, about 11 miles from port. The island's waters are renowned for walleye and perch fishing, and now for dinner tours. During the one-hour ride to the island, there's a narrated history of Saginaw Bay and the area. Upon landing you'll receive a forty-five-minute talk on the history of the island in a pavilion. Then walk ¼ mile through woods (bring bug repellant), to the light keeper's home to learn about it and the 1857 light tower attached. Enjoy a dinner of Great Lakes perch or tenderloin steak tips, and then return to the mainland. The island is an amazing stopover for migratory birds in spring and fall, hence the birding tours, and at least two pairs of eagles have made nests on the island.

## Where to Eat

See Tawas City–East Tawas listings.

## Where to Stay

**Whitestone Pointe Cabins.** 5883 South Lake Lane Dr.; (989) 876-2775 or (866) 820-6414; www.whitestonepointecabins.com. Take US 23 north from Au Gres about 8 miles and turn right onto South Lake Lane. Five cozy two-bedroom cabins including two beachfront. All bedding provided, plus volleyball and fire pit, plus swim tubes for kids and other beach toys. Arts and crafts for kids, too. Just bring a beach towel! Canoeing and golf are nearby as is Lake Huron fishing. $$

Also see Tawas City–East Tawas.

# Tawas City and East Tawas

This community used to be the quintessential tourist town that buzzed with activity in summer and curled up by the fire for winter. Not so anymore. Summer is still a busy season, but nowadays winter also finds folks out on the trails, either snowmobiling or cross-country skiing. Many of the resort cabins and motels that used to shut down for winter are staying open. Until recently this was strictly a mom-and-pop resort town, but that's changed, too, with a beachfront hotel. Tawas Bay and Lake Huron are very good producers of walleye, perch, salmon, and lake trout. Check with the Tawas Area Chamber of Commerce (see For More Information at the end of this section) for a list of current charter-boat operators. A Michigan fishing license is required for those ages sixteen and older. Tawas City and East Tawas are next to each other along US 23.

### Corsair Ski Area (all ages)

**218 West Bay St., East Tawas; (989) 362-2001; www.skinordic.org. The cross-country ski trails are in Silver Valley, about 8 miles outside town along Monument Road. From US 23, turn west on Highway 55 to Wilber Road. Follow it to Monument Road. Follow it about 7 miles to the Silver Valley and watch for the parking lot signs. Trails are free, but because it costs money to groom routes and maintain equipment (a single pass through the Corsair trail system requires twelve hours of machine operation), skiers are expected to drop something into the donation tubes at the trailhead.**

When winter comes to the dense Huron National Forest, about 6 miles outside the twin cities of Tawas City and East Tawas, it signals an entirely new season of family fun. Some 35 miles of trails on both sides of Monument Road are rated among the best in the country. They beckon cross-country ski enthusiasts of all ability levels to the series of looping courses that always begin and end at the three large parking areas. Beginners can take always-groomed, mostly flat trails that wind through the dense woods around trout-filled Silver Creek, while intermediates and advanced types can be

# Summer on **the Water**

From the time I was young, my family vacationed along the shores of Lake Huron and Tawas Bay. Long mornings were spent soaking in the odors of creosote and minnows of the perch anglers along the boardwalk dock at East Tawas. I can still remember those moonlit nights on board the old *Miss East Tawas* perch party boat, when the captain would place lights along the side of the boat to attract the fish, and we'd always come back with pails full of yellowbellies, as they're nicknamed, which we caught when we weren't munching on candy bars, untangling fishing lines, and watching the Tawas Point Lighthouse guide boats safely by the shallow waters.

Long summer days were spent diving into the clear, cold lake with my cousin, interspersed with trips to the minigolf course at neighboring Oscoda or picnicking at the lakefront. We wouldn't have stayed in fancy condos then even if there were any—we didn't have to spend lavishly to have a good time—and had a grand time at a simple resort cottage. Do yourself and your family a favor and experience this kind of vacation, too. While condos are popping up like mushrooms and shutting out the views along parts of Tawas Bay, there are plenty of other places to savor the joys of a cottage vacation on this side of the state. You owe it to your family to try it before they're gone. It's the stuff of which memories are made.

# Falling for Michigan

Hardwoods represent more than 75 percent of Michigan's 18.1 million acres of forest. And that makes the state simply spectacular when the aspen, ash, maple, and oak show what many think is their best sides come fall. The state is ablaze in color from mid-Sept through Oct, and to help you make the best of it, there are many designated fall color routes available to your family, whether you're on foot, in the family van, or on a bike. The state has weekly fall color reports, and local visitor bureaus will tell you where the best viewing is as well. As the commercial says, your trip begins at www .michigan.org.

challenged by some pretty hilly terrain with some mean curves thrown in. Young non-skiers can be towed behind in a sled.

In summer the area doubles as a great picnic and hiking spot, and a place where kids with an inexpensive fishing rod and a can of worms might have some luck catching a few brook trout in Silver Creek. Hunters walk the river valley in fall.

Gary Nelkie, owner of East Tawas's Nordic Sports shop (www.n-sport.com), can outfit your family in inexpensive rental cross-country skis and boots and will start you off with an in-store lesson ($$$) if you ask.

## Perchville USA  (all ages)

This annual festival takes place on the ice and at shore sites the first weekend of Feb. Call (800) 55-TAWAS; www.tawas.com. You can combine skiing at Corsair with this festival on the ice at East Tawas.

Some 15,000 people stroll about for fun, and many go after the schools of perch swimming underneath the bay ice. Fishing contests, arts and crafts, and a traditional demolition derby on the ice fill out the roster of events for one of the oldest winter carnivals in the state, which celebrated its fiftieth anniversary at the millennium.

One of the festival's most amusing events takes place near the state's longest wooden dock. A few hardy and normally responsible souls, who might have been cooped up in their cabins a mite too long, jump into frigid Lake Huron through a hole chopped in the ice during the Polar Bear Swim. Other events include frozen softball and children's games, plus a Fri-night, all-you-can-eat perch dinner.

## Hubie's Wondergolf  (all ages)

At 1909 East Huron (US 23), East Tawas; (989) 362-8050. Open Memorial Day through Labor Day, 10 a.m. to 10 p.m. daily. $.

The course here has eighteen holes of minigolf, with streams, waterfalls, and flowers.

A fudge shop awaits at the nineteenth hole.

### Tawas Bay Bicycle Pathway   (all ages)

**Extends from Tawas Point State Park to Alabaster; (800) 558-2927. Free.**

When you visit the Tawases, bring your bikes to pedal this great lakefront pathway extending from Tawas Point State Park to Alabaster, a small community to the south. Totaling more than 10 miles, it passes sites including a gypsum loading dock.

## Where to Eat

**Big Boy.** 1222 North US 23, East Tawas, at the north end of town; (989) 362-4403. Known for its burgers and buffet, it's a good, inexpensive family place. $

**G's Pizzeria.** 115 East Bay St., opposite the East Tawas pier; (989) 362-5946. Very good pizza and other Italian items, plus sandwiches. $$

**Marion's Dairy Bar.** 111 East Bay, East Tawas; (989) 362-2991. An old-fashioned ice cream parlor with cones, malts, and sundaes in thirty-two flavors. Open Mon through Sat 11 a.m. to 11 p.m., Sun noon to 11 p.m. $

## Where to Stay

There are scores of places to stay here along the beach, from old-time cottages and resorts (both south and north of both cities) to motels and small resorts in town.

Most resorts rent by the week and fill quickly before summer, but occasionally nightly rentals are available. If you're coming up for a week, it's a good idea to drive up in spring to check out a resort to see if it's to your liking.

**Bambi Motel.** 1100 East Bay (US 23), East Tawas; (989) 362-4582. A basic property with fifteen lakeside units. $

**Bayview Resort.** 1047 Bay, Tawas City; (989) 362-4361. Eight cottages on Tawas Bay with sand beach. $$

**East Tawas City Park.** Along US 23 at the foot of Newman Street, East Tawas; (989) 362-5562. When the state park moved to the point, the city moved into this ready-made facility. It has 174 paved campsites, with ¼ mile of sandy beach, playground, even seasonal cable TV. $

**Stoney Shores Resort.** 111 North Baldwin Resort Rd., East Tawas; (989) 362-4609. Located on Lake Huron north of town off US 23. Four cottages on the beach that usually rent by the week in summer. $$

**Tawas Bay Beach Resort.** 300 East Bay (US 23), East Tawas; (989) 362-8601. This property has 103 rooms, an indoor pool, and a 900-foot beach on the bay with great swimming. Within walking distance of downtown East Tawas's shops and movie theater, with dining. $$

**Tawas Point State Park.** At the tip of Tawas Point; (989) 362-5041 or, for reservations, (800) 447-2757. From East Tawas, take US 23 north, then jog onto Tawas Beach Road and follow it to the end. A daily ($) or annual ($$$) permit is required for vehicle entry. Camping is extra. In summer, take the family to the beach at Tawas Point, about 4 miles north of the twin cities, where you'll also find a working lighthouse, 205 very popular sandy campsites, and two minicabins with rustic accommodations. A nature trail heads to the point and is popular with birders, especially during migration times. The park, in fact, is rated one of the nation's top spots for migration watching in May. Campers have a choice of swimming in Lake Huron or warmer Tawas Bay. As the guide brochure to the hike of Sandy Hook Nature Trail explains, don't worry if the beach may look oily here and there. The dark substance is actually magnetite, iron oxide. Campers can hike past the lighthouse that's been here since 1876. Tawas Point Celebration Days, held the second weekend of June, offers family activities, arts and crafts, a fishing derby, guided hikes, and more. $

**Wooded Acres Resort.** 968 North US 23, East Tawas, 5 miles north of town; (989)

362-5188. Fourteen cottages on Lake Huron, some with fireplaces. $$

## For More Information

**Tawas Area Chamber of Commerce.** 402 East Lake St. (US 23), Tawas 48764; (989) 362-8643 or (800) 558-2927; www.tawas.com.

# Oscoda

Only 15 miles up US 23 from Tawas City and East Tawas, this beachside town offers more summer fun. The city's population grows each summer as vacationers come up to enjoy both the nearby inland lakes and Lake Huron's great sandy beaches.

Charter boats usually leave from marinas around the mouth of the Au Sable River at Bunyan Town Marina; (989) 739-2371; www.bunyantownmarina.com. The local convention and visitor bureau Web site (see For More Information) has several boats listed. The marina is near the mouth of the Au Sable River, and boats fish Lake Huron for walleye, salmon, and lake trout. Canoeing is also available.

**Three Mile Beach Park**  (all ages)
**Along US 23, about 3 miles north of town; (800) 235-4625. The park closes at 10 p.m. daily.
Free.**

A unique roadside park that includes not only a great sandy beach but a bit of nature, too. Birders head for this picnic area to watch migrating waterfowl. Wildflowers also are prevalent among the beach sands.

## Au Sable River Road National Forest Scenic Byway

Head west out of Oscoda by turning from US 23 onto River Road in the center of town. The twentieth highway in the nation to be designated a scenic byway, the Au Sable River Road National Forest Scenic Byway runs 22 miles through the Huron National Forest, on River Road and Highway 65 along the south bank of the Au Sable River, where more attractions await. For more information on byway attractions, call (989) 362-4477, (989) 739-0728, or (800) 821-6263, or go to www.oscoda.com and look under "attractions."

### *Au Sable River Queen*  (all ages)

Board at Foote Dam Pond, just upstream of Foote Site Village; (989) 739-7351; www .ausableriverqueen.net. The boats run from Memorial Day weekend through the third weekend in Oct. Times vary, so call ahead. Teens and adults $$$, ages 5 to 12 $ (for the fall color tours). Children ages 4 and under ride free, except on color tour weekends. There's also a 10 percent discount for seniors except on fall-color-season weekend trips.

Board an authentic paddle wheeler for a lazy trip through the impoundment on the river. The boat has been touring this section of river for more than forty years. The 19-mile narrated trips run about two hours. Follow the captain's running commentary about the river's history and wildlife. The area is especially beautiful and popular in fall—reservations are required for fall trips—but a trip is a wonderful, relaxing journey anytime.

### Iargo Springs  (all ages)

Along the Au Sable River Road Scenic Byway, about 15 miles west of town; (800) 235-4625; www.ausablerivermichigan.com, look under "sightseeing." Open daily, year-round. Free.

Kids and adults with stamina love to take the 227 steps down the high banks to a naturally flowing spring that Chippewa tribe members once used to quench their thirst. They also held ceremonies at the spring, which they believed had curative abilities. There's a walkway around the spring so the area won't be disturbed.

There are more platforms over Cooke Dam Pond. To help you catch your breath on the way down, and especially on the way back up, there are viewing benches. The water flows at a near-constant temperature of around fifty degrees.

### Wurtsmith Aviation Museum Yankee Air Force  (all ages)

3961 East Airport Dr.; (989) 739-7555; www.wurtsmith-yaf-museum.org. Open 11 a.m. to 3 p.m. May to Sept. $.

This is the northern wing of Ypsilanti's Yankee Air Force (see listing). See restored aircraft as well as others being restored.

## Where to Eat

**Au Sable Inn.** 100 South State St. (US 23), downtown; (989) 747-0350. Steaks, fish, and prime rib as well as sandwiches. Children's menu. $–$$$$

**Desi's Taco Lounge.** 1945 West River Rd.; (989) 739-7856. At Foote Site Village, about 6 miles west of Oscoda on River Road. Desi's has been here serving traditional Mexican meals—and American items such as burgers, chicken, and seafood—for more than twenty years. Serves breakfast, lunch, and dinner. $$

# Oscoda Annual Events and Festivals

- **Art on the Beach.** Takes place the last weekend of June at Oscoda Beach Park, at the east end of River Road. Turn east at the stoplight to the park.

- **Au Sable River International Canoe Marathon.** Runs the last full weekend of July from Grayling to Oscoda, a distance of 120 miles. They say it's "the world's toughest spectator sport." It's unknown if that's because it's tough on the spectators to follow the canoeists downstream, or because it is so wearing on the participants that many collapse and have to be lifted from their canoes at the end of the race in Oscoda. In both cases it takes dedicated spectators to follow their favorites downstream. Best places to view the race include bridges crossing the river east of Grayling, at the finish in downtown Oscoda, and the dams upstream from Oscoda (as the by-now bedraggled racers drag their canoes up and over the structures, then hop back in to continue paddling in their special racing canoes with oversize paddles). There's a hospitality tent near the finish line with refreshments, entertainment, and more. The race takes fourteen hours, starting at dusk in Grayling and running through the night until the teams finally make it to Oscoda the next afternoon.

**Wiltse's Brew Pub and Family Restaurant.** 5606 North County Road F-41; (989) 739-2231. From US 23, take F-41 northwest about 1 mile. Chicken and steak cut to order and brewed-on-premises beers for those ages twenty-one and older to sample. House-made root beer is also available. Children's menu, too. Breakfast, lunch, and dinner. $$

## Where to Stay

This resort town has scores of beachfront and woodsy choices, from motels to cottage resorts on both Lake Huron and nearby inland lakes.

**Monument Campground.** Just east of Lumberman's Monument on River Road; (989) 362-4477. This spot offers twenty sites with rustic camping. $

**Old Orchard Park.** Along River Road, on Foote Dam Pond, just west of Foote Site

Village; (989) 739-7814. Michigan's largest county campground has 500 campsites, many with water, including showers, and electricity. Rustic tent sites available, too. Located on the backwaters of Foote Dam, one of six hydroelectric dams on this stretch of river.$

**Oscoda KOA.** 3591 Forest Rd.; (989) 739-5115. Off US 23, about 1½ miles south of town and ¾ mile west on Johnson Road, 1 mile south on Forest Road. This campground has 143 sites with hookups available as well as tent sites and a fishing pond. $

**Rest All Inn.** 4270 North US 23, 1½ miles south of the city; (989) 739-8822. The inn has seventy-four rooms on Lake Huron with indoor pool and continental breakfast. Restaurant nearby. $$

**Sandy Beach Cottages.** 7462 North US 23; (941) 855-0077. About 5 miles north of downtown Oscoda along the lake, this family-owned cottage group hosts guests mid-May through mid-Sept, with five Lake Huron beachfront cottages sleeping up to six. $$$$

**Oscoda-AuSable Chamber of Commerce.** (800) 235-4625; www.oscoda chamber.com.

## For More Information

**Oscoda Area Convention and Visitors Bureau.** 4440 North US 23, Oscoda 48750; (877) 867-2632; www.oscoda.com.

# Houghton Lake

This community is located near the intersections of two of the state's major north-south routes, I-75 and US 27. With more than thirty-one square miles of surface, Houghton Lake is Michigan's largest inland body of water. Along its edges the side-by-side towns of Houghton Lake and Prudenville have been family vacation destinations for decades, and resorts, motels, and cottages practically encircle the lake. There are plenty of things to do when you're not at the beach, too, like go-kart rides and miniature and full-size golf.

Houghton Lake is one of the best places to take your family fishing. The lake abounds with panfish, pike, and walleye, with some of the best places to fish near shore, such as wild-rice weed beds. In addition, the Muskegon River, which begins on the lake's western shore, enters Reedsburg dam impoundment, also a good spot for anglers.

### Pines Theatre (all ages)

**4673 West Houghton Lake Rd. (Highway 55); (989) 366-9226; www.pinestheater.com. Two shows nightly from Memorial Day weekend through Labor Day. One show nightly after Labor Day to Memorial Day weekend. $.**

Be sure to take in a film in what is perhaps Michigan's most unusual movie theater. A handsome local landmark since 1941, it's Michigan's only movie house constructed completely of western Douglas fir logs. Inside the lobby are stuffed examples of Michigan wildlife, including deer, duck, and pheasant. Movie buffs will find such memorabilia as

## Tip-Up Town

The fun doesn't stop in winter. Snow sculptures, ice-fishing contests, snowmobiling, and a frosty parade make up the annual winter carnival that draws upwards of 60,000 people to the Houghton Lake area during the last two full weekends in Jan. The event is named for a particular type of ice-fishing rod that tips up when a fish bites and has been a winter fixture here since 1950.

# Scenic **Drives**

You've come to the right place for leisurely drives through the woods and exploring small communities. Try these on for size if you're looking for something to do. Old US 27, the same highway that cuts through Clare, Mount Pleasant, and Lansing, among other cities listed earlier in this chapter, also runs along the western edge of Houghton Lake. It's a wonderful two-lane road that is forsaken by most travelers using the US 127 freeway to the west or I-75 to the east. It edges both Houghton and Higgins Lakes, heads through wild scenic woodlands both north and south of town, and goes past public access points on both Houghton and Higgins Lakes that it seems only locals know about. And with state highway construction and repairs at their peak in summer, it's a good alternate to avoid what can be monumental traffic jams on weekends when the freeways are cut to one lane.

Another suggestion is a 32-mile loop drive around Houghton Lake. The route also gives you a good idea as to what's available for lakeside resort stays.

autographed posters of Hollywood star Charlton Heston, whose family has a cottage in nearby St. Helen and who often visited the theater. Still part of the auditorium's 500 seats are "love seats" that can fit two cuddlers.

### Zubler's Indian Craft Shop and Powwow  (all ages)

3282 West Houghton Lake Dr. (Highway 55); (989) 366-5691; www.houghtonlakechamber .com/zublers. From US 27, take the Highway 55 exit and head east around the lake. The store is on the north side of the road. Programs and demonstrations are free.

Down the street from the Pines is Zubler's, where the rhythmic sounds of drums and ancient chants once again echo each summer as they have for more than forty years.

Every Thurs from June through Aug, Native Americans from the Swan Creek and Black River bands of Chippewa and Odawa travel from the Mount Pleasant area to demonstrate Native American dances and crafts inside a circle of permanent tepees next to the store. Often, dancers will coax young audience members to join in. Native American storytelling for kids includes tales of the wise Coyote  and how ducks got their quacks. There are crafts for sale and more inside Zubler's, which specializes in Southwest Native American and Cherokee items.

### Funland Amusement Park  (all ages)

On Highway 55; (989) 422-5204. Reached from US 27 off the Highway 55 exit by heading east. Open Memorial Day through Labor Day. Cost varies, starting from five minutes on a bumper boat ($). One of two such facilities almost next door to one another.

Batting cages, go-karts, and other activities made for kids of all ages. Snacks are sold on the premises.

## Where to Eat

There are more than two dozen restaurants ringing the lake in the towns of Houghton Lake. Here are some of our favorites:

**Coyles Restaurant.** 9074 Old US 27; (989) 422-3812. Just north of Highway 55 on the west shore of Houghton Lake. Reasonably priced breakfast, lunch, and dinner with children's menu. $

**Houghton Lake Big Boy.** On Highway 55, just west of the US 27 exit; (989) 422-5193. Family-style meals and buffet, with burgers a specialty. $$

**Kilkare Inn.** 3942 Houghton Lake Dr. (Highway 55); (989) 366-5254. Soups, sandwiches, and other similar fare top the menu here. $$

## Where to Stay

More than three dozen resorts, from inns and bed-and-breakfasts to lakeside cottages, ring the lake. They are conveniently arranged by zone in the local resort finder. Most on the northeast and western edges of the lake will be farthest from traffic. Some offer beaches, but others have breakwalls only for waterfronts, and some also feature pools. It's wise to check out where you want to stay beforehand and make reservations, as accommodations fill rapidly during June, July, and Aug and for the Tip-Up Town festival in Jan.

**Best Western Beachfront Motel.** 4990 West Houghton Lake Dr. (Highway 55), Houghton Lake; (989) 366-9126. This inn has sixty rooms, most of which overlook the lake, with beach, indoor pool, and continental breakfast. $$–$$$

**Comfort Suites Lakeside.** 100 Clearview Rd., Houghton Lake; (989) 422-4000. On Old US 27, ½ mile north of Highway 55 on the western shore of Houghton Lake. This newer property has seventy rooms with indoor water park, restaurant with children's menu, Internet access, continental breakfast, and one of the best swimming beaches on the lake. $$

**Super 8.** 9580 West Lake City Rd. (Highway 55), Houghton Lake, at US 27; (989) 422-3119. This basic property has seventy rooms. Restaurants nearby. $

## For More Information

**Houghton Lake Area Tourism Bureau.** 4482 West Houghton Lake Dr. (Highway 55), Houghton Lake 48629; (800) 676-5330; www.visithoughtonlake.com.

**Houghton Lake Chamber of Commerce.** 1625 West Houghton Lake Dr., Houghton Lake 48629; (989) 366-5644; www.houghtonlakemichigan.net.

# Higgins Lake and Roscommon

Now we're talking vacation country. In the heart of the Huron-Manistee National Forest, which stretches across northern Lower Michigan, Roscommon is near what some say is the crown jewel of Michigan's more than 11,000 inland lakes. Summer, fall, winter, or spring, there's always something to do here to enjoy the season. And Roscommon's a cute little town in its own right, too. There are six golf courses within 15 miles of town and a small movie theater in town.

## North and South Higgins Lake State Parks  (all ages)   ⬡ ⬡ ⬡ ⬡

**To reach both parks, exit I-75 at Roscommon Road; head south for Higgins Lake South, or west on Roscommon Road to Higgins Lake North. For park information, call the south unit at (989) 821-6374, the north unit at (989) 821-6125; for reservations call (800) 447-2757. Entry fee is $ daily or $$$$ annually, and camping is extra.**

Consistently ranked in Michigan reader polls as having the state's favorite inland lake beaches, these two parks are both located on a body of water that members of the National Geographic Society once voted the world's sixth most beautiful lake.

Higgins Lake South is especially well liked by families with young children, as knee-high kids can wade on its shelf of hard sand and rolling bars up to 700 feet out before Mom and Dad have to worry too much about the depth. Along with 512 modern campsites and plenty of wooded picnic space, there are cross-country skiing and hiking trails starting across from the park. The park store just off the beach rents boats and pontoons and has picnic supplies.

Higgins Lake North has just as many family-friendly attributes.

## Canoe Trips  (all ages)   ⬡

**To reach downtown, take exit 239 off I-75 and turn north on Highway 18 into town. Go through the stoplight, and the river is about 1 block farther. Signs direct you to other liveries in the area as well. Call (989) 275-8760 for a list of area liveries. Trips are usually offered Memorial Day through Oct. Cost varies by trip.**

In downtown Roscommon you can take the family canoeing along the south branch of the Au Sable River. This branch, which joins the main stream about 20 miles north by water, is one of the most scenic, as much of it flows through the Mason Wilderness Tract, a 16-mile stretch of pristine natural beauty. Wildlife from deer to bald eagles and coyotes can be

# **Rules** of the River

A few words about river etiquette. In past years canoeists have been the scourge of the wading trout angler, and vice versa, because a lot of first-time paddlers don't understand that trout anglers aren't just walking around in the river to vex canoeists—that's how they fish. Nowadays, liveries restrict alcohol amounts and instruct canoeists so when they meet an angler, they're not sideways, backwards, tied in rafts, or underwater after encountering a hidden log or after squirt gun battles with fellow paddlers. Actually, most anglers are off the river when canoeists are on. But please, respect their fun, and they'll respect yours.

seen along its banks. Liveries are located in and near Roscommon and include drop-off and pickup service in the rental fee.

For a real adventure, take an overnight trip. Some liveries, including Waters Edge and Paddle Brave in Roscommon (989-275-5273 or 800-681-7092), will rent camping equipment. Paddle Brave also offers guided overnight trips. There is no camping in the Mason Tract, but Canoe Harbor forest campground is at the downstream boundary of the tract and has rustic sites.

### Cross-Country Ski Headquarters (all ages)

**9435 North Cut Rd. (Roscommon CR 100), Roscommon; (989) 821-6661; www.cross-country-ski.com. Exit I-75 at Highway 18, exit 239, and then jog south 1 block to Robinson Lake Road, also known as CR 103. Turn west and go 3 miles to the blinker light. Go north on North Cut Road for ½ mile. The outdoor gear store is open Nov through Mar. $$$ for rentals, which include a trail pass. Food also is available.**

Cross-Country Ski Headquarters has gained a national reputation for excellence in ski rentals, sales, customer service, and its own network of trails that stretches 12½ miles around the store, including great night skiing on torch-lit forest trails. The store is close to state-maintained trails as well, including the Mason Tract Trail, which doubles as a hiking path in summer. It follows the river through the tract along the north shore.

Lynne and Bob Frye will teach you how to cross-country ski if you don't know how. It's as easy as walking.

### Michigan Snowshoe Center (all ages)

**212 North Main St., Roscommon; (989) 281-1171; www.snowshoecenter.com. From I-75, exit 239, go north on Highway 18 into downtown. Go through both traffic lights. Turn left onto Main Street past the railroad tracks and go 2 blocks.**

If you're a dedicated snowshoer or want to try out this very aerobic sport, here's the place. Buy or rent equipment and try it out on either the Tisdale Triangle or Mason Tract pathways nearby.

## Where to Eat

**Fred's Dining & Cocktails.** 430 North Fifth St.; (989) 275-5366. Besides casual dining, this log-style restaurant also features a bowling alley. $$

**Matt's Lake Street Grill and Pizzeria.** 312 Lake St. (Highway 18); (989) 281-1136. Very good inexpensive meals for breakfast through dinner. $–$$

**Timbers on the Cut River.** 1136 CR 100; (989) 821-6532. Casual dining beside the Cut River flowing from Higgins to Houghton Lake. $$

**Tin Fish Restaurant and Pub.** 802 Lake St., Roscommon; (989) 275-8540. Good restaurant serving breakfast, lunch, and dinner. $–$$

## Where to Stay

Besides the two state parks, there are plenty of accommodations to choose from. Rent one of several vacation cottages and homes along Higgins Lake by the week or longer. Prices range from around $425 up to $1,500. The Higgins Lake–Roscommon Chamber of

Commerce (see For More Information) has a complete rental list. Others include:

**Great Circle Campground.** 5370 Marl Lake Rd., Roscommon; (989) 821-9486. From I-75, take exit 239 and jog south to CR 103, and then head west. Turn south on CR 101, then west on CR 104 to the campground. From US 27, exit at Higgins Lake Road, CR 104, and go east. The campground has forty-five sites, with tent sites available, too. Pets OK. $

**Great Escape Motor Lodge.** 8097 North Harrison Rd., Roscommon; (989) 821-6343. From US 27, take the Higgins Lake Road exit to Old US 27 and turn north. The property has thirty rooms with indoor pool. Restaurants nearby. $

**Higgins Lake Family Campground.** 2380 West Burdell Rd., Roscommon; (989) 821-6891. Take exit 239 from I-75, and go south on Highway 18, then 3 miles west on CR 103 and 1 mile north on CR 100. This campground has sixty modern sites, tenting area, and bicycle rentals a mile from Higgins Lake. $

**Tee Pee Restaurant and Motel.** On the I-75 Business Loop, Roscommon; (989) 275-5203 or (800) 420-5348. Fourteen rooms. Restaurant serves breakfast through dinner at inexpensive prices. Children's menu. $

## For More Information

**Higgins Lake–Roscommon Chamber of Commerce.** 709 Lake St., Roscommon 48653; (989) 275-8760; www.hlrcc.com.

# Grayling

Located just off I-75 and bisected by Business I-75 (formerly Old US 27), Grayling is one of the most storied towns in the hearts of both state historians and trout anglers.

In the midst of Michigan's vast white-pine forests, this town grew up named after the silvery fish that once inhabited the Au Sable River. Rapacious land practices destroyed the forests and caused silting in the rivers, and overfishing decimated the grayling so much that by the early 1900s, it was extinct from the river. Except for a remnant of the forests preserved forever, the trees around the area are the result of reforestation efforts in the early twentieth century.

The area survived to come back as a great vacation destination in every season, with skiing and snowmobiling in winter, fishing and waterfront fun in spring and summer, and color viewing and hunting in fall. It's one of my favorite towns in the north. Days will find my friends and me lounging on the beach at nearby Higgins Lake, or maybe walking through the pines at Hartwick Pines State Park. In the evenings we'll join other friends, lose ourselves in the sunset's afterglow, and marvel at the hues of that impressionist canvas called the Au Sable River as we wait for the hatch and the rising trout it brings. You'll find me up here or on the river almost every summer weekend.

### Trout Fishing or River Sightseeing (all ages)

**For a list of guides, call Grayling Visitors Bureau at (800) 937-8837. The cost of a day float trip is about $325 for two, $250 for one.**

Become a part of Michigan floating history while fishing, bird-watching, or just enjoying the ripple of water and quiet of the day by heading out in an authentic Au Sable River drift boat. They've been part of the river scene here for more than a hundred years, first as supply craft for riverside lumber camps. Guides in the area include Bob Andrus, a retired Grayling schoolteacher. Available through the Old Au Sable Fly Shop (200 Ingham St.; 989-348-3330; www.oldausable.com), he and others will take you on a daylong, half-day, or night float on the river to either fish or just enjoy the scenery, which is especially beautiful in fall. Usually the riverboats are 20 to 24 feet long and take one or two persons plus a guide. Passengers sit forward, and the guide steers from the stern. Part of the fun can be a shore lunch over a wood fire. Besides trout splashing after their dinners, you'll probably see beaver, deer, duck, muskrat, and an assortment of birds that might include herons and bald eagles.

## Canoeing  (all ages)

**There are at least ten canoe liveries in town and downstream from Grayling. Most are in the city, just off Business I-75. Call (800) 937-8837 for information.**

Michigan is filled with beautiful floatable rivers, but probably the best, most family fun oriented, and certainly the most popular in east Michigan is the upper Au Sable River, which flows through this former lumber town. You can canoe the main stream from several liveries in downtown Grayling. Each offers relaxing float trips as short as two hours and as lengthy as weeklong paddles to the mouth of the Au Sable in Oscoda.

Depths in the upper river range from 1 to 5 feet, and flotation devices are provided.

Canoeists also have a choice of trying the less-populous Manistee River, about 6 miles west along Highway 72.

## Wellington Farm Park  (all ages)

**6940 South Military Rd.; (888) 653-3276; www.wellingtonfarmpark.org. From I-75, take exit 251, Four Mile Road, and turn west to the end of the road. Turn south on Military Road and go about a mile. Parking is on the west side of the road. Open 9 a.m. to 5 p.m. Wed through Sun, Memorial Day weekend through Oct. $.**

The park is a new concept in historical, environmental education. It is a working replica of a 1930s Depression-era farmstead. Farming activities are conducted daily using vintage tools and practices, from blacksmithing to plowing and harvesting. The park also has a sawmill, carpenter shop, and gristmill on its sixty acres. Newest additions include a working "summer kitchen" and a locally historic church that has been moved to the grounds. A farm market sells items grown on the farm, including flour and cornmeal that are ground there. Special events include a demonstration of women's role on the farm and a walk-through history showing farming from 1760 to 1932, among many others.

There are self-guided nature trails through the woods, too. The park gets its name from a tiny farming community that once existed in the area.

## Skyline Ski and Country Club (ages 7 and up)

4020 Skyline Rd.; (989) 275-5445. From I-75, take exit 251, Four Mile Road, head east to Old US 27, then south 2 miles to Skyline Road. Follow it 1 mile to the hill. Open from 10 a.m. to 5 p.m. Fri through Mon, plus 6:30 to 10 p.m. Fri and Sat. Tickets and rentals are $$$–$$$$ per day.

Ski at one of the few ski areas in the state reliant on all natural snow. The area has fourteen runs with one chairlift and nine surface tows. Rentals, lessons, and a ski shop are available. In summer Skyline changes into a golf club with a challenging course.

## Goodale's Bakery (all ages)

500 Norway; (989) 348-8682. At the corner of Ottawa, 1 block south of Business I-75/Highway 72, the town's main street. Open daily except Sun, with extended hours Fri.

Famous for its baked goods made fresh daily, including wonderful oatmeal cookies, and its made-on-premises cakes, coffee cakes, and cinnamon and English muffin breads, which are sent across the country to loyal customers. Great sandwiches and other fare for lunch, too.

## Grayling Fish Hatchery (all ages)

On North Down River Road; (989) 348-9266; www.hansonhills.org. Off I-75, take exit 254, follow I-75 Business Loop through town, and turn north at the Clark gasoline station; then follow the signs. The hatchery is open daily from Memorial Day through Labor Day between noon and 6 p.m. $, children ages 5 and younger are admitted **free.**

Along the Au Sable's tiny east branch, take the kids to feed trout from fingerling size to several pounds at this former state trout hatchery. Dating from 1914, it was closed for production of fish in the 1960s. It reopened as a tourist attraction in 1983. Currently, ponds hold thousands of fish each summer, a sight that's sure to delight kids. There's even a special area for youngsters who want to take home some. (Parents, you pay by the inch.) There are dispensers for fish food for a quarter or two, and it's great fun to watch as your youngsters sprinkle the pellets into the water and watch as the trout, from 6-inchers to 6-pounders, gobble them up.

## Gates Au Sable Lodge (all ages)

To reach the lodge, take exit 254 off northbound I-75 and turn east on Highway 72; follow it to Stephan Bridge Road and turn north. The lodge is at the bridge. For reservation information, call (989) 348-8462; www.gateslodge.com.

Nestled by the river 6 miles east of the city, the Gates place will introduce you to the quiet joys of trout fishing up close. With sixteen rooms renting for reasonable prices, you'll get a large space with a picture-window view of the river through the trees that cover the property. Owner Cal "Rusty" Gates runs the fly shop, where you can purchase equipment and your license, while wife Julie manages the restaurant, which serves breakfast and dinner. If you're a new angler, come to the fly-fishing workshop held each spring; or arrange a float with one of the lodge's guides. Then take the kids down to the "bread hole" under a willow over the river, where huge trout gulp crusts.

Gates also supports Anglers of the Au Sable, a group that looks after the river, so patronizing his place helps ensure that the Au Sable will remain a treasured stream for generations.

### Hartwick Pines State Park (all ages)

**To get to the park, take I-75 exit 264 and drive about 2 miles east on Highway 93. For more information, call (989) 348-7068; www.michigan.gov/dnr, and then go to "Recreation, Camping & Boating." Reservations can be made online or by calling (800) 447-2757. A motor vehicle permit ($ daily or $$$$ annually) is required to enter. Camping is extra.**

Six miles north of Grayling, you'll see almost all that remains of the giants that once covered nearly all of Michigan more than a century ago in this unique 10,000-acre park, which many visitors revere as an outdoor cathedral to nature. Walk miles of trails covered by a canopy of huge white pines and hemlocks that block so much sunlight, hardly any vegetation grows on the forest floor.

There's an entrance road leading to a one-hundred-site campground (shaded sites that were a feature of the old campground across the street are few at the new one) and the Michigan Forest Visitor Center at the edge of the pines. The center provides an excellent grounding in the history of logging in the state and how it has changed from being a destructive force to a mostly beneficial practice through scientific methods that benefit both wildlife and people. Pass up the video, though.

A restored logging camp, complete with a "big wheel" (which was used to haul logs out of the forest; you'll also see a red one at the park's entrance), a bunkhouse, and a dining room, is set deep in the woods. In summer the camp comes alive twice a year as living-history portrayals explain what logging life was like in the old days.

Events take place during Wood-Shavings Days in July and Black Iron Days in Aug, and there are portrayals of lumber-camp life by costumed employees in character.

The steam-powered sawmill is fired up, and other workers are on hand selling crafts. The park also offers a woodland chapel, an extensive network of mountain biking trails, miles of great cross-country skiing in winter, a driving loop with numbered stops, and a Braille trail. Park programs include night skiing on lighted trails, snowshoe hikes, maple-syrup making, and other activities.

## Where to Eat

**The Canadian Steak & Fish Company.** About 1 mile north on Business I-75 from exit 254 on I-75; (989) 344-5555. Maybe the town's best restaurant, with steaks, fish, and other items on the menu for lunch and dinner. $$

**Dawson and Stevens.** 231 North Michigan Ave.; (989) 348-2111. Just north of the main stoplight at the intersection of Business I-75/Highway 72 in downtown Grayling. Summer hours are 11 a.m. to 8 p.m. Sun through Thurs, 11 a.m. to 9 p.m. Fri and Sat. Earlier closing in winter. Soups, salads, sandwiches, and other dishes such as vegetarian items are available, but the big draw is the old-fashioned soda fountain for outstanding phosphates, malts, coolers, cones, and shakes, all served to oldies tunes. There are plenty of 1950s and 1960s memorabilia in this onetime family drugstore. You won't find a friendlier staff. Try the mulligatawny soup. $

**Grayling Restaurant.** 211 East Michigan, just north of the Michigan Avenue/Highway 72 stoplight; (989) 348-2141. A small restaurant with good family atmosphere. Great breakfasts. $–$$

**Lone Pine.** 1164 Business I-75, about 1 mile north of downtown; (989) 348-7312. Good inexpensive breakfasts. $

**Spike's Keg O Nails.** 301 North James St. (Highway 72); (989) 348-7113. A city fixture since 1933. Great burgers and fish. $–$$

## Where to Stay

If you aren't staying at the unique Gates Au Sable Lodge, there are scores of motels in the Grayling area.

**Days Inn of Grayling.** 2556 Business I-75; (989) 344-0204. Take exit 254 from I-75. This chain hotel has sixty-five rooms, some with whirlpools. $$–$$$

**Ramada Inn Conference Center.** 2650 Business I-75; (989) 348-7611. From I-75, take exit 254. The facility is on the west side of the road. It has 151 rooms, indoor playground area and pool, and cross-country ski shop in winter. Restaurant on premises serves breakfast, lunch, and dinner, and there are others nearby. $$

## For More Information

**Grayling Visitors Bureau.** 213 North James (Business I-75), Grayling 49738; (800) 937-8837; www.grayling-mi.com.

# Gaylord

Gaylord is located 20 miles north of Grayling along I-75. Either of two exits will bring you into town. Besides its reputation as a tourism center, Gaylord has also gained a reputation as the center of nearly two dozen of the state's best golf courses, which are sprinkled throughout the woods. Downtown Gaylord also is home to the annual Alpenfest event the third week of July. Events including parades are part of the fun.

## Bavarian Falls Park & Call of the Wild Museum (all ages)

Both located at 850 South Wisconsin Ave. Park: (989) 732-4087; Open from 9 a.m. to 10:30 p.m. (or later, depending on the crowds) from May through Oct. Museum: (800) 835-4347 or (989) 732-4336; www.gocallofthewild.com; Open daily, year-round, with extended hours from mid-June to Labor Day. $$.

Bavarian Falls Park features minigolf around waterfalls and hills. There are go-karts and rides for tots, too, along with western gifts. The Call of the Wild Museum is an interactive, educational museum where kids enjoy over sixty animal displays (no, these are not live animals), listen to recorded sounds of the animals, and participate in a variety of activities.

## Treetops–Sylvan Resort (all ages)

Just east of downtown; (989) 732-6711; www.treetops.com. Take Highway 32 to Chester Road, turn north, and then continue east on Wilkinson Road. Open for golf in spring through fall and downhill in winter. Visit the Web site for discount coupons. $$$$.

The ski area boasts nineteen runs and four chairlifts, with rentals and instructions in a family atmosphere.

## Where to Eat

**Sugar Bowl.** 216 West Main St. (Highway 32); (989) 732-5524. From I-75, take exit 282, Highway 32, and go east. The restaurant is on the north side of the road. Great breakfasts, lunches, and dinners in one of the state's oldest family-run restaurants. Steak and fish are specialties. Children's menu, too. $$$

## Where to Stay

**Alpine Lodge.** 833 West Main; (989) 732-2431. Just off I-75 exit 282 on Highway 32. This lodge has 137 guest rooms with indoor pool and complimentary hot breakfast package. $$

**Baymont Inn.** 510 South Wisconsin; (989) 731-6331. Turn east from I-75, exit 282, on Highway 32 to Wisconsin, and then head about ½ mile south. The inn offers one hundred rooms, an indoor pool, and hot continental breakfast. $$

## For More Information

**Gaylord Area Convention and Tourism Bureau.** 101 West Main St., Gaylord 49735; (989) 732-6333 or (800) 345-8621; www .gaylordmichigan.net.

# Indian River

Indian River is a summer and winter resort town located along I-75 north of Gaylord.

In summer Burt, Black, and Mullett Lakes beckon with resort cottages, while in winter there are more than 180 miles of groomed snowmobile trails, not to mention miles of cross-country ski trails. The area also is near some of east Michigan's most popular ski areas. Be sure to check out the totem pole carved from a cottonwood tree planted by early settlers.

### Chillermania! (all ages)

1651 South Straits Hwy.; (888) 420-4244; www.americanchillers.com. Hours vary by season. **Free.**

Visit the store selling books, hats, shirts, and other gear related to the popular series of children's thrillers by local author Johnathan Rand. Rand often drops by, so young fans might even meet him.

### Inland Waterway (all ages)

For pontoon boat rental information, call (231) 238-9325, or the Indian River Marina at (231) 238-9373; www.indianrivermarina.com. Cost is about $190 for a full day.

Rent a pontoon boat and float along all or part of Michigan's unknown canal, the Inland Waterway. This 68-mile, partly artificial, partly natural canal cut through the tip of Michigan's "mitt" takes you to some of the state's largest inland lakes and through two locks.

The waterway was dredged in the 1800s to allow steamboats to reach the region's interior and was later improved in the 1950s.

Travelers can begin in Indian River and head all the way to Cheboygan on Lake Huron or to Crooked Lake, a few miles from Lake Michigan. While the waterway doesn't connect to the big lake, you can rent a trailer from a local marina to take your craft there.

## Where to Eat

**Cafe Noka.** On Old US 27, overlooking Mullett Lake; (231) 238-9103. From I-75, take exit 310 and head north on Old US 27 along the north shore of Mullett Lake, on the outskirts of Topinabee. The restaurant is on the north side of the road. It serves excellent breakfasts and lunches in a tiny, knotty pine building. $

**Michael's.** 5124 South Straits Hwy. (Old US 27); (231) 238-4987. Leave I-75 at exit 310. Go a mile west on Highway 68, then ½ mile south on Straits Highway. Good home-style cooking for breakfast, lunch, and dinner. $–$$$

## Where to Stay

**Burt Lake State Park.** On Burt Lake; (231) 238-9392 or (800) 447-2757. Leave I-75 at exit 310. Head west on Highway 68 to Old US 27. Go south less than a mile to the park entrance. A state motor vehicle permit is required for entry, daily ($) or annually ($$$$). Camping is extra. The park has 395 campsites with a great beach on Michigan's third-largest inland lake. $

**Holiday Inn Express.** 4375 Brudy; at exit 310 off I-75. (231) 238-3000. The inn offers fifty rooms, indoor pool, and whirlpool. $$

**Nor Gate Motel.** 4846 South Straits Hwy. (Old US 27); (616) 238-7788. Leave I-75 at exit 310. Go 1 mile west on Highway 68, then ½ mile south on Straits Highway. This little property has fourteen rooms. Restaurant nearby. $

## For More Information

**Indian River Chamber of Commerce and Tourist Bureau.** 3435 South Straits Hwy., Indian River; (800) 394-8310; www.irchamber.com or www.irtourism.com.

# Hillman

Hillman is about 45 miles east of Gaylord and about 20 miles west of Alpena along Highway 32. In fall the distinctive bugling of Michigan's elk herd can be heard for miles through the Pigeon River State Forest between Gaylord and Hillman. The herd of more than 1,000, the largest east of the Mississippi, inhabits some of the wildest forest in lower Michigan. In summer some of the best places to spot the elk are in one of several clearings they're known to frequent, especially at dusk. For information on potential spots to view elk, call the Michigan Department of Natural Resources at (989) 983-4101. For virtually guaranteed views of elk on rides (by sleigh in winter and wagon in summer) with dinner, call (989) 742-4502 or (800) 729-9375.

## Where to Eat

See Gaylord and Alpena listings.

## Where to Stay

**Thunder Bay Golf Resort and RV Park.**
27800 Highway 32, just south of town; (989) 742-4502 or (800) 729-9375; www.thunderbaygolf.com. The resort has thirty-four rooms in condo units, including some two-bedroom units as well as full hookup RV sites. Whirlpool in separate building. Great golf in summer and cross-country skiing in winter, and a restaurant for breakfast, lunch, and dinner. Ask about the great fall and winter sleigh ride/dinner package with gourmet meals cooked over century-old stoves and views of the resort's elk herd. $$

# Ossineke

Ossineke was settled in the 1840s by lumber interests. Its name was transformed by settlers from the Native American, Wasineke. It is on the southern edge of Alpena's Thunder Bay.

### Dinosaur Gardens Prehistorical Zoo  (all ages)

11160 US 23; (989) 471-5477; www.dinosaurgardensllc.com. Open from 9 a.m. to 6 p.m. daily Memorial Day through Labor Day, and from 9 a.m. to 4 p.m. weekends in Sept. $ for tours and minigolf.

A bit to the east is a low-key tourist destination that has attracted families to its wooded setting for almost seventy years—Dinosaur Gardens has been entertaining and educating youngsters since 1938. It took original owner Paul Domke thirty-eight years to sculpt the twenty-six life-size dinos set amid the pines and hardwood forest that line the winding Devil River. Storyboards at each exhibit tell visitors what scientists believe the lives of these magnificently fearsome animals were like. In one scene a towering tyrannosaur battles a horned triceratops, and in another an animal roars in frustration after being trapped in a lake of tar. A gift shop sells souvenirs, including plastic dinosaur models. It's a great exhibit and was a favorite of my kids when they were small.

## Where to Eat and Stay

See Alpena listings.

# Alpena

Built on sawmills powered by the area's abundant pine forests in the nineteenth century, Alpena is now northeast Michigan's largest city and has a great waterfront, fishing, shipwreck viewing on glass-bottom boats, scuba diving opportunities in Thunder Bay, and wildlife viewing along the lower Thunder Bay River.

### Jesse Besser Museum  (all ages)

491 Johnson St.; (989) 356-2202; www.bessermuseum.org. From US 23, go through town on Chisholm (US 23) to Alpena General Hospital. Turn right onto Johnson Street and go

300 feet. The museum is on the left. Open 10 a.m. to 5 p.m. Tues through Sat and noon to 5 p.m. Sun. Planetarium shows are at 1 p.m. and 3 p.m. Sun in July and Aug. Admission is $ and **free** for children ages 4 and younger. Planetarium shows are $1 per person extra; children ages 5 and younger are not recommended in the planetarium.

The museum highlights local history, including the concrete-block-making machine perfected here as a result of the area's rich limestone deposits used in cement making. Nineteenth-century shops and cabins line a re-created street, and outside are a cabin and a log home.

### Thunder Bay National Marine Sanctuary and Maritime Heritage Center (all ages)

500 West Fletcher St. downtown. Cross the Thunder Bay River on US 23, turn east on Fletcher Street, and follow it to the building. (989) 356-8805; www.thunderbay.noaa.gov. Open 10 a.m. to 5 p.m. Mon through Sat and noon to 5 p.m. from Memorial Day weekend to early Nov, and closed Sun from Nov to Memorial Day weekend. **Free.**

Thunder Bay is home to more than one hundred shipwrecks, and this center tells their stories. Learn which can be seen by snorkelers as well as scuba divers. The main exhibit is a life-size re-creation of the aft portion of a nineteenth-century wooden Great Lakes schooner. Climb aboard into the wheelhouse and then try the bilge pump while you experience a simulated Great Lakes storm. Another area explores what it might look like as a shipwreck, too. A Fourth of July Maritime Festival includes a tall ships gathering, live music, food, and other activities. There's also a gift shop and theater.

## Where to Eat

**Hunan Chinese Restaurant.** 1120 South State St. (US 23), 1½ miles south of town; (989) 356-6461. Great Chinese food for lunch and dinner. Children's menu and some non-Chinese food also available. $$

## Where to Stay

**Days Inn.** 1496 West Highway 32, 2½ miles west of US 23; (989) 356-6118. Another chain property with seventy-seven rooms, with indoor pool and whirlpool. Dining in Alpena. $$

**Holiday Inn.** 1000 US 23, a mile north of downtown; (989) 356-2151. This chain property has 148 rooms, indoor pool, and recreation area. Restaurant serves breakfast, lunch, and dinner. More restaurants nearby. Pets OK. $$

## For More Information

**Alpena Area Convention and Visitors Bureau.** 235 West Chisholm St., Alpena 49707; (989) 354-4181 or (800) 425-7362; www.alpenacvb.com.

# Rogers City

Located just off US 23, about 20 miles north of Alpena, Rogers City got its start in fishing, then turned to limestone mining, and is now back to fishing again, but this time as charter-boat action for salmon and steelhead. Rogers City is a hot spot for salmon fishing and also has a "secret" bass fishery along the Lake Huron shore. Salmon plants here are some of the largest in the state. Fishing is good in early summer and only gets better starting in Aug. Plan on around $350 for a trip.

For the town's size Rogers City has plenty to offer tourists. While other vacationers head to Michigan's west coast for everything from huge hotels to condoplexes, northeastern Michigan's main attraction is the lack of the same—just plenty of natural things to help you relax and keep you busy at the same time. One such area surrounds this city. At first glance the tiny town doesn't look like much, just another spot to gas up and go. But look closer.

### Harbor View  (all ages)
**Watch for signs in downtown Rogers City directing you to the overlook. Open for daylight hours. Free.**

Watch giant Great Lakes freighters pulling up to the docks to load before heading for steel mills in Indiana, Ohio, and Detroit. Take the kids into the former wheelhouse of the retired freighter *Calcite*.

### Great Lakes Lore Maritime Museum  (all ages)
**367 North Third St., downtown; (989) 734-0706; www.gllmm.org. Open 10 a.m. to 4 p.m. daily. Adults $, children through the twelfth grade admitted free.**

Dedicated to those who sailed and lost their lives on commercial ships plying the Great Lakes, the museum recently moved to Rogers City, home to many of the sailors who lost their lives in two freighter sinkings in 1958 and 1965.

### Presque Isle Lighthouse Museum  (all ages)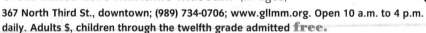
**To get to the museum, turn east off US 23 at CR 638 (East Grand Lake Road), travel past two stop signs, and turn right onto Grand Lake Road. Follow it about 9 miles, and you'll see the lighthouse on the right-hand side. Call (989) 595-2787 or (989) 595-2706 for more information. Open 9 a.m. to 7 p.m. daily from May 15 to Oct 15. $; kids under 6 are admitted free.**

A few miles to the south of Rogers City on a spit of land between picturesque Grand Lake and Lake Huron is the old lighthouse. Built in 1840, it is filled with period antiques—and some say it's haunted by a former light keeper.

### Ocqueoc Falls  (all ages)
**Head west of Rogers City along Highway 68 to reach the park, on the north side of the road. Free.**

The falls, pronounced "ock-kee-ock," is the largest in the Lower Peninsula. There are hiking and cross-country ski trails along the river as well.

## Where to Eat

**Water's Edge.** 530 West Third St., on the waterfront downtown; (989) 734-4747. Good selection of dishes for lunch and dinner. Children's menu available. $$

## Where to Stay

**Driftwood Motel.** 540 West Third; (989) 734-4777. Next to the Water's Edge restaurant downtown. The motel has forty-four rooms looking over a sandy beach. Heated indoor pool with whirlpool. Lake swimming, too. $$

## For More Information

**Rogers City Chamber of Commerce.** 292 South Bradley, Rogers City 49779; (989) 734-2535 or (800) 622-4148; www.lhi.net/chamber. Or contact Presque Isle Tourism Council; (888) 854-9700; www.presqueislemi.com.

# Cheboygan

Only 20 or so miles from the top of the Lower Peninsula, and the eastern terminus of the Inland Waterway, Cheboygan grew up on lumbering, like so many other towns in this area.

### Coast Guard Icebreaker *Mackinaw* Tours (all ages)

The new *Mackinaw* is docked at the end of Coast Guard Drive. From US 23 and Highway 27, turn south on US 23 and go across the bridge, and then turn east on Coast Guard Drive. When the ship is docked, tours are available from 1 to 4 p.m. daily, but call ahead first to the ship (231-597-2030).

Built to replace the original *Mackinaw*, which was commissioned in 1944, the new state-of-the-art, 240-foot *Mackinaw* is now moored in Cheboygan and is open for tours when it is in port along the Cheboygan River. Like the old *Mackinaw*, which now is a museum in Mackinaw City (see listing), its main role will be keeping the region's shipping lanes open during the extended winter season. For details, plus events, contact the Cheboygan Area Tourist Bureau (see For More Information).

### Cheboygan Opera House (all ages)

403 North Huron, just west of US 23; (231) 627-5432 for more information, or (231) 627-5841 for the box office to check the playbill; www.theoperahouse.org. Plays are performed all year long. Open for guided tours from 1 to 4 p.m. Tues through Fri from June through Sept. $.

A great example of structures built with lumber money in the north in the nineteenth century, the restored 1877 theater still plays host to local as well as national theater and musical groups.

### Gordon Turner Park (all ages)

At the end of Huron Street, which is the extension of Highway 27 east of US 23.

The cattail marsh that borders Lake Huron is one of the Great Lakes' largest and has been set aside as a wildlife sanctuary. Climb the viewing platform, and to the north in the distance, you'll probably be able to make out the Mackinac Bridge.

### Cheboygan River Locks  (all ages)
**Just south of Highway 27 and east of US 23, near the city's paper plant. Free.**

Stop by to watch pleasure boats using the Inland Waterway being raised or lowered 12 feet. It's one of two lock systems on the waterway.

### Cheboygan County Historical Museum  (all ages)
**At Huron and Court Streets, 1 block west of Main Street; (231) 627-5448 or (231) 627-9597. Hours are 1 to 4 p.m. Mon through Fri, June 15 to Oct 15. Call ahead for weekend hours. Adults $, preschool through high school children free.**

This museum is in the former county sheriff's home, which doubled as a jail from 1882 to 1969 and still has eight cells. New additions include a late-nineteenth-century Native American cabin and murals depicting area history.

## Where to Eat

**Boathouse.** 106 Pine St., downtown on the river, just off Highway 27; (231) 627-4316. Enjoy lunch and dinner alongside the Inland Waterway in a converted boathouse once owned by members of Detroit's infamous Purple Gang in Prohibition's rum-running days. Children's menu available. $$$

**Elias Brothers Big Boy.** 861 South Main St. (US 27); (231) 627-3661. Open 6 a.m. to 11 p.m. daily. Good family fare, from salad bar to trademark triple-decker burger. $$

**Hack-Ma-Tack Inn.** 8131 Beebe Rd.; (231) 625-2919; www.hackmatackinn.com. From downtown Cheboygan, head west on US 27 for 3¼ miles, then turn east ¼ mile on Highway 33, and then follow the signs about 2 miles to the inn. One of the best restaurant settings in the north, alongside the Inland Waterway at the eastern end of Mullett Lake. Dine in an 1894 lodge amid outdoor memorabilia. Prime rib and whitefish are not to be missed for lunch or dinner. $$$

## Where to Stay

**Best Western River Terrace Motel.** 847 South Main St. (Highway 27); (231) 627-5688. The motel has fifty-three riverside rooms, indoor pool, and exercise area. Restaurants nearby. $$

**Fleetwood Inn.** 889 South Main St.; (231) 627-3126. From US 23, head west on Highway 27 about 1⅓ miles. The inn has twenty-eight rooms on the river. Restaurants nearby. $$

## For More Information

**Cheboygan Area Tourist Bureau.** 124 North Main St., Cheboygan 49721; (231) 627-7183 or (800) 968-3302; www.cheboygan.com.

# West Michigan– South

Fruit orchards, sandy beaches, marinas, artist colonies, cities celebrating their ethnic heritage—west Michigan has a wealth of activities, spread from the Indiana state line to one of the state's most popular tourist destinations, Mackinaw City. The southern portion of this region is a great place to start your explorations.

# Bridgman

Huge dunes seen on the west side of I-94 announce the area of Michigan that's been dubbed "harbor country." It's a favorite vacation spot not only for Michiganians but for Chicago-area residents as well. From here north Lake Michigan's lakefront is nearly one big sand beach.

### Warren Dunes State Park (all ages)

**Take exit 16 off I-94 and go 2 miles south; (269) 426-4013. Open year-round. Entry is by state-issued vehicle permit ($ daily or $$$$ annually). Camping fee per night $$$.**

This is another state park that is more than just a place to stay. Covering more than 2½ miles of beautiful Lake Michigan shore near the small town of Bridgman, it has become one of the state's most popular parks, welcoming more than one million visitors annually.

Encompassing 1,507 acres, Warren Dunes is known for its continually changing sand dunes, which greet motorists as soon as they turn onto the entrance road. For many coming from Indiana or Illinois, it's the first glimpse of the magnificent Lake Michigan sand shore that stretches nearly the length of west Michigan.

Walk the beach of sugary silica sand and tell your kids to shuffle through it. It literally squeaks. Head into the dunes along 6 miles of marked hiking trails. Watch for the tops of trees long ago covered by the shifting sands. There are nearly 200 modern campsites, as well as three cabins to rent. Parts of the park are heavily wooded, but there are hundreds of acres of high sand dunes, too.

# WEST MICHIGAN–SOUTH

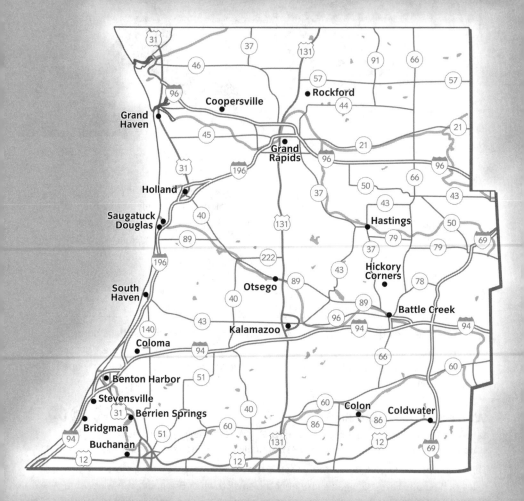

# Southwest Michigan **Wine Trail**

Yes, even unfermented grape juice for the kids is available at most of the wineries in this American Viticultural Area, classified as the Lake Michigan Shore growing area. From New Buffalo to Paw Paw, visit any of eleven wineries scattered throughout the southwest Lower Peninsula.

Most have tasting rooms, and some even have restaurants attached. For more information, including a map to the wineries, go to www.miwinetrail.com.

## Jones Blueberry Farm (all ages)

**9245 Gast Rd., exit 146 off I-94; (269) 465-4745; www.jonesberryfarm.com. Picking usually runs July 4 through Labor Day.**

Southwest Michigan is also famous for its you-pick farms, and this is one example. In July there are ten acres of blueberries to choose from. Plan on about $1.50 per pound of the heart-healthy fruit. The farm also sells jams and jellies. Farms with pick-your-own cherries and raspberries are also in the area. Ask the Joneses for directions.

## Where to Eat

**Lions Café at Weko Beach.** 5301 Lake St.; (269) 465-3800. From I-94, exit 16, go north on Red Arrow Highway to Lake Street. Go left to Weko Beach. From May through Sept, dine indoors or outside overlooking Lake Michigan. Breakfast, lunch, and dinner. Children's menu. $$

**Redamak's.** 616 East Buffalo St., New Buffalo; (269) 469-4522. From I-94, exit 4, take Pulaski Highway/US 12 west to the restaurant. This spot is billed as the burger that made New Buffalo famous. Well, maybe. But the burgers are good enough to merit a stop for the hundreds who line up for a seat. Open from Mar 1 to late Oct, Redamak's serves more than 115,000 pounds of handmade patties each season. Chicken and fish also are on the menu. $–$$

## Where to Stay

See Benton Harbor/St. Joseph listings.

# Buchanan

Settled in 1833 on a bend of the St. Joseph River, this tiny town was named for President James Buchanan. It is located north of US 12 and west of US 31.

## Bear Cave (all ages)

**4085 Bear Cave Rd.; (269) 695-3050. From Buchanan, head north 4 miles on Red Bud Trail and watch for signs. Open daily from 9 a.m. to 4 p.m. from May 1 through Labor Day. $, children 5 and younger are admitted free.**

One of the few caves in Michigan accessible to the public. Small by spelunking standards, it's a 150-foot-long cave accessible by a winding stairway. Since the temperature inside is a constant fifty-eight degrees, wear suitable clothing. Also be forewarned that the cave contains bats. Generally they won't bother you if you don't bother them.

## Where to Eat

See Benton Harbor/St. Joseph listings.

## Where to Stay

**Bear Cave Resort.** See aforementioned directions and phone number for Bear Cave.

After you've seen the cave, stay at its campground. There are eighty-five campsites and an outdoor pool, playground, movie room, and other amenities. $

See also listings for Benton Harbor and St. Joseph.

# Berrien Springs

Across the river a few miles west of tiny Eau Claire, Berrien Springs has a few surprises for travelers, too, among them the local farm owned by boxing great Mohamed Ali.

**Tree-Mendus Fruit Farm**  (all ages)
Located at 9351 East Eureka Rd., Eau Claire; (269) 782-7101; www.treemendus-fruit.com. Take I-94 to exit 41 (Highway 140). Follow Highway 140 south 12 miles to Eureka Road, then 1½ miles east to the farm. From the west, take exit 29. Go east on Meadowbrook Road 10 miles to M-140. Go south to Eureka Road, then to the farm. Hours vary by season, so call ahead.

## Sportfishing on the St. Joseph River

When it's cold outside, the best salmon and steelhead anglers head inside—inside their boats, that is. Steelhead fishing on the St. Joseph River here from just below Berrien Springs Dam downriver several miles stays hot all winter. The addition of Skamania steelhead, which spawn in summer, means some boats stay active on the river year-round.

Charter operators have specialized boats for fishing the river's holes and gravel runs. In the bow a glass cocoon heated by portable kerosene stoves keeps you warm until a fish hits one of the lines strung at the stern and extending downstream over productive areas. Salmon, steelhead, and walleye are the game. Cost per trip is about $260. To contact a guide, call either the Berrien Springs–Eau Claire Chamber of Commerce at (269) 471-2484 or the Southwestern Michigan Tourist Council at (269) 925-6301; www.swmichigan.org.

Owner Herb Teichman has created a living legend in this 450-acre orchard in the heart of Michigan's fruit belt, where you can pick your own apples, cherries, peaches, apricots, pears, raspberries, and other fruit. But in July the legend of the great pit spit lives on each year in the annual International Cherry Pit Spit. The best lips and mouths from across the world gather to see who can launch a cherry pit the farthest.

The record stands at a whopping 72 feet, 11 inches. Tours of the orchard, from May through Oct, show how fruits have evolved, and there is fresh cider in the fall.

## Where to Eat

**Daybreak Cafe.** 126 East Ferry (Old US 31), downtown; (269) 471-5605. Breakfast served all day, lunch and dinner at appropriate times. $$

See also listings for Benton Harbor and St. Joseph.

## Where to Stay

More accommodations are located near Benton Harbor and St. Joseph.

**Shamrock Park Campground.** Operated by the village on the St. Joseph River; (269) 473-5691. From downtown, head across the bridge at the north end of town and watch for the sign. Seventy-seven full-service and rustic sites plus three minicabins. No swimming. Many river fishing charters leave from here. $

## For More Information

**Berrien Springs–Eau Claire Chamber of Commerce.** P.O. Box 177, Berrien Springs 49103; (269) 471-2484.

**Niles Area/Four Flags Tourism Council.** 321 East Main St., Niles 49120; (269) 684-7444.

# Coldwater

This town grew to prominence in the 1800s as a trading center for the region's farm families and because of its location on the then-Chicago-to-Detroit turnpike, which is now US 12. Located on the western edge of the Irish Hills, it has a great Victorian downtown courthouse and other historical buildings.

### Tibbits Opera House (all ages)

14 South Hanchett St., south of US 12; (517) 278-6029; www.tibbits.org. Free theater tours offered from 9 a.m. to 5 p.m. Mon through Fri by reservation only. $–$$.

Opened in 1882, the opera house still presents professional summer stock productions June through Aug, and community plays the rest of the year. There's also a small art gallery inside.

The Tibbits also presents "Popcorn Theater," made especially for children five and up. Productions such as *Thumbelina* and *Treasure Island* take place Fri and Sat mornings at 10 a.m.

## Where to Eat

**Big Boy of Coldwater.** 556 East Chicago St. (US 12); (517) 278-5762. Open 6 a.m. to 1 a.m. daily. A wide selection of family fare, from a salad bar to its trademark triple-decker burger. $$

**Coldwater Gardens.** 432 East Chicago St. (US 12); (517) 278-3172. From I-69, head east on US 12. Daily specials for breakfast, lunch, and dinner. Ribs are a specialty. Senior discounts and children's menu. $–$$

There also are lots of places to eat just west of the I-69 exit to the city.

## Where to Stay

**Chicago Pike Inn.** 443 East Chicago (US 12), downtown; (517) 279-8744. Inside a huge, exquisitely restored 1903 Victorian home are eight rooms. Call ahead if your children are age 12 and under. $$

**Red Roof Inn.** 248 South Willowbrook; (517) 279-1199. There are sixty-five rooms with breakfast available.

**Super 8 Motel.** 600 Orleans Blvd.; (517) 278-8833. From I-69, go ½ mile west, 1 block north, and ½ block east. This budget property has fifty-eight rooms with continental breakfast included. Small pets OK. $$

# Colon

Colon is 16 miles west of Coldwater along Highway 86. If you say a visit to this tiny town is truly magical, you're right. Each year during the first weekend in Aug, thousands of professional and amateur magicians converge on the town to take part in the Magic Get-Together. For four days they pay homage to the memory of Harry Blackstone Sr., the former Colon resident who became world famous for his illusions.

Because of the festival and the famous Abbott Magic Company, Colon bills itself as the Magic Capital of the World.

### Abbott's Magic Company (all ages)

**124 St. Joseph, a block west of Highway 86; (269) 432-3235 or (800) 926-2442; www.abbott magic.com. Its retail store hours are 8 a.m. to 5 p.m. Mon through Fri and 9 a.m. to 4 p.m. Sat. Magic shows at the company's showroom on Sat afternoons during summer, during the Magic Get-Together, and at Colon High School in the evenings are open to the public. An auction/magic flea market is held in mid-May. $ for the showroom presentations and $$–$$$ for evening shows.**

Faster than you can say "abracadabra," the kids and the rest of the family can disappear inside the Abbott's Magic Company to seek out items for Halloween and tricks to dazzle their friends back home. Lacquered Chinese boxes, black top hats, magic wands, rubber chickens, and fake raccoons are among the more than 2,000 products Abbott's sells to magicians around the globe. It's the world's largest producer of handmade illusions.

## Let's Go to the Drive-In

The Capri Drive-In, just outside Coldwater, is one of the last of its kind: a real, live drive-in movie theater. Built along historic US 12 in 1964, it survives as a great family draw where the kids can curl up in their jammies while Mom and Dad cuddle in the front seat and enjoy a feature on one of two movie screens. Check out the Capri at www.capridrive-in.com, or call (517) 278-5628. To find more drive-ins, go to www.michigandriveins.com.

## Where to Eat

**River Lake Inn.** 767 Ralston Rd.; (269) 432-2626. Family buffet dinner served Wed, Thurs, and Sun along with other items daily. A bonus is a butterfly and hummingbird garden in summer, a birding trail, and other wildlife. $$

See more under Coldwater listings.

## Where to Stay

**Palmer Lake Lodges.** 52970 Burr Oak Rd.; (269) 432-2825; www.magicgettogether.com/ hotels. Six lakeside cottages featuring boats, tackle shop, and a play area for kids. $$ See Coldwater listing for more places to stay.

## For More Information

**Branch County Area Chamber of Commerce and Branch County Tourism Bureau.** 20 Division St., Coldwater 49036. For the chamber, (517) 278-5985; www .branchareachamber.com. For the tourism bureau, (517) 278-0241.

# Stevensville

Stevensville is perched atop the now-grassy dunes, just off I-94 and just south of Benton Harbor and St. Joseph.

### Red Arrow Hobbies  (all ages)

5095 Red Arrow Hwy.; (269) 429-8233; www.redarrowhobbies.com. Open Mon through Fri 10 a.m. to 6 p.m., 10 a.m. to 3 p.m. Sat.

Got a budding rocket scientist in the house? This is the place to take him or her. Red Arrow Hobbies caters to kids of all ages interested in rockets and rocketry and other science projects. The store carries more than 1,000 rocketry items and even has information on weekend rocket launches, where as many as 500 enthusiasts gather to blast off their creations up to 3 miles high.

### Grand Mere State Park  (all ages)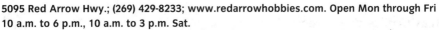

On Red Arrow Highway; (269) 426-4013. From I-94, take the Stevensville exit and go south to Thornton Road. It soon becomes Willow Road. The park entrance is about ½ mile away.

**Warren Dunes State Park administers the facility. Entrance is by state park permit ($ daily or $$$$ annually).**

This stately old park (*grand-mère* is French for "grandmother") offers a glimpse of what the lake's sand dunes were like before towns and cities sprang up along the shore. Mostly undeveloped, the park has hiking trails through tree-covered and bald dunes and is a great place for bird-watching and enjoying the seclusion.

## Where to Eat

**Grand Mere Inn.** 5800 Red Arrow Hwy.; (269) 429-3591. From I-94, take exit 22 and go east. Great view of Lake Michigan, with seafood and steak specialties. Children's menu available. $$$

For less expensive fare, try the restaurant at Park Inn International (see Where to Stay), or see listings under Benton Harbor and St. Joseph.

## Where to Stay

**Baymont Inns and Suites.** I-94, exit 23; (269) 428-9111. Basic motel has one hundred rooms. Restaurants nearby. Two rooms are available for guests traveling with pets. $$

**Park Inn International.** 4290 Red Arrow Hwy.; (269) 429-3218. Just south of St. Joseph. Take I-94, exit 23 at Stevensville and go ½ mile north on Business I-94. The inn has ninety rooms, indoor and outdoor pools, and exercise areas. Restaurant on premises serves moderately priced breakfast, lunch, and dinner. Pets OK. The hotel also offers **free** breakfasts for guests plus **free** high-speed Internet lines. $$

# Benton Harbor and St. Joseph

If you've got a Sears appliance in your home, chances are it came from these towns, home of the Whirlpool Corporation. This is indeed a tale of two cities. While Benton Harbor is attempting to lift itself up by its bootstraps, sister city St. Joseph, just across the St. Joe River bridge, is prospering. One-way brick streets route traffic past shops downtown. Down the hill toward Lake Michigan is the old part of town, with many historic homes and a great beach. The two towns are accessible just off I-94.

## Krasl Art Center (all ages)

707 Lake Blvd., in downtown St. Joseph; (269) 983-0271; www.krasl.org. Open from 10 a.m. to 4 p.m. Mon, Tues, Wed, Fri, and Sat, 10 a.m. to 9 p.m. Thurs, and 1 to 4 p.m. Sun. Admission is **free.**

The museum features regional artists and traveling exhibits with works from other museums around the country, such as the Detroit Institute of Arts. Exhibits change about every six weeks. There is also a permanent collection of sculpture on the grounds outside. There are occasional one-day workshops for children as well.

### Curious Kids Museum (all ages)

415 Lake Blvd., in downtown St. Joseph; (269) 983-2543; www.curiouskidsmuseum.org. Reach the museum by taking exit 27 off I-94 and heading north on Niles Avenue; turn west on Broad, go 2 blocks, and then proceed south on Lake Boulevard. The museum is open daily, but hours vary by season. Kids ages 12 and younger must be accompanied by an adult. Admission is $ for anyone age 1 or older.

Southwest Michigan's own hands-on children's museum features interactive displays and ways for kids to learn about everything from serving customers to listening for a heart-beat in a teddy bear.

## Where to Eat

**Broad Street Cafe.** Corner of Main and Broad, St. Joseph; (269) 983-7646. Great bagel sandwiches, soups, and coffees throughout the day, starting around 6:30 a.m. $

**Clementine's.** 1235 Broad St., downtown St. Joseph; (269) 983-0990. Looks over a marina and serves a wide variety of lunch and dinner items. Children's menu available. $–$$$

**Schu's Grill and Bar.** 501 Pleasant St., downtown St. Joseph; (269) 983-7248. Good American-style food. Children's menu available for lunch and dinner. $$

## Where to Stay

The shoreline between Indiana and Benton Harbor and St. Joseph literally has hundreds of choices for travelers and vacationers, from bed-and-breakfasts to large motels and inns. Here are a couple of favorites:

**Boulevard Inn.** 521 Lake Blvd., St. Joseph; (269) 983-6600. From I-94, take exit 33 into Benton Harbor and across the bridge to St. Joseph. At the first light, turn left onto Main. Go to the next light and turn right onto Broad. Go to the second stop sign and turn left onto Lake. The hotel, 2 blocks down on the left,  offers eighty-three suite-style rooms and restaurant serving breakfast, lunch, and dinner. $$$

**Silver Beach Hotel.** 100 Main St., St. Joseph; (269) 983-7341. On Business I-94 just across the bridge from Benton Harbor. The hotel has 149 rooms, indoor pool, whirlpool, and restaurant serving breakfast through dinner. Also close to downtown St. Joseph shopping, fishing piers, and beachfront. $$$

## For More Information

**Southwestern Michigan Tourist Council.** 2300 Pipestone Rd., Benton Harbor 49022; (269) 925-6301; www.swmichigan.org.

# Coloma

Founded in 1834, this village, once called Dickerville, was renamed after a West Coast wildflower. It's now a familiar stop on I-94.

### Deer Forest (all ages)
**Take the I-94 Coloma exit, then go north 2½ miles; (269) 468-4961; www.deerforest.com. Open daily from 10 a.m. to 6 p.m. from Memorial Day weekend through Labor Day. Admission includes rides on the train, Ferris wheel, child-size roller coaster, and more. $$$.**

More than 300 tame animals await the kids to pet and feed them. The kids also can ride a Ferris wheel and take a railroad ride through the woods or play on a huge playscape. Snacks and picnic area with grills are available.

## Where to Eat and Stay
See Benton Harbor and St. Joseph listings.

# Battle Creek

While the city that cereal built no longer features tours of the Kellogg Company, Ralston Purina, and Post—protecting trade secrets was the reason, the companies said—Battle Creek has other great events to bring you down.

### International Festival of Lights (all ages)
**Downtown Battle Creek centered around Main Street; (269) 962-2240; www.bcfestivals.com. To reach the festival area, take exit 98B off I-94 and go north into downtown. Free.**

More than one million holiday lights grace downtown, ice sculptures go up around Millrace Park, and other activities help welcome the holiday season to the city. The event includes International Children's Day one Sat (check to determine the day) with interactive activities for kids that include crafts and games.

### Field of Flight Air Show and Balloon Festival (all ages)
**Takes place in early July at W. K. Kellogg Airport; (269) 962-0592; www.bcballoons.com. The airport is reached by exiting I-94 at Helmer Road and following the signs. Admission $, parking $.**

Each July, Battle Creek residents turn their eyes to the skies for eight days, starting the Sat before the Fourth of July holiday. The competition draws up to 200 balloon fliers to the city for takeoffs, weather permitting. During the air show, see aerobatics teams perform precision maneuvers. Your kids will love the wing walkers and stunt planes, not to mention their chance to inspect aircraft up close during on-the-ground displays.

### Binder Park Zoo (all ages)
**7400 Division Dr.; (269) 979-1351; www.binderparkzoo.org. The zoo is 3 miles south of I-94, exit 100. It is normally open from the last Sat of Apr through mid-Oct. Hours are 9 a.m. to 5 p.m. Mon through Fri (until 8 p.m. on Wed only from June through Aug), 9 a.m. to 6 p.m. Sat, and 10 a.m. to 6 p.m. Sun. Stroller accessible. $$.**

The zoo contains more than eighty animal exhibits with more than 250 animals in natural settings, including snow leopards, an interactive exhibit on insects, and the new Wild

Africa exhibit. Eighty African animals roam **free** in a fifty-acre exhibit. There's a gift shop offering nature books, stuffed animals, and the like. A restaurant serves snacks and sandwiches indoors and out. There's also a hands-on playground at Miller Children's Zoo, part of Binder Park that includes a dinosaur replica.

### Leila Arboretum (all ages)

928 West Michigan Ave., at Twentieth Street; (616) 969-0270. To get there, take exit 95 off I-94 and travel north on Helmer for about 6 miles to West Michigan Avenue; from there, head east 1½ miles, then north into the arboretum. The arboretum is open daily from dawn to dusk and is **free.**

The seventy-two-acre arboretum, built with the help of Post Cereal money in 1922, was left dormant during the Great Depression and remained that way until 1982, when it was revived once more. There are massive floral displays in season, a children's adventure garden, a sunken garden, and a visitor center.

### Battle Creek Bombers (all ages)

1392 Capital Ave. Northeast; (269) 660-2255; www.battlecreekbombers.com. Take exit 98B off I-94 and go north. The road becomes Capital Avenue, which will take you through town to Bailey Park and the stadium. Field box seats and box seats $$, reserved seats and bleachers $. Senior citizens and ages 14 and younger $. Many nights feature special promotions, such as **free** hats or balls, or fireworks.

Like baseball? This Northwoods League affiliate features collegiate players hoping to catch the eye of major-league scouts. The team plays in the 6,200-seat C. O. Brown Stadium. Special theme games include **free** bats and jersey giveaways.

### Full Blast (all ages)

35 Hamblin Ave.; (269) 966-3667; www.fullblast.org. From I-94, take I-194/Highway 66 north into town. Turn left at the first light onto Hamblin, and you're there. Hours are 6 a.m. to 9 p.m. Mon through Fri, 8 a.m. to 9 p.m. Sat, and 11 a.m. to 8 p.m. Sun, Memorial Day weekend to Labor Day. Depending on the amount of fun you want, prices range $–$$$. Children 10 and under must be accompanied by someone 18 years or older.

One of the largest outdoor and indoor exercise areas in the state goes right along with the reputation of Battle Creek from its early days as a health-spa location. Included in the fifteen attractions are a full-service health club, an indoor playground, a food court, and Gully Washer, an indoor park with two waterslides, "river" float, and other amenities. Next to it is Flash Flood, for outdoor fun, with two 200-foot waterslides and a playground. There's also a gym with three basketball courts and indoor walking track.

## Where to Eat

**Arcadia Brewing Co.** 103 West Michigan Ave., downtown; (269) 963-9690. From I-94, head north on I-194/Highway 66 to Michigan Avenue, and turn west. Enjoy house-made brews with wood-fired pizza for lunch and dinner. $$

**Clara's on the River.** 44 North McCamly; (269) 963-0966; www.claras.com. From I-94, head north on I-194/Highway 66 to downtown. Turn west on Michigan to McCamly and north to the riverside. Large and varied selection of foods for lunch and dinner. Chicken Caesar salad is great. Children's menu. $$

## Where to Stay

**Days Inn.** 4786 Beckley Rd.; (269) 979-3561. From I-94, take exit 97 and head east to Beckley. The motel has eighty-four rooms. Pets OK at extra charge. **Free** continental breakfast; restaurants nearby. $$

**McCamly Plaza Hotel.** 50 Capital Ave., downtown; (269) 963-7050. From I-94, take I-194/Highway 66 north. Turn west on Hamblin to Capital, and then go north. The hotel has 242 rooms, indoor pool, exercise area, and restaurant serving breakfast through dinner. Small pets OK at extra charge. $$$

## For More Information

**Greater Battle Creek–Calhoun County Convention and Visitors Bureau.** 77 East Michigan Ave., Suite 100, Battle Creek 49017; (269) 962-2240 or (800) 397-2240; www .battlecreekvisitors.org.

# Hickory Corners

Named for a hickory tree found in the 1840s, Hickory Corners is home to about 3,000 people.

**Gilmore Classic Car Club of America Museum** (all ages) 6865 Hickory Rd.; (269) 671-5089; www.gilmorecarmuseum.org. Take Highway 43 north from Kalamazoo to Hickory Corners. Museum hours are 9 a.m. to 5 p.m. early May through late Oct. Adults and seniors $$; children ages 7 to 15 $, 6 and under **free.** Parking is also **free.**

You'll find more than 140 preserved beauties that epitomize the term *rolling sculpture.*

They're all on display in antique barns in the tiny town of Hickory Corners, just northwest of Battle Creek. The collection includes a rare 1899 Locomobile Steamer as well as Packards, Cadillacs, and cars made in Kalamazoo. Along with the autos and a replica of a 1930s Shell filling station, there's a picnic area where the kids can blow off steam. The newest building addition is the Blue Moon Diner, the precursor of the modern fast-food restaurant. It was moved from Meriden, Connecticut, and now is open for lunch (call for dates). On at least two weekends a month in summer, the museum hosts shows highlighting vintage motorcycles, tractors, and cars from sports models to specific makes.

## Where to Eat and Stay

See Battle Creek and Kalamazoo listings.

# Kalamazoo

From maple sugaring in season to a walk-by history of aviation at its "Air Zoo" and a stroll through the campus of Western Michigan University, this city along I-94 delivers a memorable visit for the entire family. Sports fans can enjoy not only WMU's great football program but also professional baseball and hockey.

### Kalamazoo Nature Center (all ages)

**7000 North Westnedge; (269) 381-1574; www.naturecenter.org. Go north from I-94 at US 131 and get off at exit 44 (D Avenue); drive east to Westnedge, then south less than a mile. The visitor center is open from 9 a.m. to 5 p.m. Mon through Sat and from 1 to 5 p.m. Sun. The grounds are open one hour later. $–$$, children ages 3 and under free.**

A recently renovated interpretive center greets visitors to the 1,000 acres of dense hardwood forest awaiting exploration. Kids can walk through tree trunks and learn about animals through lots of hands-on exhibits. There's also a butterfly house open in summer, where you can watch the entire life cycle of butterflies, plus a hummingbird garden and a bug house. The Delano pioneer homestead, with depictions of early Michigan farm life, operates during warm weather. The dense woodlands include a glen that was a favorite inspiration for nineteenth-century author James Fenimore Cooper.

### Kalamazoo Air Zoo (all ages)

**6151 Portage Rd., Portage; (269) 382-6555; www.airzoo.org. Take I-94, exit 78 south onto Portage Road and go about 1½ miles to Milham Road, and then head east ½ mile. Open 9 a.m. to 5 p.m. Mon through Sat, noon to 5 p.m. Sun. Adults $$, children ages 6 to 15 $, ages 5 and younger free.**

The Air Zoo showcases Michigan's and America's history in flight and is one of the state's best air museums. More than fifty aircraft are displayed in a large hangar, an adjacent annex, and outside. Let the kids climb in and "fly" a flight simulator.

Go up in a former air force propeller-driven trainer on summer weekends. You'll also see military uniforms and model aircraft, and there's a gift shop, too. In place of the annual air shows given in previous years, the museum presents summer weekend events highlighting aircraft and past air shows. A unique "4-D" theater takes you on an almost-real flight in a four-engine bomber, complete with vibrations and other planes flying by thanks to a 180-degree, 60-foot-high screen. In another area, take a 3-D trip to the International Space Station, or hop in a flight simulator for a trip in a fighter jet.

Two recent additions are the Guadalcanal National Museum, which focuses on that famous World War II Pacific island battle, and the Michigan Aviation Hall of Fame.

### Kalamazoo Valley Museum (all ages)

**230 North Rose St.; (269) 373-7990 or (800) 772-3370; www.kvm.kvcc.edu. From I-94, take the Westnedge Avenue exit north. Jog onto Park Street, then turn east on Michigan Avenue to Rose, and head north. Hours are 9 a.m. to 5 p.m. Mon through Sat, and 1 to 5 p.m. Sun. Admission is free, but there are charges for some of the museum's exhibits and programs, including a fee for children ages 13 and up for the Challenger Learning Center ($) and for the Universe Theater and Planetarium ($).**

A hands-on science center for the kids is combined with local history lessons in this museum, created with the largest capital contribution campaign in the history of the city. More than 11,000 persons contributed to its construction. The core gallery features exhibits from the museum's collection of 45,000 local artifacts. There are also antiques.

A Trail of History explores local history with the help of items found in home attics. And, of course, there's the mummy, which has been part of a museum here since 1927. The mummy is that of a woman who lived more than 2,300 years ago. In the Interactive Learning Hall, a computer drives a fully interactive theater that creates programs based on audience ideas, while the *Challenger* Learning Center focuses on space exploration.

### Echo Valley  (all ages)

**8495 East H Ave.; (269) 349-3291; www.echovalleyfun.com. To reach Echo Valley, take I-94, exit 85, Thirty-fifth Street. Turn right. At the first stop, turn left on Highway 96 and drive to Thirty-third Street. Turn right and go 3 miles to H Avenue. Turn left. Open in winter from 6 to 10 p.m. Fri, 10 a.m. to 10 p.m. Sat, and noon to 7 p.m. Sun. Toboggans, an all-day pass, or inner tubing $$.**

The family fun in Kalamazoo doesn't stop for winter. Remember those butterflies in your stomach at just the moment your sled or toboggan moved down your neighborhood winter hill? You and your kids can experience the same roller-coaster thrill at Echo Valley, east of the city. Eight iced tracks await. You'll get to use a wooden toboggan.

Load it onto one of the tracks, and you'll be launched down a 120-foot hill at up to 60 miles per hour, on more than ¼ mile of curves and straights. A rope tow gets you back to the top. Cold noses and toes can be warmed at the lodge while you sample the offerings at the snack bar. Then strap on a pair of rental skates and try the 43,000-square-foot outdoor rink ($).

# Theater Choices in the Kalamazoo Area

For a city its size, Kalamazoo and its surroundings have an outstanding selection of live theater choices throughout the year. They include the **Kalamazoo Civic Theatre** (269-343-1313; www.kzoocivic.com) at 329 South Park St. at South Street downtown, just off Bronson Park, the only location where Abraham Lincoln spoke in Michigan, four years before becoming president. From I-94, take Westnedge downtown, and then turn north onto Park.

The **Barn Theatre** (269-731-4121; www.barntheatre.com) is along Highway 96, west of downtown Kalamazoo in Auga. From downtown, head east on Michigan 96. It features summer stock. The theater has been performing plays and musicals for local crowds for more than fifty years.

The **New Vic Theatre** (269-381-3328; www.newvictheatre.org) is at 134 East Vine. From I-94, head north on Westnedge to Vine and turn east. The theater is a professional stock company that produces and performs plays year-round except Jan. *A Christmas Carol* is performed each Nov and Dec. $$$

### Michigan K-Wings (all ages)

The Wings play at Wings Stadium, 3620 Van Rick Dr.; (269) 345-9772; www.kwings.com. From I-94, take the Sprinkle Road exit and head south to Van Rick. Adults $$–$$$, children 12 and younger $. Public skating rentals $.

Watch the Wings, a farm team for the Dallas Stars in the NHL, take on other International Hockey League teams in forty-one home games between Oct and Apr.

### Kalamazoo Kings Baseball (all ages)

The team plays at the Homer Stryker Field, 251 Mills St., off King Highway; (269) 388-8326; www.kalamazookings.com. Box seats $$, general admission $; there are lots of "give-away" nights scheduled each season.

Everybody's getting into the act for sports teams, including Kalamazoo. The city's Class A baseball team plays in front of up to 5,300 fans late May through late Aug, including the Frontier League All-Star game. If one of your family members is a player, you can even try out for the team each May.

## Where to Eat

**Antique Kitchen Family Restaurant.** 6215 South Westnedge, Portage, off I-94; (269) 327-4014. Great for breakfast and lunch. $$

**Olde Peninsula Brew Pub & Restaurant.** 200 East Michigan Ave.; (269) 343-2739. Pasta and seafood complement house-made beers and root beer inside a great restored building. Children's menu. $$–$$$

## Where to Stay

**Radisson Plaza Inn & Suites at Kalamazoo Center.** 100 West Michigan Ave., at the junction of Michigan and Rose; (269) 343-3333. Upscale hotel has 281 rooms with restaurants, health club, indoor pool, whirlpool, and sauna. Attached to shopping mall. $$$

**Red Roof Inn West.** 5425 West Michigan, at I-94 and Sprinkle Road; (269) 375-7400. This economical property has 108 rooms. Restaurants nearby. Small pets OK. $

**Stuart Avenue Inn Bed and Breakfast.** 229 Stuart Ave.; (269) 342-0230; www.stuart aveinn.com. Located in the Stuart Avenue Historic District, which along with the South Street District, west of South Westnedge, and the Vine Historic District, just south and west of downtown, is in a historic walking-tour brochure. The B&B has seventeen rooms in two historic Victorian homes with English gardens. $$–$$$

## For More Information

**Kalamazoo County Convention and Visitors Bureau.** 141 East Michigan Ave., Kalamazoo 49007; (800) 888-0509; www .discoverkalamazoo.com.

# Otsego

North of Kalamazoo off US 131, Otsego is the location of another ski area.

### Bittersweet Ski Area (ages 7 and up)

North of Otsego along US 131; (269) 694-2032; www.skibittersweet.com. The season generally runs from Dec through Mar. The ski runs are usually open until 11 p.m. $$$$.

Bittersweet features sixteen runs with six chairlifts, snowmaking instruction for kids as young as 4, night skiing, and rentals. Food is available on the premises.

## Where to Eat and Stay

See Kalamazoo listings.

# South Haven

From I-196, take exit 20 west into this lakeside town, which will remind you a lot of New England. South Haven's businesses abut the Black River, which flows right through town. Harborfest, South Haven's annual summer festival, is in mid-June.

### Michigan Maritime Museum (all ages)

260 Dyckman Rd., in downtown South Haven, on the banks of the Black River; (269) 637-8078 or (800) 747-3810; www.michiganmaritimemuseum.org. $–$$, with family admission prices available. Hours vary seasonally, so call ahead.

With its shipping and Great Lakes heritage, South Haven is the perfect location for this museum, which tells the story of the role ships played and still play on the Great Lakes. A recent addition to the museum's holdings is a replica of the nineteenth-century sloop *Friends Good Will*. Beginning life in Detroit as a trading ship, the original *Friends* figured in the War of 1812 and Perry's victory in the Battle of Lake Erie, which determined control of the Great Lakes for the Americans. The sloop had been part of the British fleet, having been captured earlier. Now, kids can step on board to see what life on a real sailing vessel was like. The museum also features a former Coast Guard lifesaving station, a collection of antique outboard motors, a commercial fishing boat, a light keeper's house, and the South Haven south harbor pier light. It's also on the South Haven Harbor Walk, with historical markers set along the Black River telling the history of the town.

## Where to Eat

**Magnolia Grille.** 515 Williams St.; (269) 637-8435. In the Old Harbor Village area. From I-196, head west at exit 20 on Phoenix Street, and then go 1 block north on Center. Floating restaurant at Nichols Landing for lunch and dinner. Children's menu. $$$$

**Sherman's Dairy Bar.** 7328 CR 388; (269) 637-1148. Open mid-Mar through Oct. Featuring forty ice-cream flavors, a great summer dalliance after a day at the beach. No other food. $

**Thirsty Perch.** 268 Broadway; (269) 639-8000. Enjoy fresh fish and other items from salads to sandwiches. $–$$

## Where to Stay

**Great Lakes Inn and Suites.** 9817 Highway 140, a mile north of exit 18 on I-196;

(269) 637-8700. This motel has sixty rooms, indoor pool, exercise area, and restaurant serving breakfast, lunch, and dinner. $$

**Old Harbor Inn.** 515 Williams St.; (269) 637-8480. From I-196, head west at exit 20 and go 1 mile on Phoenix, then 1 block north on Center to Williams. The inn has forty-four rooms downtown on the banks of the Black River in the Old Harbor Village shopping area. Indoor pool and whirlpool. Restaurant. $$$

**Seymour House Bed & Breakfast.** 1248 Blue Star A-2 Hwy.; (269) 227-3918. Seven miles north of town on Blue Star Highway, this B&B offers five rooms and one log cabin, plus swimming, fishing, and nature trails. $$$

**Van Buren State Park.** 23960 Ruggels Rd.; (269) 637-2788, or for reservations, (800) 447-2757. From South Haven, go south on Blue Star Highway (Old US 31) to Ruggels Road and head west. A daily ($) or annual ($$) permit is required for entry. Camping is $ nightly. The park has 220 campsites, a picnic area, and its main attraction, the large, duned beach.

## For More Information

**South Haven Visitors Bureau.** 546 Phoenix St., South Haven 49090; (269) 637-5252 or (800) 764-2836; www.southhaven.org. Also see South Haven Chamber of Commerce's Web site at www.southhavenmi.com.

# Saugatuck

Saugatuck is west of I-196 (also known as A-2, or the Blue Star Highway) at exit 41.

Originally a lumber shipping town, it was discovered in the late 1800s by Chicagoans who hopped quick passage on steamboats for the area's magnificent beaches and lakeshore inns. Saugatuck, which means "river's mouth" in Native American, still holds a quaint, quiet atmosphere and is now known as an artists' colony. Be sure to visit some of the area's twenty-four galleries for locally produced art. There are so many that the region bills itself as the Art Coast of Michigan.

The annual Taste of Saugatuck/Douglas takes place in mid-June in downtown Saugatuck along Water Street. Up to thirty area restaurants take part in setting up booths to serve their best.

### Mount Baldhead (all ages)

**Along the river near Oval Beach. From Saugatuck, take Blue Star Highway across the river to Douglas, and then turn west on Center and north on Park.**

Everyone has to climb the 279 steps up this giant dune for a view of the area and Lake Michigan beyond town.

### Star of Saugatuck (all ages)

**Leaves from 716 Water St.; (269) 857-4261; www.saugatuckboatcruises.com. Operates early May to late Oct. Children ages two and under ride free.**

Take a scenic ninety-minute cruise on the Kalamazoo River with a short turnaround in Lake Michigan aboard this two-deck paddle wheeler. The 80-foot boat offers snacks and

# Take the **A-2**

The A-2, also called the Blue Star Highway, is a wonderful alternative to the freeway grind. Many who travel it have labeled it Michigan's version of New England's US 1. Traveling through tiny towns with frequent glimpses of sparkling Lake Michigan, the highway traverses some of the state's most picturesque country and passes country inns tucked in the woods, you-pick fruit farms, and roadside stands, which in summer brim with homegrown peaches, blueberries, and other goodies. If you have the time, take the drive, which runs from the Indiana state line nearly all the way north. Some of my best vacation finds have been on this forgotten former major highway. It's also become the latest state Heritage Route. You won't be disappointed.

drinks during the trip along with live narration. The craft conforms to all Coast Guard safety regulations; it's safe for younger kids.

### Sand Dune Rides (all ages)

**6495 Washington Rd., Saugatuck; (269) 857-2253; www.saugatuckduneride.com. Take exit 41 (Saugatuck) from I-196 and go south on Blue Star Highway about ½ mile. Rides start in May at 10 a.m. Mon through Sat and at noon on Sun; the last ride leaves at 5:30 p.m. In July and Aug there are extended hours. Rides run through mid-Oct. Adults $$$, children age 10 and under $$.**

Visitors can take sightseeing trips skimming over the nearby dunes in dune buggies that hold up to eighteen people. Trips last about thirty-five minutes and are safe for babies and tots.

## Where to Eat

Saugatuck is so compact that most of the town's eateries don't even need a street address. Just watch for them. The main business district is along Water Street.

**Coral Gables.** 220 Water St., overlooking the harbor downtown; (269) 857-2162; www.coral-gables.com. Serves lunch and dinner—from burgers to chicken and seafood—seasonally, with dockside open-air dining in warmer weather. $$

**Crane's Pie Pantry & Restaurant.** 6054 124th Ave., between Saugatuck and Fennville; (269) 561-2297. As the name implies,

Crane's specializes in fresh-baked pies and other items for lunch and dinner. $

**Ida Red's Cottage.** On Water Street; (269) 857-5803. Serves breakfast all the time and lunch from burgers to pasta. $

**M&M's Ice Cream Treats & Stuff to Eat.** On Blue Star Highway, Saugatuck; (269) 857-1030. One of several sweet shops in the area. Ice cream, burgers, and other items served from breakfast onward. $

**Pumpernickel's Eatery.** 202 Butler Street, Saugatuck; (269) 857-1196. Enjoy breakfast, lunch, and dinner downtown. $$–$$$

## Where to Stay

The twin towns of Saugatuck and Douglas plus neighboring Fennville together hold one of the most extensive concentrations of Victoriana and early-twentieth-century bed-and-breakfasts and cottages in the state, as well as modern motels and campgrounds.

**Goshorn Lake Cottage Condos.** 3581 Sixty-fifth St.; (269) 857-4808 or (800) 541-4210; www.saugatuck.com/sbonline.htm. From I-196, take exit 41 and turn west to Sixty-fifth. The resort offers nineteen housekeeping cottages on Goshorn Lake, a few minutes from downtown Saugatuck. Cottages usually rent weekly. $$

**Lake Shore Resort.** 2885 Lakeshore Dr.; (269) 857-7121. From Highway A-2, head west on Wiley Road, then a mile south on Lakeshore Drive. The resort offers thirty motel rooms on the lake as well as an outdoor pool. Restaurant nearby. $$$

**Park House Bed & Breakfast Inn.** 888 Holland St.; (269) 857-4535. From I-196, take exit 41 and go west. This inn has eight rooms in a restored 1857 home plus four cottages. $$–$$$$

**Shangrai-la Motel.** 6190 Blue Star Hwy.; (269) 857-1453. The motel has twenty rooms, with outdoor pool. $$

## For More Information

See Douglas listing.

# Douglas

Just across the mouth of the Kalamazoo River is this small town, home of one of the last great overnight steamers afloat in the Great Lakes.

## Keewatin Maritime Museum (all ages)

At Blue Star Highway and Union Street, just south of the Saugatuck-Douglas bridge in Douglas; (269) 857-2464; www.keewatinmaritimemuseum.com. Open 10 a.m. to 4:30 p.m. Memorial Day weekend to Labor Day. Adults $–$$$, children ages 6 to 14 $–$$, under age 6 **free.**

Step on board and tour the last of her kind, a classic Great Lakes passenger steamer.

Show the kids the 105 passenger cabins and how travel used to be around the lakes before the advent of expressways put this boat out of business in 1965. The adjacent Red Dock Cafe offers lunch and dinner.

## Where to Stay and Eat

See the Saugatuck listing, earlier in this chapter.

## For More Information

**Saugatuck–Douglas Convention and Visitors Bureau.** 303 Culver, Douglas 49453; (269) 857-1701; www.saugatuck.com.

# Holland

A visit to this quaint city gives you a taste of the area's history. As you'd guess by its name, it was settled by the Dutch in the nineteenth century. They brought all their customs with them, many of which remain today and are highlighted in the annual Tulip Time Festival in May. Its series of street performers and **free** concerts run all summer in the city park. The city was also a famous furniture-making center—like its neighbor, Grand Rapids, 30 miles to the east.

### Windmill Island (all ages)

**The thirty-acre island is downtown at Seventh Street and Lincoln Avenue; (616) 355-1030; www.windmillisland.org. Open from May through Oct. Hours vary through the summer. Adults $$, ages 5 to 12 $, and ages 4 and younger free.**

Cross an authentic Dutch drawbridge to see the 240-year-old De Zwann windmill, which still operates and where North America's only Dutch-certified miller produces flour sold at the park. There's also a miniature Dutch village where there are dancing demonstrations and guided tours in summer.

A carousel and farm animals can entertain the kids, too.

### De Klomp Wooden Shoe and Delftware Factory and Veldheer Tulip Gardens (all ages)

**12755 Quincy St., at US 31, 3 miles north of the city; (616) 399-1900; www.veldheertulip .com. Hours are 8 a.m. to 6 p.m. Mon through Fri and 9 a.m. to 5 p.m. Sat and Sun from Apr through Dec; 9 a.m. to 5 p.m. Mon through Fri from Jan through Mar. Admission to the shoe factory is free. Admission to the gardens is $.**

As many as 90 percent of the locals you'll see are of Dutch descent, left from when the area was settled in 1846 by religious-freedom seekers. The immigrants brought their crafts with them, and two examples can be seen here. Artisans continue to create the blue and white delftware ceramics produced at De Klomp, the only delft factory in the nation, while in another area skilled experts gouge, carve, and shape blocks of wood into shoes. Next door at the gardens, more than a hundred varieties of tulips bloom in neat rows each spring along US 31, and visitors who stop can purchase bulbs. The best times to see the tulips in bloom are the last week of Apr and the first week of May. Veldheer is the largest tulip grower in the Midwest.

### Dutch Village (all ages)

**At US 31 and James Street; (616) 396-1475 or (800) 285-7177; www.dutchvillage.com. Hours vary by season, which runs from mid-Apr through Labor Day Adults $$; children ages 3 to 11 $, ages 2 and younger free.**

Wooden shoe carving, folk-dancing demonstrations, and imported gifts are set amid Dutch architecture in a miniature village and gardens. For the kids, head for the petting zoo, the antique carousel, or the swing ride, and make your last stop the delft shop.

# Tulip Time Festival

The Holland area is a major producer of tulip bulbs, and its Dutch heritage is celebrated each May during one of Michigan's first warm-weather outdoor events. If you're planning to come for the event, make your reservations early, as this is a popular festival.

Each spring, the city's streets are lined with 8 miles of blooming tulips. Thousands of visitors come out to watch parades, which feature the traditional washing of the streets by costumed, dancing scrubbers. For information, call (616) 396-4221 or (800) 822-2770; www.tuliptime.org.

### Craig's Cruisers Family Fun Center (all ages)

**US 31 and Chicago; (616) 392-7300; www.craigscruisers.com. Open 10 a.m. to 11 p.m. in summer. The indoor arcade is open all year. Food is available. Open noon to 10 p.m. Fri, 11 a.m. to 10 p.m. Sat, and noon to 8 p.m. Sun in fall and winter. $.**

Go-karts, minigolf, carts for younger children, batting cages, and other fun activities are offered here.

## Where to Eat

**New Holland Microbrewery.** 66 East Eighth St.; (616) 355-6422. Good selection of sandwiches, pizza, and other pub grub, plus house-made beers and spirits. Children's menu. $$

**The Piper.** 2225 South Shore Dr., Macatawa, overlooking Lake Macatawa; (616) 335-5866. From US 31, take Sixteenth Street west through town. It becomes South Shore Drive. Pastas and wood-fired pizzas are specialties for lunch and dinner. $$$

**Russ's Restaurants.** Three different locations in Holland: 210 North River, (616) 392-6300; 1060 Lincoln, (616) 396-4036; and 361 East Eighth, (616) 396-2348; all west of US 31. Serves breakfast, lunch, and dinner. Traditional family fare from pancakes to burgers. Try the pie. $$

## Where to Stay

Most accommodations will be along or just off US 31, which skirts the town's eastern edge.

**Comfort Inn.** 422 East Thirty-second St. at US 31; (616) 392-1000. This hotel has seventy-one rooms, with continental breakfast included. $$

**Doubletree Hotel.** 650 East Twenty-fourth, just east of US 31; (616) 394-0111. This hotel has 168 rooms, indoor pool, sauna, exercise room, hot tub, recreation area, and restaurant. $$–$$$

**Hampton Inn.** 12427 Felch St., just off US 31; (616) 399-8500. This hotel features 178 rooms and what's billed as west Michigan's largest indoor recreational area. $$

**Holland State Park.** Seven miles west of US 31 on Ottawa Beach Road; (616) 399-9390; www.michigan.gov/dnr, then look for the "parks" tab. From US 31, turn west onto Lakewood, and then follow Douglas. It becomes Ottawa Beach Road. The park has 142 campsites on mostly open area near the road, but the real draw is the park's Lake Michigan beach around the corner. Camping is available here, too, but there is little shade. The beautiful beach is what brings folks out. At sunset, be sure to bring your camera for stunning shots of the bright red lighthouse.

## For More Information

**Holland Area Convention and Visitors Bureau.** 76 East Eighth St., Holland 49423; (616) 394-0000 or (800) 506-1299; www .holland.org.

# Grand Rapids

While the rapids that gave this city its name are long covered under dams, you can see one of the state's minor-league baseball teams in action, explore a museum portraying the city's past, stroll through sculpture gardens, and perhaps even wet a fishing line downtown. The city is at the intersection of US 131, I-96, and I-196, named the Gerald R. Ford Freeway. Most of the addresses outside the city are divided by geographical quadrant, with NE, NW, SE, or SW after them meaning northeast, northwest, southeast, or southwest. Use those designations to help find locations of accommodations or attractions.

In the 1800s Grand Rapids was the nation's capital of furniture design, as it is today, with huge annual shows that drew buyers from across the country. Logs from the surrounding hardwood forests floated down the Grand River to mills that brought European craftsmen here to create the industry. Lots of office furniture is still made in town, but most of the home-furniture factories have gone south.

## Public Museum of Grand Rapids and Van Andel Center (all ages)

272 Pearl St.; (616) 456-3977; www.grmuseum.org. Located on the west bank of the Grand River. Hours are 9 a.m. to 5 p.m. Mon through Sat and noon to 5 p.m. Sun. Adults $$, seniors and children age 3 to 17 $. Kids under age 3 are admitted free.

The complex traces the city from its start as a trading post to its peak as an industrial center known worldwide for furniture production. One of the first things you'll see, though, isn't furniture. It's a 76-foot-long finback whale skeleton hanging from the museum's three-story entrance Galleria. The museum shows the city's furniture-manufacturing heyday through artifacts, photos, and videos.

Inside, a huge flywheel of a 1905 steam engine powers a replica furniture factory, where docents explain the hours of work that went into making the finely crafted furniture that the "Furniture City" was known for. Antiques buffs will like the more than 120 types of finished furniture representing several periods, including pieces designed by Frank Lloyd Wright. Other exhibits include a re-creation of downtown at the turn of the twentieth century and one on west Michigan's first inhabitants, Native American Anishinabes.

For kids and the young at heart, a 1928 carousel is set in a pavilion over the river, accompanied by an old Wurlitzer organ ($). Also inside is a gift shop and cafe.

The museum also houses the Roger B. Chaffee Planetarium (616-456-3663). There's an extra charge ($$$) for planetarium and laser shows. The planetarium is not recommended for children ages three and younger, but your grade schooler will enjoy it.

## Gerald R. Ford Museum (all ages)

**303 Pearl St., on the west bank of the Grand River; (616) 451-9263; www.geraldfordmuseum .org. From I-196, take the West Ottawa Street exit. Go south on Ottawa to Pearl. Go west on Pearl to the museum lot. Open daily 9 a.m. to 4:45 p.m. $, free for children younger than 16.**

This stunning mirrored-glass building, reflecting most of downtown and the Grand River, houses memorabilia of the private and public life of local boy made good, President Ford, who assumed office when President Richard Nixon resigned and to whom some credit was given as the leader who began the country's healing following years of conflict at home and overseas. You will see not only glimpses into the Ford White House years but also changing interactive exhibits on the life and times of America during that period of conflict and resolution. There's also a re-creation of the Ford Paint & Varnish Company, where he worked as a boy.

## Frederik Meijer Gardens and Sculpture Park (all ages)

**3411 Bradford NE; (616) 957-1580; www.meijergardens.org. From I-96 take the East Beltline exit and go north to Bradford, and then turn east and drive about ½ mile. The gardens are open daily from 9 a.m. to 5 p.m. Mon, Wed, and Thurs, and 9 a.m. to 9 p.m. Tues and noon to 5 p.m. Sun. From June through Aug, they stay open until 9 p.m. Thurs. $.**

Take in some greenery at this seventy-acre sanctuary of tropical and other plants from five continents.

At five stories tall the indoor Lena Meijer Conservatory is Michigan's largest. Mixed in with coconut palms from the Pacific, ficus from India, and orchids from South America is a desert garden. In spring butterflies flutter in the conservatory.

Outside is a sculpture park with more than fifty sculptures by renowned artists, such as the late Marshall Fredericks, one of Michigan's own. The largest sculpture is the huge da Vinci horse by Nina Akamu, with its own football-field-size, open-air space. It's the world's largest horse sculpture.

Outdoor tours include tram rides (adults $, children under 5 free, weekends only) that focus on woodlands and wetlands. The gardens also feature a gift shop and restaurant inside, plus free tours and docents to answer questions. The newest aspect is the Lena Meijer Children's Garden. As an added treat for kids, butterflies "bloom" each Mar and Apr in an annual indoor show featuring more than forty species from around the world.

## West Michigan Whitecaps (all ages)

**The Whitecaps' Fifth Third Ballpark is at US 131 and West River Drive, Comstock Park; (616) 784-4131; www.whitecaps-baseball.com. The exit is about 5 miles north of downtown.**

**Season runs from Apr through Sept. Box and reserved seats, the U.F.P. deck, and family section $$, bleachers and lawn $.**

Completed in 1994, Fifth Third Ballpark has been home ever since to the Whitecaps, a Class A baseball farm team for the Detroit Tigers. Up to 10,000 fans can watch each of the seventy home games a year. Take your lawn chair and wait with the kids for that foul ball in a special grassy area set aside for folks who want to watch the game the way spectators did when it was invented. Special youth-oriented events include clinics and giveaway games, and there's even a playground.

### Millennium Park  (all ages)

**1415 Maynard Ave. SW; (616) 336-3697; www.millenniumpark.org. Park hours are 8 a.m. to dusk. Beach hours are 10 a.m. to 8 p.m. Beach access $.**

The Grand Rapids area's newest park features a one-hundred-acre lake with beach, hiking and nature trails, picnic areas, and a splash pad with water attractions for kids.

### Grand Rapids Children's Museum  (ages 3 to 10)

**11 Sheldon Ave. NE, at the corner of Fulton and Sheldon Streets, east of the river on Fulton; (616) 235-4726; www.grcm.org. Open 9:30 a.m. to 5 p.m. Tues, Wed, Fri, and Sat; 9:30 a.m. to 8 p.m. Thurs; and noon to 5 p.m. Sun. $, free for children younger than 2.**

Hands-on exhibits for kids to explore and learn, including the Rapids, where kids can try on waders or design a bridge across the river.

### John Ball Park Zoo  (all ages)

**1300 West Fulton St.; (616) 336-4300 or (616) 336-4301; www.johnballzoosociety.org. East of I-196 and Highway 45, 2 miles west from downtown on Fulton. Open daily from 10 a.m. to 6 p.m. from mid-May to Labor Day and from 10 a.m. to 4 p.m. daily the rest of the year. Wheelchair and stroller accessible. Children ages 4 and younger get in free—and so does everybody else from Dec through Feb, when the entrance fee ($) is waived.**

The 140-acre park is the state's second largest, with more than 800 animals from around the world. The zoo's Van Andel Living Shores Aquarium features penguins, seabirds, and underwater viewing. Be sure to see the lions, tigers, bears, warthogs, the African Forest Edge, and the Mokomoboso Valley Champanzee exhibits. There's also a petting corral with farm animals for kids, plus food and a gift shop.

### Celebration Village  (all ages)

**2121 Celebration NE, off Knapp and East Beltline; (616) 530-SHOW; www.celebrationvillage .com. $.**

The first IMAX big-screen theater in west Michigan, plus the added attraction of seventeen regular movie screens, makes this cineplex unique in the state. Shopping is adjacent in the development's village-themed area.

## Where to Eat

Downtown alone features nearly forty restaurants, from diner food to Spanish. Here's a selection:

**Cottage Bar and Restaurant.** Fulton Street and LaGrave, 5 blocks east of Monroe; (616) 454-9088. Next door to One Trick Pony, it's the city's oldest bar and restaurant. Good burritos and chili, along with other items for lunch and dinner. $$

**Grand Traverse Pie Company.** 3224 Twenty-eighth St. SE, off I-96; (616) 977-7600. Fare includes great sandwiches, potpies, and quiche, and always great fresh-baked pies. $

**One Trick Pony.** 136 East Fulton, downtown; (616) 235-7669. Pizza tops the list, along with Cajun and Caribbean fare for lunch and dinner. $$

**Pal's Diner.** 6502 Twenty-eighth St. SE, off I-96; (616) 942-7257. A 1950s stainless-steel diner that serves breakfast, lunch, and dinner all day. $$

**Pietro's Ristorante.** 2780 Birchcrest Dr. SE, off I-96 and the Twenty-eighth Street exit; (616) 452-3228. Very good Italian food. Children's menu. $$

## Where to Stay

Choose from among nearly fifty places to stay, including four bed-and-breakfasts in the historic Heritage Hill area. Here are some good bets for families:

**Amway Grand Plaza Hotel.** 187 Monroe; (616) 774-2000. At the corner of Pearl downtown, east of the US 131 Pearl exit. This establishment has 682 rooms in both renovated and new portions of the hotel. Indoor pool, racquetball and exercise area, six restaurants. $$–$$$$

**Days Inn Downtown.** 310 Pearl St., at the US 131 exit; (616) 235-7611. The property has 175 rooms, indoor pool, and restaurants. Small pets OK. $$

**Fairfield Inn.** At 3930 Stahl Dr. SE; (616) 940-2700. Take exit 43 off I-96. Go west on Highway 11, and then turn north onto East Paris to the hotel. The property has eighty-two rooms, indoor pool, and continental breakfast. Restaurants nearby. $$

**Quality Inn Grand Rapids North.** 2171 Holton, Walker, south of the I-96 Walker Avenue exit; (616) 791-8500. The inn has sixty rooms and an indoor pool. Restaurant nearby. $$

## For More Information

**Grand Rapids/Kent County Convention and Visitors Bureau.** 140 Monroe Ave. NW, Suite 300, Grand Rapids 49503; (616) 459-8287 or (800) 678-9859; www.visitgrandrapids.org.

# Rockford

Just north of Grand Rapids off Highway 44 and east of US 131, Rockford's downtown is filled with interesting places to shop, browse, and dine.

**Cannonsburg Ski Area** (ages 7 and up)
6800 Cannonsburg Rd., Cannonsburg; (616) 874-6711; www.cannonsburg.com. $$$$.

# Favorite Events in West Michigan–South

- **Discover Michigan Skiing** (Jan), at various ski areas including those in southwest lower Michigan, (810) 620-4448

- **Icebreaker Festival** (Feb), downtown South Haven, (269) 637-5252; www .southhaven.org

- **Fishing and Travel Show** (Mar), Grand Center, Grand Rapids, (616) 530-1919

- **Derrick Edwards Bicycle Safety Program** (Apr), Kellogg Arena, Battle Creek, (616) 963-4800

- **Blossomtime Festival** (May), Benton Harbor and St. Joseph, (269) 926-7397; www.blossomtimefestival.org

- **Mayfaire Renaissance Festival** (May), Calhoun County Fairgrounds, Marshall, (269) 382-6120

- **Berrien Auto Fair** (June), Berrien County Youth Fairground, Berrien Springs, (616) 463-5532

- **Coast Guard Festival** (July), downtown Grand Haven, (616) 846-5940

- **Krasl Art Fair** (July), Lake Bluff Park in downtown St. Joseph, (269) 926-0271

- **Kustom Kemp of America Street Custom Car Show** (Aug), on Windmill Island in Holland, (616) 394-0000 or (800) 506-1299

- **Celebration on the Grand** (Sept), downtown Grand Rapids, Ah-Nab-Awen Park, (616) 456-1613

- **International Festival of Lights** (Nov), downtown Battle Creek, (616) 962-2240, (616) 963-3830, or (800) 397-2240

- **Holiday parade** (Dec), St. Joseph, (269) 983-6739

The facility has ten runs with three chairlifts, lessons, and equipment rental. Cannonsburg offers ski school for all ages of learners. Food and drink are available in the cafeteria.

There is no babysitting per se, but youngsters can sign up for lessons while their parents ski. Both daylight and night skiing are available.

## AAA Canoe Rentals (all ages)

12 East Bridge St., downtown; (616) 866-9264. The livery opens in mid-May and closes in late Oct after fall color-viewing season, starting at 9 a.m. daily. There are two- and four-

hour trips available. Life preservers are standard issue for young children, and flotation seat cushions are provided also. Children as young as 2 months have gone on the trip. Parents should judge as to whether they are competent enough paddlers to bring along the youngest children, since canoes can be tippy. The river is calm with no rapids. $$$; children 5 and younger ride **free.**

Canoe on the Rogue River, a trout stream that runs through town. Near the end of the trip, a dam downtown halts the upstream spawning run of salmon in fall and steelhead trout in spring. Anglers catch them below the dam.

## Where to Eat

**Herman's Boy.** 63 Courtland, downtown; (616) 866-2900. Hand-roasted custom coffee blends that might be the state's best, bulk leaf teas, fresh-baked goods, and fudge make this place a "must-stop." $

**Peppermill.** 7 Squires St., downtown; (616) 866-7778. Open Mon through Sat 6 a.m. to 3 p.m. and Sun 8 a.m. to 2:30 p.m. Specializes in big breakfasts, such as scrumptious omelets, and lunch items such as hamburgers. $$

**Rosie's Diner.** 4500 Fourteen Mile Rd. NE, downtown; (616) 866-3663; www.rosiesdiner .com. Remember Rosie and her "quicker picker-upper" paper towels? The diner used in those TV commercials was moved here. Food includes classic pot roast and salads, plus malts. Breakfast served, too. $$

## Where to Stay

See Grand Rapids listings.

## For More Information

**Rockford Area Chamber of Commerce.** P.O. Box 520, Rockford 49341; (616) 866-2000; www.rockfordmichamber.com.

# Coopersville

This small community lies 15 miles west of Grand Rapids along I-96. Take the Coopersville exit, of course.

### Coopersville & Marne Railway (all ages)

**Departs from downtown Coopersville; (616) 997-7000; www.coopersvilleandmarne.org. Themed train schedules vary by season, so call ahead for times. General excursions depart at 11 a.m. and 1 p.m. and cost $$; kids under 2 ride free. No rides from Jan through mid-Mar.**

Besides the summer rides there are special theme rides for kids, including a Pumpkin Train on Oct weekends and a Santa Train on Dec weekends. The train makes a slow tour to Marne, about 5 miles away, and returns on the same route, which runs through west Michigan's farm country. It's a chance for kids to experience rail travel in slow motion.

## Where to Eat and Stay

See Grand Rapids listings.

# Hastings

Named after a local landholder, Hastings was settled in 1836 on the banks of the Thornapple River. It's the seat of Barry Country.

### Charlton Park Village, Museum, and Recreation Area
(all ages)

2545 South Charlton Park Rd.; (269) 945-3775; www.charltonpark.org. A ¼ mile north of Highway 79 between Hastings and Nashville. Travel north from I-94 on Highway 66, turn west on Highway 79, and then head 2 miles south and 4 miles east on Highway 79. From mid-May through Sept, hours are 9 a.m. to 4:30 p.m. daily. Admission is $, with children 4 and younger admitted **free.** Special-events costs vary.

Southeastern Michigan has Greenfield Village and the Henry Ford. Flint has Crossroads Village. And Hastings, population only 6,500, has a historic village that is on a par with the big boys. Seventeen buildings help re-create an 1890s Michigan town; in addition, you'll find a beach, a playground, and a boat launch, on more than 300 acres. In the village there's everything from a blacksmith's to a schoolhouse.

Christmas is one of the most decorative times, as buildings are lit by candlelight from noon to 5 p.m., starting on the first two weekends in Dec. The Thornapple Trail Park, a nonmotorized linear park, joins Charlton Park with another Barry County park. It's open for hiking, skating, biking, cross-country skiing, and other sports.

## Where to Eat

Besides concession stands at Charlton Park, local restaurants include fast-food chains along with the following:

**Elias Brothers Big Boy.** 915 West State St.; (269) 948-2701. Open Sun through Thurs 7 a.m. to 10 p.m., Fri and Sat 7 a.m. to 11 p.m. Serves a variety of family fare from salads to its trademark triple-decker burger. $$

## Where to Stay

**Bay Pointe Inn and Restaurant.** 1156 Marsh Rd., Shelbyville, about twenty-five minutes west of Hastings on Gun Lake; (269) 672-8111; www.baypointeinn.com. The inn has thirty-eight guest rooms overlooking the lake, plus continental breakfast, indoor pool, and fitness area. The great restaurant has a children's menu. There is lake swimming nearby at Yankee Springs State Park. Weekly rates available. $$–$$$$

**Parkview Motel.** 429 North Broadway (Highway 43), about ⅓ mile north of the town center; (269) 945-9511. There are eighteen rooms in this economy motel. $$

## For More Information

**Barry County Chamber of Commerce.** 221 West State St., Hastings 49058; (269) 945-2454 or (800) 510-2922; www.barry chamber.com. Information also is available at www.hastings.mi.us.

# Grand Haven and Spring Lake

Grand Haven is reached by taking exit 9 (Highway 104) off I-96 and heading west.

The town is one of a successive string of beachside communities along Lake Michigan that help make this part of the state one of the most appealing to summer vacationers from across the Midwest. Its simple, compact downtown is one of the most picturesque in the area, as the end of the Grand River sweeps past boats moored in the harbor to the great beach. US 31 acts as a second business district, and many motels are located along it. It's only a few blocks from the water. Walk the 2½-mile boardwalk along the river and lakefront, or take the trolley that runs all summer.

Spring Lake is mentioned in the same breath because it's right next to Grand Haven on the lake that is formed by the Grand River.

Sportfishing charters in the Grand Haven–Spring Lake area focus on big-lake fishing for salmon and steelhead from summer through fall. Call (616) 842-4910 or (800) 303-4096 for more information.

### Musical Fountain  (all ages)

**In downtown Grand Haven on the riverfront. Bursts to life nightly about 9:45 p.m. from Memorial Day through Labor Day and on Sept weekends. Free.**

Families start gathering just before sundown, and by nightfall the grandstand, which holds 2,500, is usually filled. The harbor, where the Grand River ends its journey across lower Michigan at Lake Michigan, is dotted with boat lights as—suddenly—a dune erupts in color, water plumes, and music. The fountain spews jets of water up to 125 feet in the air—and best of all, the show's free.

### Grand Haven/Spring Lake Trolley  (all ages)

**(616) 842-3200 or (800) 303-4096; www.grandhaven.com/harbortransit. Runs from 11 a.m. to 10 p.m. daily from Memorial Day through Labor Day, through Grand Haven. Pick it up at several locations, including the state park and Chinook Pier. Fare $, children 2 and younger ride free.**

Trolleys, actually converted minibuses, transport visitors up and down the beachfront.

### Harborfront Place  (all ages)

**In downtown at Harbor Drive and Washington Street; (616) 846-5711. Open 10 a.m. to 6 p.m. Mon through Sat. Some stores open on Sun.**

Built out of the relic of a century-old piano company, this enclosed, three-story contemporary shopping and dining mall is one of the reasons for the city's revitalization. There are more than a dozen shops, Porto Bello Restaurant (see Where to Eat), and a coffeehouse.

Later take the kids to Imagination Station (at Harbor Drive and Y Drive), a playscape designed by kids.

# Great Lakes **Kite Festival**

Viewing the championships is **free** with admission to Grand Haven State Park (see Where to Stay). If you come here in mid-May and someone in town tells you to go fly a kite, he or she just might be directing you to the golden-sand beach, with blue Lake Michigan as the background, where you'll join up to 40,000 spectators to watch kites up to half a football field long fill the air during this annual event.

You'll see kites here that are a bit different than the ones you buy at the local hardware store for your kids—you know, kites that eventually end up in your front-yard tree. The ones here include wildly decorative models as well as sport kites controlled by two lines that pilots use to steer. Individuals and teams fly the kites through maneuvers, executing some pretty spectacular aerial ballets.

Events run Fri through Sun and include a Fri-night fly at which lights attached to the kites and lines create a spectacular show.

Relive your childhood and try your own hand during **free** stunt kite lessons for beginners. For more information, call the event's sponsor, the Mackinac Kite Company, at (616) 846-7501; www.mackite.com.

### Musketawa Rail-to-Trail Bike Path (all ages)

**Connecting with Grand Haven, it runs between Marne and Muskegon. For more information, call Ottawa County Parks at (231) 853-5746 or (888) 731-1001, ext. 4810.**

This 26-mile paved trail, which was formerly a railroad right-of-way, connects the towns of Marne, Conklin, Ravenna, Grand Haven, and Muskegon. Walk, skate, bike, or hike. From the trail you can plan side trips to the Gillette Sand Dune Visitor Center at P. J. Hoffmaster State Park, between Grand Haven and Muskegon. There are also miles of other bike paths in the Grand Haven area. Check the local visitors bureau for maps or view the Web site (see For More Information).

## Where to Eat

**Bil-Mar Restaurant.** 1223 Harbor Ave., on the beach; (616) 842-5920; www.grandhaven .com/~bil-mar. Lake perch is the specialty at lunch and dinner. Outdoor seating available. Children's menu. $$$

**Porto Bello Restaurant.** 41 Washington St., west of US 31, in Harborfront Place; (616) 846-1221. Italian food for lunch and dinner. $$

**Stable Inn.** 118880 US 31, 5 miles south of town; (616) 846-8581. Serves lunch and dinner, with Mexican food a specialty. Children's menu. $$

## Where to Stay

**Days Inn.** 1500 South Beacon; (616) 842-1999. This economical motel offers one hundred rooms, indoor pool, and restaurant. $$

**Grand Haven State Park.** 1001 South Harbor Dr., on the beach; (616) 798-3711 or, for guaranteed reservations, (800) 447-2757. A daily ($) or annual ($$) permit is required for vehicle entry. Camping is $14 nightly. Like your camping sandy and close? This is the place. It's one of the state's most popular campgrounds despite the fact there's little shade. You're camping right on the beach sand at any of the 174 sites. $

**Grand Haven Waterfront Holiday Inn.** 940 West Savidge (Highway 104), Spring Lake, just east of US 31; (616) 846-1000. This property has 121 rooms overlooking the river and Spring Lake, indoor and outdoor pools, exercise area, and restaurant. $$$

**Lakeshore Bed & Breakfast.** 11001 Lakeshore Dr.; (616) 844-2697; www.bbonline .com/mi/lakeshore/. The B&B has three rooms with private beach on Lake Michigan. Cottages are also available for families. $$

**Rodeway Inn.** 1010 South Beacon (US 31); (616) 846-1800 or (800) 745-8660. The inn has forty-seven rooms and is 1½ miles from the beach. $

**Yogi Bear Jellystone Park.** 10990 US 31 North; (616) 842-9395; www.ghjellystone .com. Seven miles south of Grand Haven, this park has 240 sites, two swimming pools, and a beach. $

## For More Information

**Grand Haven/Spring Lake Area Visitors Bureau.** 1 South Harbor Dr., Grand Haven 49417; (616) 842-4910 or (800) 303-4092; www.visitgrandhaven.com, or www.grand havenchamber.org.

# West Michigan–North

T he northern part of west Michigan takes in some of the state's most inviting places to visit, from former industrial towns on the verge of finding new life as tourist destinations, to small towns that are growing by leaps and bounds, to others that nearly close in winter.

## Top
# FamilyAdventures
### in West Michigan–North

1. Michigan's Adventure Amusement Park, Muskegon. Ride Michigan's only wooden roller coaster.

2. Mac Wood's Dune Rides, Silver Lake Dunes, Shelby. Ride the ride that started the dune buggy craze.

3. SS *Badger*, Ludington. Sail away on a day trip to Wisconsin in the state's last remaining overnight car ferry. Rides can taken be during the day, or book passage on a night trip.

4. Sleeping Bear Dunes National Lakeshore, Empire. Walk up the dune; then see if you can keep from running down.

5. Mackinaw City. Historic parks, great views, and more at this gateway to the Upper Peninsula and Mackinac Island.

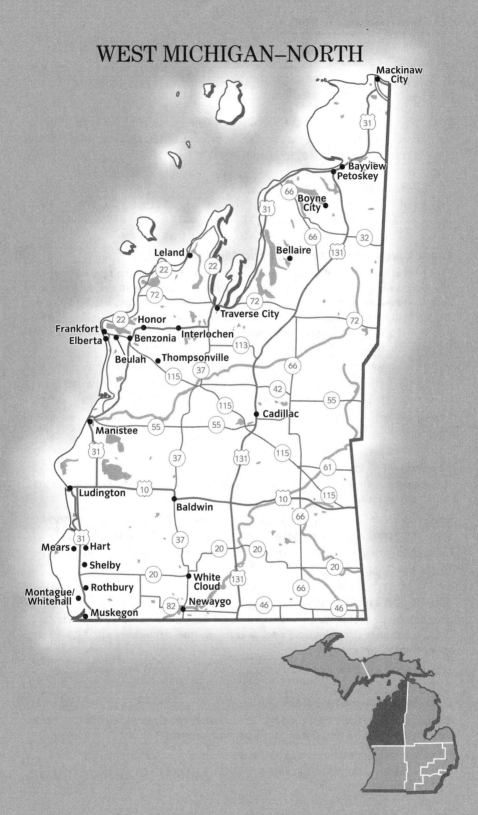

# WEST MICHIGAN–NORTH

# Muskegon

Welcome to Muskegon, the Lumber Queen City, at the intersection of I-96 and US 31. In the nineteenth century Muskegon's now-razed mills and surrounding forests of white pine provided the lumber to rebuild Chicago after its 1871 fire and to construct homes in much of the West. Some of that heritage remains in historic homes-turned-museums.

The city knows how to throw a beach party, too, with nine public beaches along 26 miles of shoreline in the county, four beachfront state parks within a few miles of downtown, and more natural beauty than you can shake a sand dune at.

### Great Lakes Naval Memorial and Museum  (all ages)

**1346 Bluff at Pere Marquette Park, on the south side of the Muskegon Lake channel; (231) 755-1230; www.glnmm.org. Open from Apr through Oct. Hours are 10 a.m. to 5:30 p.m. daily from June through Aug; 1 to 5:30 p.m. Mon through Fri and 10 a.m. to 5:30 p.m. on weekends in May and Sept. In Apr and Oct the museum is open only on weekends from 10 a.m. to 5:30 p.m. Children ages 4 and under are free. Group rates available. Ask about the overnight encampment program.**

Along the Muskegon River outlet, board the *Silversides,* billed as the country's most famous surviving World War II submarine. You'll climb below deck to see how its crew shared bunk space in shifts and how they lived on patrol, and learn how it ranked third highest among all World War II subs in number of ships sunk. The exhibit also includes the Coast Guard cutter *McLane.*

### LST 393  (all ages)

**Moored downtown at 560 Mart St., just off Shoreline Drive. (231) 730-1477; www.lst393 .org. Open for tours 10 a.m. to 4 p.m. daily May through Sept. $$.**

Of the more than 1,100 LSTs (standing for *landing ship tank,* or, by some who served on them, "long slow target) launched, there are two remaining. The ships that could beach themselves to off-load equipment played a prominent role in World War II to transport troops and cargo.

### Muskegon Lumberjacks  (all ages)

**The Lumberjacks play in Walker Arena downtown along the waterfront area; (231) 726-2400; www.muskegonlumberjacks.com. Season runs from Oct through Apr. $–$$, children younger than 2 get in free.**

The city's entry in the United Hockey League plays thirty-seven home games.

### P. J. Hoffmaster State Park  (all ages)

**Just south of Muskegon; (231) 798-3711. To reach Hoffmaster State Park, exit US 31 at Pontaluna Road and drive west 2 miles. Daily permit $, annual $$$.**

One of the state's most beautiful parks, with 333 shaded campsites amid the rolling dunes of Lake Michigan. The park encircles 2½ miles of lake shoreline and 10 miles of hiking trails through dunes and the forests that have taken hold behind them. Picnicking and swimming are available.

### Muskegon Winter Sports Complex (ages 8 and up)

**Inside Muskegon State Park; (231) 744-9629; www.msports.org/luge.htm. The track is open to the public on Fri night, Sat, and Sun. Cost of the orientation session is $17. All-day track passes are $$$–$$$$.**

In cold weather, hold your own family Winter Olympics and ride a luge at the complex.

Here's a place for the kids to live up to their "No Fear" hats and slip down an ice-covered, banked track on a sled barely a yard long, faster than Dad or Mom. The beginners' run starts a ways down the track, and when you've got some experience, you can work your way up to the top for the full trip down one of only two luge runs in the nation. After instruction that includes a video, sliders can hit around 25 miles per hour on the lower track and up to 45 miles per hour on the upper. The sports complex also features a skating rink and lighted cross-country ski trails.

### Duck Lake State Park (all ages)

**About 15 miles north of Muskegon; (231) 744-3480. From Muskegon State Park, take Scenic Drive, itself a great tourist attraction as it slips past expensive lakefront homes and scenic views and passes Duck Lake. The day-use park is open daylight to dusk. Daily permit $, annual $$$.**

The park is fairly undeveloped, but you'll find a wonderful public beach on Lake Michigan at the mouth of Duck Lake and another on Duck Lake. There are designated swimming areas on Lake Michigan and Duck Lake but no lifeguards.

### Lake Express Ferry (all ages)

**The dock and terminal are just off US 31 at the Great Lakes Marina, 1920 Lakeshore Dr.; (866) 914-1010; www.lake-express.com. The ferry runs late Apr through Oct 1, generally**

## Away for the **Weekend**

Pick a beach, any beach, in summer. There are so many in this region to choose from. My favorites include Ludington's miles of secluded dunes, along with its great city park beach. Other top spots to enjoy during summer include Muskegon and Grand Haven. There are lots of inexpensive places to stay in each area. Check a few miles inland, where prices are more moderate, and all you have to do is drive a few minutes to find the shore.

Trying skiing this winter? Head for Crystal Mountain, near Thompsonville, with one of the state's best children's programs. Farther north, Shanty Creek Resort's children's learn-to-ski program also rates highly.

with three sailings daily. Passengers are $$$$, with children 4 and under free. Call or check the Web site for vehicle rates.

The second ferry service to return to Lake Michigan began service in 2004 and runs from Muskegon to Milwaukee in about two and a half hours. Climb on board this high-speed giant catamaran, which also will take your car and trailer. Even if you're not going, it's quite a sight to see at the dock.

## Michigan's Adventure Amusement Park and Wild Water Adventure (all ages)

On US 31, 4750 Whitehall Rd. at Russell Road, 8 miles north of town; (231) 766-3377; www.miadventure.com. Open daily from Memorial Day through Labor Day; then limited hours to mid-Sept. The admission price ($$$$, free for children under 2) gets you into both Michigan's Adventure and Wild Water Adventure.

Summer fun awaits you at the state's largest amusement park. Stare down from the 90-foot crest of the first hill on the Wolverine Wildcat, a wooden roller coaster, one of five in the park. The newest is Shivering Timbers, the third-largest wooden coaster in the country and more than a mile long. Or try tamer rides, too, among the thirty available, seven of which are just for youngsters. Kids' rides include Zach's Zoomer, a pint-size coaster named after the owner's son.

The park also includes Wild Water Adventure. If getting wet on a hot summer day sounds like fun, visit the state's largest water park, with a wave pool, the state's longest waterslide, the Grand Rapids raft ride, and the meandering Lazy River inner tube ride. Play areas and a tree house are just for kids.

## *Port City Princess* (all ages)

Sailing from the waterfront at Hartshorn Marina, 1133 West Western Ave.; (231) 728-8387 or (800) 853-6311; www.portcityprincesscruises.com. From Business US 31 (Seaway Drive), follow the signs and take it downtown to Shoreline Drive, and then head left to Western Avenue, the first light. Turn west onto Western to the marina entrance. Ninety-minute sightseeing cruises leave at 3:30 p.m. daily from Memorial Day through Labor Day. $$$, children ages two and under board free. There are also brunch, lunch, and dinner cruises at higher prices, plus summer holiday cruises at special prices. Reservations are required for all cruises.

The *Princess* takes passengers onto Muskegon Lake, through the channel, and, if weather permits, briefly onto Lake Michigan. On the way you'll see the lake's shoreline, the *Milwaukee Clipper* (an old steamship), and the *Silversides* (see Great Lakes Naval Memorial and Museum listing).

# Where to Eat

**Frosty Oasis.** 2181 West Sherman, west of Business US 31; (231) 755-2903. Great ice-cream dishes. $

**Grand Traverse Pie Co.** 5817 Harvey St.; (231) 799-3399; www.gtpie.com. Made-on-premises soups, wraps, sandwiches, potpies, and baked goods, such as great cream and fruit pies. $

**The Hearthstone.** 3350 Glade; (231) 733-1056. At the corner of Seaway (Business US 31) and Norton. Great soups and sandwiches and pasta for lunch and dinner. Children's menu. $$

**Tony's Bistro.** 212 Seaway Dr.; (231) 739-7196. Good variety of well-prepared lunch and dinner items. $$$

## Where to Stay

**Comfort Inn.** 1675 East Sherman Blvd., at the US 31 Sherman exit; (231) 739-9092. The inn has 117 rooms, free continental breakfast, indoor and outdoor pools, exercise area and sauna, and restaurant nearby. $$

**Holiday Inn–Muskegon Harbor.** 939 Third St., downtown; (231) 722-0100. From Business US 31, turn west on Third. The hotel is just 2 blocks from Muskegon Lake. It has 200 rooms, indoor and outdoor pools, exercise area, sauna and whirlpool, and restaurant. $$

**Seaway Motel.** 631 West Norton Ave., at Business US 31, south of downtown; (231) 733-1220; www.muskegonseawaymotel.com. This economical motel has twenty-nine modest rooms and an outdoor pool. Restaurant nearby. Kids under sixteen stay free. Small pets OK. $

**Victory Inn & Suites.** 2967 Henry St., west of Business US 31, south of downtown; (231) 733-2651. This hotel has 112 rooms, indoor pool, and restaurant. $$

## For More Information

**Muskegon County Convention and Visitors Bureau.** 610 West Western Ave., Muskegon 49440; (231) 724-3100 or (800) 250-WAVE; www.visitmuskegon.org.

# Rothbury

Settled in 1865, Rothbury is a quiet suburb of the Muskegon/Whitehall area. The town is heavily wooded.

**Rothbury Music Festival** (all ages)

**On the grounds of Double JJ Resort, 5900 South Water Rd.; for tickets and other information, www.rothburyfestival.com. Tickets are $$$$.**

The first such four-day music festival, which took place in 2008, is being reprised each July. Thousands of fans gather to hear the likes of performers such as John Mayer, Bob Dylan, Willie Nelson, and others. The theme of the festival is to be earth friendly, hence its goal to be zero-waste producing, and to educate concertgoers about recycling.

# Montague and Whitehall

Located just north of Muskegon, these twin towns, separated by the outlet of the White River into White Lake, were founded on lake shipping in the 1800s, first sending lumber, then fruit, and supporting a brisk trade in summer vacation passengers. They still count tourism as the top export, but nearly all come by car nowadays. Lake Michigan provides the beaches, and there also are boating and fishing on White Lake.

Both towns share various events, including arts-and-crafts fairs in June, Aug, and Oct.

## World's Largest Weathervane (all ages)

**Located at the corner of Dowling and Water Streets in Montague; (231) 893-3030. Free.**

At 48 feet high, 14 feet long, and 4,300 pounds, it has no peer, and it actually works.

It's located in a new park. At its base is a small weather station that tells you if it's cloudy, rainy, or sunny if you don't want to look up.

## White River Light Station Museum (all ages)

**Located at 6199 Murray Rd., beside the mouth of the White River and Lake Michigan, at the west end of White Lake, Whitehall; (231) 894-8265; www.whiteriverlightstation.org. The museum is open Memorial Day through Sept. Hours are 11 a.m. to 5 p.m. Tues through Fri, noon to 6 p.m. June through Aug, and noon to 6 p.m. on Memorial Day weekend and weekends in Sept. Adults $, children under 10 free.**

Built in 1875, the light station started life by guiding lumber and passenger ships into the entrance to White Lake, and its light still works to help pleasure boaters and anglers to safe harbor. Inside the brick and limestone structure are many Great Lakes nautical artifacts, including light keepers' paraphernalia. You can also learn about the history of some of the ships that first brought tourists to the area from Chicago.

## Hart-Montague State Park Bicycle Trail (all ages)

**Located along Business US 31 in Montague; (231) 893-4585 or (231) 873-3083; www.white lake.org/recreation/biketrail.htm. Free. Bicycle rentals and maps are available (check with the White Lake Area Chamber of Commerce, below, for information).**

The trail is Michigan's first linear state park, along a former railroad grade between Montague and Hart, 22 miles north. Picnic areas are at most cities. It's paved and draws more than 60,000 users a year. Rangers patrol the trail each day.

## Where to Eat

**Crosswinds.** At 302 South Lake St., Whitehall; (231) 893-4655. Casual fine dining, from prime rib to vegetarian, overlooking White Lake. Outdoor dining in season. Children's menu. $$–$$$

## Where to Stay

Lodging from B&Bs to cabins is available in the area. Here is a sample:

**Maple Tree Inn.** 323 South Mears, Whitehall; (231) 894-4091; www.themapletreeinn .com. This inn has eleven rooms, two with whirlpools, all with refrigerators and microwaves, plus continental breakfast. Open from Memorial Day weekend through Labor Day. $$

**Montgomery Inn.** 10233 North US 31, Montague; (231) 894-4339. Adjacent to the Hart-Montague State Park bike trail (see listing). This motel has nine rooms; three are suites with fireplace and hot tub. A whirlpool

# Favorite Events in West Michigan–North

- **Winterfest** (Jan), downtown Mackinaw City, (888) 455-8100

- **North American Snow Festival** (Feb), Cadillac, (231) 755-0657 or (800) 225-2537; www.michiweb.com/cadillac

- **Spring Fling** (Mar), Crystal Mountain Ski Area, Thompsonville, (231) 378-2000

- **National Trout Festival** (Apr), Kalkaska, (231) 258-9103

- **Trillium Festival** (May), Gillette Visitor Center, P. J. Hoffmaster State Park, Muskegon, (231) 798-3573

- **Mesick Mushroom Festival** (May), Mesick, (231) 885-1675

- **Summer Arts and Crafts Fair** (June), Mackinaw City, (231) 436-5664

- **National Forest Festival** (July), Manistee, (231) 723-2575

- **National Coho Festival** (Aug), Honor, (231) 882-5801 or (231) 882-5802

- **Logging and Harvest Days** (Sept), White Pine Village, Ludington, (231) 843-4808

- **Hemingway Weekendfest** (Oct), downtown Petoskey, (231) 348-2755 or (800) 845-2828; www .MichiganHemingwaySociety.org

- **Festival of Trees** (Nov), Muskegon Museum of Art, Muskegon, (231) 720-2570

- **Victorian Sleighbell Parade** (Dec), Manistee, (231) 723-2565

and kids' play area also available. Bike rentals nearby. Prices drop drastically after the summer tourist season. $–$$$

**Ramada Inn.** 2865 Colby Rd. at US 31, Whitehall; (231) 893-3030. This motel has sixty-six rooms, with indoor pool, sauna, and **free** continental breakfast. $$$

## For More Information

**White Lake Area Chamber of Commerce.** 124 Hanson St., Whitehall 49461; (231) 893-4585 or (800) 879-9702; www .whitelake.org.

# Newaygo

Located on the river valley banks above the Muskegon River, Newaygo is famed for salmon and steelhead fishing in the river below in fall and spring, for morel mushroom hunting in the surrounding woods in May, and other outdoor fun the rest of the year. The Newaygo Logging Fest takes place downtown each year on Labor Day weekend to celebrate the area's logging history. It features an arts-and-crafts fair, sidewalk sales, chicken dinners, and a lumberjack competition, along with a custom-car show.

### River Float Trips  (all ages)

**There are several liveries in the area. One is Wisner Canoes, 25 East Water St. (Highway 37), Box 101, Newaygo 49337, at the Muskegon River Bridge; (231) 652-6743; www.wisner canoes.com. Day trips are $$$–$$$$ for canoes, large inner tubes, and two-, three-, and four-person inflatable rafts.**

Canoe, or float in a tube, down the wide, lazy Muskegon River. Day or overnight trips can be booked. Life vests are provided. For families, owner Bob Wisner recommends the inflatables for comfort and safety. Start from High Rollway public access and paddle/float back to his business. Or go to Croton Dam for a 12-mile, four-hour float, by canoe only.

## Where to Eat

**Cory's Family Restaurant.** On Highway 37, just south of town; (231) 652-7222. Serves breakfast, lunch, and dinner along with take-out. $$

## Where to Stay

Besides local motels, mostly along Highway 37, plenty of campgrounds are available.

**Little Switzerland Resort and Campground.** 254 Pickerel Lake Dr.; (231) 652-7939. From Highway 37, head to the signal light at Eighty-second, and turn west. The next street is Old Highway 37. Turn right and go about 1½ miles, and turn in on Pickerel Lake Drive. The resort has eighty campsites and seven housekeeping cottages open from May through Oct. Named after the area's old nickname because of its rolling hills and river valleys. $$

**Newaygo State Park.** 2793 Beech; (231) 745-2888 (summer), (231) 845-4452, or (800) 44-PARKS (for reservations). The park offers ninety-nine sites on the east shore of Hardy Dam Pond, all rustic. Most of the park is undeveloped, and there is no swimming in the lake, but the park has a boat launch.

**Wisner Canoes.** 25 East Water St.; (231) 652-6743; www.wisnercanoes.com. The canoe livery (see listing above) also rents three cottages, two on area lakes. $$

## For More Information

**Newaygo County Tourist Council.** 4686 South Evergreen, Newaygo 49337; (231) 652-9298; www.newaygocountytourism.com.

# White Cloud

If you don't come here to see or fish for salmon and steelhead in the nearby Muskegon or White Rivers, then you ought to come to say you've roomed at a shack.

### The Shack Country Inn  (all ages)

2263 West Fourteenth; (231) 924-6683; www.theshackbandb.com. **From the stoplight in downtown White Cloud, head 5½ miles west and then watch for the signs; the lodge is ¼ mile off the main road. The Shack is 8 miles northeast of Fremont. Open year-round. Rates start at $$ per room (single or double occupancy) for weekday stays.**

It doesn't have the most inviting name, but this bed-and-breakfast is far from what its moniker and even its weird location—in the heart of downtown "Jugville," as its ads say—connote. Families who stay here for a night or a long weekend are bathed in rustic luxury, from the forty-five beautiful log-cabin rooms, thirty with hot tubs and eighteen with fireplaces inside, to the inexpensive rates, which include full breakfast, dinner, and even a 9 p.m. banana split on Fri and Sat. Sun brunch is available. Kids like the beach on Robinson Lake, too. The lodge, rebuilt to original detail after a fire in 1943 and added to over the years, is one of the north's surprising secrets.

## Where to Eat

See the Shack Country Inn and the Newaygo listings.

## Where to Stay

If you're not up for the Shack, here's another option:

**Sandy Beach Campground.** 6926 Thirtieth St., on Hardy Dam Pond; (231) 689-7383. From Highway 37, go east on Thirteenth Street. The campground has 150 sites with swimming beach open from mid-May through mid-Sept. Run by the Newaygo County Parks Commission. $

# Baldwin

Located along Highway 37, this small town is busiest in summer, when canoeists and others come to enjoy the surrounding lakes and rivers of Lake County, and during fall hunting season.

### Shrine of the Pines  (all ages)

The shrine is 2 miles south of Baldwin, off Highway 37; (231) 745-7892; www.shrineofthe pines.com. Open from 10 a.m. to 6 p.m. daily from May 15 through Oct 15. $.

Raymond W. Overholzer's legacy, carved in the woods south of Baldwin, is demonstrated in the impressive collection at this shrine, dedicated to the virgin white-pine forest that once blanketed the state. Over a period of thirty years, Overholzer, a hunting and fishing guide, gathered tree stumps, limbs, roots, and trunks. Then, using such simple tools as

## Pere Marquette **River Activities**

Step outside the log cabin, or stop at the public access along Highway 37, and you're along the fabled "PM," where in spring the river's gravel becomes a nursery for steelhead trout. It was the first stream in the nation to receive a planting of German brown trout, and a historic marker along the river tells the story. In fall salmon take over. Anglers come for all three. Part of the river is for fly-fishing only. Canoe liveries are nearby for those who want to tackle the twists and turns of the stream, which can be paddled by beginners.

broken glass, brushes, and deer hide, he hand-chiseled and rubbed smooth the wood to create natural works of art in the form of beds, chairs, and even chandeliers and candlesticks.

The centerpiece of the display here is a huge table carved from a single stump, complete with drawers. There's also a short nature trail through the woods.

## Where to Eat

**Government Lake Lodge.** 4953 South Highway 37; (231) 745-3000. Open 11 a.m. to midnight Mon through Sat, noon to midnight Sun. Casual dining 1 mile north of town. Children's menu. $$

## Where to Stay

There are several good places to stay in town and its environs, from lodges to cabins to motels. Here's one:

**Pere Marquette Lodge.** 8841 South Highway 37; (231) 745-3972; www.pmlodge .com. Cozy lodge rooms, plus homes and rustic cabins are available on or near the Pere Marquette River. Guided river fishing trips are available. $$

## For More Information

**Lake County Chamber of Commerce.** 911 Michigan Ave., Baldwin 49304; (231) 745-4331; www.lakecountymichigan.com.

# Shelby, Hart, and Mears

Named for a War of 1812 general who recaptured Detroit from the British, Shelby was settled in 1866. It's in the middle of west Michigan farm country. Hart, settled in 1856, was named after a local pioneer and is the seat of Oceana County. Mears is named for Charles Mears, a nineteenth-century pioneer settler of the area. Each June the area celebrates its spring asparagus crop with the National Asparagus Festival.

### Shelby Man-Made Gemstones (all ages)

1330 Industrial Dr., Shelby; (231) 861-2165; www.shelbygemfactory.com. The store is minutes off US 31 from either the Hart or Shelby exits; just follow the signs east. Showroom is open from 9 a.m. to 5:30 p.m. Mon through Fri and from noon to 4 p.m. Sat. Theater admission is **free**, and the facility is wheelchair accessible.

You don't have to spend a lot for a "diamond," a "ruby," a "sapphire," or some other gem at the showroom in this tiny town near the Lake Michigan shoreline. The company is the world's largest maker of synthetic and simulated gems. It got its start producing industrial rubies to make lasers and then branched out to create crystals for science and other uses.

In the fifty-seat theater you'll learn about the manufacturing process.

### Mac Wood's Dune Rides (all ages)

629 North Eighteenth Ave., Mears; (231) 873-2817; www.macwoodsdunerides.com. Nine miles west of US 31 at the Hart or Shelby exit—depending on whether you're driving north or south. Rides run daily from 9:30 a.m. to dusk between Memorial Day and Labor Day. From mid-May through the day before Memorial Day and for fall tours from Labor Day through early Oct, the hours are 10 a.m. to 5 p.m. daily. $$–$$$, **free** for children ages 2 and under.

In 1930, on the Silver Lake dunes here, Malcolm "Mac" Wood invented the sport of dune buggying when he fitted a Model A Ford with oversize tires and a big engine to travel the sands between Silver Lake and Lake Michigan. The craze he originated carries on across the country—and so does his Michigan attraction.

The forty-minute "dune scooter" rides in modified convertible trucks take visitors on an 8-mile route through one of the Midwest's largest dune complexes. En route, drivers provide a running narrative on the history of the dunes, and at one point zip along the hard sand beach to make sure everyone on board gets "cooled off" by a wave or two.

### Silver Lake State Park (all ages)

Exit US 31 at Shelby Road and drive west 6 miles, and then go north on Scenic Drive and follow the signs; (231) 873-3083; www.michigan.gov/dnr, then click on "Recreation, Camping & Boating." For reservations, call (800) 447-2757. A motor vehicle permit ($ daily, $$$$ annual) is required for entry.

Near the dune rides this park is one of Michigan's most popular. Besides camping at one of nearly 250 sites and swimming on Lake Michigan or Silver Lake, you can run your own registered dune buggy within the designated 600-acre off-road-vehicle area on the dunes. The big Silver Lake dune is inching eastward with each wind gust.

### Country Dairy (all ages)

3476 South Eightieth Ave., in New Era; (231) 861-4636; www.countrydairy.com. Near Hart, take the New Era exit off US 31. Travel east 2 miles on Highway 20. Turn north onto Oceana Drive and go north ½ mile. The store is on the right about ½ mile. Open 7 a.m. to 8 p.m. Mon through Sat. Tours ($) available by appointment in winter. There are four tours daily in summer.

Climb aboard a tractor-pulled wagon and tour this working dairy farm where 1,000 cows help produce milk, ice cream, cheese, and other items sold at the farm store. Lunch items are available, too, in the deli. The bottling plant is included as is the milking parlor. The farm has been run by the Van Gunst family for more than a century.

## Where to Eat

**Sands Restaurant.** 8448 West Hazel Rd., Mears; (231) 873-5257. Salads, sandwiches, and the half-pound "duneburger," sans sand, are on the menu, along with a full list of dinner entrees. $–$$$

**Silver Lake Whippydip.** 591 Eighteenth Ave., Shelby; (231) 873-4715. Next to Mac Wood's Dune Rides, 9 miles west of US 31 at the Hart or Shelby exits. Open Sun through Thurs 11 a.m. to 11 p.m., Fri and Sat Memorial Day to Labor Day until midnight, and weekends in May and Sept 11 a.m. to 11 p.m. Known for its turtle sundaes and pizza. $

## Where to Stay

**Gateway Motel.** 3781 North Oceana Dr., Hart; (231) 873-2125; www.oceana.net. Take the Hart exit off US 31 and go east about 1½ miles to Oceana and turn left. Nineteen units with picnic and play areas and cable TV. Ten minutes from Silver Lake State Park. $$

**Yogi Bear's Jellystone Park Camp Resort.** At 8329 Hazel Ave., Hart; (231) 873-4502. From US 31, go west from the Hart exit and follow the signs to Silver Lake for about 6 miles. There are 200 campsites, heated outdoor pool, playground, organized games, and arts and crafts. $

## For More Information

**Hart–Silver Lake/Mears Chamber of Commerce.** 2388 North Comfort Dr., Hart 49420; (231) 873-2247, or (800) 870-9786; www.hartsilverlakemears.com.

**Silver Lake Sand Dunes–Hart Visitors Bureau.** Same address as chamber of commerce; (800) 874-3982; www.silverlakecvb.org.

# Ludington

It's hard to find a more picturesque Lake Michigan town. Located west of US 31 and at the Michigan terminus (the highway continues in Wisconsin) of US 10, Ludington is a favorite for summer vacationers and for salmon and steelhead anglers.

## SS *Badger* (all ages)

700 South William, at the end of US 10 in Michigan; (231) 843-1509 or (888) 337-7948; www.ssbadger.com. The ferry runs from mid-May through mid-Oct; departure times vary by date. Pets are OK in the owner's vehicle or in a portable kennel provided by the owner. $$$$, children ages 4 or younger ride free. Ask about special rates and discounts.

If you can't afford that Caribbean cruise for the family, here's a Great Lakes alternative.

Welcome aboard the only coal-fired cross–Great Lakes car ferry still operating, for a relaxing four-hour cruise between Ludington and Manitowoc, Wisconsin. The 410-foot

# Sportfishing in Ludington

At the charter-boat harbor, book a trip for salmon and steelhead fishing on the big lake, or launch your own boat at the mouth, near the Coast Guard station.

Small boats can fish in Pere Marquette Lake when it's too rough to go onto the big lake. The best salmon action is from Aug onward, but there's good steelhead fishing most of the summer offshore. A 19-foot boat or larger with radio and fish-finding equipment is recommended for Lake Michigan, as storms can blow out of Wisconsin in a hurry. For sportfishing charter information on just a few of the boats, go to www.fish-ludington.com or contact the convention and visitor bureau listed at the end of this section.

*Badger* accommodates more than 100 vehicles and 600 passengers. It was built in 1952 and features onboard cafeteria service, live entertainment, a family movie lounge, bingo, special children's activities, and a ship's store. There are special two-hour shoreline cruises ($$$$) also scheduled in early June and around Labor Day in Ludington. The ship is part of the national Heritage Travel program.

### White Pine Village (all ages)
**1687 South Lakeshore Dr.; (231) 843-4808; www.historicwhitepinevillage.org. Three miles south of Ludington, west of Old US 31 (Pere Marquette Highway). Head west on Iris, Hesslund, or Chauvez Roads and north on South Lakeshore Drive. Open 10 a.m. to 5 p.m. Tues through Sat from early May to mid-Oct and 1 to 5 p.m. Suns from Memorial Day to Labor Day. $.**

On a wooded hill south of town, White Pine Village is a reconstructed 1800s Mason County town of twenty-nine buildings on a bluff. Events centered around the buildings are scheduled throughout the summer. Gift shop and ice-cream parlor on premises, too.

### Ludington City Beach (all ages)
**Along North Lakeshore Drive, downtown at the lakefront; (231) 845-0324. Open during daylight hours Memorial Day through Labor Day. The city beach is free.**

Fun in Ludington includes a beautiful city beach. You'll find great swimming, as well as beachfront minigolf and shuffleboard.

## Where to Eat

**House of Flavors.** Downtown on the north side of US 10; (231) 845-5785. Great made-on-the-premises ice-cream treats plus grilled items. $

**Jamesport Brewing Company.** At 410 South James St., downtown; (231) 845-2522; www.jamesportbrewingco.com. Ludington's first brewpub features up to eleven house-made brews, plus bottled root beer and food. Try the beef tenderloin salad, the fish of the day, or the salmon sandwich. Children's menu. $$–$$$

**P. M. Steamers.** 502 West Loomis; (231) 843-9555. Just south of Ludington Avenue, along the waterfront. My favorite for dinner because of the harbor view and entrees such as prime rib and walleye. $$$

**Scotty's.** 5910 East Ludington Ave. (US 10), about 2 miles west of US 31; (231) 843-4033. Good American menu for lunch and dinner, such as steak and seafood. $$$

## Where to Stay

**Four Seasons Lodging and Breakfast.** 717 East Ludington Ave. (US Highway 10); (231) 843-3448 or (800) 968-0180; www.lodgingandbreakfast.com. The motel has thirty-three rooms. Continental breakfast included with stays and package lunches upon request at extra charge. Bicycles for guest use. $$–$$$

**Ludington State Park.** At the end of Highway 116, which runs from Ludington about 8 miles through the dunes; (231) 843-8671 or (231) 843-2423. Camping is $ nightly. The park has 344 campsites and 3 minicabins that each sleep four, with electric heat. There are beaches on both Lake Michigan and Hamlin Lake. One of the popular things to do at the Lake Michigan beach is to surf the water coming out of Hamlin Lake at the mouth. There

also are 18 miles of hiking trails through the dunes and woods, as well as a unique canoe trail.

**Nova Motel.** 472 South Pere Marquette Rd. (Old US 31); (231) 843-3454 or (800) 828-3162; www.novamotel.com. From US 10, turn south on Pere Marquette and go about ½ mile. The motel has thirty-two rooms and outdoor pool. $$

**Ramada Inn.** 4079 West US 10, just west of US 31; (231) 845-7311 or (800) 707-7475. Here you'll find 116 rooms and an indoor pool. $$

**Sauble Resort.** 3443 North Stearns Ave.; (231) 843-8497; www.saubleresort.com. Thirty lodge rooms and cottages on Hamlin Lake with pool and marina as well as pontoon and boat rentals. Beach nearby. Rooms and lodges rent weekly late June to mid-Aug, and nightly other times.

**Snyders Shoreline Inn.** 903 West Ludington Ave., on the lakefront; (231) 845-1261; www.snydersshoreinn.com. The inn has forty-four rooms, outdoor pool, and beach access, with breakfast room. Other dining is nearby. $$

## For More Information

**Ludington and Scottville Convention and Visitors Bureau.** 5300 US 10, Ludington 49431; (231) 845-5430 or (800) 542-4600; www.ludingtoncvb.com.

# Manistee

Manistee prides itself on its beautiful Victorian-era downtown (listed on the National Register of Historic Places). Located along US 31 and nicknamed the Victorian Port City, it is surely one of the most charming towns in the nation. Blocks of its quaint buildings are lit by antique-style street lamps. The Manistee Trolleys take visitors on a tour of town and leave from several points downtown from mid-June through Labor Day. Call (231) 723-6525 for schedules.

Street fests take place in Manistee throughout the year. The National Forest Festival takes place over the Fourth of July. Parades, dances, a midway, antique-boat and custom-car shows, a boat parade, and fireworks over Lake Michigan are among the features of this festival. The Victorian Sleighbell Parade is the first weekend in Dec. Call (231) 723-2575, or go to www.visitmanistee.com.

The Port City Street Fair takes place downtown over Labor Day weekend. Among its highlights are an antique- and classic-car show, Native American arts and dance perfor-mances, and an arts-and-crafts fair. Call (231) 723-3541 for more information.

Manistee is also one of the lake's prime salmon- and trout-fishing charter ports, with fishing available throughout the summer. Call the Manistee Area Charterboat Associa-tion or the Onekama Charterboat Association (231-398-9355) to find out how to get on board.

## Lake Michigan Recreation Area (all ages)

**West of US 31, south of the Manistee city limits, 10 miles south of the junction with High-way 55; (231) 723-2211 or, for reservations, (877) 444-6777. Usually open daily during day-light hours from Apr 1 through Oct 1. Free. Camping is $ per night.**

There are ninety-nine campsites at this gem of a recreation area, supervised by the Man-istee National Forest. It has 3½ miles of gravel biking and hiking trails, a great beach on Lake Michigan, and a picnic area with a playground, all adjoining the Nordhouse Dunes Wilderness Area to the south. The campground is extremely popular on weekends, and each site can take up to eight people and two vehicles.

## Manistee River Trail and "Little Mac" Bridge (all ages)

**Located east of Manistee. From Manistee, take Highway 55 east to Highway 37. Turn north about 9 miles. Turn west onto 26 Road for about 1½ miles. Bear right on O'Rourke Drive and go about 1⅓ miles to FR 5993, to Seaton Creek Campground. Follow the trail about 1 mile to the bridge. For more information, contact the Manistee National Forest offices, (231) 723-2211.**

# Cabins for Rent

Cottage vacations are one of my favorite family ways to have fun. A comfy pine cottage looking over a lakefront, with a rowboat that's usually available, and outboard rentals, too. Swimming, fishing, and plenty of relaxin'.

Mind you, the usual cabin is not a fancy condo. There may be plenty of makeshift items, nonmatching dinnerware, and the like, but that's all part of the fun. Cottages are a dying breed with the increasing "condoization" of the north. If you can find a good one, stick with it. It deserves your business, and you deserve the good time you'll have.

The 12-mile Manistee River Trail connects with the 4,400-mile-long North Country Trail. Hike in to see the 167-foot-long suspension bridge known as "Little Mac," over the Manistee River just downstream from Hodenpyl Dam.

## Where to Eat

**Big Al's Pizza.** 2211 Parkdale Ave.; (231) 723-6239. As the name implies, pizza rules here. $$

**The Boathouse Grille.** 440 West River St.; (231) 723-7902. Waterfront dining along the Manistee River. $$–$$$

**The Bungalow Inn.** 1100 Twenty-eighth St.; (231) 723-8000; www.thebungalowinn.com. Very good location for breakfast, lunch, and dinner. Try the deep-fried asparagus. Children's menu. $$$

## Where to Stay

There are at least eight bed-and-breakfasts operating in the Manistee County area, including five in Manistee. For descriptions and locations, call the Manistee Area Convention and Visitors Bureau (see For More Information). Other accommodations include the following:

**Days Inn of Manistee.** 1462 US 31 South, about 1⅓ miles south of town on US 31; (231) 723-8385; www.daysinnofmanistee.com. Ninety-four rooms with indoor pool and continental breakfast. $$–$$$

**Manistee National Golf & Resort.** 4797 US 31 South; (231) 398-0123; www.manisteenational.com. Forty-two rooms on two golf courses. $$ winter, $$$ summer. Packages available.

**Orchard Beach State Park.** The park is 2 miles north of Manistee on Highway 110; (231) 723-7422. Camping is offered at 174 campsites on dunes looking over the lake, with a great Lake Michigan beach. $

## For More Information

**Manistee County Convention and Visitors Bureau.** 310 First St., Manistee 49660; (231) 398-9355 or (877) 626-4783; www.visitmanisteecounty.com.

# Cadillac

This former lumber town, founded in the nineteenth century, has switched gears to log tourist dollars instead. You'll find everything here—skiing, what's billed as North America's largest snowmobile festival, summer activities from fishing to beachfront fun, and a great summertime jazz series in its downtown waterfront park. There's also a 9-mile-long bicycle trail around Lake Cadillac.

## Caberfae Peaks Ski Area (ages 3 and up)

Located about 12 miles west of Cadillac; (231) 862-3000; www.caberfaepeaks.com. Go west on Highway 55, and then turn north on Caberfae Road. Ski and snowboard school available, as well as children's programs on weekends for kids as young as 3. $$$$, children ages 6 and under ski free with full-fare adult.

The oldest ski resort in the Midwest and third oldest in the entire nation, Caberfae offers a limited amount of at-slope lodging in its Mackenzie Lodge, but most skiers make the short drive in from Cadillac. The resort features some of the state's highest slopes, made so by adding to the natural hills. It boasts one of the largest ski and snowboard rental fleets in the Midwest, too. Adjacent cross-country ski trails can be found throughout the surrounding hardwoods.

### Carl T. Johnson Hunting and Fishing Center (all ages)

6093 East Highway 55, near the entrance to Mitchell State Park; (231) 779-1321; www .michigan.gov/dnr." Open 10 a.m. to 6 p.m. daily Memorial Day through Thanksgiving; then noon to 5 p.m. Fri and 10 a.m. to 5 p.m. weekends. **Free.**

Named for the founder of the Michigan Conservation Foundation, the center teaches visitors about Michigan's outdoor heritage through displays on wildlife. New interactive displays let kids fight a salmon or bass through a fishing simulator, test their marksmanship at archery and pellet-gun ranges, or, in winter, use the 2½-mile hiking trail for cross-country skiing. There are guided walks in summer. Bring bug repellent, however.

### North American Snowmobile Festival (all ages)

Usually takes place the first weekend of Feb across Cadillac; (231) 755-0657 or (800) 225-8537; www.cadillacmichigan.com/northamericansnowmobilefestival/. **Free,** except for private events.

Take hundreds of miles of snowmobile trails in and around the city, plenty of hotels and motels as hosts, and events from fireworks to snowmobile trail runs, and you've got what's billed as North America's largest snowmobile festival. Thousands of machines converge on the city when the weather cooperates. Snowmobile drags on Lake Cadillac, motorcycle races on the ice, sleigh rides, ice sculptures, and other fun are scheduled each year.

### Lakes Mitchell and Cadillac (all ages)

Accessed best through Mitchell State Park, 6093 East Highway 55; (231) 775-7911.

Two watery gems anchor Cadillac and the surrounding area. Both lakes feature several resorts and great fishing year-round. Most public access is through Mitchell State Park, which offers beachfront on both lakes, along with small-boat access to both through a canal. The lakes are known for bass, walleye, and pike fishing.

### Jazz in the Park (all ages)

Takes place Thurs from mid-June through Aug in Rotary Park in downtown Cadillac. For schedule updates, call (800) 225-2537; www.cadillacmichigan.com. **Free.**

Like jazz and blues? Each Thurs at 7 p.m., downtown's park features some of the Midwest's best jazz and blues groups. While you're there, look at the Shay locomotive. Invented by a Cadillac resident, this steam engine figured prominently in the logging industry across North America.

## Sound Garden (all ages)

**On Chestnut Street (no street address); (231) 775-0567. Take Mitchell Street north from downtown (Business US 131) to Pine Street. Turn west and go through the light. The park is a ½ mile on the right. Free.**

A unique metal art sculpture park on the bridge over the headwaters of the Clam River. Created by a local artist of maple and other native trees, plus scrap metal, the pieces move with the wind.

## Johnny's Wild Game and Fish Park (all ages)

**Located at 5465 46½-Mile Road on Tobacco Road; (231) 775-3700; www.johnnyspark.com. Turn west off Highway 115 at the first intersection south of the junction with Highway 55 and follow the signs. Open 10 a.m. to 6 p.m. daily, Memorial Day through Labor Day. $.**

A landmark in the area. Kids will enjoy seeing and feeding game animals like deer and bison, llamas, sheep, and small animals, as well as catching trout from a pond.

## Adventure Island (all ages)

**Located ¼ mile north of the Highway 55/Highway 115 intersection between Lakes Cadillac and Mitchell, near the state park; (231) 775-5665; www.cadillacmichigan.com/adventure island/. Open 10 a.m. to 10 p.m. Memorial Day through Labor Day, then weekends through Oct, and May 1 through Memorial Day, weather permitting. $.**

Treat the family to a few hours here and play minigolf (under three free), float in a bumper boat ($, priced by the minute; must be 48 inches tall to ride), ride in a go-kart (five-minute rides, $; must be ten years old, 52 inches tall). Other fun includes a waterslide and batting cages.

## Pine River Paddlesports (ages 8 and up)

**9590 South Highway 37, in Wellston, about 12 miles west of Cadillac; (231) 862-3471; www .thepineriver.com. Rates vary by distance on the river and type of craft. $$$$.**

Canoe, raft, or kayak down the Lower Peninsula's fastest river, complete with rapids in some spots. Pine River Paddlesports will give you a careful primer on handling the river's twists and turns and will transport you to the spot where you'll put in. Trips as short as a few hours are available.

# Where to Eat

**Herman's European Café.** 214 North Mitchell, downtown; (231) 775-9563. Elegant dining in a relaxed setting. $$$$

**Lakeside Charlies.** 301 South Lake Mitchell St.; (231) 775-5332. Great Sun brunch and menu items, focusing on beef and seafood, in three dining rooms overlooking Lake Mitchell, next door to the Sun 'n Snow Motel (see listing). Children's menu. $$–$$$

## Where to Stay

Choose from more than two dozen accommodations. They include:

**Birchwood Resort.** 6545 East Highway 115; (231) 775-9101; www.birchwoodresortmi.com. This resort offers six cabins and an RV park with full hookups on Lake Cadillac. $$

**Cadillac Sands Resort.** 6319 East Highway 115; (800) 647-2637; www.cadillacsands.com. Fifty-five rooms overlooking Lake Cadillac. Restaurant on premises. Indoor pool and beach with docks, boat, snowmobile, and paddleboat rental. $$–$$$

**Laura Lee's Landing.** 1749 North Blvd.; (231) 775-2648; www.lauraleeslanding.com. Knotty-pine interiors grace one- and two-bedroom cabins adjacent to Lake Cadillac, with furnished kitchens and cable TV. The resort includes a beach, boat rentals, boat launch, and dock, plus a small restaurant open in summer. Cabins are open year-round and rent by the night or week during summer. $$

**McGuire's Resort.** 7880 Mackinaw Trail; (231) 775-9947; www.mcguiresresort.com. At the US 131 exit for Cadillac, go ½ mile west, and then go north to the top of the hill. A Cadillac-area landmark for decades, it has 123 rooms, twenty-seven holes of golf on one of the North's top courses, lighted cross-country skiing in winter, tennis courts, indoor pool, restaurant, and other amenities. $$–$$$$

**Mitchell State Park.** 6093 East Highway 55, at the entrance to Mitchell State Park; (231) 775-7911; www.michigan.gov/dnr. The park has 215 campsites with two beaches, a boat launch, and one rustic minicabin for those without tents that sleeps up to four (bring your own sleeping bags or linens).

**Sun 'n Snow Motel.** At the corner of Highways 115 and 55; (800) 477-9961; www.michiweb.com/cadillac/sun&snow. From US 131 go west on Highway 115 to the intersection with Highway 55. The motel is at the stoplight. The motel has twenty-nine rooms, including two suites. On Lake Mitchell with beach, boat dock, and great restaurant next door. $$

## For More Information

**Cadillac Area Visitors Bureau.** 222 Lake St., Cadillac 49601; (231) 775-0657 or (800) 225-2537; www.cadillacmichigan.com.

# Thompsonville

Settled in the late 1800s and named for a local lumberman, the small town of Thompsonville now sees hundreds heading for the resort just north of town along Highway 115.

### Crystal Mountain Resort & Spa (all ages)

**Just north of Thompsonville along Highway 115; (231) 378-2000 or (800) 968-7686; www.crystalmountain.com. The resort is open year-round, for golf and swimming in summer and skiing generally from early Dec through late Mar. $$$–$$$$.**

With a national reputation as one of the region's best places for families, Crystal has learned to cater to kids, with lots of programs both on the slopes and off. You'll find great kids' facilities and activities. The resort features an indoor pool, outdoor hot tubs, and forty-five ski runs. It also has more than 300 rooms, including new cottage-style facilities, condos, and an on-site restaurant ($$). Package stays can include breakfast and instruction. Cross-country ski trails also are available.

## Where to Eat and Stay

Besides the resort, which has its own restaurant, see Cadillac and Frankfort listings.

# Benzonia, Frankfort, Elberta, Honor, and Beulah

A fantastic beach, great accommodations, and super salmon fishing make this cluster of small towns along US 31 a vacation winner.

### Sportfishing (all ages)

**At East Shore Marina, Elberta, across Betsie Lake from Frankfort; (734) 422-0933. Cost is about $85 per person with a minimum of four, $400 for five, $450 for six for a half day, or $530 for a full nine-hour day.**

If you know how to fish steelhead, you're a "scum." Captain Greg Sheremeta and other charter-boat operators take anglers into the lake starting in June to search for the lake-run rainbow trout under what anglers have termed the "scum line"—tiny rivers of bugs and other debris that signal different water temperatures where steelhead themselves like to fish. Chinook-salmon-fishing action runs June through Aug.

### Platte River State Fish Hatchery (all ages)

**East of Honor along US 31; (231) 325-4611. Open for free self-guided tours daily 8 a.m. to 4 p.m. year-round.**

In fall families can watch as thousands of salmon darken the river bottom at the hatchery. There also are interpretive trails and an ecology information center.

## Where to Eat

**Cherry Hut.** Along northbound US 31, Beulah; (231) 882-4431. Open daily from early May through Oct. Great regional foods focusing on cherries, including cherry pie. $$

## Where to Stay

There are many choices here, from B&Bs to campgrounds and cottages throughout the area. Here are just a few:

**Betsie Bay Inn.** 231 Main, Frankfort, downtown; (231) 352-8090; www.betsiebayinn .com. Extra-large rooms with a Scottish flair, some with in-room saunas and all with private bath and wireless Internet. Restaurant and gift shop, too. $$

**Betsie River Campsite.** 1923 River Rd., Frankfort, at Highway 115; (231) 352-9535. There are one hundred campsites along the lower Betsie River, with playground and recreation room. $

# Sleeping Bear Dunes **National Lakeshore**

Roll or run down a giant sand dune or trek across it and learn how it got there. It's all waiting at the state's first national lakeshore, north of Frankfort.

Named by Native Americans who said one of the hulking formations was actually a slumbering mama bear, the dunes are among the largest freshwater sand piles in existence, rising to nearly 500 feet. At the visitor center, find out how they were formed; then head for the dune slide, where you can make the climb to the top and have fun coming back down.

Before you go, tour the 7-mile Pierce-Stocking Scenic Drive, with overlooks on Lake Michigan. You can also visit a restored station of the U.S. Lifesaving Service, forerunner of the Coast Guard, at the edge of the lake. For more information, call the headquarters (9922 Front St., Empire) at (231) 326-5134; www.nps.gov/slbe.

## For More Information

**Benzie County Chamber of Commerce and Benzie County Visitors Bureau.** P.O. Box 505, Beulah 49617; (231) 882-5801; www.benzie.org or www.visitbenzie.com.

**Frankfort/Elberta Area Chamber of Commerce.** P.O. Box 566, Frankfort 49635; (231) 352-7251.

# Interlochen

Named for two lakes it sits between, Interlochen was settled around 1900 and soon became known as an artist's retreat.

## Interlochen Arts Festival (all ages)

On Highway 137, south of the US 31 intersection; (231) 276-7800 or (800) 681-5920 for ticket information; www.interlochen.org for general information; www.tickets.interlochen.org for tickets. Outdoor summer concert series usually runs from mid-June to late Aug. There are fall and winter arts festivals indoors as well. $–$$$$.

Every summer since 1928, talented young persons from across the nation have converged on this unique wood-shrouded campus to learn from the best teachers that music, theater, and written and visual arts have to offer. The National Music Camp was established by an arts teacher who also founded the full-time arts academy here in 1962.

Performers who once studied here come back to teach students and play. The Interlochen Arts Festivals feature more than 600 concerts each year with student and faculty performers and dozens of professional concerts each year. In summer there are five concert venues, and visitors can also sit in on classes, rehearsals, and impromptu performances on the grounds of the 1,200-acre campus.

**Free** guided tours of the campus are available in summer at 10 a.m. and 2:30 p.m. Tues through Sat, 4 p.m. Sun, and other times by appointment.

### Fun Country Water Park  (all ages)

**Intersection of US 31 and Highway 137, at the entrance to the Interlochen area; (231) 276-6360. Open 11 a.m. to 11 p.m. daily Memorial Day through Labor Day. The waterslides close at 6:30 p.m. An all-day pass entitles you to unlimited waterslides, amusement rides, one go-kart ride, and one minigolf round. $$–$$$.**

Splashy fun awaits. The park features two 330-foot-long waterslides, along with water fun for the smallest youngsters, including bumper boats. There's also a small carousel.

### Michigan's Gifts and Treasures

**2511 Highway 137; (231) 632-8175; www.michigansgiftsandtreasures.com. Open 10 a.m. to 7 p.m. daily.**

This store specializes in locally made items, from jewelry and cutlery, to furniture and blown glass.

## Where to Eat

Besides the Stone Student Center (see Where to Stay), see listings under Frankfort and Traverse City.

## Where to Stay

**Interlochen State Park.** A mile south of US 31 on Highway 137; (231) 276-9511 or (800) 447-2757 for reservations; www.michigan.gov/dnr. Camping is $ nightly. The park has 490 sites on both Green and Duck Lakes, near Interlochen's performing arts center. The first campground to open in Michigan's state parks, it offers a beach on the lake, bathhouse, and boat rentals. As you might imagine, the park is very popular in summer during the concert series at Interlochen, so reserve well in advance. Daily permit $, annual $$$.

**Stone Student Center.** On the Interlochen campus, overlooking Green Lake; (231) 276-7570 or (231) 276-7200. There are a limited number of rooms and cottages with kitchens available. Inexpensive campus meals also are available. $$

## For More Information

**Interlochen Area Chamber of Commerce.** (231) 276-7141; www.interlochenchamber.org.

# Leland

This small town along scenic Highway 22 has developed a good reputation as a place to browse its small shops, many of which have been transformed from former fishing wharves below the town dam. There are lots of good restaurants as well. Visit the Leland Web site at www.leelanau.com.

### Fishtown (all ages)
**In Leland, below the dam.**

Shop for smoked fish at Carlson's, visit a quaint shop, or book a fishing charter from one of the craft moored at the docks in this picturesque former fishing village.

### North and South Manitou Islands (all ages)
**The ferry leaves the Fishtown wharf at 10 a.m. The trip across takes about ninety minutes. For island transportation, tips, days of operation, and other information, call (231) 256-9061; www.leelanau.com/manitou/. $$$.**

The most remote part of the Sleeping Bear Dunes National Lakeshore, these islands are reached by ferry from Leland, the fishing-village-turned-tourist-town. According to a Native American legend, the islands are the cubs of the mother bear that became Sleeping Bear Dune, and she eternally waits for them to come ashore. The islands feature primitive hiking. South Manitou has a restored 1839 U.S. Coast Guard lighthouse as well as one modern shipwreck. Don't forget your mosquito repellent; these pesky insects can be terrors at times. Tours of South Manitou Island are available ($–$$), as are rustic campgrounds. Camping on North Manitou is primitive.

## Where to Eat

**The Cove.** 111 River, just west of Main (Highway 22); (231) 256-9834. It'll be hard to find a more romantic spot for lunch and dinner, with the waterfall from the Leland River splashing merrily. Children's menu. $$$

## Where to Stay

**Falling Waters Lodge.** 50 West Cedar St. (Highway 22); (231) 256-9832; www.falling waterslodge.com. A favorite location for TV commercials, this picturesque lodge has twenty-one rooms and suites overlooking Leland's Fishtown area. $$$$ in summer, $$ in fall and spring.

**Homestead Resort and Ski Area.** Along Highway 22, north of town; (231) 334-5000; www.thehomesteadresort.com. More than 115 rooms and condos on the beach and in the wooded dunes overlooking Lake Michigan. The Homestead's historic inn was recently remodeled to include seventeen rooms with continental breakfast. $$$

For other places to eat and stay nearby, see entries for Traverse City or go to the Web site listed under For More Information.

## For More Information
**Leland Chamber of Commerce.** (877) LELAND1 or (231) 256-0079; www.lelandmi .com.

# Traverse City

Named for the traverse, or portage, that voyagers made between the bays, the region retains its reputation as the nation's largest tart-cherry-growing district. While many of the orchards have been plowed under for expensive homes and condos, there are still plenty around. Michigan still produces about 75 percent of the nation's tart-cherry crop.

# Cherry, Cherry Baby!

If Michigan's west side is orchard country, you're in the heart of the cherry orchard here. Many of the nearly four million cherry trees in Michigan are all around you and in the neighboring Leelanau Peninsula to the west. Each tree holds enough cherries for twenty-eight pies. Come summer, many of the farms sport roadside stands where they sell still-warm pies right out of the oven to take back to your campground or room. Beaches, like Lighthouse Park at the end of the Old Mission Peninsula, entice you to spend the day or the week with a slice of fresh pie while you enjoy beautiful scenery, great water, and great cherries.

Apr and May are great times to visit and watch for the annual cherry-blossom opening. This rapidly growing city has become the spot to vacation for many Michigan families. With great shopping downtown and plenty of waterfront accommodations on East and West Grand Traverse Bays, it's no wonder.

Traverse City is at the intersection of Highway 72 and US 31.

## Amon Orchards (all ages)

**It's 2 miles north of the northern Traverse City limit on US 31 at 8066 US 31 North, Acme; (231) 938-9160 or (800) 937-1644; www.amonorchards.com. Open daily for tours May through Oct.**

Despite creeping urban sprawl the area is still America's tart-cherry capital. This orchard, just north of the city, offers visits to its tree lots, both to handpick the fruit and to see how it's done commercially. Besides cherries, which usually are ready in July, the adjacent eighty-acre orchard has you-pick apricots, peaches, nectarines, and other fruits. Also on-site are a market offering nearly everything cherry, from salad dressing to ice-cream toppings, and a petting farm for the kids.

## National Cherry Festival (all ages)

**Takes place annually starting around July 4, with its focus on downtown. For information, call (231) 947-4230; www.cherryfestival.org.**

This festival is truly a cherries jubilee. The cherry harvest usually coincides with the festival, which features a carnival downtown, activities on the waterfront, and fresh-baked cherry pies sold everywhere, both in town and from farm roadside stands approaching the city. Big parades are part of the festival, the biggest of which is the Cherry Royale. Usually there is an air show scheduled, along with concerts, arts-and-crafts fairs, and more.

### Traverse City Beach Bums Baseball (all ages)

**The Bums play in 3,500-seat Wuerfel Park, at US 31 and Highway 37, south of Traverse City; (231) 943-0100; www.traversecitybeachbums.com.**

Brooklyn had its "Bums" before the Dodgers moved west. Now Traverse City has its aptly named team, part of the Frontier League. Cheer them on from a comfortable bowled stadium with extensive casual lawn seating as well as seats and boxes. The team plays nearly one hundred games from late May to Labor Day, with postseason play through mid-Sept, if the Bums make it into the playoffs.

### Traverse City Film Festival (check movies for appropriate ages)

**Takes place in late July at six locations around the city, including the restored opulent State Theatre downtown and in Cherry Festival Open Space along the waterfront on a huge inflatable screen; (231) 392-1134; www.traversecityfilmfest.org.**

Since it began in 2004, this festival has become one of the largest such events in the Midwest. Some of the best independently produced films, including U.S. and world premiers, make up the screenings, and part of the fun are the classic movies that are shown **free** at the inflatable outdoor screen at the Cherry Festival Open Space downtown, where the kids can run amok—within reason—while you enjoy the flick. Home screen of most movies is the State Theatre, built in 1923 and restored in 2005, which also shows movies year-around.

### Old Mission Peninsula Lighthouse (all ages)

**Along Highway 37, Old Mission, which bisects the Old Mission Peninsula separating the east and west arms of Grand Traverse Bay; www.oldmission.com. $**

Your kids can stand halfway between the equator and the North Pole outside of this nineteenth-century lighthouse. It's a highlight of a 37-mile drive on Highway 37 north. There's also a great beach with a very gradual drop-off.

### The Village at Grand Traverse Commons (all ages)

**1200 West Eleventh St.; (231) 941-1900; www.thevillagetc.com. Most shops are open 10 a.m. to 6 p.m. daily from Memorial Day to Labor Day.**

Currently sixteen specialty retailers. Surrounded by more than 300 acres of parkland with hiking and some serious mountain biking trails affording amazing views of downtown and Grand Traverse Bay.

### Clinch Park (all ages)

**Across from downtown Traverse City along US 31 at Cass; (231) 922-4904. Free parking is across the street. The free park is reached via an underground pedestrian walkway from the parking lot.**

There's a large beach with lifeguards on duty. The beach is one of several parks along both arms of the bay.

## Pirate's Cove (ages two and up)

**1710 US 31 North; (231) 938-9599; www.piratescove.net. Open 11 a.m. to 11 p.m. daily, weather permitting, from Memorial Day through Labor Day, except the minigolf courses, which stay open Apr and May weekends and Sept and Oct, usually until the first snow.**

Give the kids a time-out here and let them play on the waterslide, zip-line and ropes course, go-karts, and, for the smallest youngsters, battery-operated four-wheeler replicas. You must be 42 inches tall to go on the waterslide, 58 inches to drive go-karts, and 40 inches to be a passenger. Nearly all the rides use tokens, purchased at the gate. Five tokens ($), twenty-five tokens ($$).

## Tall Ship *Manitou* (all ages)

**On Grand Traverse Bay's west arm at 13390 South West Bay Shore Dr. For cruise schedules, call (231) 941-2000 or (800) 678-0383; www.tallshipsailing.com. $.**

Try a cruise on one of the Great Lakes' largest sailing crafts. In summer the 114-foot *Manitou* plies the bay during the day and also acts as a floating bed-and-breakfast that includes an evening sail.

## Vasa Pathway (all ages)

**Reach the pathway at Acme Township Park; (231) 947-1120; www.vasa.org. From US 31, take Bunker Hill Road east to Bartlett. Free.**

Used in winter for the giant Vasa cross-country ski race that brings in competitors from across the country, the trail is used by mountain bikers and hikers in summer. There are three loops ranging from 3 to 16¾ miles through the woods.

## Sand Lakes Quiet Area (all ages)

**East of Traverse City; (231) 922-5280. Take Highway 72 east to Broomhead Road and turn south. The area is open year-round, all the time. Free. Parking is available at the entrance to the area.**

Slow your pace, take a breath, and listen to the quiet. All motorized vehicles are banned in this heavily wooded preserve. There are nearly 10 miles of trails with fishing and camping available, but mostly for hikers who pack in. It's a wonderfully quiet place to visit and just enjoy what the area must have looked like to early settlers. Trails wind through the woods, so bring a child backpack since strollers are not of much use here.

# Where to Eat

There are literally hundreds of restaurants in town, from fast food to elegant. Here are just a few:

**Apache Trout Grill.** 13671 South West Bay Shore Dr.; (231) 947-7079; www.apachetrout grill.com. Named after a fish, you'd expect fish to be a specialty here, and it is, but beef is also on the menu. Children's menu. $$–$$$

**Boone's Long Lake Inn.** 7208 Secor Rd.; (231) 946-3991; www.booneslli.com. About 5½ miles southwest of Traverse City. Take US 31 south, and then head 4 miles southwest on Silver Lake Road, and 1½ miles west on Secor and watch for the signs. Open Mon through Sat 4 to 11 p.m. and Sun noon to 10 p.m. Vegetarians, beware. For the money it's one of the best places for steak, including eighteen-ounce New York strips. Children's menu. $$$

**Grand Traverse Pie Co.** 525 West Front St., downtown; (231) 922-7437; www.gtpie .com. Open 7 a.m. to 7 p.m. Mon through Fri, 8 a.m. to 6 p.m. Sat. You're in cherry country, so you'd better make a dent here in a crumble-top cherry pie. Owners Mike and Denise Busley opened it in 1996, and shops have spread across Michigan since. Great handmade fruit and cream pies (what else?), along with tasty sandwiches, breakfast items, potpies, and quiches. $

**La Senorita.** 1245 South Garfield Rd.; (231) 947-8820. About a mile south of the junction of Highways 37 and 72 at the Old Mission Peninsula turnoff. Open Mon through Thurs 11 a.m. to 11 p.m., Fri and Sat until midnight, and Sun noon to 10 p.m. Good Mexican food for lunch and dinner. $$

**Moomers.** 7263 North Long Lake Rd.; (231) 941-4122; www.moomers.com. Moomer's features more than twenty of its hundred-plus ice-cream flavors daily in its shop on a working dairy farm. $

## Where to Stay

Choose from scores of lodgings that ring both the east and west arms of Grand Traverse Bay. The majority are along US 31, which skirts the bottoms of both arms.

Besides those mentioned there are about a dozen bed-and-breakfasts operating in the area as well.

**Days Inn and Suites Traverse City.** 420 Munson Ave.; (231) 941-0208 or (800) 982-3297. Two miles east of downtown on US 31. This economical chain property offers 183

rooms, some whirlpool rooms, indoor pool, and adjacent restaurant. $$

**Driftwood Resort.** 1861 US 31 North; (231) 938-6100. The resort has thirty-nine rooms, indoor pool, and recreation area. You can also swim in the bay. Restaurants nearby. $$

**Grand Beach Resort Hotel.** 1683 US 31, about 4½ miles east of downtown; (231) 938-4455; www.tcbeaches.com. The hotel has ninety-five rooms on Grand Traverse Bay, with swimming in the bay or an indoor pool. Exercise room and continental breakfast included in the room rate. $$$

**Grand Traverse Resort and Spa.** 100 Grand Traverse Village Blvd., Acme; (231) 938-2100 or (800) 748-0303; www.grandtra-verseresort.com. From Traverse City, head north on US 31, just past the intersection with Highway 72. This grand resort has 669 rooms, suites, and condos surrounding three golf courses, including ones designed by Gary Player and Jack Nicklaus. $$$

**Great Wolf Lodge.** 3573 North US 31 South, on the south side of Traverse City; (231) 941-3600 or (866) GR8-WOLF; www .greatwolflodge.com. This resort has it all, from a spa for Mom, to the huge indoor water park for everyone. There are 281 rooms, as well as two restaurants, an arcade, and an outdoor pool. You have to be a hotel guest to use the water park. $$$

**Park Place Hotel.** 300 East State St.; (231) 946-5000 or (800) 748-0133; www.park-place-hotel.com. The city's venerable downtown classic, with 140 restored rooms in the town's tallest building. Indoor pool, exercise area, and packages. $$

**Pineview Resort.** 2275 Pinehurst Trail, Mayfield; (231) 947-6792. Just south of US 31, 6 miles southeast of Traverse City. Weekly rates range from $525 to $610. One of a vanishing breed of cottage resorts in the con-doland of west Michigan, it has twelve two- to three-bedroom units on Arbutus Lake, some with fireplaces. Small pets OK. $$

**Timber Ridge Campground.** 4050 Hammond Rd., 7½ miles southeast of the city; (231) 947-2770. Head east about 4¼ miles on US 31, then south 2 miles on Four Mile Road and east 2 miles on Hammond. Here you'll find 231 sites and 15 log cabins in a well-run, quiet location, with pool, wading pool, arcade, minigolf, and children's programs. $

**Traverse City State Park.** 1132 US 31, on the eastern edge of downtown; (231) 922-5270 or (800) 447-2757. Camping is extra. The park has 343 sites opposite Grand Traverse Bay. A pedestrian bridge over US 31 connects the campground with 700 feet of sandy beach. Located near the highway and tourist attractions, it's not the quietest park, but it's convenient to all things happening in the area. Daily permit $, annual $$$

**Waterfront Inn.** 2061 US 31 North; (231) 939-1100. The inn has 128 rooms on Traverse Bay's east arm, with beach, indoor pool, and restaurant. $$$

## For More Information

These organizations can provide information for the entire Grand Traverse area:

**Leelanau Peninsula Chamber of Commerce.** 5046 South West Bayshore Dr., Suttons Bay 49682; (231) 271-9895; www .leelanauchamber.com.

**Traverse City Convention and Visitors Bureau.** 101 West Grandview Parkway, Traverse City 49684; (231) 947-1120 or (800) 872-8377; www.mytraversecity.com.

# Bellaire

The Antrim County seat was founded in 1879 and was so named for its pleasant air. The name still applies. There are several large lakes within a few minutes' drive of the city.

### Shanty Creek Resort (all ages)

1 Shanty Creek Road; (800) 678-4111; www.shantycreek.com. The resort is off Highway 88, just south of Bellaire and 12 miles west of Mancelona. From I-75, take Highway 72 west to US 131 north, which leads to Highway 88 west. The resort is open year-round. It has an excellent children's ski school, and babysitting is available. Midweek deals abound, especially for families with kids. During ski season up to four children 17 and under sleep and ski **free** when in the same accommodations as their parents. $$$$.

The resort has three bases: Summit Mountain, which underwent a multi-million-dollar renovation to open in 2009, Schuss Mountain, and Cedar River Village.

The Lodge at Cedar River has eighty-five one-bedroom condo suites and ten two-bedroom suites, all ski-in, ski-out, including a ski-through tunnel that kids love, plus a two-lane tubing hill that's a blast. There are forty-six downhill runs with equipment rental and instruction, plus lots of cross-country ski trails. **Free** shuttles connect the resort bases. Summer brings golfers to the complex's four courses, including its Arnold Palmer–designed Legend and the Tom Weiskopf–designed Cedar River Golf Club.

## Where to Eat and Stay

**Shanty Creek Resort.** See the listing for directions and address; (800) 678-4111; www .shantycreek.com. Schuss and Summit Mountains and Cedar River Village have a total of 600 rooms, 400 of them condos to suit everyone, from one to five bedrooms. They also have four good restaurants, with Summit's Lakeview Dining Room buffet dinners and Sun brunch overlooking great northern Michigan countryside highly recommended. Children's menu. $$$

# Boyne City, Boyne Falls, and Walloon Lake

Settled in 1865, the Boynes were named after Ireland's Boyne River. Walloon Lake was settled about seven years later. The area now is known as a vacation destination.

### National Morel Mushroom Festival (all ages)

**Takes place the weekend after Mother's Day in downtown Boyne City; (231) 582-6222; www.morelfest.com. Free admission. Rides $.**

It happens each spring. Just as the wild white trilliums sprout delicately to cover the forest in greenery once again, morel mania takes over during the festival. Pickers from across the country converge here to head for the rolling hardwood hills around Boyne, an ideal habitat for morels. It takes a little effort at first, but once you find one, their trademark caps with furrows and pockets are easy to spot. Since there are false morels that some people are allergic to, attend the festival to learn what you're looking for. Guided hunts and contests take place each day.

### Boyne Mountain and Mountain Grand Lodge (all ages)

**Just south of Boyne Falls off US 131, Boyne Falls; (231) 549-2441 or (800) 462-6963; www .boyneusa.com.**

Get ready for four seasons of fun at one location. Boyne Mountain is what many regard as the Lower Peninsula's premier ski area. The lodge features more than 200 rooms overlooking sixty-one runs, rentals, condos in the woods and slopeside, and Michigan's largest indoor water park, Avalanche Bay. Kids love the attractions there, including the surfing pool—just wear a snug-fitting suit—and waterslides galore, where it's always eighty-four degrees. In summer Boyne features championship golf courses and excellent golf instruction. In winter there's a great ski school for kids and adults alike, plus babysitting.

## Where to Eat

There are restaurants at Boyne Mountain and others in town.

## Where to Stay

**Brown Trout Motel.** 2510 Nelson, Boyne Falls, along US 131, south of Highway 75;

(231) 549-2791. The motel has fifteen rooms and an indoor pool. $$

## For More Information
**Boyne City Chamber of Commerce.** 20 South Lake St., Boyne City; (231) 582-6222; www.boynechamber.com.

# Petoskey

Located on the shores of Little Traverse Bay, Petoskey features modern accommodations and unique shopping. Petoskey's Historic Gaslight District downtown is worth a look. The Petoskey harborfront, with its Bayfront Park, is a pleasant location to bring the family, and the state park's rolling dunes, clear water, and sandy beach are great places to visit.

### Kilwin's Candy Kitchens (all ages)
**355 North Division Rd.; (231) 347-3800 or (800) 255-0759; www.kilwins.com. From Mitchell Street, the main downtown thoroughfare, go east about a block, then north on Division. Free tours lasting about twenty minutes are offered from June through Aug (times vary; call first).**

What more delicious thought can there be to a child than a candy-factory tour? In Petoskey, a great vacation city, they can watch and sniff as the chocolates are formed, and then buy some in the shop.

## Where to Eat
There are scores of places to dine, from resorts to restaurants. For more, go to www.petoskeyarea.com.

**City Park Grill.** 432 East Lake St.; (231) 347-0101. This restaurant serves lunch and dinner. $$–$$$

**Villa Ristorante Italiano.** 887 Spring St. (US 131, just south of US 31); (231) 347-1440. Open 4:30 to 11 p.m. nightly. Children's menu. Save money and order a pizza. $$

# Highway 119 Scenic Drive

The drive starts north of downtown Petoskey. From US 31, head north on Highway 119. You'll soon discover why state residents have many times voted it to be Michigan's most scenic highway. The highway has breathtaking overlooks on bluffs high above blue Lake Michigan. The roadway is nicknamed the "Tunnel of Trees" because of the thick foliage. It can be twisty in spots, so follow the low speed limit and enjoy.

## Where to Stay

**Apple Tree Inn.** 915 Spring (US 131), Petoskey, just south of town; (231) 348-2900. The inn has forty rooms, indoor pool, play area, continental breakfast, and dining nearby. $$

**Baywinds Inn.** 909 Spring (US 131), Petoskey, a mile south of town; (231) 347-4193. The inn has forty-eight rooms, indoor pool, and exercise area. Restaurant nearby. $$

**Best Western Inn.** 1300 Spring (US 131), Petoskey, 1⅓ mile south of town; (231) 347-3925. The inn has eighty-five rooms and indoor pool. Restaurant nearby. $$

**Best Western of Harbor Springs.** 8514 Highway 119, Harbor Springs, north of the US 31 and Highway 119 intersection; (231) 347-9050. The property has forty-six rooms, indoor pool, and breakfast room. $$

**Econo Lodge.** 1858 US 131 South, Petoskey, 2 miles south of the US 31/US 131 intersection; (231) 348-3324. This property has sixty rooms and indoor pool. $$

**Stafford's Bayview Inn.** 2011 Woodland Ave. (US 31), Bayview, down the hill from downtown Petoskey; (231) 347-2771; www.staffords.com. You'll find eight rooms in a historic 1886 inn in the heart of the Bayview historic home district. $$$

**Petoskey State Park.** Along Highway 119, north of downtown, 4 miles north of the US 31 junction; (231) 347-2311 or (800) 447-2757. The park has ninety campsites nestled in the dunes along Lake Michigan's Little Traverse Bay. A great beach, nature trails, and programs. Daily permit $, annual $$$

## For More Information

**Petoskey Area Visitors Bureau.** 401 East Mitchell St., Petoskey 49770; (231) 348-2755 or (800) 845-2828; www.petoskeyarea.com.

**Petoskey Regional Chamber of Commerce.** 401 East Mitchell St., Petoskey 49770; (231) 347-4150; www.petoskey.com.

# Bayview

North on US 31 from downtown Petoskey is this area of magnificent 1870s Victorian summer homes and marvelous bed-and-breakfasts and inns that originally were part of a religious settlement connected with the Methodist Church. Turn north on Highway 119 for a scenic drive you'll never forget.

## Boyne Highlands and Nubs Nob (all ages)

**From Bayview, head north on US 31, and then turn north on Highway 119 to Pleasantview Road, head north, and follow the signs. For Boyne Highlands, (231) 526-3000 or (800) 462-6963; www.boyne.com. For Nubs, (231) 526-2131 or (800) 754-6827; www.nubsnob.com.**

These two downhill ski areas are across the street from each other. Nubs Nob has thirty-eight runs. It has rentals and instruction, but it has no slopeside lodging. Boyne Highlands is a genteel ski area that caters to families. Slopeside rooms surround a large, heated outdoor pool that's warm even when the air's fifteen degrees below zero in winter. It also offers rentals, instruction, children's programs, and babysitting.

Nubs has children's programs but no babysitting.

## Charlevoix Smurf Houses and Beaver Island Adventures

Reached by ferry and air from the picturesque lakeside town of Charlevoix, the island has a unique history. It holds title as America's only kingdom, under Mormon leader James J. Strang, and now is a heaven for boaters mooring at its harbor, and vacationers looking to get away for a few days. Fishing both on Lake Michigan and its inland lakes is available, along with biking and walking its miles of beachfront. A great marine museum, potters and artists, and even a golf course are also on the island.

Take a tour with Beaver Island Ecotours (231-448-2194; www.beaverislandecotours.com. $$$$). From May through Aug, go with Inland Seas Kayak Tours (231-448-2221; www.inlandseaskayaking.com. $$$$) to really enjoy this unique getaway. Stay at the Laurain Lodge (231-448-2099; www.laurainlodge.com), the Beaver Island Lodge (231-448-2396; www.beaverislandlodge.com), or several others. Back on the mainland, enjoy shopping in downtown Charlevoix, and then drive past the several homes that remind some of Smurfs and others of Hobbits. These unique stone homes designed by late resident Earl Young can be seen on Park Avenue, Grant and Clinton Streets, and along Round Lake. Homes feature gracefully curving roofs and walls made of native limestone. Find out more from the Charlevoix Area Convention and Visitors Bureau at (800) 367-8557 or through www.charlevoixlodging.com, and the Beaver Island Chamber of Commerce by calling (231) 448-2505, or going to www.beaverisland.org.

## Where to Eat

**La Senorita.** At the junction of US 31 and Highway 119; (231) 347-7750. Good Mexican food. $$

**Stafford's Bay View Inn.** 2011 Woodland Ave. (US 31); (231) 347-2771. Serves breakfast, lunch, and dinner plus Sun brunch in a cozy dining room. $$$

## Where to Stay

See listings under Petoskey, above.

# Mackinaw City

Ask even a local here why the island is spelled *Mackinac* but the city is *Mackinaw*, and he or she probably won't know (they're both pronounced "Mackinaw"). The answer is lost with the 300-odd years since the first European settlers arrived here, first the French, then the British (probably the reason for the spelling differences). A few beautiful state parks and family attractions abound in this town, which comes alive in summer and hibernates in winter. Three ferry lines serve Mackinac Island: Arnold Line, (906) 847-3351 or (800) 542-8528, www.arnoldline.com; Shepler's, (906) 847-6124 or (800) 638-9892, www.sheplersferry.com; and Star, (906) 643-7635 or (800) 638-9892, www.mackinacferry.com. They leave regularly from docks in downtown Mackinaw City. Got a fall leaf-peeping trip in mind? Plan on being here around mid-Oct for the annual show's peak.

## Colonial Michilimackinac State Historic Park (all ages)

Under the southern ramp of the Mackinac Bridge in Mackinaw City; (231) 436-5563; www.mackinacparks.com. Admission is $–$$, children ages 5 and younger are admitted **free**. You can also purchase a pass for entrance into other area historic state parks for $$–$$$.

This park stands on the location of the fort used by the French, then the British, until a larger, more defensible fort (or so everyone thought) on Mackinac Island was completed. In summer interpretive programs with costumed docents in character tell about life at the fort in the seventeenth century. There are demonstrations of musket and cannon firing, cooking, and blacksmithing. Archeological digs for artifacts are also held within the fort each summer. The annual Memorial Day weekend historical pageant, in which locals reenact a famous battle between the French, British, and Indians, is the longest-running historical pageant in the nation. Evening fireworks accompany the show.

## Historic Mill Creek Discovery Park (all ages)

9001 US 23, south of Mackinaw City; (231) 436-4100; www.mackinacparks.com. Admission $$ adults, $ ages 5 through 17, and under 5 **free**.

One of the area's five state parks, this one features a replica working water-powered sawmill like that used near here in the eighteenth and nineteenth centuries. Nature trails and an adventure tour that includes a zip-line ride, plus a kid's play area, also are at the park.

## Seashell City (all ages)

At I-75 exit 326 (Levering Road) in Cheboygan; (231) 627-2066; www.seashellcitymi.com. Hours are 9 a.m. to 6 p.m. daily from May 1 through Labor Day and 9 a.m. to 5 p.m. daily from the day after Labor Day.

This place is a must for any tourist-attraction aficionado. Just a few miles south of Mackinaw City along I-75 is Seashell City, where, besides what's billed as a "Giant Man-Eating Clam" (it actually is just a big shell and never ate anybody), you'll discover thousands of shells from across the world. It's a gas.

## Thunder Falls Water Park (all ages)

1028 South Nicolet; (231) 436-6000; www.thunderfalls-waterpark.com. Open early June through Labor Day. Admission: adults $$$$, children under 48 inches $$$, ages 2 and under **free**.

With twelve waterslides (including one that's nearly seven stories tall), a tube float for Mom and Dad on the Lazy River, and a wave pool that generates 4-footers, Thunder Falls is wet and wild. When you get out of the water, try the arcade, the midway, or the food court. Check out the Web site for discount tickets in combination with stays at a partner motel/hotel.

### Mackinaw Outfitters (all ages)

220 South Huron Ave.; (231) 436-4066; www.mackinawoutfittersstore.com. **Hours vary by season, so call ahead.**

This store has everything for fun in the outdoors, including an indoor climbing wall and a 10,000-gallon aquarium stocked with Michigan game fish.

### Mackinac Bridge (all ages)

You'll know it when you see it from I-75; (906) 643-7600. $.

This huge structure leads north to Michigan's Upper Peninsula. Before the bridge was built, ferries crammed the lakefront there, taking cars and trucks across the straits. On busy weekends traffic jams stretched for miles as vacationers waited for passage.

The bridge celebrated its fiftieth anniversary in 2007. From cable anchorage to cable anchorage, it's the Western Hemisphere's longest suspension bridge, measuring 5 miles. The only time you can walk it is the annual Labor Day Bridge Walk, when Michigan's governor leads more than 80,000 people on foot across the bridge. You can picnic at **free** parks on both the south and north ends of the bridge, including beautiful Bridge View Park on the St. Ignace side. A **free** museum dedicated to the bridge's construction is on the second floor of MaMa Mia's Pizzeria, 231 East Central Ave.

### Mackinaw Crossings

248 South Huron St. (US 23); (231) 436-5330; www.mackinawcrossings.com.

After browsing through more than fifty stores, you can stay late and watch the laser light show on summer evenings.

### Jack Pine Lumberjack Show (all ages)

Located 1½ miles south of Mackinaw City on US 23; (231) 436-5225; www.jackpinelumberjack shows.com. **Performances take place at 7:30 p.m. Thurs through Sun, Memorial Day through mid-June, and 7:30 p.m. daily mid-June through Labor Day. $$, kids 4 and under free.**

After you've seen the sawmill at Mill Creek, take the family to see how logs got to the sawmill before machinery did much of the dangerous work. Watch from covered grandstands as lumberjacks compete in cutting, log rolling, tree climbing, and other woodsman skills.

### Icebreaker *Mackinaw* Maritime Museum (all ages)

Moored at the ferry docks in Mackinaw City; (231) 436-9825; www.themackinaw.org. **Open for tours 10 a.m. to 8 p.m. in July, 10 a.m. to 6 p.m. in Aug. $$ adults and ages 6 through 17; $$$$ for a family.**

Tour the other "Mighty Mac," a 290-foot-long icebreaker that served Great Lakes shipping before its retirement in 2001, when a new ship took its place.

## Where to Eat

**Audie's Family Restaurant and Chippewa Room.** 314 North Nicolet Ave.; (231) 436-5744; www.audies.com. Good choice for breakfast, lunch, and dinner, with fresh whitefish fixed several ways. Within sight of the bridge. The Chippewa Room features higher-end casual dining. $–$$$$

**MaMa Mia's Pizzeria Restaurant.** 231Central, downtown; (231) 436-5930. Good family-style food. The Mackinaw Bridge Museum, with the story of the building of the bridge, is on the second floor. $$

## Where to Stay

Many of the city's accommodations close in winter, so call ahead to be sure your favorite is open.

**America's Best Value Inn–Mackinaw City.** 112 Old US 31; (231) 436-5544 or (800) 647-8286; www.abvinn.mackinawcity.com. From I-75, take either exit 338 or 337 and go into town. The property has seventy-three rooms with indoor pool. Continental breakfast included in room rates. Restaurants nearby. $$

**Anchor Inn.** 138 Old US 31; (231) 436-5553 or (888) 262-4679. Just north of exit 337 from I-75. The inn has thirty-two rooms, outdoor pool, and playground. $

**Best Western Dockside Waterfront Inn.** 505 South Huron Ave.; (231) 436-5001. The inn is 3 blocks south of Central, the town's main east-west road, along US 23. It has eighty-eight rooms with indoor pool. Beach and restaurants nearby. $$

**Chief Motel.** 10470 US 23, a mile south of town; (231) 436-7981. This little motel has sixteen rooms, outdoor pool, picnic area, and beach access. $

**Days Inn.** 825 South Huron (US 23), South Huron; (231) 436-5557 or (800) 329-7466. The inn has eighty-four rooms, indoor pool, restaurant, putting green, and shuffleboard. Located next to one of the ferry lines to the island. $$

**Mackinaw Mill Creek Camping.** On US 23, 3 miles south of the city; (231) 436-5584. Privately owned, with 600 sites, pool, playground, and minigolf. $

**Northpointe Inn.** 1027 South Huron St. (US 23); (231) 436-9812; www.northpointeinn .com. This ninety-eight-room motel features a 23,000-square-foot indoor waterpark near the island ferry docks. $$

**Wilderness State Park.** About 12 miles west of Mackinaw City via CR 81 and Wilderness Park Drive; (231) 436-5381 or (800) 447-2757. Choose from 210 campsites or, in the heart of the park, six trailside cabins (and three group-style bunkhouses) reached by short hikes. They don't have electricity and are equipped with a woodstove for cooking and warmth, a hand pump for water, and a pit toilet. Cabins and campsites available. Daily permit $, annual $$$.

## For More Information

**Mackinaw Area Visitors Bureau.** 10800 West US 23, Mackinaw City 49701; (800) 666-0160; www.mackinawcity.com. For more on the area, contact the Mackinaw City Chamber of Commerce, (888) 455-8100; www.mackinawchamber.com, or even www .mackinawcity.com.

# Upper Peninsula– East

Michigan's Upper Peninsula, the UP for short, can be divided into two distinct regions. The eastern part is where farms mix with forest, cities, and other attractions that make this section of the state unique. The western region is more rugged and wild. Bear, deer, moose, wolves, and even cougar roam there.

## Mackinac Island

Mackinaw City, the Mackinac Bridge's southern anchor, is one of the two spots to catch the high-speed ferry services that run to this unique vacation island. The other is St. Ignace, on the north end of the bridge. Those whom the islanders call "fudgies" (because most leave with its most popular export, fudge) are part of the hundreds of thousands who visit here annually. Historic spots around the island include War of 1812 battlefield sites, now occupied by one of the country's oldest golf courses, Wawashkemo. It's one of three on the island, and, in a nod to modern times, there is also a disc-golf course. The island is also home to old fur-trading posts and churches.

Winter visitors arrive by plane and find a decidedly slower tempo, with only a few hotels operating. They can cross-country ski on the trails that host mountain bikers in summer, or snowmobile in other areas.

Tourists in search of cool breezes invade this island each summer day to walk its streets, ride its bike trails, and enjoy the jewel of a lake that surrounds it. Nearly the entire island is a state park. The pace slows on the island, and except for the clothes, it could be one hundred years ago, as the only modes of transportation here are horses, bicycles, and feet.

To get to Mackinac Island, leave from either the Mackinaw City side or the St. Ignace side of the bridge. Don't worry about missing the boat, unless it's late at night and you're due for an overnight stay. Ferries leave continuously from three docks and take about sixteen minutes to get across. Parking is generally **free.** Call Arnold Line at (906) 847-3351 or (800) 542-8528, Shepler's at (800) 828-6157, or Star at (800) 638-9892.

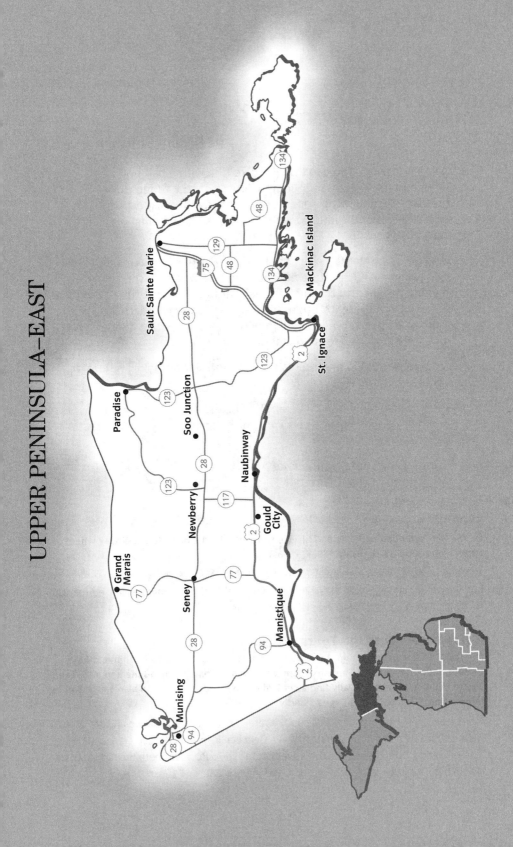

UPPER PENINSULA–EAST

# Top
# FamilyAdventures
### in Upper Peninsula–East

1. **Mackinac Island.** You can't beat a bike ride with a half pound of fudge and the kids as your companions. Why the fudge? Silly question. For the more adventurous, rent a mountain bike and explore the island's little-traveled dirt trails in the bluffs. Maps are available.

2. **Soo Locks and Valley Camp, Sault Sainte Marie.** Grown-ups and kids alike will gawk at the huge freighters just inches from the sides of the locks, at the trip through on the tour boats, and at the enormity of the water flowing through the area each second. Boarding one of those freighters to see how they work and to get an idea of how huge they actually are is educational and great fun.

3. **Pictured Rocks National Lakeshore, Munising.** Another of nature's wonders in the UP.

4. **Great Lakes Shipwreck Museum, Paradise.** Learn about just how treacherous the lakes can be and why even seagoing vessels fear their storms.

5. **Tahquamenon Falls, Tahquamenon Falls State Park, Paradise.** The twin falls are a scenic wonder.

## Skull Cave  (all ages)
**On the Garrison Road pathway and bicycle trail, actually the only state highway where autos aren't allowed, Highway 185. Free.**

This natural cave, which resembles a skull from the outside, served as a Native American burial chamber and also was the hiding place of local settlers during the Native American revolt in 1763. It's part of Mackinac Island State Park.

## Horse-Drawn Carriage Tours  (all ages)
**(906) 847-3573; www.mict.com. Tours run from 8:30 a.m. to 5 p.m. daily from mid-June through Labor Day and 8:30 a.m. to 4 p.m. daily from mid-May to mid-June and after Labor Day to mid-Oct. You can usually find a seat when you land, but you can also call ahead for information. $$–$$$, children ages 3 and younger ride free.**

Tours leave daily from the ferry dock and several other points downtown and are great ways to become acquainted with the island. Between jokes and the clip-clop (and other noises) coming from the horses, the driver will tell you a lot about both the history of the island, before it became a vacation spot, and the present.

Tours take in Arch Rock and Skull Cave and historical stops, along with a drive-by of the governor's mansion, where he stays when he's on the island, and the grand dame of summer hotels, the Grand Hotel.

You can also rent drive-it-yourself carriages, but the narrated tour is the best way for newcomers to see the sights.

## Fort Mackinac State Park  (all ages)

**The fortress on a bluff above downtown Mackinac Island is part of the state park; (906) 847-3328; www.mackinacparks.com. If you plan on spending time in the area and seeing the sights, a combination ticket (for Fort Mackinac and the mainland's Colonial Michilimackinac and Historic Mill Creek) is a good buy. Parks are open daily from 9:30 a.m. to 6 p.m. from June 15 to Aug 25, with reduced hours in spring and fall except for Labor Day, Memorial Day weekend, and some dates in early June. $$–$$$; children ages 5 and under enter free.**

Peer inside the quarters at Fort Mackinac State Park, which dates from 1780, when the British moved here from the mainland. They lost the fort after the Revolutionary War, regained it after invading the island during the War of 1812, and lost it for good afterwards.

In summer the fort is "patrolled" by actors who portray uniformed soldiers. They demonstrate cannon firing and musket practice and tell what life was like on station in the wilderness of the 1790s.

## Grand Hotel  (all ages)

**(906) 847-3331 or (800) 334-7263. www.grandhotel.com. $$$$.**

Gleaming white on a hill looking toward the Lower Peninsula, the Grand is nearly the only structure one can easily identify from the mainland. Elegant it is, and summery, with its predominant colors of green, white, and yellow. There are 385 air-conditioned, high-

# Attack of the **10,000 Fudgies**

The myriad fudge shops downtown and in many of the hotels are the attraction that helped coin the word *fudgie,* used to describe most of the visitors who take home a pound or two, and the shops are just about everywhere downtown. One reason they're so popular? As employees cool and form the confection on marble tables strategically located in the front windows, shops also blow the sugar-sweet-laced exhaust air directly onto the streets, tempting your neurons to come inside for a sample. No fools, they. Warning: There's no known antidote.

You'll find everything from peanut butter to pistachio, and chocolate walnut, too. My favorite brand? JoAnne's. Make the rounds and choose which you like best. **Free** samples are usually waiting inside.

# **Bicycle Rentals** on Mackinac Island

The number of bikes for rent on the island are legion, and they need to be. Biking tours of the island are fun, leisurely ways to enjoy the sights.

Just make sure that when you get back on, it's the one you've rented, as many look alike. There are rental booths downtown. $

ceilinged rooms and an outdoor pool. The 660-foot-long porch has plenty of wicker chairs and rockers to pass the day on. The film *Somewhere in Time* was shot here, and a few years ago, the hotel became so popular for drop-ins that it began charging nonguests just to come in, but the fee can be charged off to lunch, which is open to all comers.

Dinner and breakfast are for guests only, and there's a coat-and-tie dress code after 6 p.m.

Package stays are the best, most inexpensive ways to enjoy the Grand Hotel, usually including two meals and two nights. Just ask your travel agent. Booking not using a package can be expensive. Rooms feature simple elegance, and some are themed, including a few that honor Hollywood greats who've made films here, complete with framed autographs. Early season, usually the weeks after opening in early May, and late season in Oct offer the best prices, which often feature theme weekends, from decorating to murder mysteries.

Young guests age 5 and older can join children's group programs while the adults enjoy lunch and dinner. They can take hayrides, play games, visit island attractions, and enjoy special kids' meals. Sign up your children when you arrive. Babysitters are available for the even younger set. Cribs are available. There is no tipping.

One of the best parts about a stay here is being awakened in the morning by the clip-clop of horse hoofbeats on the pavement outside. Theme weekends include the *Somewhere in Time* Festival, when fans of the movie flock to the island.

## **Haunted Theater**  (ages 6 and up)

**Located along Main Street downtown; (906) 847-6545. Open May through Oct. Not recommended for very small children. $.**

You'll see dead people as well as scary scenes as animated monsters and ghouls pop out of caskets and doors. Scenes also depict eerie monsters that are island legends.

## **Original Mackinac Island Butterfly House**  (all ages)

**1308 McGulpin St., east of downtown; (906) 847-3972; www.originalbutterflyhouse.com. Open 10 a.m. to 7 p.m. Memorial Day to Labor Day, and 10 a.m. to 6 p.m. before and after those holidays until close. $.**

Visit the third-oldest butterfly exhibit in the United States, with more than 800 of these brightly colored insects flitting about and landing on young shoulders, toes, and fingers—if the kids can stand still long enough. The cost is cheap, and the fun for the kids is well worth it.

## Where to Eat

Tourists do not live by fudge alone. There are plenty of places to grab a burger or other meal on the island. Most are downtown.

**Mustang Lounge.** 8 Astor St., off Main; (906) 847-9916. The hangout for locals, it serves lunches and dinners that include burgers, hot dogs, and chicken. $$

**Pink Pony.** 1 Main St., in the Chippewa Hotel, downtown; (906) 847-3343. Burgers and other items available. Children's menu. $$

## Where to Stay

Besides Grand Hotel, which is *the* place to stay, accommodations range from hotels to cozy bed-and-breakfasts, and most offer package stays that greatly trim the per-night charge. Inquire at each about them.

**Island House.** 1 Lakeshore Dr., about 3 blocks east of the ferry dock; (906) 847-3347 or (800) 626-6304; www.theislandhouse .com. Here you'll find ninety-four rooms in an 1850s-era hotel with pool and dining. Children's programs in summer. $$$

**Lakeview Hotel.** 1 Huron St., downtown; (906) 847-3384; www.lake-view-hotel.com. This restored 1862 hotel offers eighty-five rooms, pools, and restaurant. $$$

## For More Information

**Mackinac Island Tourism Bureau.** P.O. Box 451, Mackinac Island 49757; (800) 454-5227; www.mackinacisland.org. More information is available at www.mackinac.com.

# St. Ignace

St. Ignace was founded by Father Jacques Marquette in the 1600s (Father Marquette National Memorial, http://www.nps.gov/fama/, overlooks the Straits). Besides being the other town to catch the ferry to Mackinac Island, St. Ignace hosts lots of special events. The Straits Area Antique Auto Show literally takes over town during the last full weekend of June each year. Avoid the hassle of finding a parking spot by heading for the **free** parking lot just west of the bridge and taking a shuttle ($). For further details, call ((906) 643-8087, or visit the Web site at www.nostalgia-prod.com. There are at least two other waterfront car shows each summer. Another waterfront car show is in mid-Sept. In winter come to enjoy the quiet and nearby cross-country ski and snowmobile trails.

## Castle Rock  (all ages)

**Off I-75 at exit 348 north of downtown; (906) 643-8268; www.stignace.com/attractions/ castlerock/. Open 9 a.m. to 9 p.m. from May 1 to Oct 15. $.**

This is one of two tourist attractions that were here before the Mackinac Bridge was built. This ancient lookout used by Native Americans is one of the most inexpensive attractions you'll visit here. It features a nearly 200-foot-tall limestone formation that you can climb via a set of stairs, plus a souvenir shop, a campground, and a statue of Paul Bunyan and his blue ox, Babe, for photo-ops with the kids.

## Mystery Spot  (all ages)

**Along US 2, 5 miles west of the bridge; (906) 643-8322; www.mysteryspot.org. Open 8 a.m. to 9 p.m. daily from early May through Labor Day and from 9 a.m. to 7 p.m. daily after Labor Day until late Oct. $, children ages 4 and younger get in free.**

The spot is one of the region's first tourist draws, and it still brings in the curious (some would say gullible). Inside, see where the laws of physics are supposedly turned upside down by clever use of gravity and optical illusions.

## Weird Michigan Wax Museum  (all ages)

**At Martin Lake Road and US 2, 6 miles west of the bridge; (906) 643-8760 or (800) 331-3530; www.weirdwax.com. $$, children ages 5 and under get in free.**

As the name implies, you'll find lots of weird characters in wax here, from the Michigan "dog man" to some state history thrown in with the fictional.

## Fort De Baude Indian Museum  (all ages)

**334 North State St., downtown; (906) 643-6622. Open 9 a.m. to 9 p.m. May 30 to Oct 1. $.**

The museum concentrates on the early French, English, and American inhabitants and the Native Americans of the area. A block or two north, also visit the Museum of Ojibwa Culture (906-643-6076) for more on Native American culture. Admission to the second is by donation.

## Deer Ranch  (all ages)

**Located 4 miles west of St. Ignace and the bridge along US 2; (906) 643-7760; www.deer ranch.com. Open daily 10 a.m. to 4 p.m. May through Nov. $, kids under 4 free.**

Kids can feed live whitetail deer and see them with fawns in a natural setting. There's also a gift shop.

## Totem Village  (all ages)

**About 2½ miles west of the Mackinac Bridge along US 2; (906) 643-8888. Generally open daily 9 a.m. to 10 p.m. (hours vary by season) May 1 to Oct 31. $, ages 5 and under free.**

This shop, which has been hosting visitors since about 1950, has an Indian lore museum, with folk art, and a small petting zoo. The gift shop features handcrafted items by local Native Americans and other artisans.

# Where to Eat

**Clyde's Drive-In.** Along west US 2, west of downtown; (906) 643-8303. Known for its three-quarter-pound burgers. $

**The Galley.** 241 North State St., downtown; (906) 643-7960. Features Great Lakes perch, whitefish, and a special Upper Peninsula delicacy, tasty sautéed whitefish livers, as well as chicken and burgers. $$

**State Street Bar & Grill.** 250 South State St., downtown; (906) 643-9511. Menu features pizza, burgers, and whitefish. $$

# US 2 Scenic Drive

Starting at the intersection with I-75, this two-lane highway has been called one of the nation's most beautiful regardless of the season, but especially in summer and fall. Follow it along bluffs for scenic overviews of the Lake Michigan shore and freighters a few miles off the coast. The highway then opens into miles of sandy beachfront where you can pull the car off the road and take a swim. US 2 is a scenic wonder for its entire length.

## Where to Stay

This is motel central, if there ever was one. More than forty of them are spread along I-75, US 2, and downtown Business I-75, or State Street. There also are bed-and-breakfasts and nearby cottage resorts. During the height of the tourist season, plan on paying top dollar in town for a room with amenities such as a pool or beach. Prices start dropping as you travel west along US 2.

**Aurora Borealis Motor Inn.** 635 West US 2; (906) 643-7488. This motel has fifty-six rooms. Discounts for persons fifty and older. **Free** shuttle to and from Mackinac Island ferry dock. $

**Castle Rock Mackinac Trail Campark.** Four miles north of St. Ignace off I-75 at exit 348; (906) 643-9222 or (800) 333-8754. Here you'll find eighty campsites on Lake Huron beach with playground and laundromat. $

**Holiday Inn Express.** 965 North State St.; (906) 643-0200. This economical chain property offers eighty-five rooms and indoor pool. $$

**Kewadin Shores.** 3015 Mackinaw Trail; (906) 643-8411. Take the downtown St. Ignace exit and follow Mackinaw Trail. The motel has eighty-one rooms and indoor pool. Restaurant nearby. $$

**K-Royale Motor Inn.** 1037 North State St. (Business I-75); (906) 643-7737 or (800) 882-7122. The inn has ninety-five rooms on Lake Huron beachfront, with **free** continental breakfast, playground, and picnic area. Restaurants nearby. $

**Lake Michigan Forest Campground.** On the lake, 16 miles west of town on US 2; (906) 643-7900. The campground has thirty-six rustic sites operated by the National Forest Service; on the beach. $

## For More Information

**St. Ignace Chamber of Commerce.** 560 North State St., St. Ignace 49781; (800) 970-8717; www.saintignace.org.

**St. Ignace Visitors Bureau.** 6 Spring St., St. Ignace 49781; (800) 338-6660; www.st ignace.com.

# Naubinway

Naubinway is located along US 2, about 40 miles west of St. Ignace. Settled in 1879, the town's name, in local Native American language, means "place of echoes." No, I haven't

## Pass de Pasties

No visit to the UP is complete without a taste of that peninsular delicacy, the pasty. The original UP fast food, pasties are handheld meat pies filled with meat, rutabaga, carrots, potatoes, onions, and spices. Miners used to take pasties with them into the pits because they were easily eaten and stayed warm. You'll see pasty signs all over the UP, including the outskirts of Marquette and surrounding cities. Have fun holding your own taste contest to see which purveyor is best. If you get hooked, many will ship frozen pasties to your home.

heard any. Its past was in lumbering, and present business focuses on tourism. A beach at the rest stop on US 2 is the northernmost point of Lake Michigan.

### Garlyn Farm and Zoological Park  (all ages)

Six miles east of Naubinway on US 2; (906) 477-1085; www.garlynzoo.com. Open from 11 a.m. to 7 p.m. from Apr through Dec 24. $, children ages 3 and under free.

The peninsula's largest collection of live animals in a parklike setting. More than two dozen species—including reindeer, wolves, sitka deer, llamas, ostrich, pheasants, and more—can be seen and fed. There's also a gift shop with wildlife-related items.

### Top of the Lake Snowmobile Museum  (all ages)

W11595 Center St., 2 blocks south of US 2; (906) 477-6298; www.exploringthenorth.com/naubinway/museum.html. Open noon to 6 p.m. Thurs through Mon. $ adults, $$ per family.

This museum displays more than seventy antique snowmobiles and gear dating back from when the sport was new, including the first production snow machine.

# Sault Sainte Marie

Commonly called "the Soo," this city was founded by Father Jacques Marquette. Michigan's oldest city, it is now one of the state's most popular destinations for its natural and historical attractions. The waterway through town that looks like a river is actually a canal. It feeds the world's longest power plant and doubles as a fisheries research station for Lake Superior State University in town. The main tourist attractions are located along Portage Street.

### Soo Locks Information Center
### and Locks Park Historic Walkway  (all ages)

Downtown along Portage Street; (906) 253-9101; www.soolocksvisitorscenter.com. The center is open daily 7 a.m. to 11 p.m., and the park is open daily 6 a.m. to midnight mid-

May to mid-Oct. The park is open year-around. Shipping season runs from late Mar to mid-Jan. Stroller access everywhere except the second-story observation platform. **Free.**

See the locks up close from the riverside. Step up alongside the concrete ditches and watch as ships inch their way inside and then are either raised or lowered without pumps to the level of Lake Superior or Huron. The visitor center explains how it's done.

### Soo Locks Boat Tours (all ages)

515 and 1157 East Portage Ave.; (906) 632-6301 or (800) 432-6301; www.soolocks.com. Ships depart daily from mid-May through Oct starting at 9 a.m. Call ahead for times of the last trip. $$–$$$, **free** for children ages 4 and younger.

For a real family treat, take a tour to see the giant Soo Locks up close and personal.

Two-hour trips leave from two locations along the swift St. Marys River and travel up to and through the locks.

Captains narrate as you travel, explaining the history of how the raging St. Marys Rapids, dropping Lake Superior waters 22 feet into Lake Huron, forced ships to portage around the rapids on rails, and how the locks evolved from a wooden structure in 1855 to the longest in the world, handling 1,000-foot-long Great Lakes freighters. You'll drift by giant Canadian steel mills and past the Canadian shoreline before returning. Dinner cruises also are available at extra cost.

### SS *Valley Camp* Museum (all ages)

501 East Water St.; (906) 632-3658 or (800) 744-7867; www.thevalleycamp.com. Open mid-May through mid-Oct. Admission: adults $$, ages 6 to 16 $, kids 5 and under **free.**

See what life was and is like on board a lake freighter. This ship steamed literally millions of miles hauling iron ore. You can tour the ship from stem to stern and visit two major artifacts from the sinking of the *Edmund Fitzgerald,* that ship's two battered lifeboats. A souvenir shop is in the ship's main hold.

## Away for the **Weekend**

Make your eastern UP headquarters for vacationing in either St. Ignace or the Soo. There are plenty of accommodation choices, and attractions, from Mackinac Island and the Soo Locks, along with neighboring Canada, are close by. Tahquamenon Falls and Whitefish Point also are short drives away, as is Seney and the trout of the Fox River, where Ernest Hemingway fished and wrote about it in the Nick Adams stories. He tried to hide his fishing spot, however, or just liked the name when he called his story's river the Big Two-Hearted, after the stream to the north. For accommodations families can't beat cottages for economical stays, as long as you check them out first.

**Twilight Walking Tours** (all ages)
Tours leave from downtown Soo; (906) 495-7122; www.twilightwalkingtours.com. Tours take place most weekends from Memorial Day weekend through Sept. Tour cost is by donation.

Starting from the Soo Locks, join Jim Couling on walks down Water Street past historic buildings, as he spins yarns interwoven with fact and lore. There's even a ghost walk.

## Where to Eat

**Abner's.** 2865 Business I-75, off exit 392; (906) 632-4221. Turn toward town. Look for the restaurant on the right. Good selection of American-style food in a rustic setting, including ample dinner buffets and a breakfast buffet in summer. $$

**Antlers.** 804 East Portage St., east of Business I-75; (906) 253-1728. In a nondescript building is one of the most unusual eateries you'll ever encounter, right down to the snake curling up a tree built into one end of the bar. Canoes hang from the rafters, along with animal heads and other items bartered for meals by locals or found at estate sales. Pick out steaks from a cooler, or enjoy other items. It's a fun spot. $$

**Applebee's.** 4478 Business I-75, off exit 392; (906) 253-0532. Good American-style food from this chain pub and grill. $$

**Freighters.** 240 West Portage St., inside the Ramada Plaza Ojibway; (906) 632-4100. Here you'll find what is probably the best dining view of the locks, except for the tour-boat dinner cruises. Enjoy breakfast, lunch, or dinner as the ships go by outside the panoramic windows. $$$

**Studebaker's.** 3583 Business I-75, off exit 392; (906) 632-4262. On the westbound side of the road. Cute 1950s theme restaurant with lunch and dinner. Breakfast buffet on weekends. $$

## Where to Stay

**Best Western Sault Sainte Marie.** 4281 Business I-75, off exit 392; (906) 632-2170. The motel offers 111 rooms and indoor pool. Restaurant nearby. $$

**Hampton Inn.** 3295 Business I-75, just east off exit 392; (906) 635-3000. The inn has eighty-two rooms and indoor pool. Restaurants nearby. $$

**Ramada Plaza Ojibway.** 240 West Portage St.; (906) 632-4100; www.waterviewhotels .com. Take Business I-75 into town to Portage Street and turn west. This restored 1928 hotel is on the north side of the street. It has seventy-one modern rooms, indoor pool, exercise room, and a great view of ships passing through the Soo Locks right outside its restaurant windows (see Freighters in Where to Eat). $$$

## For More Information

**Sault Sainte Marie Convention and Visitors Bureau.** 2581 I-75 Business Spur, Sault Sainte Marie 49783; (906) 632-3366 or (800) 647-2858; www.saultstemarie.com.

# Newberry and Soo Junction

These two towns are located along Highway 28 west of Sault Sainte Marie. Soo Junction was settled in the 1890s and named for its location at the junction of two rail lines. Newberry, a logging town, was named for a Detroit industrialist. Logging still plays a role here, but much of the focus of both towns is now on bringing tourists to see the two Tahquamenon Falls. Even though Newberry and Soo Junction are a few miles away from the cataracts, they call themselves the home of the falls.

### Toonerville Trolley and Riverboat Ride to Tahquamenon Falls

(all ages)

**Rides leave from Soo Junction, just north of Highway 28 (watch for the sign); (906) 876-2311 or (888) 77-TRAIN (778-7246); www.trainandboattours.com. Adults $$$$; children ages 4 to 8 $$$, 9 to 15 $$$$, under 3 free. Train ride only children ages 4 to 8 $, 9 to 15 $$, and adults $$$.**

See the falls that inspired Longfellow's epic poem "Hiawatha," either by car or on all-day adventures that combine trains and riverboat rides, which have been running more than seventy years.

Near this map-dot town is an excursion lovingly nicknamed "the trolley." The six-and-a-half-hour trip combines a 5½-mile, thirty-five-minute railroad trip on board the narrow-gauge train hauling up to 250 persons, followed by a 21-mile river cruise accompanied by narration and lots of wildlife from beaver to deer. After the boat docks it's a short hike to the upper falls, where 50,000 gallons of tea-colored water spews over the lip each second. At 100 feet high, it's Michigan's largest falls and the second largest east of the Mississippi. It's one of nearly 150 waterfalls in the Upper Peninsula. If you're in a hurry, the trolley also offers a less-expensive train ride only, a one-and-three-quarter-hour trip.

### Tahquamenon Falls State Park   (all ages)

**On Highway 123, Paradise; (906) 492-3415 for information or (800) 447-2757 for reservations; www.michigan.gov/dnr. Then go to ""Recreation, Camping & Boating." From the Soo Junction area, head east on Highway 28, then north on Highway 123 about 22 miles to Paradise. The state park is 5 miles west of Paradise. Open daily, year-round. Camping is $ nightly. Daily permit $, annual $$$.**

You can drive to see both the upper and the cataract-like lower falls at this park, where camping is available at 180 sites near the falls and another 130 sites in its river mouth unit along Lake Superior. This park offers picnicking and hiking trails. Parking is available a short walk from both falls. The park also features great short hiking trails that become cross-country ski loops in winter.

### Oswald's Bear Ranch   (all ages)

**13814 CR 407, north of Newberry; (906) 293-3147; www.oswaldsbearranch.com. Open 10 a.m. to 6 p.m. from the Fri of Memorial Day weekend to Sept 30. $$ per car.**

If you don't see any of the UP's thousands of wild bears elsewhere on your visit, you're guaranteed to see them here. Almost thirty bears, including cubs and big bruins, roam the grounds in three natural habitats.

## Where to Eat

**Tahquamenon Falls Brewery and Pub.** Highway 123, Paradise, on private property within the boundaries of the state park; (906) 492-3300. Lunch and dinner, along with house-brewed beer and also root beer, are served in this log lodge near the river. $$

**Timber Charlie's Food 'n Spirits.** 110 Newberry, Newberry, on the west side of Highway 123; (906) 293-3363. Local eatery serving lunch and dinner in a rustic setting. $$

## Where to Stay

**America's Best Value Inn Tahqua- menon Country.** 12956 Highway 28, Newberry; (906) 293-4000. An economical chain motel offering sixty-six rooms and indoor pool. **Free** continental breakfast. $$

**Comfort Inn Newberry.** At the intersection of Highways 28 and 123, Newberry; (906) 293-3218. This basic motel has fifty-four rooms and a twenty-person hot tub with sauna. Restaurant nearby. $$

# Paradise

Some may not think of it as paradise in Feb, but after all, it was named for its site along Lake Superior, which is inviting to summer vacationers and winter snowmobilers.

Activities also include cross-country skiing, dogsled rides, and even a bear park.

## Great Lakes Shipwreck Museum (all ages)

**110 Whitefish Point, just north of town; (906) 635-1742 or (888) 397-3747; www.shipwreck museum.com. Open from 10 a.m. to 6 p.m. daily from May 15 through Oct 15. $–$$.**

A lighthouse at Whitefish Point, 20 miles north of Tahquamenon Falls, is now the museum, a haunting tribute to the more than 5,000 ships that ventured onto what explorers called the Great Northern Seas, never to make port.

Accompanied by the eerie words of Canadian singer-songwriter Gordon Lightfoot's ballad "The Wreck of the *Edmund Fitzgerald*," you'll see exhibits on many of the ships claimed by the lake's storms and other mishaps. From the wreck of the sailing schooner *Invincible* in 1816, to the great storm of 1913, to the loss of the *Fitzgerald* with twenty-nine hands on board only a few miles west in the 1970s, your family will get a feel of what fury the lakes can hold and how even saltwater sailors fear them in bad weather. The working lighthouse is the oldest on Lake Superior, guiding ships around the point since 1849. The present structure has been there since 1861.

## Where to Eat

See Tahquamenon Falls Brewery and Pub (Newberry and Soo Junction listings).

## Where to Stay

**Best Western Lakefront Inn & Suites.**
8112 North Highway 123; (906) 492-3770. The
inn has forty-one rooms with indoor pool and
**free** continental breakfast. $$

## For More Information

**Paradise Michigan Chamber of Commerce.** P.O. Box 82, Paradise 49768; (906)
492-3219; www.paradisemichigan.org.

# Seney

In the 1800s this tiny map-dot of a town was one of the most notorious lumber camps in
the nation. Later, it figured in the Nick Adams short stories of novelist Ernest Hemingway,
who vacationed and explored this area. It's also the eastern end of the "Seney stretch,"
a 20-plus-mile length of Highway 28 that's straight as an arrow and features no services
between Seney and Shingleton, to the west.

### Seney Historical Museum (all ages)
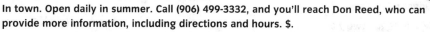

**In town. Open daily in summer. Call (906) 499-3332, and you'll reach Don Reed, who can
provide more information, including directions and hours. $.**

The small museum explores Seney's colorful and often raucous past, when local charac-
ters reportedly bit the heads off snakes for fun, turned city folk just off the train upside
down to shake out loose change, or, it was rumored, shanghaied the unsuspecting to
work in lumber camps in the surrounding forests. There's also an exhibit on author Ernest
Hemingway, who came here and wrote "The Big Two-Hearted River" after his visit.

### Seney National Wildlife Refuge (all ages)

**Just south of town along Highway 77; (906) 586-9851; http://midwest.fws.gov/seney/. The
refuge is open during daylight hours only. The visitor center is open daily from 9 a.m. to 5
p.m. mid-May through mid-Oct. Free.**

This refuge contains nearly 96,000 acres of wetlands and woods. From a visitor center off
Highway 77, take a scenic drive through part of the refuge and get a chance to spot bald
eagles, deer, Canada geese, and other wildlife. Adventurous types can canoe through the
refuge by renting craft from Northland Outfitters in Germfask (906-586-9801), just south of
the refuge.

## Where to Eat

**Seney Trailz.** Downtown along Highway
28; (906) 499-3100. Fresh-made pasties
(meat pies) and other dishes from breakfast
onward. $

**Weber's Rustic Inn.** 24896 County High-
way 98 (Ten Curves Road), south of Seney

and 10 miles east of Germfask; (906) 586-
6635 or (877) 586-6635; www.chefbarbies
.com. Fine dining with a rustic twist. Half
orders available. Try the grilled walleye in
Cajun, lemon pepper, or Asian style, beef
stroganoff, or white chicken chili. Children's
menu. $$–$$$

## Where to Stay

**Fox River Motel.** On the corner of Highway 28 at Highway 77; (906) 499-3332 or (906) 499-3337; www.foxrivermotel.com. This local motel offers thirteen rooms. Restaurant nearby. $

# Munising and Grand Marais

Munising is along Highway 28. Grand Marais also lies along the Superior shore and is reached via Highway 77 from Seney. It's considered the eastern gate to the Pictured Rocks, since CR H-58 begins here, and Munising is the western entrance.

### Pictured Rocks Cruises (all ages)

**Departure times vary by month, so call ahead at (906) 387-2379; www.picturedrocks .com; or write P.O. Box 355, Munising 49862. Boats run daily from the Munising city dock Memorial Day weekend through Oct 10. Adults $$$$; children ages 6 to 12 $$, ages 5 and younger ride free.**

In Munising are two waterborne attractions you shouldn't miss. This is one of them.See the lakeshore formations up close on board the tour boats, leaving daily from Munising's downtown harbor, weather permitting. The 37-mile trips last nearly three hours and take you almost within touching distance of the rocks.

## Pictured Rocks National Lakeshore (all ages)

Shaped by wind and water over eons, the spectacular cliffs can be seen on both land and water. Administered by the National Park Service, the lakeshore encompasses 70,000 acres of wilderness along 42 miles of Lake Superior. Glacier-carved rocks and waves and wind have created rock formations that resemble battleship prows and castles, in multicolored hues from minerals seeping from the soil and rock. CR H-58 through the lakeshore from Grand Marais to Munising is open from May until the first large snowfall. It's about 25 paved miles and 30 miles of gravel, so inquire about its condition, especially at the eastern end.

Drivers can stop at platforms at spots like Grand Sable Dunes and the Miners Castle to look down onto the lake 200 feet below. Three rustic campgrounds plus backpack camps for backcountry hikers are available here. A visitor center is in Munising at Highway 28 and CR H-58. For information, call (906) 387-3700; www.nps.gov/piro.

# It's Always **Christmas** Here

In the town just over the hill, west from Munising on Highway 28, it's Christmas every day. The town got the name "Christmas" from an old toy factory that no longer exists. Stop to have your picture taken in front of the giant Santa.

### Grand Island Shipwreck Tours (all ages)

1204 Commercial St., Munising; (906) 387-4477; www.shipwrecktours.com. Watch for the signs along Hwy. 8, west of downtown. Tours leave at 10 a.m., 1 p.m., and 4 p.m. in July and Aug, 10 a.m. and 1 p.m. in June and Sept. Adults $$$$; children ages 6 to 12 $$, ages 5 and under sail **free.**

A few blocks west of the Pictured Rocks Cruises departure point is the other don't-miss attraction, the Grand Island Shipwreck Tours. Step on board Michigan's only glass-bottomed boat for a view of three of the 5,000 shipwrecks at the bottom of the Great Lakes. The 42-foot boat also takes up to one hundred passengers on two-and-a-half-hour narrated tours while sailing past Grand Island National Recreation Area. Wrecks you'll see include an intact 1860s-era, 160-foot-long cargo schooner.

### Munising Falls (all ages)

On Sand Point Road, Munising, about 3 miles east of town. Open anytime. Access is via a paved path. **Free.**

One of six waterfalls within the city limits, the Munising Falls' water here drops over the lip of a huge natural amphitheater.

## Where to Eat

**Dogpatch.** 820 East Superior, downtown Munising, a block east of Highway 28; (906) 387-9948. Good family dining for breakfast, lunch, and dinner in a rustic setting. Serves items from pancakes to steak. $$$

## Where to Stay

**America's Best Value Inn Cherrywood Lodge.** On Highway 28, Wetmore, east of downtown Munising about 3 miles; (906) 387-4864. This chain motel has eighty rooms, an indoor pool, and a restaurant that serves breakfast through dinner. $$$

**Camel Riders Restaurant and Resort.** On Forest Highway (FH) 13, Wetmore, south of Munising; (906) 573-2319; www.schoolcraftcountychamber.com/camelriders. Take Highway 94 south to FH 13, head south to CR 440, and then turn east. Located on this area's version of the chain of lakes. Cabins with boats provided for stays by the week or, if available, overnight. Towels aren't provided, so bring your own. The adjacent restaurant is open for breakfast, lunch, and dinner in winter, and dinner only in summer. $$

**Terrace Motel.** 420 Prospect, Munising, east of Highway 28; (906) 387-2735; www.terracemotel.net. The motel has eighteen rooms, sauna, and wireless Internet. Restaurant nearby. Pets OK. $

## For More Information

**Alger County Chamber of Commerce.** 422 East Munising Ave., Munising 49862;

(906) 387-2138; www.algercounty.org or go to www.exploremunising.com.

# Manistique

US 2 now bypasses downtown Manistique to go closer to the Lake Michigan shoreline. There's a great, nearly 2-mile-long boardwalk that connects to other pathways along the beach. Be sure to drive into town on Business US 2, too. The town's 150th anniversary is 2010.

### Palms Book State Park, Big Spring (all ages)
**Turn north from US 2 onto Highway 149 and follow it and the signs about 10 miles; (906) 341-2355; www.stateparks.com/palms_book.html. Daily permit $, annual $$$.**

It was called Kitch-iti-kipi, or "Mirror of Heaven," by Native Americans, and it's easy to see why when you stare into this pool of crystal-clear spring water. Board the rope-tethered raft with a center viewing area and let the kids pull your family across the 200-foot-wide spring. About halfway across, look down. Some 60 feet below you, huge trout are being tickled by the 16,000 gallons of water that flow out of the boiling bottom each minute, at a constant temperature of forty-five degrees. It empties into a river that feeds nearby Indian Lake. Sorry, no fishing's allowed, and there's no camping here. However, there are hiking trails and a gift shop.

## Where to Eat

**Cedar Street Café & Coffee House.** 220 South Cedar St.; (906) 341-2469; www.cedarstreetcafe.com. Good selection of signature sandwiches and European specials on Fri. $–$$$

**Clyde's Drive-In.** 201 Chippewa Ave.; (906) 341-6021. Great burgers. $

**Floyd's.** 2835 South Cedar; (906) 341-0245. Good selection of well-priced items. $$

**Sunny Shores Restaurant.** Along US 2, Manistique; (906) 342-5582. Open from mid-Apr through midwinter, this restaurant offers inexpensive meals for breakfast, lunch, and dinner. $

## Where to Stay

**Beachcomber Motel.** 751 East Lakeshore Dr.; (906) 341-2567. Twenty rooms with Internet access. Restaurants nearby. $

**Cottages and Resorts.** There are quite a few to choose from, especially along Indian Lake's shoreline. Compare before you reserve so you won't be disappointed. Don't expect ritzy accommodations at many, but there are also quite a few comfortable, inexpensive

# Favorite Events in Upper Peninsula–East

- **Valley Spur Ski Bash** (Jan), Munising, (906) 387-4918, or www.valleyspur.org
- **Michigan Icefest** (Feb), Munising, www.downwindsports.com/ice_fest.html
- **I-500 Snowmobile Race** (Feb), Sault Sainte Marie, (800) 647-2858
- **Tahquamenon Falls Nordic Invitational Ski Race** (Mar), Newberry, (906) 293-5562
- **Spring Show** (Apr), Sault Sainte Marie, (906) 632-3301
- **Memorial Day Celebration** (May), Mackinac Island, (906) 847-3783
- **Straits Antique and Classic Auto Shows** (June), St. Ignace, (800) 970-8717
- **Folk Fest** (July), Manistique, (906) 341-5010
- **Antique Wooden Boat Show** (Aug), Hessel, (906) 484-3935 or (888) 364-7526
- **Mackinac Bridge Walk, Tractor Parade and Show, and Semi-Truck Show** (early and mid-Sept), St. Ignace, (906) 643-7600
- **Autumn Apple Days** (Oct), St. Ignace, (800) 970-8717
- **Christmas Parade of Lights** (Nov), Sault Sainte Marie, (906) 632-3301
- **Red Cross Tour of Homes** (Dec), Sault Sainte Marie, (906) 632-8111

places. A list is available from the local tourism council (see For More Information).

**Econolodge.** Along US 2, Manistique, 1½ miles east of town; (906) 341-6014. This property has thirty-one rooms. Restaurant nearby. Small pets OK at extra charge. $$

**Gray Wolf Lodge.** Two miles east of town on US 2; (906)341-2410. Forty rooms with indoor pool and beach access. Restaurant nearby. $$

## For More Information

**Manistique Tourism Council.** 1000 West Lakeshore Dr. (US 2), Manistique 49854; (800) 342-4282; www.visitmanistique.com.

**Schoolcraft County Chamber of Commerce.** (888) 819-7420; www.schoolcraft countychamber.com.

# Upper Peninsula— West

Y ou want wilderness? It's got wilderness. You want big cities? It's got the biggest in the region. The western Upper Peninsula is a mix of the historic and the present day, from ghost towns where copper and iron ore once ruled to modern cities where iron ore still plays a big part in the economy. Tourism is also important here, especially in winter and summer. This region is what many people think of when they talk about the Upper Peninsula, or the UP for short. For general UP information, call the Upper Peninsula Tourism and Recreation Association in downtown Iron Mountain at (906) 774-5480 or (800) 562-7134; www.uptravel.com.

## Marquette

Marquette was fortunate enough to prosper from the right combination of time and the growth of America. When surveyors Douglass Houghton and, later, William Burt reported crazy readings coming from iron-ore outcroppings on the surface in Negaunee, the rush was on. Combined with the copper country in the far western UP, it caused a land rush that rivaled California's gold rush in the mid-1840s.

They still mine iron ore here, but emphasis also is on the rich vein of tourism that the area attracts. You'll be surprised at the town's beauty. Downtown and only a few miles outside, moose, bear, and mountain lion roam.

### Presque Isle Park (all ages)
**At the north end of the city in the area called the Upper Harbor, at the end of Lakeshore Boulevard; (906) 228-0460, ext. 3. Open daily from 7 a.m. to 11 p.m. Admission is free.**

Presque Isle Park is a jewel, designed by Frederick Law Olmsted, the same landscape architect who created New York's Central Park and Detroit's Belle Isle. A small road leads around the 328-acre facility perched on a rock outcropping jutting into Lake Superior. At the entrance you might see a Great Lakes ore freighter tied up to Marquette's huge ore

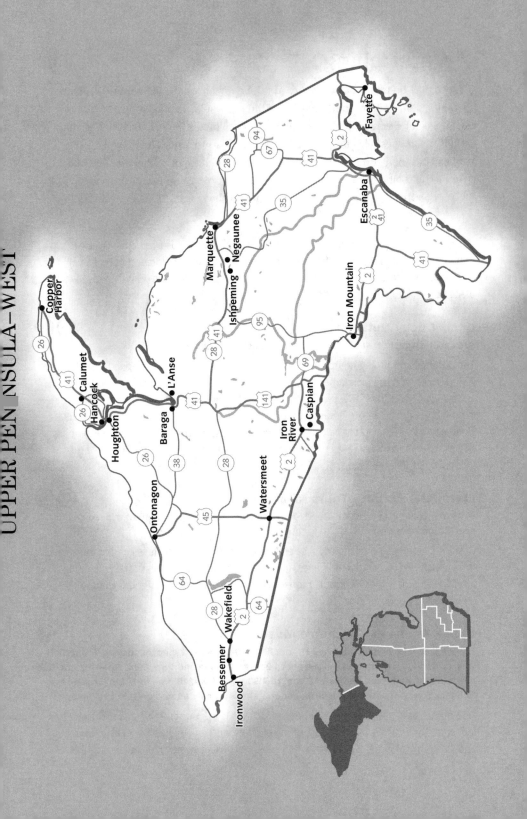

UPPER PENINSULA–WEST

# "Waterfalling"

There may be more, but there are at least a dozen waterfalls within Marquette County, some of the hundreds across the peninsula. Typical is Warner Falls, which can be viewed from the highway as it plunges 20 feet. To reach it, take Highway 28 west about 5 miles, and then turn south onto Highway 35. Drive 9 miles, and then continue about ½ mile beyond the town of Palmer. The falls are on the right side of the road. Find more listed on a **free** map from the local visitors bureau (see For More Information at the end of the Marquette section).

dock, where high-grade iron-ore pellets thunder into ship holds from bins. Overlooks in the park are countless. Picnic facilities and an outdoor pool are located here as well. The pool and a waterslide are open daily from noon to 8 p.m. They are **free.** Art shows take place here in late July, and, yes, in Feb.

## Uncle Ducky Outfitters  (all ages)
**434 East Prospect St.; (877) 228-5447; www.uncleducky.com.**

The outfitter and fishing charter service with the unlikely name was begun by Bill Duck-wall, who earned the nickname "Uncle Ducky" from his name, will tackle everything you ask for in a UP outdoor adventure, from stream fishing for trout to fishing for lake trout in one of the most remote areas of Lake Superior. Not into fishing? He'll also take you on sightseeing cruises and canoe or kayak trips into remote lakes and rivers where loons, eagles, bear, and moose are common sights. In winter he'll make sure you have fun on a guided ice fishing trip, too.

## Marquette Country Tours  (all ages)
**809 West College Ave.; (906) 226-6167. Prices vary depending on type of trip, so call for specific information.**

Besides canoeing and hiking trips, operators also take visitors on less-rugged four-wheel-drive trips to waterfalls, to old mines, and on historic tours, as well as on sightseeing treks after the elusive Upper Peninsula moose. Trips may be custom designed according to your family's needs and desires.

## Upper Peninsula Children's Museum  (ages 3 to 11)
**123 West Baraga Ave.; (906) 226-3911 or (888) 590-UPCM; www.upcmkids.org. From Highway 28/US 41, go north on Front Street to Baraga Avenue and turn west. Open 10 a.m. to 6 p.m. Mon through Wed and Sat, 10 a.m. to 7:30 p.m. Thurs, 10 a.m. to 8 p.m. Fri, and noon to 5 p.m. Sun. Admission $, children under 3 free, family admission rate available.**

One of the city's newest family-friendly attractions is the Upper Peninsula Children's Museum, located downtown. Most of the exhibits were suggested by local youngsters and illustrate concepts such as the importance of groundwater. Kids love it.

**Marquette Mountain Ski Area** (ages 7 and up)
Just south of town on CR 553; (906) 225-1155; www.marquettemountain.com. From US 41/
Highway 28, turn west on Furnace near the Pizza Hut. Follow it to Division and go south
until it ends. Then take 553 south to the ski area. Adults $$$$; children under 6 $$. Equip-
ment rental $$$–$$$$.

One of the state's higher ski areas, this one has twenty-five runs, a snowboard half-pipe,
and two terrain parks. Instruction for adults and children also available.

## Where to Eat

**Jean Kay's Pasties & Subs.** 1639 Presque
Isle Ave.; (906) 228-5310 or (800) 727-2922;
www.jeankays.com. Leave US 41/Highway 28
and continue north on Front Street to Wash-
ington Street. Turn west to Fourth Street
and go north. It jogs to become Presque Isle.
Authentic UP pasties, an enclosed meat pie
that was a favorite of UP miners and now is
something everybody's at least got to taste.
They're made vegetarian-style, too. $

**Sweetwater Café.** 517 North Third St.;
(906) 226-7009; www.sweetwatercafe.org.
North and west of downtown, bordering the
campus of Northern Michigan University.
Innovative meals for breakfast, lunch, and
dinner in a university-style setting. $$

**Thill's Fish House.** At the end of East Main
Street, 1 block east of Front Street; (906) 226-
9851. Fresh-caught and smoked fish are a
specialty. $

**Up North Lodge.** 215 South CR 557,
Gwinn, south of Marquette and 3 miles west
of downtown Gwinn; (906) 346-9815; www
.theupnorthlodge.com. Closed Mon. Known
for its ribs, this restaurant also serves up
burgers, wraps, pasta, steaks, and whitefish.
Children's menu. $$–$$$

**Vierling Restaurant and Marquette
Harbor Brewery.** Corner of Front and Main
Streets, downtown; (906) 228-3533; www
.thevierling.com. The Vierling, established by
Martin Vierling in 1883, is a brewpub with a
family atmosphere and a children's menu to
prove it. Open for lunch and dinner. $$–$$$

## Where to Stay

**Days Inn.** 2403 East US 41; (906) 225-1393;
www.superioroasis.com. This economical
motel has sixty-five rooms, indoor pool,
sauna, and **free** continental breakfast. Res-
taurants nearby. $$

**Landmark Inn.** 230 North Front St., down-
town; (906) 228-2580 or (888) LAND–MARK;
www.thelandmarkinn.com. A classic down-
town hotel with sixty-two guest rooms, most
decorated with items that look back on Mar-
quette's history, some even tongue-in-cheek.
The Abbott and Costello Room was named,
for instance, after the appearance that the
comedy pair made here during World War II.
Another is decorated like a UP hunting cabin.
The inn has a health spa, plus a restaurant
that serves breakfast, lunch, and dinner. $$

## For More Information

**Marquette Country Convention and
Visitors Bureau.** 2552 US 41 West, Suite
30, Marquette 49855; (906) 228-7749 or (800)
544-4321; www.marquettecountry.org.

# Negaunee

This is the city that began it all for the state's iron industry, when the area's first iron mine opened here in 1846.

### Michigan Iron Industry Museum  (all ages)

**73 Forge Rd.; (906) 475-7857; www.sos.state.mi.us/history/museum/museiron/index.html. From US 41, take Highway 35 south to CR 492. Go west to Forge Road and turn north to the museum. Hours are 9:30 a.m. to 4:30 p.m. from May through Oct. Wheelchair access also is available. Admission is free.**

This unique museum chronicles the life both above and below the earth of the immigrant miners who came to the UP's Marquette Iron Range and two other mining sites.

Using a special timeline motif, exhibits tell the range's past from prehistory to the present. Mining cars and other equipment are also on display. Hands-on exhibits for the kids include a model of the Soo Locks and a working model of an ore freighter and loading dock. Visitors walk to the museum on paths through part of a typical UP forest to give them a sense of what the country was like when it was new.

## Where to Eat and Stay

See Marquette listings.

# Ishpeming

Mine headframes still tower over the city that was the center of the area's mining industry, where the ground still bleeds red after a rain from the iron it contains. Nearly all of the town lies south of US 41/Highway 28. The historic downtown area is along Division Street. Take Lakeshore Drive south from US 41/Highway 28.

### U.S. National Ski Hall of Fame and Museum  (all ages)

**610 Palms Ave. at US 41; (906) 485-6323; www.skihall.com. Open 10 a.m. to 5 p.m. Mon through Sat. Admission is by donation.**

See the greats of skiing and its history, from its birth to present-day snow heroes.

### Da Yoopers Tourist Trap  (all ages) ⬤

**490 US 41/Highway 28; (906) 485-5595; www.dayoopers.com. West of town; watch for the signs. Open 9 a.m. to 9 p.m. Mon through Fri from Memorial Day until Dec; shorter hours thereafter.**

You've got to see this store to believe it. Da Yoopers, a singing group who pokes fun at UP life, right down to "da accent," opened a shop to sell souvenirs, oddities, and other folderol, hence the unabashed name. The group's irreverent music has become so popular around the state that Da Yoopers tour each year.

Outside, someone's built a "replica" UP deer camp, and there are other items unique to the peninsula, including a giant mosquito and nowhere-else-but-the-UP contraptions like a snowmobile on motorcycle wheels to ride in summer. It's a fun place to visit, and a tape or CD of Da Yoopers to play in the car will help put you in a "Yoo P frame-a-mind, you betcha."

## Where to Eat

See Marquette listings.

## Where to Stay

**Best Western Country Inn.** 850 US 41 West, north of town; (906) 485-6345; www.countryvillageresort.com. This chain property offers sixty rooms, indoor pool, and restaurant. Or try its campground. It's all part of Country Village Resort, which also includes a restaurant, shopping, and bowling. $$

**Van Riper State Park.** Seventeen miles west of Ishpeming on Highway 41; (906) 339-4461 for information or (800) 447-2757 for reservations. There are 189 sites, with a boat launch and swimming on Lake Michigamme. Fishing has taken somewhat of a downturn on the lake, but it's in a beautiful park in the midst of moose country. A plaque erected by the Michigan Outdoor Writers Association tells visitors of the moose lift that used helicopters to transplant Canadian animals to the woods here to reintroduce the species to this part of the UP. Hiking trails go past old mine sites. Daily permit $, annual $$$. Camping costs extra.

## For More Information

**Ishpeming–Negaunee Chamber of Commerce.** 661 Palms Ave., Ishpeming 49849; (906) 486-4841; www.marquette.org.

# Escanaba

Besides its historical importance as a Great Lakes port and center for iron-ore shipment, Escanaba also is a favorite for anglers. Big and Little Bays de Noc are popular for walleye salmon, and it's one of the few areas of the state known for "coaster" brook trout, larger than their stream cousins because they live in the open lake. The county has the most freshwater shoreline of any in the nation. Lots of things in town and the area are named "Ludington," including the city's main street, after Nelson Ludington, an early lumberman.

### Rapid River Knifeworks  (all ages)

Located along US 2 in Rapid River, north of Escanaba; (906) 474-9444; www.rapidriverknifeworks.com.

Whether you're shopping for a gift or just curious about how they're made, step inside and watch as craftsmen create handmade knives of all types. You can view the whole process through windows looking into the factory.

# Fishing the "Nocs"

If you've got fish on your mind, you've come to the right spot. From spring through late fall, the Escanaba area is one of the stops you'll want to make. For trout, try the middle to upper Escanaba River. In spring Little Bay de Noc is a hot spot for smallmouth bass in the shallows right along US 2. And the bay proper holds huge numbers of walleye from summer right through autumn. Nov is an especially hot time for catching walleye from boats. And when the ice forms, the entire bay becomes a minicity as ice shanties crop up everywhere housing anglers after walleye. And don't forget salmon. Contact skippers like Dick Stafford (906-789-0110; www.takefivecharters .com), or go to the visitor bureau Web site at the end of this listing for more information.

### Upper Peninsula State Fair  (all ages)

Takes place in mid-Aug each year at the fairgrounds at the eastern outskirts of Escanaba, at 2401 Twelfth Ave.; (906) 786-4011; www.upstatefair.net. Adults $, free for children younger than 5. Grandstand shows are extra. Parking is $.

Michigan is so large that we need two state fairs to cover the bounty that summer brings. This one comes first, and then the Michigan State Fair, in Detroit, takes place the week before and including Labor Day weekend. Tilt-A-Whirl and tractor-pull fans can get their fill here with such thrills among the daily entertainment, and plenty of offbeat, family-fun attractions make this state fair an exciting event for the entire family, from pig racing to baking and homemaker-of-the-year contests. With respect for the peninsula's heritage, Native American Day is celebrated with traditional tribal dances and other activities. At the grandstand, watch for big-name country and rock stars, as well as motorcycle racing.

## Where to Eat

**Dobber's Pasties.** 827 North Lincoln (US 2/US 41), just north of the intersection with Ludington Avenue; (906) 786-1880; www .dobberspasties.com. Lots of pasty gourmets contend that these are the Upper Peninsula's best. I've had both meat and veggie varieties, and they're great. They also ship. $

**Hereford & Hops Restaurant & Brew-pub.** 624 Ludington St., inside the Delta Hotel downtown; (906) 789-1945. Four varieties of home-brewed beer, plus home-brewed root beer for the kids. Eat there or carry out. Food ranges from burgers to chicken and fish. $$

**Swedish Pantry.** 819 Ludington St.; (906) 786-9606. Sweeter-than-sweet Swedish pancakes for breakfast topped with butter and syrup or other toppings, such as jam or spiced peaches; lunch sandwiches; and Swedish dinner entrees top the menu. Buy some cardamom bread to take with you from the bakery. $$–$$$

## Where to Stay

**Fishery Pointe Beach Cottages.** E5041 Highway 35, 5 miles south of town; (906) 786-1852 or (800) 473-3410; www.fisherypointe.com. Nine cottages on Lake Michigan, beach, and sauna. Usually rents weekly. $$

**Sleepy Hollow Motel.** 7156 US 2/US 41, Gladstone; (906) 786-7092 or (800) 473-3410. Eighteen clean rooms near access to the bay. $$, $ in winter.

**Super Eight Motel.** 2415 US 2/US 41; (906) 786-1000. Ninety rooms with continental breakfast and indoor pool. $$

**Terrace Bay Inn Budget Host.** 7146 P. Road, just off US 2/US 41, Gladstone; (906) 786-7554. www.terracebay.com. Seventy-one units with restaurant, indoor and outdoor pools, lake access, and meeting center. $$

## For More Information

**Bays de Noc Convention and Visitors Bureau.** 2401 Twelfth Ave. North, Escanaba 49829; (906) 789-7862 or (800) 533-4FUN; www.travelbaysdenoc.com.

# Fayette

You don't have to travel to the West to see a real ghost town—just go to Fayette, now a state park. Located along Lake Michigan's Bay de Noc, the former iron-smelting town once was home to more than 500 employees of the Jackson Mine Company and their families from 1867 to 1891. Raw ore was brought to the town, where it was refined into blocks of iron called "pigs" in its charcoal-fired furnaces. The pig iron was later shipped down the lake to Chicago, Detroit, and Cleveland for steelmaking. Once the trees for charcoal making disappeared, and larger ships were built to carry raw ore south, the town slowly died out.

### Fayette State Historic Park  (all ages)

To reach the park, turn south off US 2 onto Highway 183 and follow the signs about 17 miles to the town of Garden; (906) 644-2603 for information or (800) 447-2757 for reservations; www.michigan.gov/dnr, then go to "Recreation, Camping & Boating." The historic site is open daily 8 a.m. to 8 p.m. from May 15 through Oct 15. Camping is extra. Daily permit $, annual $$$.

About 10 miles from Escanaba, one of the peninsula's largest cities, this historic site will take you back more than a century. Pilings that once supported the docks that Great Lakes schooners called home still dot the shoreline of the bay.

In the visitor center a scale model of the city at its heyday will orient you to what's outside. Along with reconstructed kilns and furnaces are twenty restored original buildings. There are sixty-one campsites as well, plus miles of easy hiking and cross-country ski trails at another part of the park.

## Where to Eat and Stay

See Escanaba listings.

## Favorite Events in Upper Peninsula–West

- **Michigan Tech Winter Carnival** (Jan), Houghton, (906) 487-2818
- **Winter Fun Fest** (Feb), Ishpeming, (906) 486-4841
- **Camper, RV, and Travel Show** (Mar), Superior Dome, Marquette, (906) 227-1032
- **Kiwanis Sports and Recreation Show** (Apr), Escanaba, (800) 437-7496
- **Arts and Crafts Show** (May), Marquette, (906) 226-8864
- **Annual Riverfest** (June), Ontonagon, (906) 884-4735
- **Art on the Rocks Show and Sale and Outback Art Show and Sale** (July), Marquette, (906) 225-1952
- **Keweenaw Bay Indian Community Powwow** (July), Ojibwa Campground near Baraga, (906) 353-6623
- **Upper Peninsula Rodeo** (July), Iron County Fairgrounds, Iron River, (906) 265-5605
- **UP Vintage Tin Antique Car Show** (July), Ludington Park, Escanaba, (906) 786-2192 or (800) 437-7496
- **Waterfront Art Festival** (Aug), Ludington Park, Escanaba, (906) 786-2192 or (800) 437-7496
- **Porkiefest** (Sept), Porcupine Mountains State Park, Ontonagon, (906) 885-5885
- **Leif Erickson Fall Festival** (Oct), Norway, (906) 563-7172
- **Christmas Tree Galleria** (Nov), Caspian, (800) 225-3620
- **Old Fashioned Christmas Fair** (Dec), Wakefield, (906) 224-8151

# Baraga and L'Anse

### Sturgeon River Gorge Park (all ages)

Along the west side of US 41, 17 miles south of Baraga. Open all year daylight to dusk. **Free.**

See the Sturgeon River surge through sheer rock cliffs at the river and falls. A path takes walkers on a short hike through the woods from the parking area along the river as the noise from the falls gets closer. Rapids culminate in the falls, where the river, colored like tea from the natural tannic acid it's carrying, enters the rock gorge. Keep track of young children near the river. There is no stroller access, so bring your child backpack.

### Alberta Village Museum (all ages)

**Located 8 miles south of L'Anse on US 41; (906) 524-6181; www.fordcenter.mtu.edu. Open 9:30 a.m. to 3:30 p.m. Tues through Sat mid-June through mid-Oct. $.**

This living museum, overseen by Michigan Technological University, traces the history of this Ford Motor Company facility. The site containing a sawmill was one of Henry Ford's "village industries," producing wood for the company's famed "woodie" station wagons. There's also a gift shop.

## Where to Eat

**Carla's.** On US 41, Baraga; (906) 353-6256. Six miles north of Baraga on US 41, inside Carla's Lake Shore Motel. Fresh fish and steaks for dinner. Children's menu. $$

**The Hilltop.** On US 41, L'Anse, 1 mile south of town; (906) 524-7858; www.sweetroll .com. Cinnamon buns ($) bigger than your fist await on the north side going into L'Anse, looking over the scenic Keweenaw Bay. The restaurant also serves breakfast, lunch, and dinner. $

## Where to Stay

**Baraga State Park.** A mile south of town on US 41, Baraga; (906) 353-6558 for information or (800) 447-2757 for reservations; www .michigan.gov/dnr. Along Keweenaw Bay near Baraga. Camping is $ nightly. The park offers 119 sites and a minicabin that sleeps four. As one might guess, road noise can keep light sleepers awake, as US 41 travels right by the park along the bay. You can swim in Lake Superior, if you dare, from a beach. The lake temperature rarely rises above fifty degrees Fahrenheit in late summer. There's also a short hiking trail. Daily permit $, annual $$$

**Best Western Baraga Lakeside Inn.** 900 US 41, Baraga; (906) 353-7123. The inn has thirty-six rooms, indoor pool, and restaurant. $$

**Carla's Lake Shore Motel.** On US 41, Baraga, 6 miles north of town; (906) 353-6256. This basic motel has ten rooms. Pets OK at extra charge. $

**Ojibwa Campground.** Two miles north of Baraga; watch for the sign and turn west; (906) 353-6623. This tribal-run campground has fifty sites. Beach nearby. $

# Houghton

Located along US 41 in the middle of the Keweenaw Peninsula, Houghton and several nearby cities—Hancock to the south and Lake Linden, Laurium, and Calumet to the north—are at the heart of hundreds of years of Upper Peninsula history revolving around the decades when copper was the main export here. When Horace Greeley coined the famous phrase "Go west, young man" in the mid-1800s, he wasn't talking about California. He was referring to the massive copper strikes in the UP. In all, the Keweenaw Peninsula produced more than eight and a half billion—yup, billion—pounds of copper. The sites in this area will tell you the story. Houghton also is home to Michigan Technological University, or Michigan Tech for short.

## Michigan Tech Winter Carnival (all ages)

**Held in late Jan to early Feb on the campus of Michigan Tech. For information and directions, call (906) 487-2818.**

The Keweenaw gets a lot of winter, sometimes running from Nov well into May, and holds one of the oldest celebrations of all that snow, dating from 1922. It brightens up the campus and is run by students. The four-day event's highlight is the construction of huge snow and ice sculptures to conform with the particular year's chosen theme. The structures extend along US 41 for more than 1½ miles. Be prepared for cold, as temperatures can reach a balmy minus twenty degrees Fahrenheit. Dorms provide convenient warming shelters.

## Where to Eat

**The Library.** 62 North Isle Royale; (906) 487-5882. This brewpub features steaks, pizza, seafood, and Mexican dishes, along with house-made beers and root beer. $$–$$$

**Suomi Home Bakery & Restaurant.** 54 Huron St., downtown, "under the covered street"; (906) 482-3220. Serves breakfast all day along with other meals, including Finnish dishes, great pasties, and other items. $

## Where to Stay

If you want inexpensive lodging, this is the region. You'll still find plenty of local motels with few amenities where three persons can still get change back from $50.

**Best Western Franklin Square Inn.** 820 Shelden Ave. (US 41); (906) 487-1700; www.houghtonlodging.com. The inn has 102 rooms, restaurant, and indoor pool. Pets OK. $$

**Budget Host Inn.** 46995 US 41, 2 miles south of Houghton; (906) 482-5351 or (800) 283-4678; www.bhihoughton.com. This motel features twenty-four rooms with outdoor pool (summer only) and continental breakfast. $$

## For More Information

**Keweenaw Convention and Visitors Bureau.** 56638 Calumet Ave., Calumet 49913; (906) 337-4579; www.keweenaw.info.

# Keweenaw National **Historical Park**

At the core of three towns in the Keweenaw Peninsula is this national park, actually a public-private mix of attractions ranging up and down the peninsula, including the Quincy Mine Hoist in Hancock and the Coppertown USA Museum in Calumet. For general information on the park, call (906) 337-3168, or write Keweenaw National Historical Park, P.O. Box 471, Calumet 49931; www.nps.gov/kewe/.

# Hancock

This former mining town is just north of Houghton along US 41. From Hancock north, the highway is considered one of the state's most scenic, traveling past lakes and through groves of hardwoods that nearly blot out the sun. The drive is spectacular any time of year but is especially so in summer and fall.

### Quincy Mine Hoist (all ages)

Part of the Keweenaw National Historical Park, the Quincy Mine is atop the hill on the Hancock side of the Keweenaw shipping canal, along US 41; (906) 482-3131; www.nps.gov/kewe/, then go to "links" to find individual attractions like the mine hoist, or go directly to www.quincymine.com. Open 9:30 a.m. to 5 p.m. Mon through Sat, 11 a.m. to 5 p.m. Sun May through Oct, reduced hours after Labor Day. Surface tour and tram ride $–$$, full mine surface tour $$–$$$; children under age six enter **free.**

The machinery comprises the world's largest ore hoist, on display at the old Quincy mine. The famed shaft operated from 1848 to the 1960s, producing 300 million pounds of copper.

When the last load of ore was hauled up, its shafts had reached nearly 2 miles under the city and Lake Superior. Visit the hoist room, where you'll see the hoist and photos of what it was like working deep in the mine, where temperatures were in the nineties. The shaft house is the area's most recognizable structure, standing 150 feet tall.

As part of the park displays, you can also step into a portion of the mine worked in the 1960s and then used by Michigan Tech for classes. You'll travel 2,000 feet into the hill to view original workings from the Civil War era, and into the huge stopes, or mined-out underground rooms. A gift shop features historical photos, books, and paintings.

## Where to Eat

See Houghton listings.

## Where to Stay

**Best Western Copper Crown Motel.** 235 Hancock Ave. (US 41); (906) 482-6111. The motel has forty-seven rooms, indoor pool, and saunas. Restaurants nearby. $

**F. J. McLain State Park.** North of Hancock 10 miles along Highway 203; (906) 482-0278 for information or (800) 447-2757 for reservations; www.michigan.gov/dnr. There is a daily ($) or annual ($$$) vehicle entry fee. Camping is $ nightly. The park has 103 campsites along the bluffs on the Lake Superior shoreline, with a beach and swimming. Also hiking paths. $

# Calumet

Founded in the 1860s, the town for decades was, along with nearby Houghton and Hancock, the center of copper mining on the Keweenaw Peninsula area.

### Coppertown USA Museum (all ages)

**On Red Jacket Road, 2 blocks west of US 41; (906) 337-4354; www.uppermichigan.com/coppertown/main.html. Open from 10 a.m. to 5 p.m. Mon through Sat from mid-June to mid-Oct and also from 1 to 4 p.m. Sun in July and Aug. $, free for children younger than 12.**

This museum is at the core of the Keweenaw National Historical Park. It acts as a visitor center for the entire Keweenaw Peninsula. You can follow the evolution of the mines, beginning when Native Americans extracted pure copper with stone hammers and continuing with the "copper rush" that brought thousands of immigrants to the area, and walk into a mine replica.

# Copper Harbor

Take a drive north on US 41 from Houghton, and you'll know why the tip of the Keweenaw Peninsula is, in summer, one of the UP's most popular tourist destinations.

## Isle Royale National Park

Michigan's only national park lies some 50-plus miles off Copper Harbor in Lake Superior. The *Isle Royale Queen* leaves from Copper Harbor from mid-May to Sept 30 on four-and-a-half-hour trips. The larger *Ranger III* leaves from Houghton on six-and-a-half-hour journeys from early June to mid-Sept, and floatplane service runs from mid-May to late Sept.

For lodge information, call (906) 337-4993 or, in preseason, (502) 773-2191. For information on the park itself, call (906) 482-0984; www.isle.royale.national-park.com or www.nps.gov/isro/.

The nation's only island national sanctuary is accessible only by boat or seaplane. But don't think you have to rough it when you visit. True, most people come with a pack to explore the island's hundreds of miles of hiking trails and backcountry campgrounds, but Rock Harbor Lodge offers excellent accommodations for those without backpacks. Lodge rooms with meals included or modern housekeeping cabins where you cook (bring your groceries with you; the island's store has limited provisions) are perfect for driving travelers.

Rent a canoe, charter a lake-trout fishing trip, go after panfish and pike on the island's many lakes, or take a sightseeing trip on the boat *Sandy* to see secluded lighthouses and a re-created Great Lakes fishing camp. You can also just take day hikes on the well-marked but secluded trails. Wildlife you might meet includes 1,400 or so—the number varies annually, depending on the severity of the winter. Use caution.

# Eagle River

On your way to Copper Harbor, you'll pass Eagle River. This town is the Keweenaw County seat and site of the state's oldest courthouse and a monument to Douglass Houghton, who started it all. It sits like a New England fishing village on the shore of Lake Superior. If you or your kids are into free souvenir collecting, stop along one of the Superior stone beaches here and search for agates and greenstones.

Most vacationers save the area for late July and Aug, since biting black flies and cold weather can be a problem here in early summer. In late summer you'll find beautiful scenery and lots to do. For more information visitin www.copperharbor.org.

## Fort Wilkins State Park (all ages)

**About a mile east of Copper Harbor on US 41; (906) 289-4215 for information or (800) 447-2757 for reservations; www.michigan.gov/dnr. Open in summer. Historic buildings are open from mid-May to mid-Oct. There's also a modern 165-site campground. Camping is extra. Daily $.**

Built in 1844 to protect rugged copper miners more from themselves than from local tribes, the fort lies along fish-rich Lake Fanny Hooe at the tip of the Keweenaw. It's purported to be the last remaining all-wooden fort east of the Mississippi. Amazingly, it was abandoned two years after it was built, then regarrisoned in 1867, and decommissioned in 1870.

Eighteen buildings, twelve of them original, survive. From mid-May to mid-Oct, living-history workers, with help from video presentations and other exhibits, portray life in the mid-1800s in this then-remote part of the nation.

## Eagle Harbor Lighthouse Museum (all ages)

**Located in Eagle Harbor, off Highway 26. There is no phone; www.keweenawhistory.org. $.**

Open from mid-June through Oct, the lighthouse and adjacent lifesaving station figured in the rescue of the crews of two ships that had run aground on the Keweenaw's rugged shore. One of the ships carried a cargo of then-new 1926 Chryslers, and one of those vehicles is displayed. The light still protects mariners on the big lake.

## Copper Harbor Lighthouse Boat Tours (all ages)

**Tours run from Copper Harbor Marina between 10 a.m. and 5 p.m. Hours vary, and tours are weather dependent, so call ahead: (906) 289-4966. Adults $$$; children 12 and under $$.**

Attached to Fort Wilkins State Park is the Copper Harbor Lighthouse, and the only way to see it is by this tour. The boat leaves the public marina ¼ mile west of downtown.

# **Brockway** Mountain Drive

West of Copper Harbor, point your car up. Up, that is, on this scenic highway.

One visit, and your family will know what an eagle must feel like contemplating its domain. Via the winding road with plenty of turnoffs, travel to the top, 700 feet above the town. If you're lucky, you'll see passing freighters cruise shimmering Lake Superior. It's the highest above-sea-level drive in the country between the Rockies and the Alleghenies. You'll be looking at nearly fifty types of trees and 700 species of wildflowers.

The hardwood and conifer mix of trees along the drive makes this a spectacular spot for fall color. On the way down west, and along Highway 26 back to Copper Harbor, you'll pass waterfalls and roadside parks along the Superior shoreline that are perfect places for picnics or for kids with energy to burn.

On seventy-five- to ninety-minute narrated tours, you'll learn the history of the town and visit the light, built in 1866. Take a walk down a short trail to the first copper-mine shaft—or at least the first attempt at the mine shaft—in the Keweenaw Peninsula, dating from 1844. Spectacular sunset cruises are also available in summer.

### **Delaware Copper Mine Tours** (all ages)

**Located on US 41, 12 miles south of Copper Harbor; (906) 289-4688; www.copperharbor .org/site_files/del_mine.html. Tours last forty-five minutes and take place daily from 10 a.m. to 6 p.m. June through Aug and from 10 a.m. to 5 p.m. Sept and Oct. $.**

Step 110 feet into a former operating copper mine, which produced more than eight million pounds of ore between 1847 and 1887. See veins of native copper still in its walls.

## Where to Eat

**The Jam Pot.** Along Highway 26, 3 miles north of Eagle River. There is no phone. Open mid-May through the mid-Oct fall-color season. Run by members of the Society of St. John, a small Orthodox mission. The store's brothers cook up great sweet treats, from thimbleberry jam, a UP favorite, to blueberry muffins, cakes, and other delights. It's definitely worth a stop.

**Pines Restaurant.** On US 41; (906) 289-4222 or (906) 289-4229. Good, inexpensive, family-style food. Save room for one of "Red's" huge cinnamon rolls. $

**Shoreline Resort.** 201 Front St., Eagle Harbor; (906) 289-4441. This resort has eight rooms with an inexpensive restaurant. $$

**Tamarack Inn.** At US 41 and Highway 26; (906) 289-4522. Children's menu and local dishes, including fresh whitefish. $$

## Where to Stay

**Eagle River Inn.** 100 Front St., south of Copper Harbor in Eagle River, 2 blocks off Highway 26; (906) 337-0666 or (800) 352-9228; www.eagleriverinn.com. This inn overlooking Lake Superior has twelve rooms, whirlpool, beach, and restaurant. $$–$$$

**Keweenaw Mountain Lodge.** On US 41, at the hill above Copper Harbor; (906) 289-4403 or (800) 685-6343; www.atthelodge.com. This Depression-era lodge is a UP gem, with well-kept log cabins sprinkled around a golf course, and there's also a restaurant. $–$$

**Minnetonka Resort and Astor House Museum.** 560 Gratiot; (906) 289-4449; www.minnetonkaresort.com. This motel and resort features rooms and cabins, plus a museum featuring antique dolls and Native American artifacts dealing with the area's history. Restaurant nearby. $$

**Pines Resort.** On US 41; (906) 289-4573; www.pinesresort.net. The resort has fifteen motel and cabin units. Restaurant on premises. $

**Shoreline Resort.** South of Copper Harbor along Highway 26, Eagle Harbor; (906) 289-4441; www.shorelineresort.com. The resort has just eight rooms, each with a view of Lake Superior. Continental breakfast included. $

# Ontonagon

Ontonagon is located along Highway 38 in Ontonagon County, on Lake Superior. If you're not a Michiganian, you probably never thought that Michigan had mountains until you read this book. You'll find them here, in another of Michigan's finest parks.

### Porcupine Mountains Wilderness State Park (all ages)

At the end of Highway 107, west of town; (906) 885-5275 for information or (800) 447-2757 for reservations; www.michigan.gov/dnr. Then click on "Recreation, Camping & Boating." Camping is available. Bring plenty of repellent for biting black flies in early summer. Open daily all year. Camping is $ nightly. Daily permit $, annual $$$.

Take a gander off the edge of the rock escarpment and down at Lake of the Clouds.

You'll be looking over just part of the 60,000-acre park, Michigan's largest. There's hiking, including an easy walk down to the lakeshore of Lake of the Clouds or a bit farther to Mirror Lake, beyond the next ridge. A visitor center features a slide show and more information to help orient you.

There are two campgrounds for auto campers, one near the escarpment on Union Bay, which features a great beach, and another, primitive site at the west end of the park at Presque Isle, reached by a road off Highway 28. There's also camping along the nearly 90 miles of hiking trails through the park.

Want a unique experience? Rent one of the park's sixteen primitive cabins and treat the family to a rugged overnight stay indoors. Cabins have bunks, a wood-burning cooking and heating stove, and basic table and cooking utensils. Those on lakes also come with boats. Toilets are outdoors. You bring bedding and towels, food, lighting, and other utensils. You'll also be drawing your own water. A cookstove is recommended in summer to use outside. The cabins are very popular, so reserve in advance. And remember, the park has many black bears. Most of them are shy, but some have turned into Yogis, looking for your food. Take care with your food and cooking utensils, as well as toiletries, especially when using a cabin or camping in the backcountry, or you may have an unwelcome visitor knocking at your door, not to mention a park ranger with a citation book. The park also features cross-country and downhill skiing in winter.

## Mead Lake Mine Site (all ages)

**Along Highway 107. Free.**

The former mine features a horizontal shaft and is home to about 14,000 hibernating bats in fall. In summer they fly out at dusk to dine on those pesky UP mosquitoes and black flies, thank goodness. If you're not afraid of them, head there at dusk to see the flights. There's a historical marker at the site, along with a picnic area on a pond formed from the mine seepage.

## Where to Eat

**Paul's Restaurant.** Inside Americinn Porcupine Mountain Lodge in Silver City, about 16 miles west of Ontonagon; (906) 885-5311. Serves breakfast, lunch, and dinner from 7 a.m. to 9 p.m. A full menu and nightly specials are available. $$

**Syl's Country Kitchen.** 713 River St., downtown; (906) 884-2522. Serves breakfast (anytime), lunch, and dinner. Enjoy specialties such as pasties, desserts, and the biggest pancakes around. $

## Where to Stay

**Americinn Porcupine Mountain Lodge.** In tiny Silver City, about 16 miles west of Ontonagon, at the entrance to the Porkies; (906) 885-5311. The lodge has seventy-one rooms on Lake Superior with pool and restaurant. Small pets OK at extra charge. $$

**Inn Towne Motel.** 314 Chippewa, at Highway 64 and US 45; (906) 884-2100; www .ontonagonmotel.com. This basic motel has nineteen rooms. Restaurant nearby. $

**Rainbow Lodging.** 2900 Highway 64, east of Highway 107, near the entrance to the Porkies, Silver City; (906) 885-5348; www .rainbowlodging.com. The property has sixteen rooms and three chalets, including one that rents weekly on the Lake Superior beach, mountain bike rentals, whirlpool, and beach access. Restaurant on premises open June through Sept. $$–$$$

**River Pines RV Park & Campgrounds.** 600 River Rd., ½ mile south from Highway 64 on the Ontonagon River; (906) 884-4600 or (800) 424-1520. The park has thirty sites with marina and Lake Superior access, playground. Pets OK. $

**Scott's Superior Inn & Cabins.** 277 Lakeshore Rd. (Highway 64), about 1½ miles west of Ontonagon; (906) 884-4866; www.ontonagon.net/scotts. The facility has eighteen rooms along Lake Superior with whirlpool, beach, and nearby restaurants. Pets OK at extra charge. $$–$$$

**Sunshine Motel and Cabins.** 1442 Highway 64, 3 miles west of Ontonagon; (906) 884-2187; www.ontonagonmi.com. This property offers fifteen motel rooms and five cabins with beach access and fifteen campsites. $–$$

**Union River Campground.** In Silver City, about 16 miles west of Ontonagon, on Highway 107, near the entrance to the Porkies; (906) 885-5324. Open roughly from early June to early Oct, depending on the weather. Here you'll find sixty sites along Lake Superior. Pets OK. $

## For More Information

**Ontonagon County Chamber of Commerce.** P.O. Box 266, Ontonagon 49953; (906) 884-4735; www.ontonagonmi.org.

**Porcupine Mountains Convention and Visitor Bureau.** P.O. Box 1, Ontonagon 49953; (906) 884-2047; www.porcupine mountains.com.

# Ironwood, Bessemer, and Wakefield

The state's westernmost group of cities are only a few miles from one another along Highway 28 and US 2 and claim a particular soft spot among waterfall lovers because of the Black River Scenic Byway. It's also known among skiers for the three ski areas within a few miles of each other, including one that's the state's highest.

## Black River National Scenic Byway (all ages)

Take CR 513 from US 2/Highway 28. Watch for the unique wooden "Indianhead" signs that mark scenic locations here in Gogebic County. For more information, call **(906) 667-0261**. **Free.**

Of Michigan's dozen or so Black Rivers, this one is by far the most beautiful. The highway weaves past trails through the woods to the five waterfalls up to 40 feet high that this restless river tumbles over in a stretch only 11 miles long. Names, such as Conglomerate (dropping over a rock ledge), Sandstone (named for the red rock riverbed), and Gorge (which roars into a chasm 22 feet below), are given to the cascades that range from close by the road to a distance along a trail from which you can faintly hear the water.

Two of the falls are wheelchair accessible, with paved sidewalks. The drive ends at a Lake Superior shoreline park, with a kid-friendly swinging bridge over the now-gentle river.

Along the Black River Scenic Byway, about 10 miles northwest of Ironwood, you'll also pass Copper Peak Ski Flying Hill, the only ski flying hill in the Americas and the largest artificial slide in the world. There are tours to the top in summer and events that feature skiers from around the world in late Jan.

## Pines & Mines Mountain Bike Trail System (ages 4 and up)

In the forests around Ironwood and in neighboring northern Wisconsin; **(800) 522-5657.**

The trail system offers more than 200 miles of marked and mapped routes in Iron County, Wisconsin. In Michigan, pathways such as the Pomeroy/Henry Lake Mountain

Bike Complex feature 100 miles of routes, mainly on gravel roads, from beginner routes to moderate pedals of 7 to 16 miles. An accompanying system, the Ehlco Tract, is more remote, taking bikers deep into the area's forests.

### Indianhead Mountain Ski Area (all ages)

**500 Indianhead Rd., Wakefield, just outside downtown; (906) 229-5181 or (800) 346-3426; www.indianheadmtn.com. Open twenty-four hours a day from mid-Nov to mid-Apr. Lift tickets $$$$, one child age 6 or younger per paid adult skis free. Rentals are available (call for price information).**

Many skiers say this might be the state's best ski resort, with twenty-two runs, five chair-lifts, rentals, instruction, and on-slope lodging. Babysitting is available. It's one of two ski resorts in the area.

### Copper Peak Adventure Ride (all ages)

**Located at Copper Peak Ski Flying Hill, north of Ironwood; (906) 932-3500; www.copper peak.org. Open 10 a.m. to 5 p.m. Weekends from Memorial Day to mid-June, then daily through Labor Day except Mon. Adults $$, children 14 years and under $.**

Ride the chair lift up eighteen stories to the top of the Copper Peak Ski Flying Hill, similar to ski jumping but resulting in jumps of 500 feet or more. You'll see as far as the Canadian shore. There's also a gift shop.

## Where to Eat

**Big Boy.** 111 East Cloverdale Dr. (Highway 28), Ironwood; (906) 932-8400. Open daily 7 a.m. to 10 p.m. Offers a variety of family fare, from salads to the trademark triple-decker burger. $–$$

## Where to Stay

Besides these and other Michigan accommodations, there are more in neighboring Wisconsin. You'll find most along US 2 from Wakefield west. During ski season many motels also offer discount lift tickets to individual ski areas they're closest to.

**Armata Motel.** 124 West Cloverland, Ironwood, on US 2; (906) 932-9906. The motel has twelve rooms. Restaurant nearby. Pets OK at extra charge. $

**Big Powderhorn and Indianhead Mountain.** Both of these ski areas offers restaurants and accommodations from ski chalets to motels. With nearby Whitecap in Wisconsin and Porcupine Mountains ski area near Ontonagon, the resorts make up the Big Snow Country group. Call each individually. Powderhorn: (906) 932-4838; www.bigpow-derhorn.net. Indianhead: (800) 356-6326; www.indianheadmtn.com. $$

**Black River Campground.** Near Bessemer at the end of the Black River Scenic Byway; (906) 932-7250 for information or (800) 280-2267 for reservations. The campground has forty sites in a beautiful setting along Lake Superior. Flush toilets. $

**Black River Lodge.** N12390 Black River Rd., Ironwood; (906) 932-3857. www.blackriver-lodge.net The lodge has twenty-four rooms, condos, and suites on the Black River Scenic Byway, along the river. Indoor pool, cross-country ski and hiking trails, and restaurant. $$

**Crestview Motel.** 424 Cloverland (US 2), Ironwood; (906) 932-4845. www.crestview motel.com The inn has twelve inexpensive but well-kept rooms and sauna. Restaurant nearby. Pets OK at extra charge. $

**Davey's Motel.** Along US 2, Ironwood; (906) 932-2020; www.daveysmotel.com. The motel has twenty-three rooms, sauna, and hot tub. Restaurants nearby. $

**Ottawa National Forest Campgrounds.** There are rustic campgrounds scattered in the forest throughout the area, most on lakes or rivers. In early summer, be aware that some campgrounds may be bothered by biting insects, including black flies and "no-see-ums," pepper-grain-size chompers. Make sure tents have windows with "no-see-um" netting, or you'll be harried at night. By early July most biting bug populations are reduced. Contact the Forest Supervisor's office for locations at (906) 932-1330 and for reservations at (800) 280-2267. $

**Powdermill Resort.** 11330 Powderhorn Rd., Bessemer, near the base of Big Powderhorn, at 1½ miles north of US 2 near Bessemer; (906) 932-0800; www.powdermillresort .com. The inn has fifty rooms, indoor pool, restaurant, whirlpool, and playground. $$

**Regal Country Inn.** On US 2, Wakefield, east of downtown; (906) 229-5122; www .westernup.com/regalinn. The inn has eighteen themed rooms from historical, furnished with local antiques, to country and Victorian. Adjacent ice-cream parlor. $$

## For More Information

**Western UP Convention and Visitor Bureau.** P.O. Box 706, Ironwood 49938; (906) 932-4850 or (800) 272-7000; www .westernup.com.

# Iron River, Caspian, and Stambaugh

State fisheries biologists call the waters around these towns some of the best brook trout fishing in Michigan, including the Iron River, which flows at the bottom of the hill, just east of the downtown that shares its name. Iron mining was big in the area, but now the mines are closed.

### Iron County Historical Museum (all ages)

In the former mining town of Caspian, off Highway 189 about 2 miles south of US 2 in Iron River; (906) 265-2617; www.ironcountymuseum.com. Open mid-May through Sept from 9 a.m. to 5 p.m. Mon through Sat, 1 to 5 p.m. Sun. $.

This museum is built around the old mine site in Caspian, the headframe of the old Caspian Mine, which at its peak was the area's largest iron-ore producer. It's the oldest steel headframe in the Midwest. The museum also features twenty locally historic buildings, from settlers' cabins to a school. The Lee LeBlanc Wildlife Art Gallery displays work by the nationally known artist. The Carrie Jacobs–Bond Home was the home of the composer of those late-nineteenth-century hits that you can still occasionally hear today, "I Love You Truly" and "Perfect Day." It's part of the Heritage Trail of Iron County, a collection of twelve sites of historic interest in the county. See For More Information at the end of this listing for contact information.

# Keep That Camera Handy!

The area around Iron River is wild country indeed, containing one of the state's largest deer populations, and it pays to have your camera at the ready. On a fishing trip there to try for walleye in catch-and-release Winslow Lake with champion angler Mark Martin, I was traveling between my accommodations near Chicaugon Lake and downtown Iron River when I noticed something black along the roadside that looked like a Labrador retriever at first. But when I pulled up, I saw about a one-hundred-pound black bear sniffing the weeds on that June afternoon. Just as I was rolling down the window to snap a picture, however, he hightailed it into the woods. As I said, have your camera ready. You never know what you may come across.

### George Young Recreational Complex (all ages)

On Youngs Lane, Iron River, off CR 424; (906) 265-3401; www.georgeyoung.com. From Iron River, head south on Highway 189, then east on CR 424 to Youngs Lane, and then turn north. Hours are 10 a.m. to 9 p.m. daily. Use of the nature trails is free, but registration is required at the clubhouse. There is a charge for golf ($$$$) and use of the indoor pool ($). There is also a driving range. In winter there is cross-country skiing, with rentals $$.

Set deep in the woods on the western side of Chicaugon Lake and near so many skeletons of the area's heyday of heavy mining operations is this gem of a recreational complex, which you have to see to believe. The land and complex were donated to the city and area by George Young, a local boy who made it big in the Chicago brick-making business. He wanted to give something back to his community, so he did: a 3,300-acre recreational center that is unique. Each year, according to the will, improvement must be made to make it even more attractive.

A beautiful eighteen-hole public golf course, where both golfers and wildlife from deer to bear play, is the centerpiece. Each hole is based on the late George Young's favorite holes from championship courses across the nation.

The clubhouse also doubles as a community center, with indoor swimming pool, whirlpool, and sauna. There are nature trails for hiking, biking, and cross-country skiing, including a 1½-mile Wolf Track Nature Trail with interpretive signs. Even if you don't golf, it's worth driving into the complex.

## Where to Eat

**The Depot and the Station.** 50 Fourth Ave. (Highway 189) in downtown Iron River; (906) 265-6341, (906) 265-5657 for the Depot. Some of the best food north of Chicago, bar none, served in restored railroad passenger cars and across the street at the Station. The Depot specializes in breakfast, and the Depot, lunch and dinner. A surprising find in the north country. Try the breakfast crepes, burgers for lunch, and for dinner, whitefish or T-bone steaks. $$–$$$$

**Mr. T's Family Restaurant.** On US 2, Iron River; (906) 265-4741. Open for breakfast, lunch, and dinner daily. $$

## Where to Stay

There are plenty of resort cottages on area lakes as well as motels. Call (906) 265-5605 for more.

**Americinn Lodge and Suites.** 40 East Adams St. (US 2), downtown; (906) 265-9100 or (800) 634-3444. This chain lodge has sixty-five rooms with indoor pool, whirlpool, and full breakfast. Restaurants nearby. $$–$$$

**Chicaugon Lake Inn.** 1700 CR 424, Gaastra, at the southern end of Chicaugon Lake; (906) 265-9244; www.iron.org/biz/chicaugon/chicaugon.html. The nearest post office is in tiny Alpha, population 229, southeast of Iron River and east of Caspian. Seemingly in the middle of nowhere, this is a quiet and well-kept motel with twenty-four rooms, some with whirlpools. Restaurant across the street and others nearby. Within a block of the public boat launch for Chicaugon Lake, with fishing for walleye and other species. The inn is a popular spot for snowmobilers and skiers in winter. $$

**Hillberg's Cabins.** On the north end of Chicaugon Lake, 2 miles south of US 2, Iron River; (906) 265-2982. Four cabins on seventy acres of forested lakeshore with beach, playground equipment, and fishing for walleye and lake trout in the lake. $

**Iron Inn Motel.** 211 Cayuga St.; (906) 265-5111. This basic motel has ten rooms. $

**Lac O'Seasons Resort.** 1176 Stanley Lake Dr., Iron River, on Stanley Lake; (906) 265-4881; www.lacoseasons.com. From Iron River, head south on Highway 189 about ½ mile to Hiawatha Road. Turn west and follow the signs. The resort has two- and three-bedroom cottages, indoor pool, canoes, and boats. $$

**Pentoga Park.** On Chicaugon Lake; (906) 265-3979. Go south on Highway 189 to CR 424 and go east to the park. Or, from US 2 east of town, head south on scenic Pentoga Trail to CR 424 west. This campground has one hundred wooded sites and a fascinating highlight, an authentic Native American burial ground where Ojibwa had camped since pre-European times.

# Iron Mountain

Iron Mountain was founded on the city's backbone of ore. Mines operated here continuously from the 1800s through the 1930s.

### Iron Mountain Iron Mine (all ages)

**The mine is actually in Vulcan, along US 2 about 9 miles east of Iron Mountain; (906) 563-8077; www.ironmountainironmine.com. Open 9 a.m. to 5 p.m. daily Memorial Day to mid-Oct. Last tour leaves at 4:25 p.m. $.**

Don a raincoat (to protect yourself from the dripping water) and a hard hat to go hundreds of feet belowground through 2,600 feet of tunnels for a glimpse of the inside of the mine, which operated until 1945. As a guide explains, you'll go by the same train that used to ferry miners into this underground world.

### Menominee Range Historical Museum (all ages)

300 East Ludington, a block east of US 2; (906) 774-4276. Open from 10 a.m. to 4 p.m. Mon through Sat and noon to 4 p.m. Sun in summer. Admission is $; children ages 9 and under **free.**

Inside a former Carnegie library, the museum features more than one hundred exhibits on life in the iron range at the turn of the twentieth century, including displays of the area's Native American heritage.

### Millie Mine Bat Cave (all ages)

On Park, just off East A Street; (906) 774-5480. Best viewing times are late Apr and Sept. Open anytime. **Free.**

This former mine is 350 feet deep, and with a constant forty-degree temperature, it is perfect for bats. In fact, it's the second-largest known colony of hibernating bats in North America. The bats move out in Apr and settle in for winter come Sept, so those are the only viewing times when you're bound to see clouds of the creatures.

Informational plaques are situated near benches, where you can sit and watch the flights.

## Where to Eat

**Dobber's Pasties.** 1400 South Stephenson (US 2); (906) 774-9323. Traditional Cornish and veggie pasties, too. $

**Romagnoli's.** 1620 North Stephenson, downtown along US 2; (906) 774-7300. Not only did Finns and other Scandinavians come to the UP's mines, but the Italians did, too, and some opened restaurants. This is one of the best, for lunch and dinner. $$

## Where to Stay

**Best Western Executive Inn.** 1518 South Stephenson Ave., near US 2 and US 141; (906) 774-2040. The inn offers fifty-seven rooms and indoor pool. Restaurant nearby. Pets OK at extra charge. $$

**Days Inn.** W8176 South US 2, about 2 miles east of town; (906) 774-2181. This economical motel has forty-four rooms, indoor pool, and continental breakfast. Restaurant nearby. Pets OK for an extra charge. $–$$

**Lake Antoine County Park.** N3393 Quinnesec Lake Antoine Rd.; (906) 774-8875. The park has eighty campsites and a beach. $

## For More Information

**Upper Peninsula Travel and Recreation Association.** P.O. Box 400, Iron Mountain 49801; (906) 774-5480; www.uptravel.com or www.ironmountain.org (for Iron Mountain).

# Index

# About the Author

Bill Semion is a freelance writer and full-time public relations specialist and has been involved in magazine and newspaper travel and outdoor writing for more than twenty-five years. He has explored Michigan for as long as he can remember. One of Bill's earliest memories is taking a car-ferry ride with the family cat across the Straits of Mackinac (prior to the completion of the Mackinac Bridge) and vacationing with his parents in Michigan's Upper Peninsula.

Bill has won a number of writing awards, including the 1998 Mark Twain Award for Best Travel Book for *Fun with the Family in Michigan*. He is also the author of *Winter Trails Michigan: The Best Cross-Country Ski & Snowshoe Trails*. A father of two, Bill lives in Canton Township, a Detroit suburb.